JTH COUNTY

 03

STORY AND ART BY
RIKDO KOSHI

EXCEL SAGA 03

STORY AND ART BY
RIKDO KOSHI

ENGLISH ADAPTATION BY
DAN KANEMITSU & CARL GUSTAV HORN

TRANSLATION
DAN KANEMITSU

LETTERING & TOUCH-UP BY
CATO

COVER DESIGN
BRUCE LEWIS

GRAPHIC DESIGNER
CAROLINA UGALDE

EDITOR
CARL GUSTAV HORN

MANAGING EDITOR
ANNETTE ROMAN

EDITOR IN CHIEF
WILLIAM FLANAGAN

DIRECTOR OF LICENSING & ACQUISITIONS
RIKA INOUYE

VP OF SALES & MARKETING
LIZA COPPOLA

SR. VP OF EDITORIAL
HYOE NARITA

PUBLISHER
SEIJI HORIBUCHI

EXCEL SAGA ©1997 Rikdo Koshi. Originally published in Japan in 1997 by SHONENGAHOSHA CO., LTD. Tokyo. English translation rights arranged with SHONENGAHOSHA CO., LTD.

New and adapted artwork © 2003 VIZ, LLC
All rights reserved.

Printed in Canada.

Published by VIZ, LLC
P.O. Box 77064
San Francisco, CA 94107

Action Edition
10 9 8 7 6 5 4 3 2 1
First printing, October 2003

For advertising rates or media kit, e-mail advertising@viz.com

www.viz.com

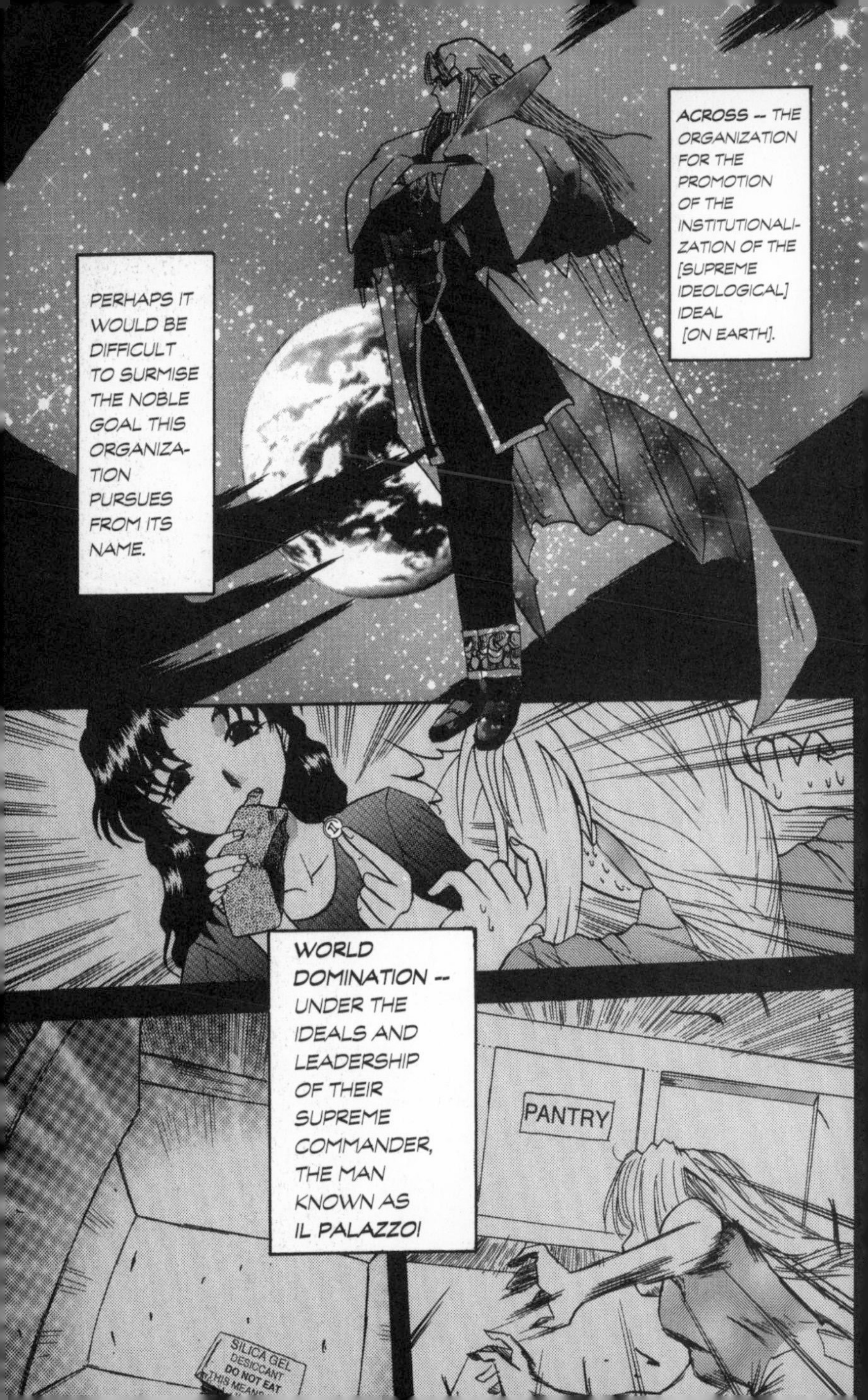
ACROSS -- THE ORGANIZATION FOR THE PROMOTION OF THE INSTITUTIONALIZATION OF THE [SUPREME IDEOLOGICAL] IDEAL [ON EARTH].
PERHAPS IT WOULD BE DIFFICULT TO SURMISE THE NOBLE GOAL THIS ORGANIZATION PURSUES FROM ITS NAME.
WORLD DOMINATION -- UNDER THE IDEALS AND LEADERSHIP OF THEIR SUPREME COMMANDER, THE MAN KNOWN AS IL PALAZZO!
PANTRY
SILICA GEL
DESICCANT
DO NOT EAT

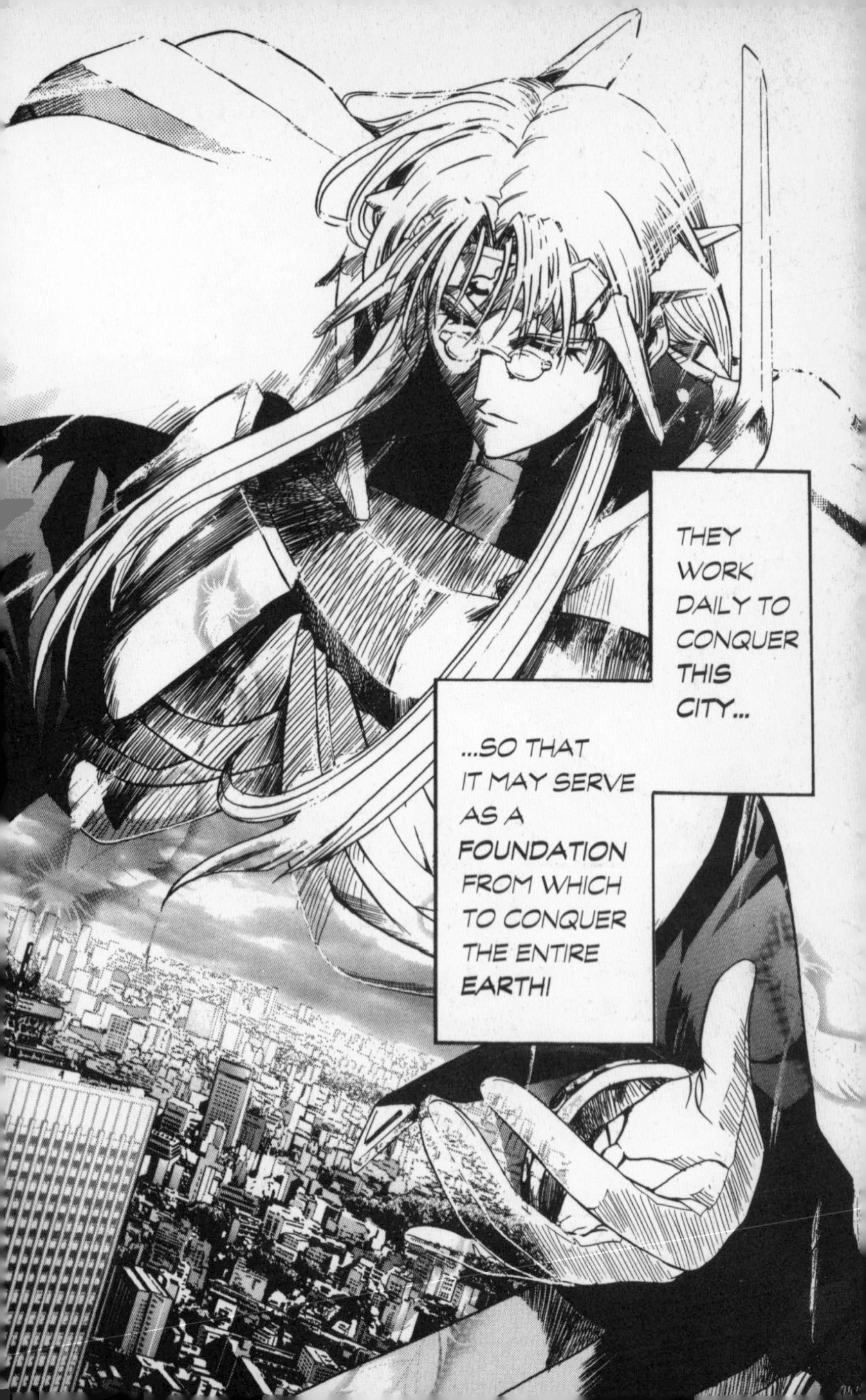
THEY WORK DAILY TO CONQUER THIS CITY...
...SO THAT IT MAY SERVE AS A FOUNDATION FROM WHICH TO CONQUER THE ENTIRE EARTH!

MISSION 1
CHOSE BROKEN

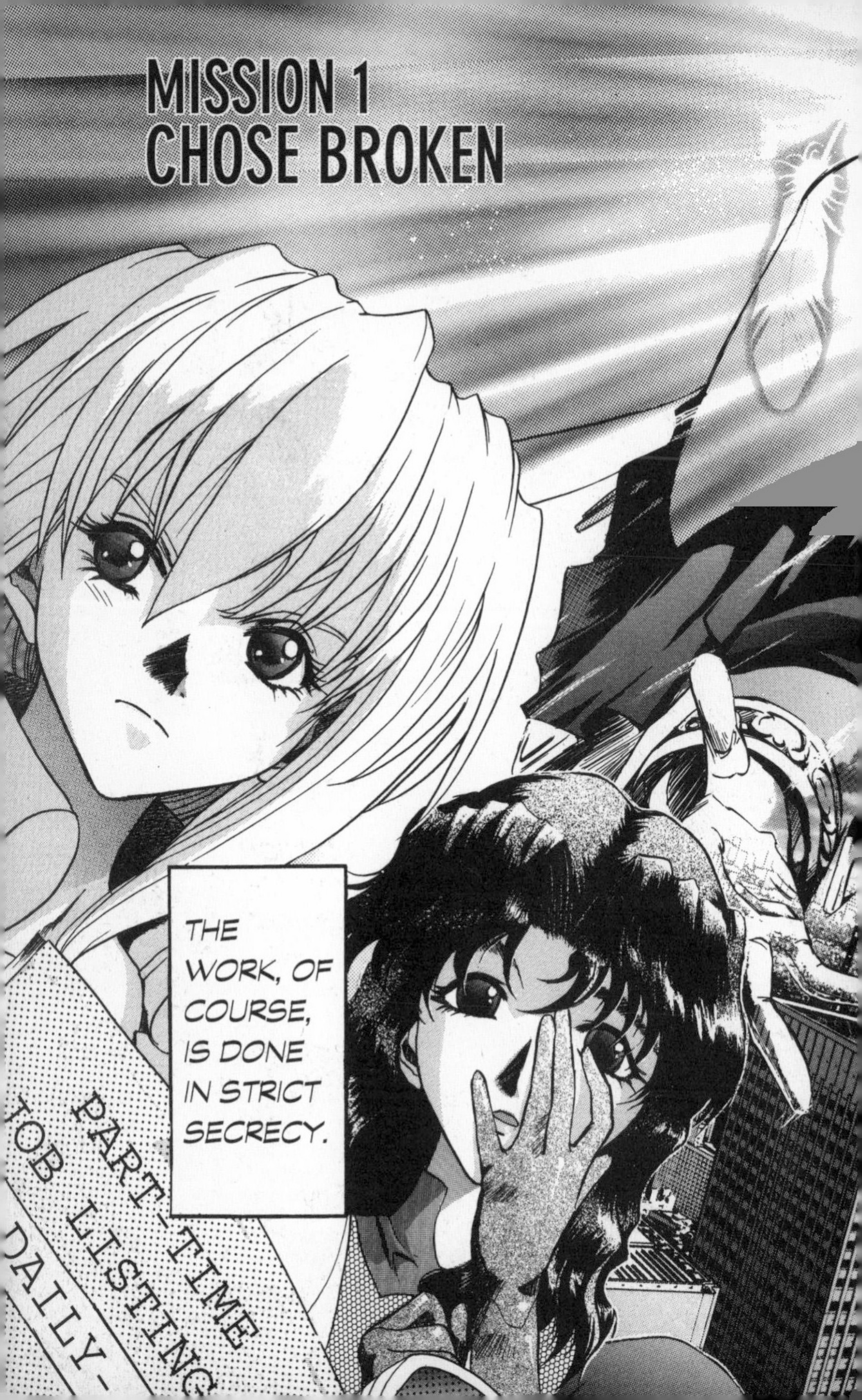
THE WORK, OF COURSE, IS DONE IN STRICT SECRECY.
PART-TIME JOB LISTING
DAILY-

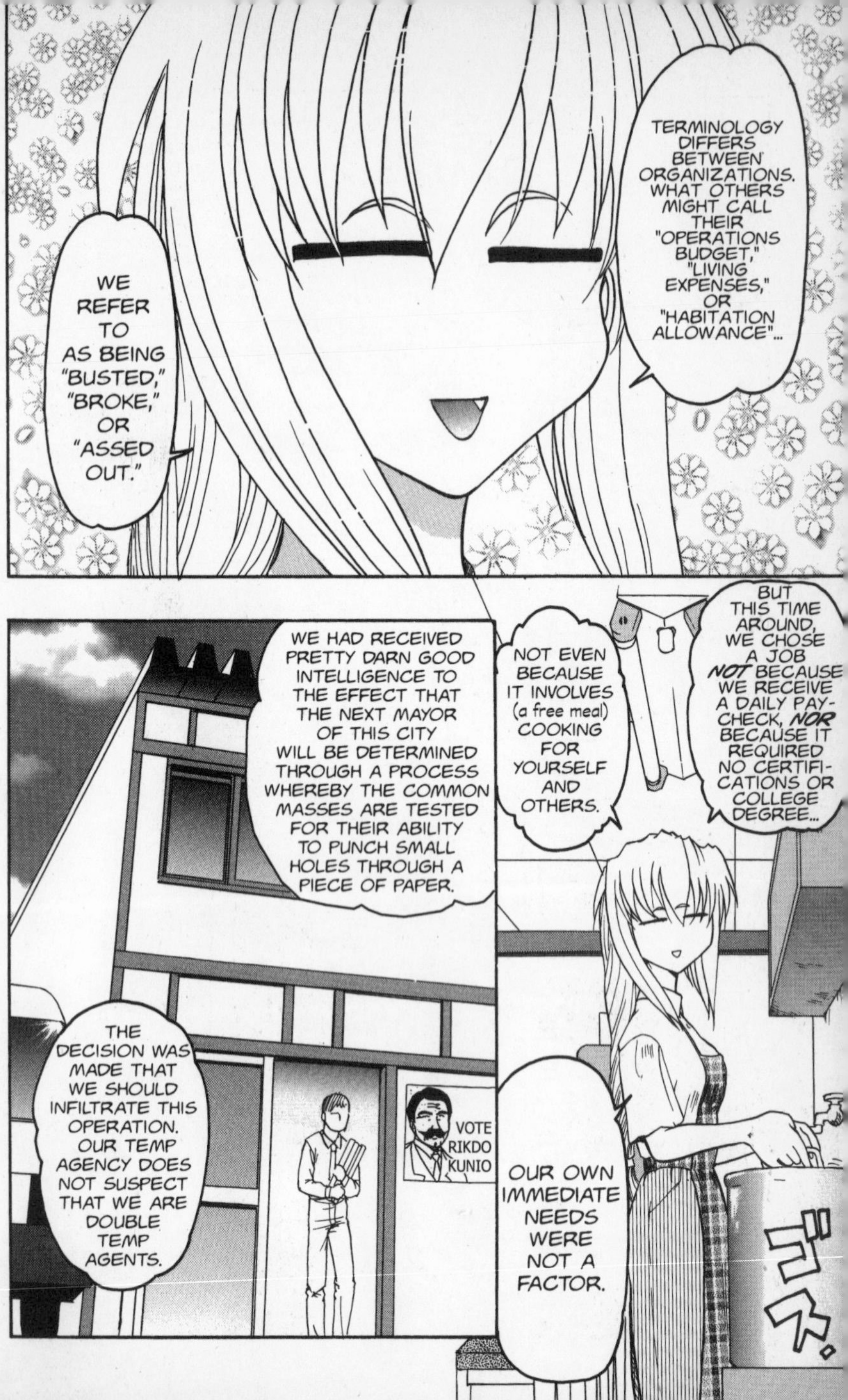
TERMINOLOGY DIFFERS BETWEEN ORGANIZATIONS. WHAT OTHERS MIGHT CALL THEIR "OPERATIONS BUDGET," "LIVING EXPENSES," OR "HABITATION ALLOWANCE"...
WE REFER TO AS BEING "BUSTED," "BROKE," OR "ASSED OUT."
BUT THIS TIME AROUND, WE CHOSE A JOB *NOT* BECAUSE WE RECEIVE A DAILY PAY-CHECK, *NOR* BECAUSE IT REQUIRED NO CERTIFI-CATIONS OR COLLEGE DEGREE...
NOT EVEN BECAUSE IT INVOLVES (a free meal) COOKING FOR YOURSELF AND OTHERS.
OUR OWN IMMEDIATE NEEDS WERE NOT A FACTOR.
ゴス。
WE HAD RECEIVED PRETTY DARN GOOD INTELLIGENCE TO THE EFFECT THAT THE NEXT MAYOR OF THIS CITY WILL BE DETERMINED THROUGH A PROCESS WHEREBY THE COMMON MASSES ARE TESTED FOR THEIR ABILITY TO PUNCH SMALL HOLES THROUGH A PIECE OF PAPER.
VOTE RIKDO KUNIO
THE DECISION WAS MADE THAT WE SHOULD INFILTRATE THIS OPERATION. OUR TEMP AGENCY DOES NOT SUSPECT THAT WE ARE DOUBLE TEMP AGENTS.

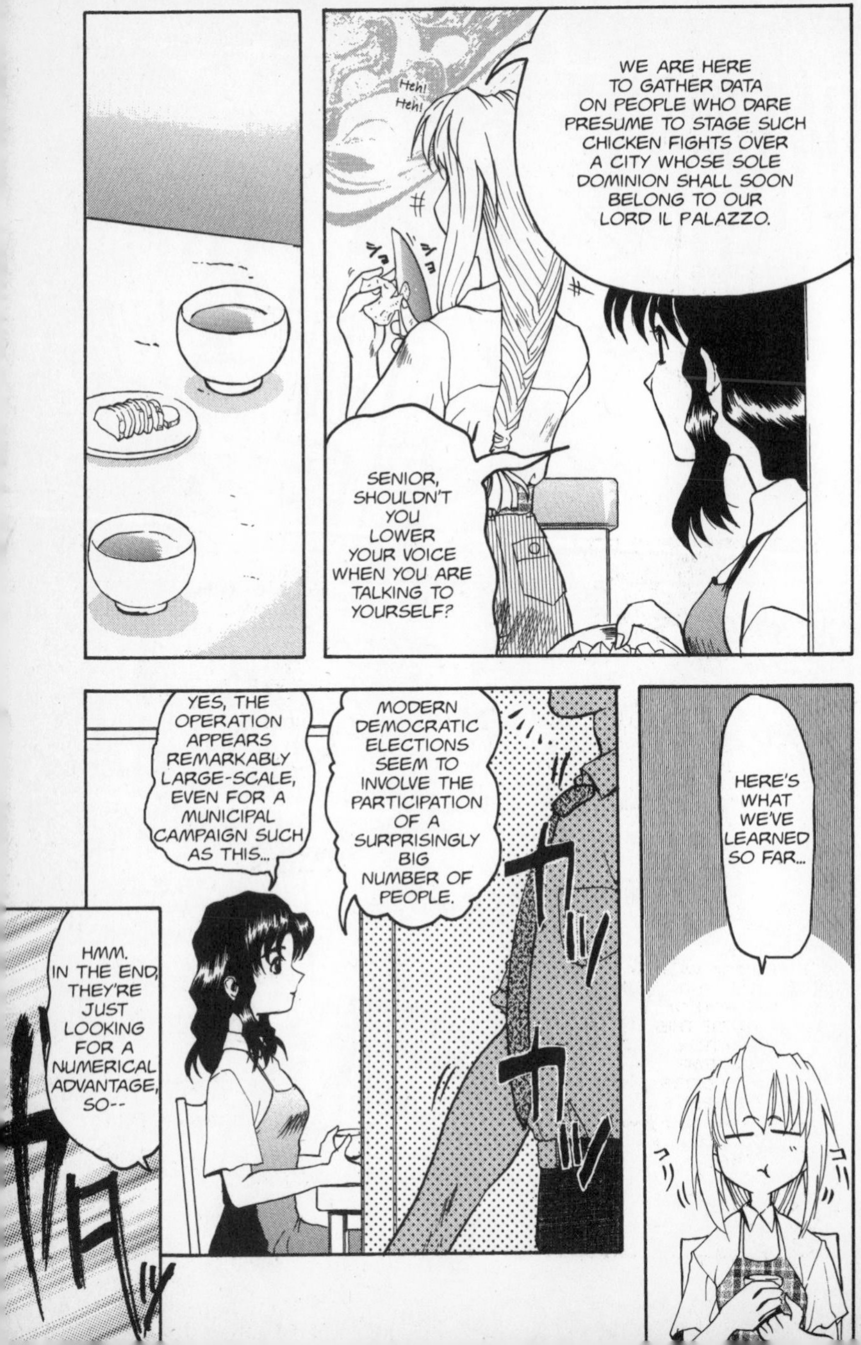
WE ARE HERE TO GATHER DATA ON PEOPLE WHO DARE PRESUME TO STAGE SUCH CHICKEN FIGHTS OVER A CITY WHOSE SOLE DOMINION SHALL SOON BELONG TO OUR LORD IL PALAZZO.
Heh! Heh!
SENIOR, SHOULDN'T YOU LOWER YOUR VOICE WHEN YOU ARE TALKING TO YOURSELF?
HERE'S WHAT WE'VE LEARNED SO FAR...
MODERN DEMOCRATIC ELECTIONS SEEM TO INVOLVE THE PARTICIPATION OF A SURPRISINGLY BIG NUMBER OF PEOPLE.
YES, THE OPERATION APPEARS REMARKABLY LARGE-SCALE, EVEN FOR A MUNICIPAL CAMPAIGN SUCH AS THIS...
HMM. IN THE END, THEY'RE JUST LOOKING FOR A NUMERICAL ADVANTAGE, SO--

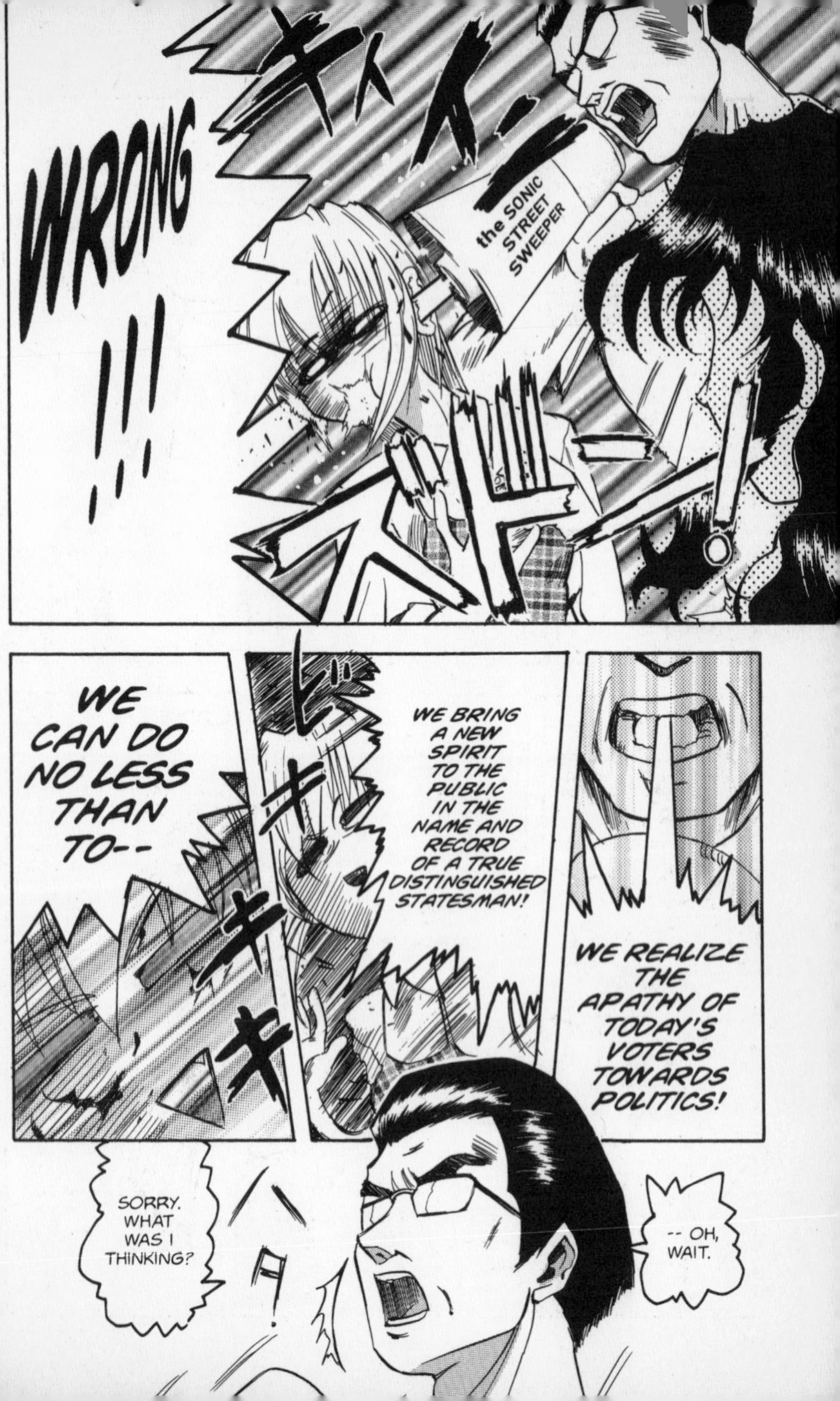
WRONG!!!
the SONIC STREET SWEEPER
WE REALIZE THE APATHY OF TODAY'S VOTERS TOWARDS POLITICS!
WE BRING A NEW SPIRIT TO THE PUBLIC IN THE NAME AND RECORD OF A TRUE DISTINGUISHED STATESMAN!
WE CAN DO NO LESS THAN TO--
-- OH, WAIT.
SORRY. WHAT WAS I THINKING?

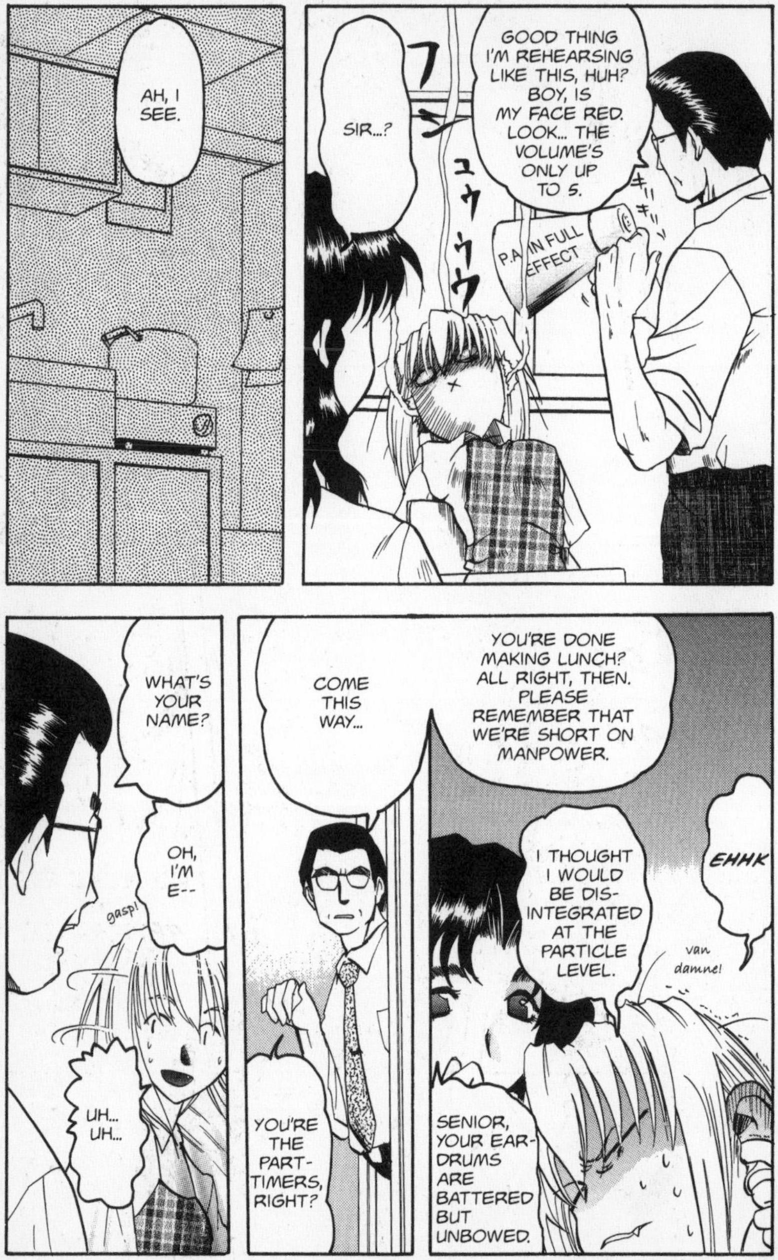

GOOD THING I'M REHEARSING LIKE THIS, HUH? BOY, IS MY FACE RED. LOOK... THE VOLUME'S ONLY UP TO 5.
P.A. IN FULL EFFECT
フン
ユウウウ
SIR...?
AH, I SEE.
EHHK
I THOUGHT I WOULD BE DIS-INTEGRATED AT THE PARTICLE LEVEL.
van damne!
SENIOR, YOUR EAR-DRUMS ARE BATTERED BUT UNBOWED.
YOU'RE THE PART-TIMERS, RIGHT?
YOU'RE DONE MAKING LUNCH? ALL RIGHT, THEN. PLEASE REMEMBER THAT WE'RE SHORT ON MANPOWER.
COME THIS WAY...
WHAT'S YOUR NAME?
OH, I'M E--
gasp!
UH... UH...

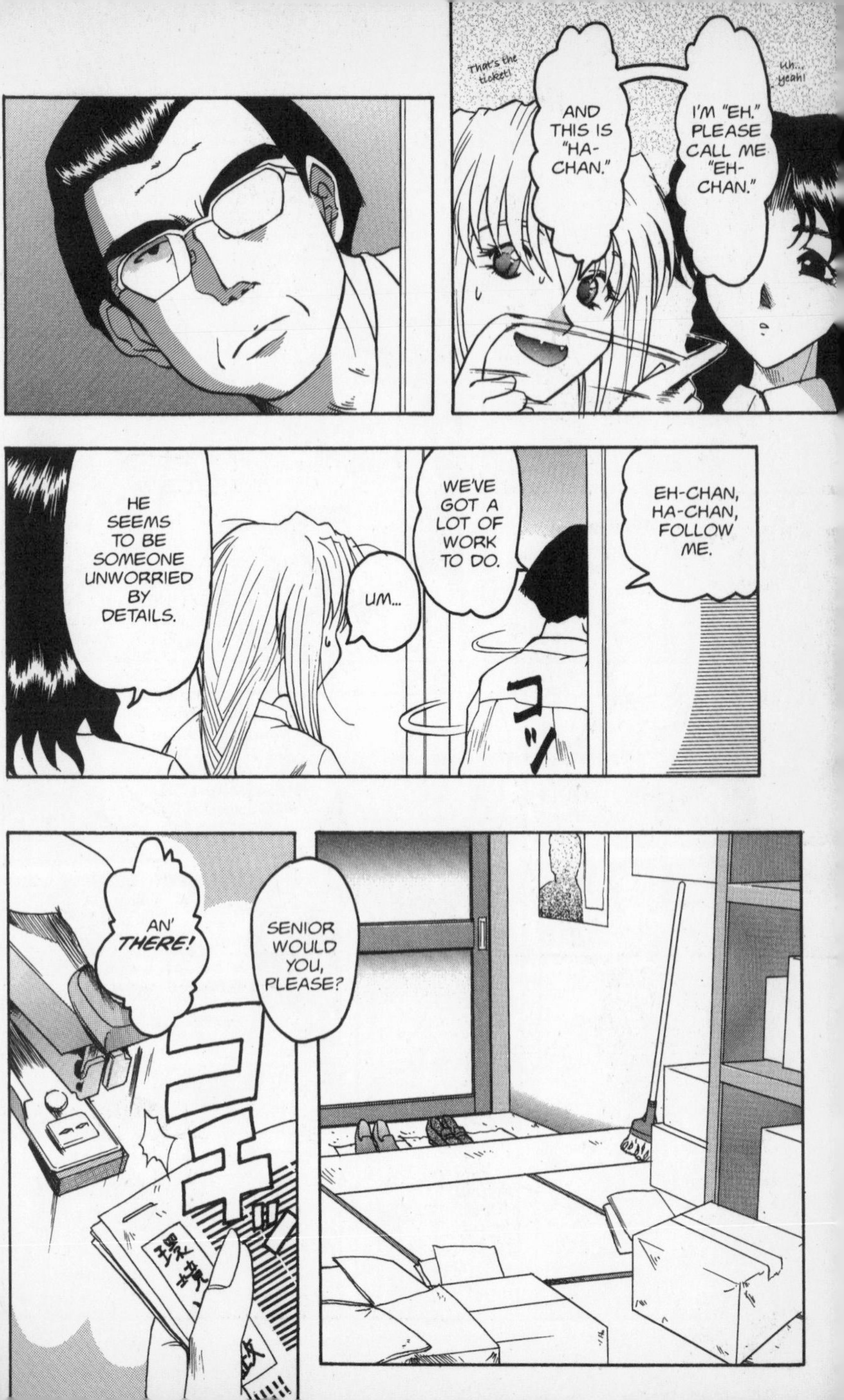
Uh... yeah!
I'M "EH." PLEASE CALL ME "EH-CHAN."
AND THIS IS "HA-CHAN."
That's the ticket!
EH-CHAN, HA-CHAN, FOLLOW ME.
WE'VE GOT A LOT OF WORK TO DO.
UM...
HE SEEMS TO BE SOMEONE UNWORRIED BY DETAILS.
SENIOR WOULD YOU, PLEASE?
AN' *THERE!*

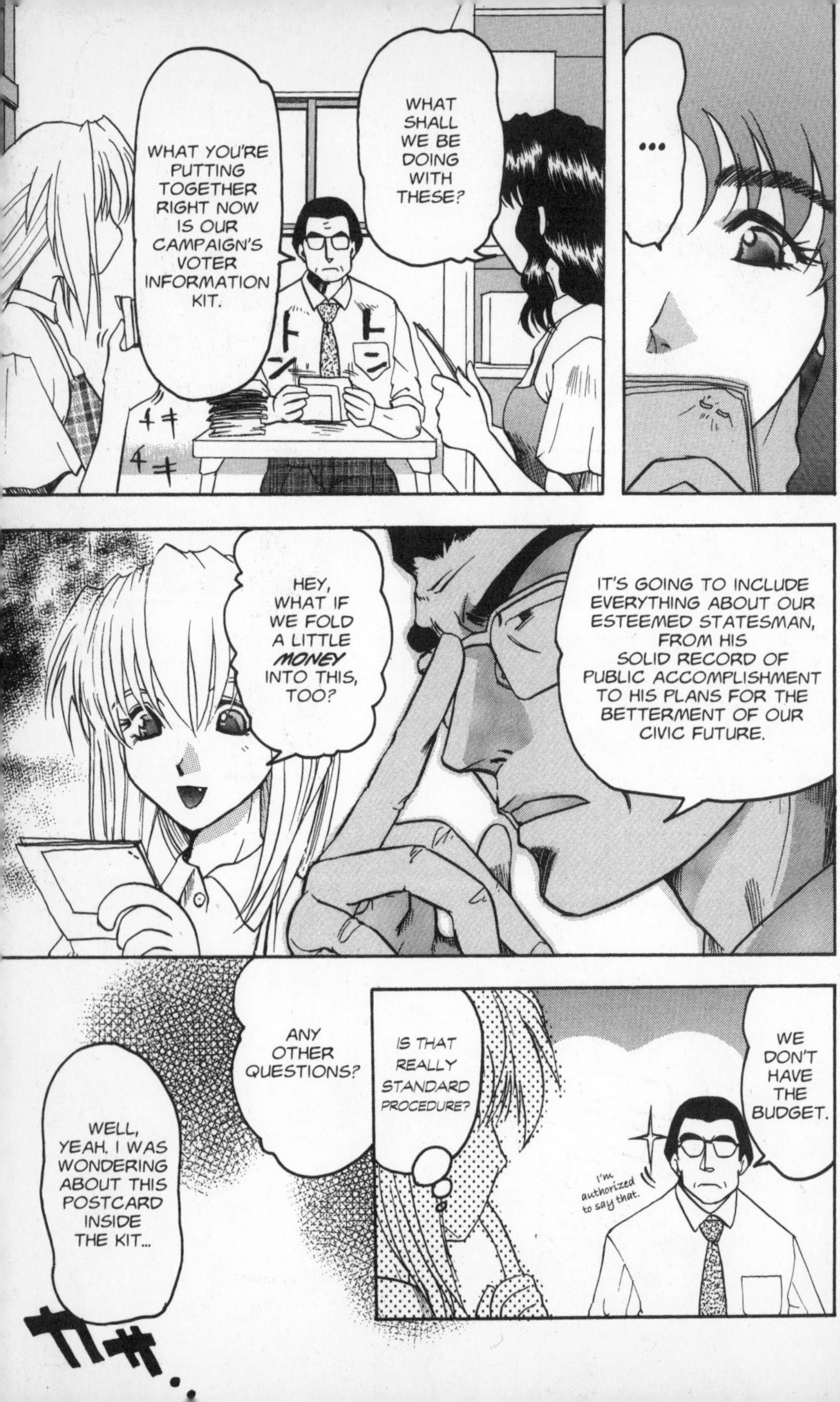
...
WHAT SHALL WE BE DOING WITH THESE?
WHAT YOU'RE PUTTING TOGETHER RIGHT NOW IS OUR CAMPAIGN'S VOTER INFORMATION KIT.
IT'S GOING TO INCLUDE EVERYTHING ABOUT OUR ESTEEMED STATESMAN, FROM HIS SOLID RECORD OF PUBLIC ACCOMPLISHMENT TO HIS PLANS FOR THE BETTERMENT OF OUR CIVIC FUTURE.
HEY, WHAT IF WE FOLD A LITTLE *MONEY* INTO THIS, TOO?
WE DON'T HAVE THE BUDGET.
I'm authorized to say that.
IS THAT REALLY STANDARD PROCEDURE?
ANY OTHER QUESTIONS?
WELL, YEAH. I WAS WONDERING ABOUT THIS POSTCARD INSIDE THE KIT...

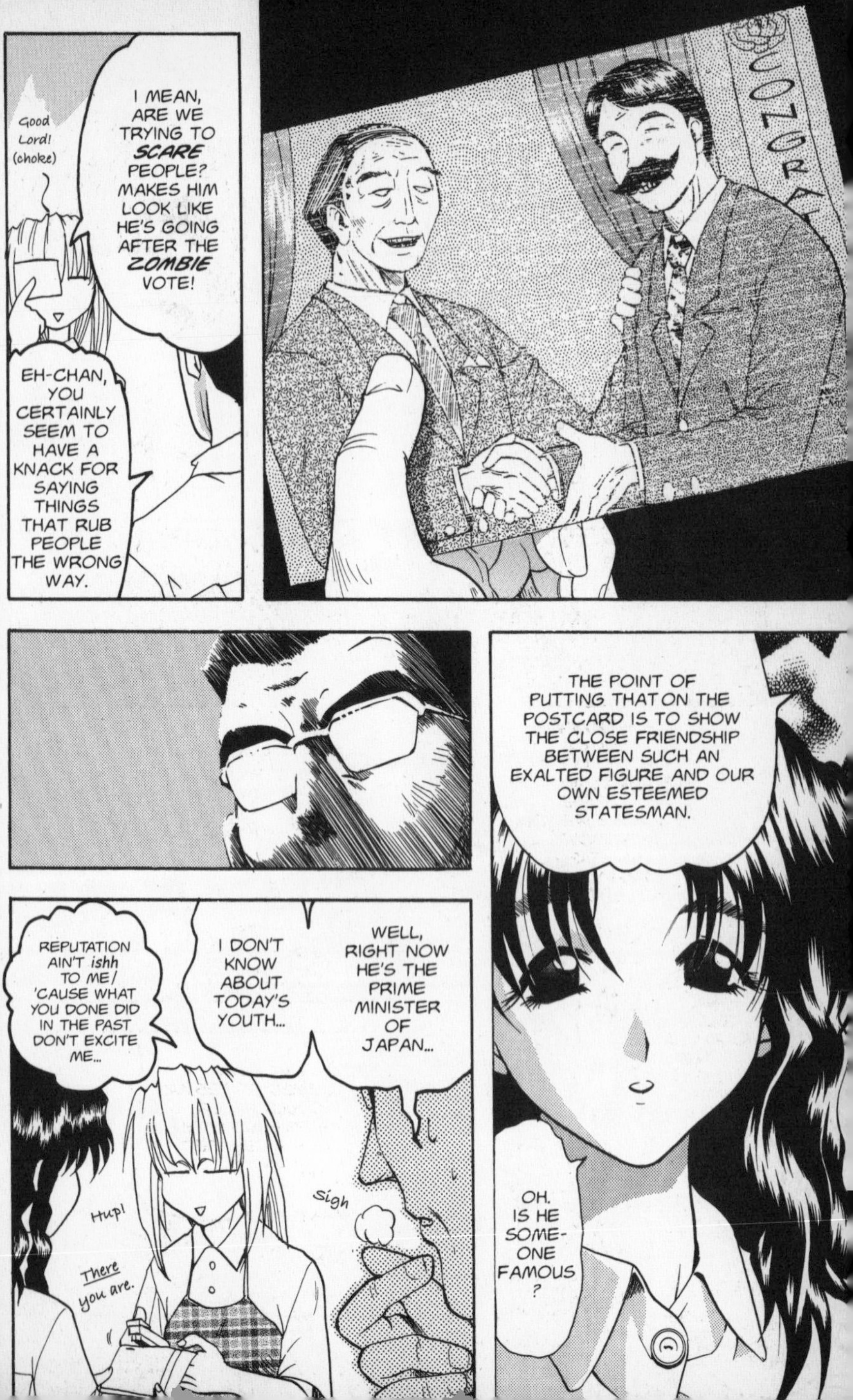
I MEAN, ARE WE TRYING TO SCARE PEOPLE? MAKES HIM LOOK LIKE HE'S GOING AFTER THE ZOMBIE VOTE!
Good Lord! (choke)
EH-CHAN, YOU CERTAINLY SEEM TO HAVE A KNACK FOR SAYING THINGS THAT RUB PEOPLE THE WRONG WAY.
THE POINT OF PUTTING THAT ON THE POSTCARD IS TO SHOW THE CLOSE FRIENDSHIP BETWEEN SUCH AN EXALTED FIGURE AND OUR OWN ESTEEMED STATESMAN.
OH. IS HE SOME-ONE FAMOUS?
WELL, RIGHT NOW HE'S THE PRIME MINISTER OF JAPAN...
I DON'T KNOW ABOUT TODAY'S YOUTH...
Sigh
REPUTATION AIN'T ishh TO ME/ 'CAUSE WHAT YOU DONE DID IN THE PAST DON'T EXCITE ME...
Hup!
There you are.

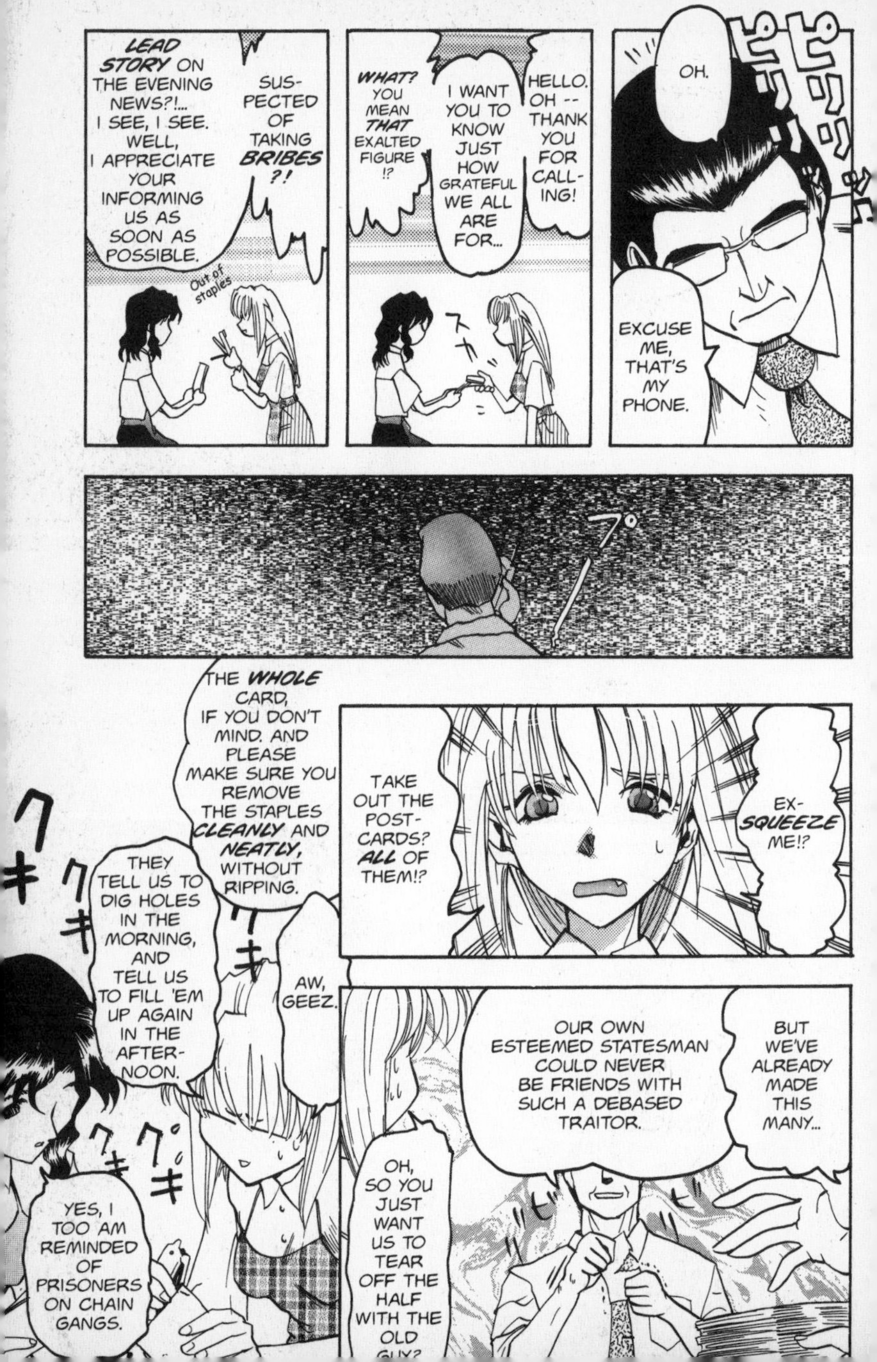
OH.
EXCUSE ME, THAT'S MY PHONE.
HELLO. OH -- THANK YOU FOR CALLING!
I WANT YOU TO KNOW JUST HOW GRATEFUL WE ALL ARE FOR...
WHAT? YOU MEAN THAT EXALTED FIGURE !?
SUS-PECTED OF TAKING BRIBES?!
LEAD STORY ON THE EVENING NEWS?!... I SEE, I SEE. WELL, I APPRECIATE YOUR INFORMING US AS SOON AS POSSIBLE.
Out of staples
EX-SQUEEZE ME!?
TAKE OUT THE POST-CARDS? ALL OF THEM!?
THE WHOLE CARD, IF YOU DON'T MIND. AND PLEASE MAKE SURE YOU REMOVE THE STAPLES CLEANLY AND NEATLY, WITHOUT RIPPING.
BUT WE'VE ALREADY MADE THIS MANY...
OUR OWN ESTEEMED STATESMAN COULD NEVER BE FRIENDS WITH SUCH A DEBASED TRAITOR.
OH, SO YOU JUST WANT US TO TEAR OFF THE HALF WITH THE OLD
AW, GEEZ.
THEY TELL US TO DIG HOLES IN THE MORNING, AND TELL US TO FILL 'EM UP AGAIN IN THE AFTER-NOON.
YES, I TOO AM REMINDED OF PRISONERS ON CHAIN GANGS.

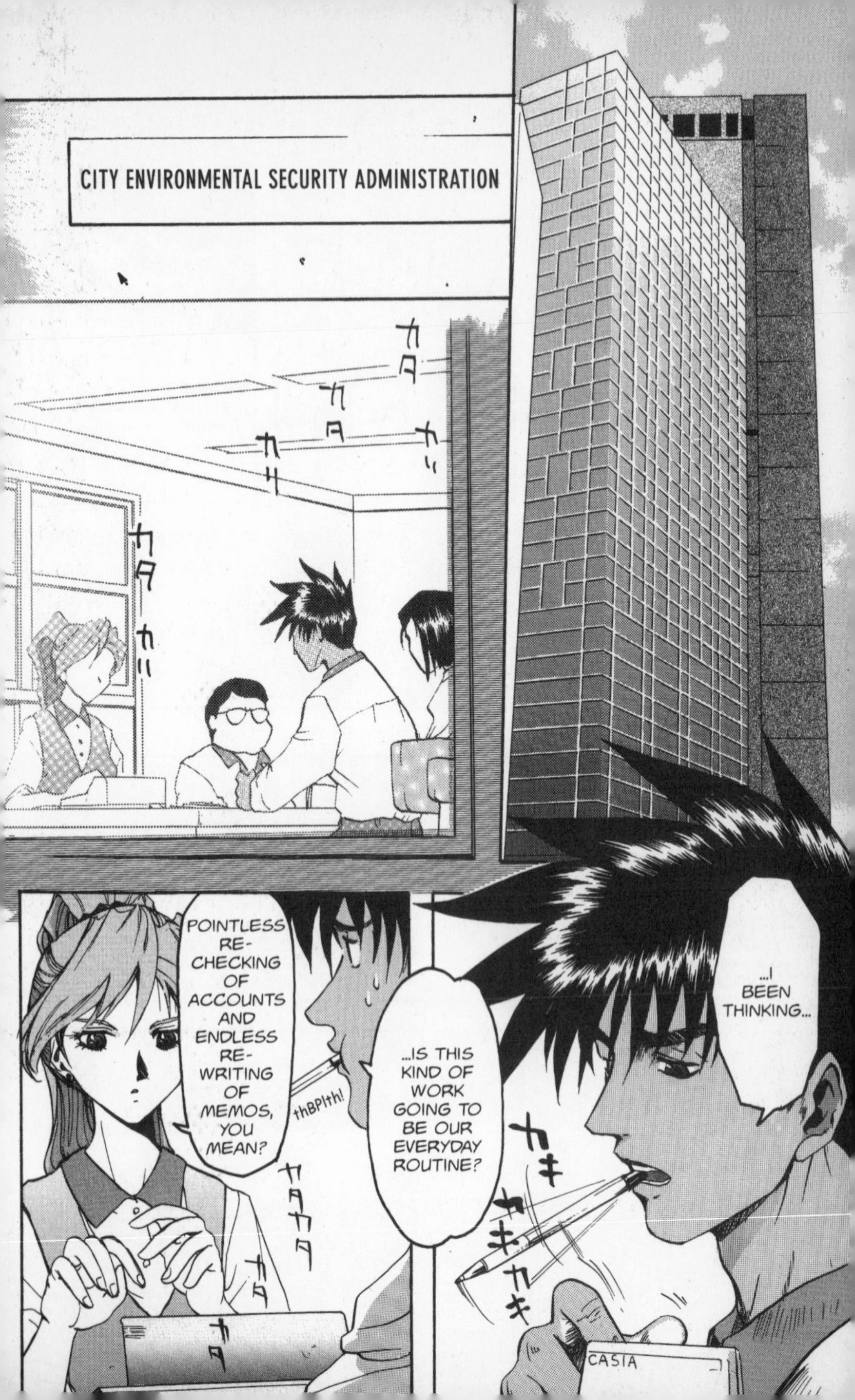

CITY ENVIRONMENTAL SECURITY ADMINISTRATION
...I BEEN THINKING...
...IS THIS KIND OF WORK GOING TO BE OUR EVERYDAY ROUTINE?
POINTLESS RE-CHECKING OF ACCOUNTS AND ENDLESS RE-WRITING OF MEMOS, YOU MEAN?
thBPlth!
CASIA

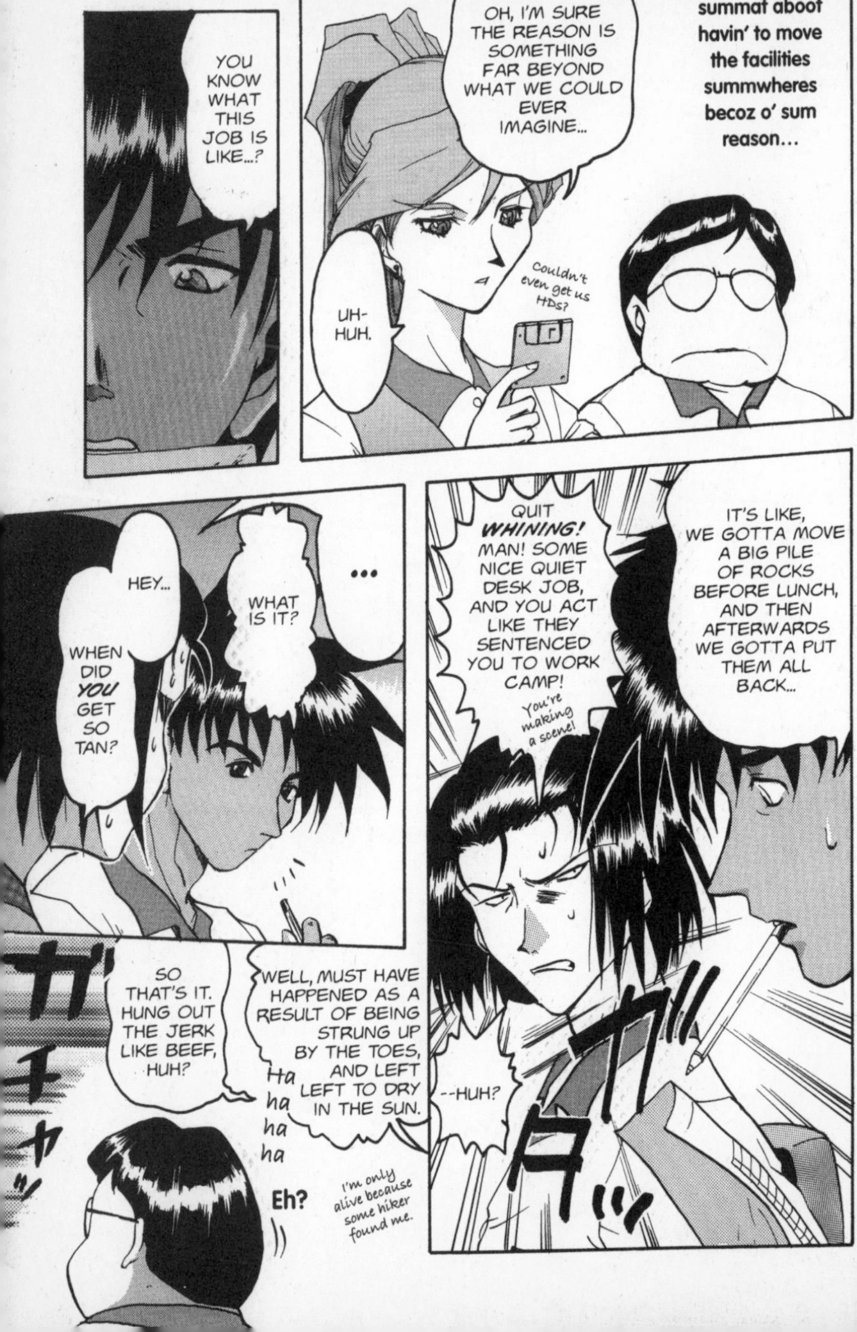
The Dokta tolt us summat aboot havin' to move the facilities summwheres becoz o' sum reason...
OH, I'M SURE THE REASON IS SOMETHING FAR BEYOND WHAT WE COULD EVER IMAGINE...
Couldn't even get us HDs?
UH-HUH.
YOU KNOW WHAT THIS JOB IS LIKE...?
IT'S LIKE, WE GOTTA MOVE A BIG PILE OF ROCKS BEFORE LUNCH, AND THEN AFTERWARDS WE GOTTA PUT THEM ALL BACK...
QUIT *WHINING!* MAN! SOME NICE QUIET DESK JOB, AND YOU ACT LIKE THEY SENTENCED YOU TO WORK CAMP!
You're making a scene!
ガタッ
--HUH?
...
WHAT IS IT?
HEY...
WHEN DID *YOU* GET SO TAN?
WELL, MUST HAVE HAPPENED AS A RESULT OF BEING STRUNG UP BY THE TOES, AND LEFT LEFT TO DRY IN THE SUN.
SO THAT'S IT. HUNG OUT THE JERK LIKE BEEF, HUH?
Ha ha ha ha
ガチャッ
Eh?
I'm only alive because some hiker found me.

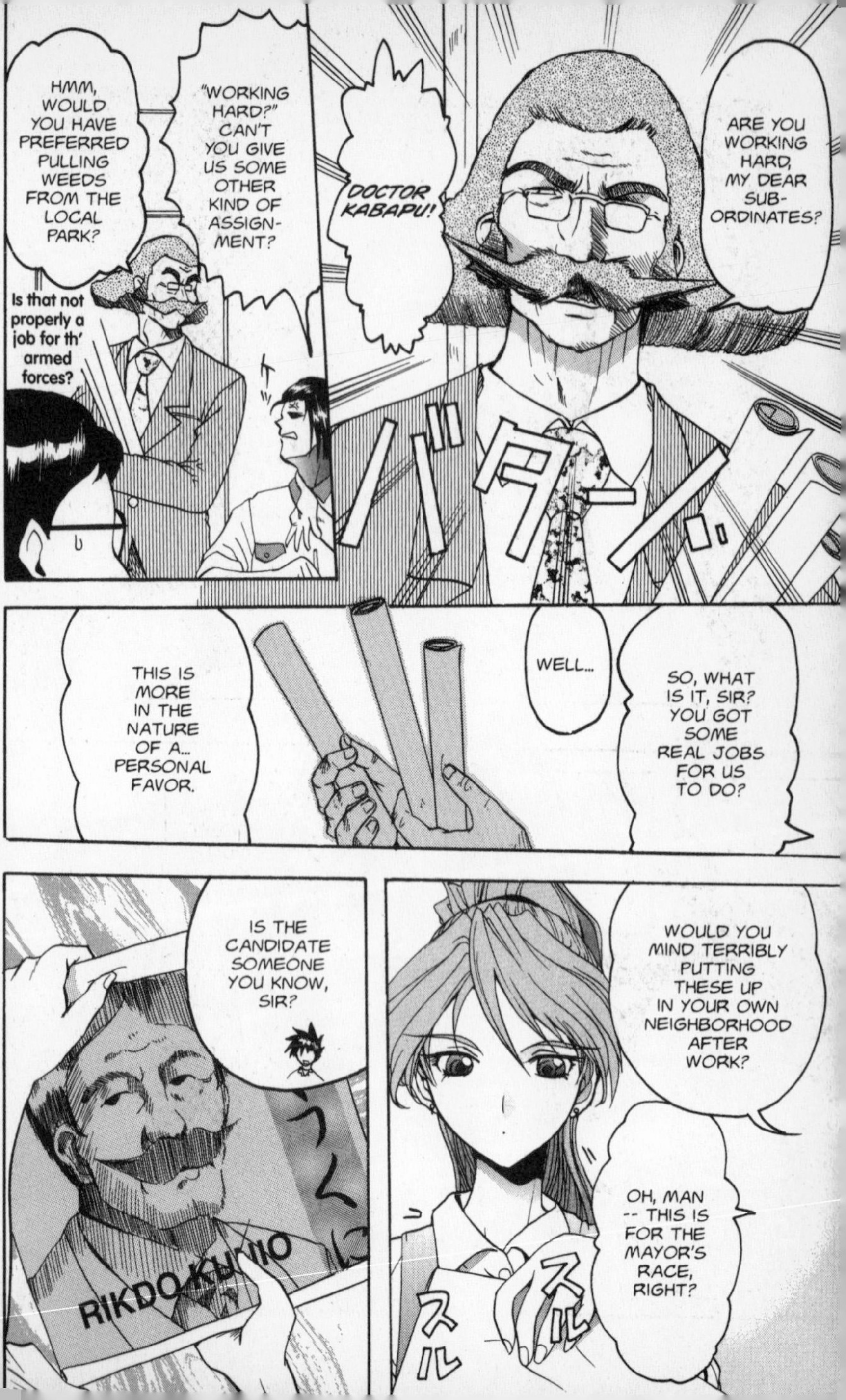
ARE YOU WORKING HARD, MY DEAR SUB-ORDINATES?
DOCTOR KABAPU!
"WORKING HARD?" CAN'T YOU GIVE US SOME OTHER KIND OF ASSIGN-MENT?
HMM, WOULD YOU HAVE PREFERRED PULLING WEEDS FROM THE LOCAL PARK?
Is that not properly a job for th' armed forces?
SO, WHAT IS IT, SIR? YOU GOT SOME REAL JOBS FOR US TO DO?
WELL...
THIS IS MORE IN THE NATURE OF A... PERSONAL FAVOR.
WOULD YOU MIND TERRIBLY PUTTING THESE UP IN YOUR OWN NEIGHBORHOOD AFTER WORK?
OH, MAN -- THIS IS FOR THE MAYOR'S RACE, RIGHT?
IS THE CANDIDATE SOMEONE YOU KNOW, SIR?
RIKDO KUNIO

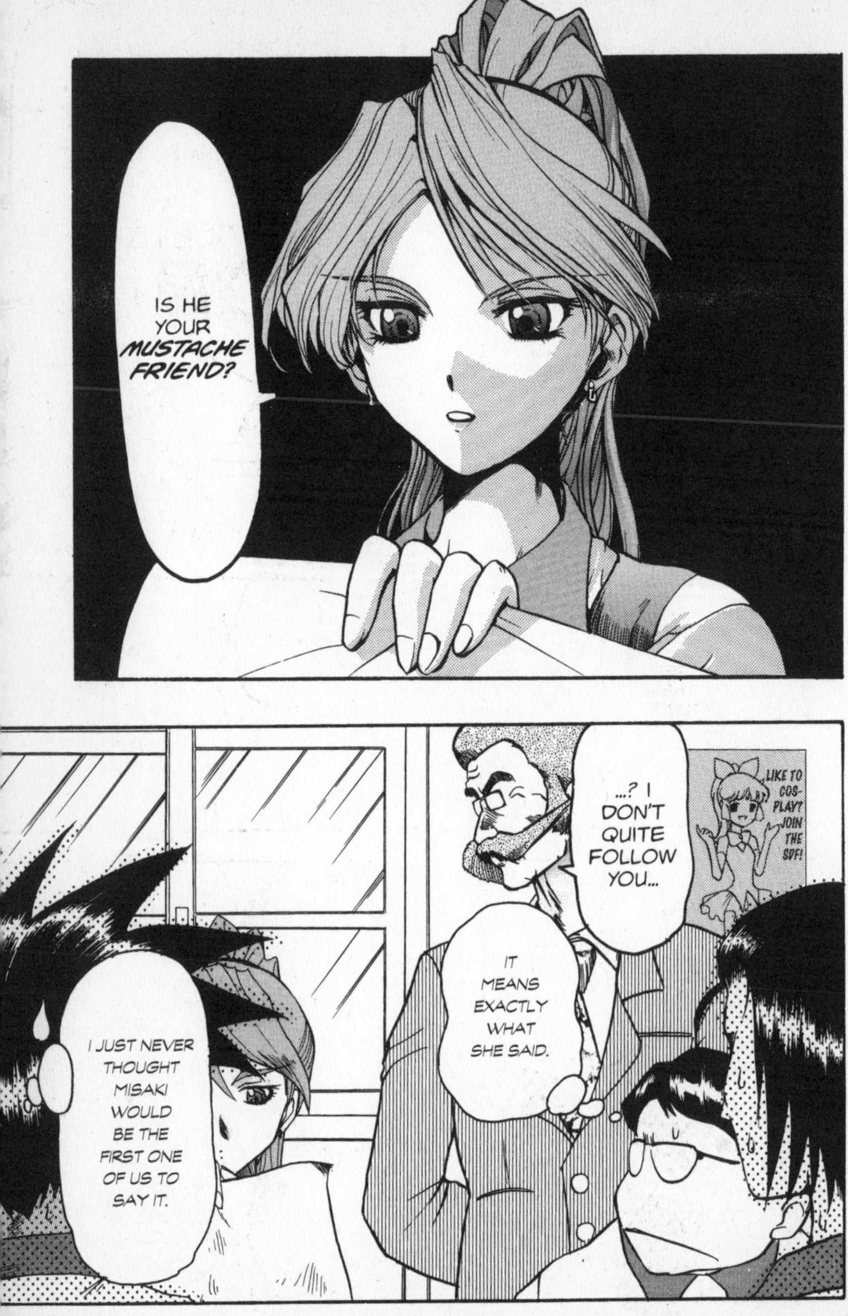
IS HE YOUR MUSTACHE FRIEND?
...? I DON'T QUITE FOLLOW YOU...
LIKE TO COS-PLAY? JOIN THE SDF!
IT MEANS EXACTLY WHAT SHE SAID.
I JUST NEVER THOUGHT MISAKI WOULD BE THE FIRST ONE OF US TO SAY IT.

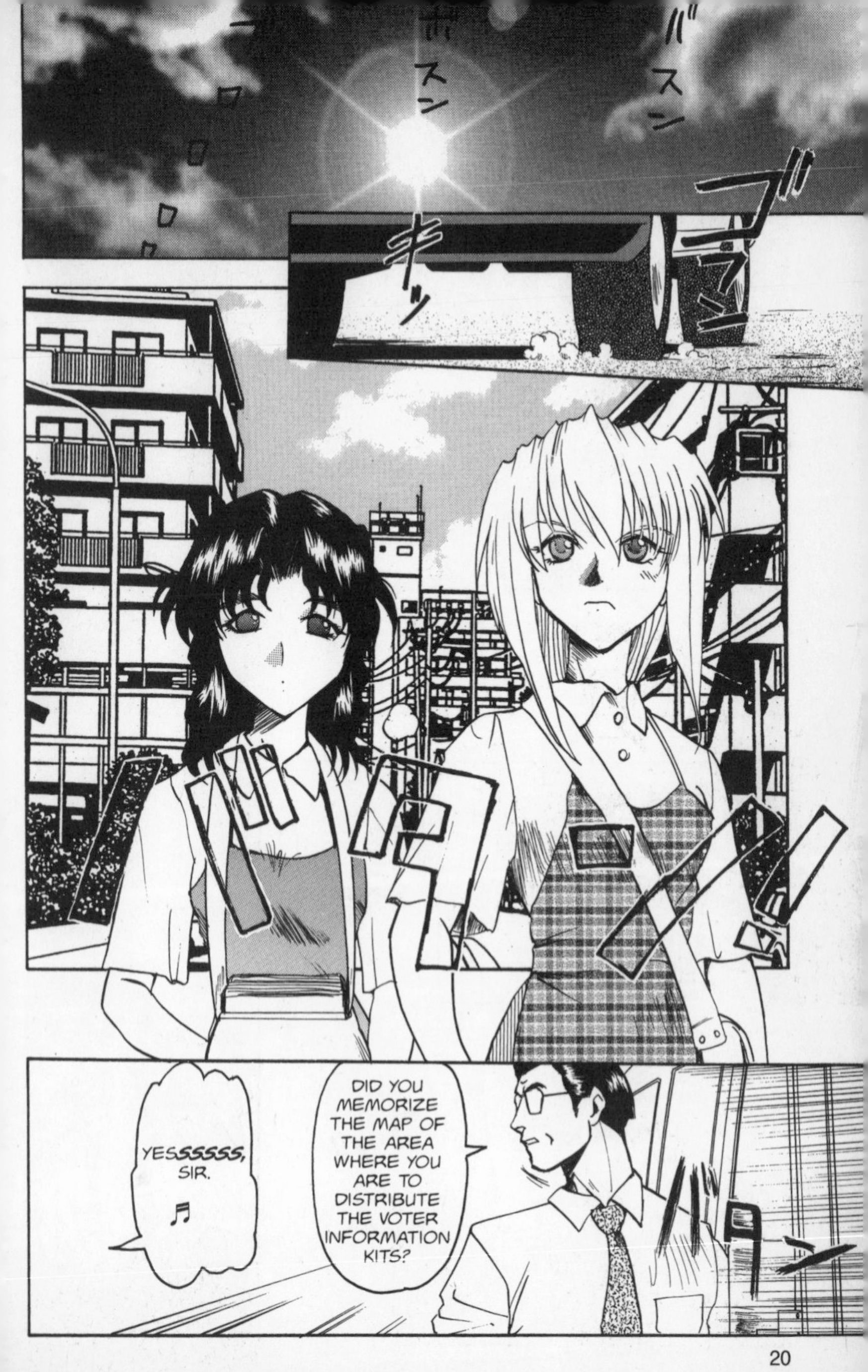
バスン
ボスン
キッ
DID YOU MEMORIZE THE MAP OF THE AREA WHERE YOU ARE TO DISTRIBUTE THE VOTER INFORMATION KITS?
YESSSSSS, SIR. ♪

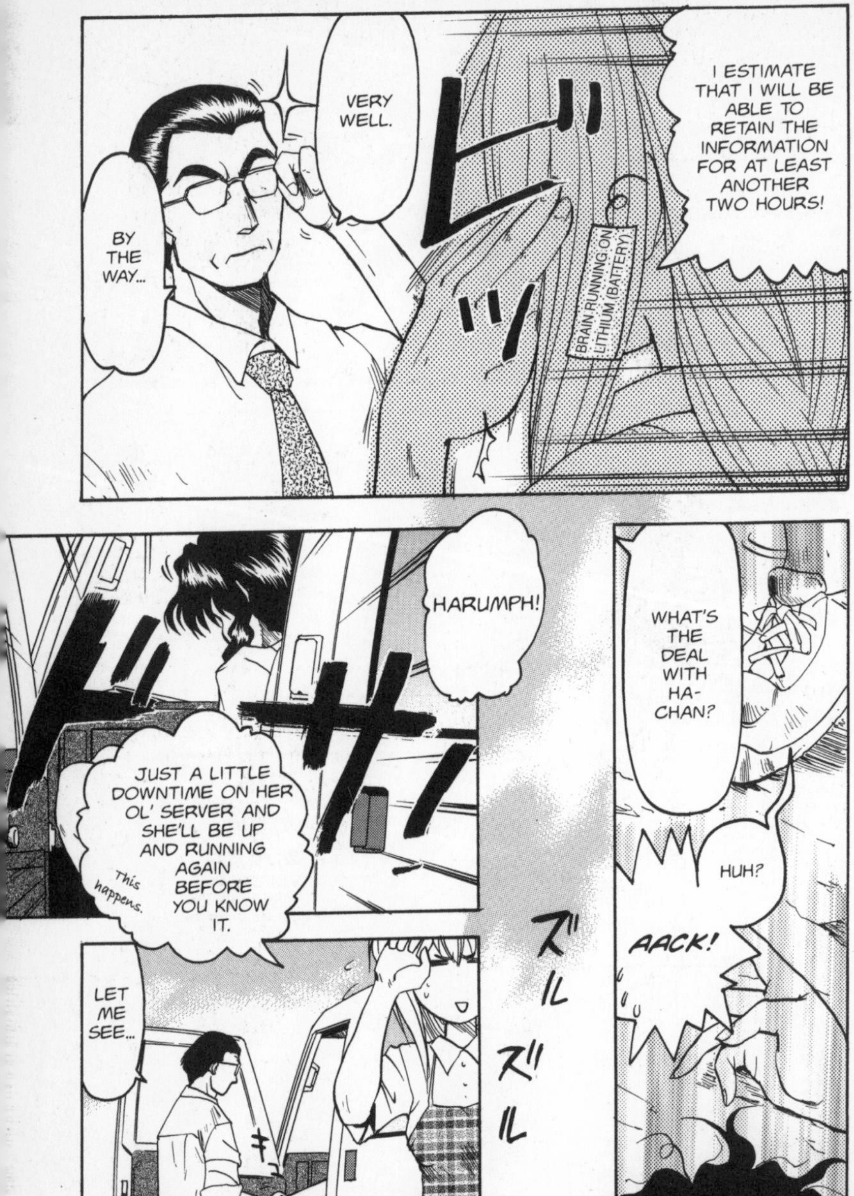
I ESTIMATE THAT I WILL BE ABLE TO RETAIN THE INFORMATION FOR AT LEAST ANOTHER TWO HOURS!
BRAIN RUNNING ON LITHIUM (BATTERY)
VERY WELL.
BY THE WAY...
WHAT'S THE DEAL WITH HA-CHAN?
HUH?
AACK!
ズル
ズル
HARUMPH!
JUST A LITTLE DOWNTIME ON HER OL' SERVER AND SHE'LL BE UP AND RUNNING AGAIN BEFORE YOU KNOW IT.
This happens.
LET ME SEE...

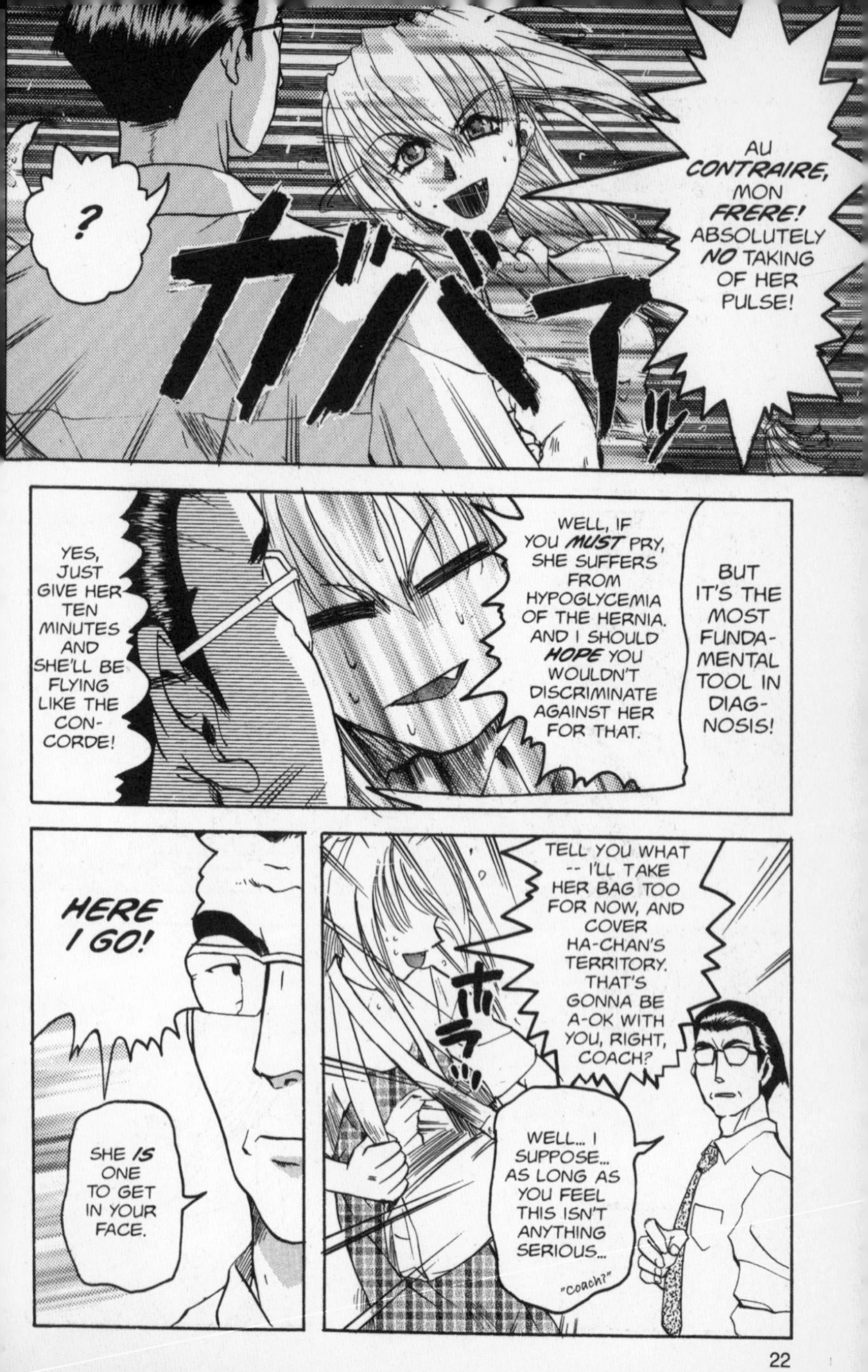

AU CONTRAIRE, MON FRERE! ABSOLUTELY NO TAKING OF HER PULSE!
ガバァッ
?
BUT IT'S THE MOST FUNDAMENTAL TOOL IN DIAGNOSIS!
WELL, IF YOU MUST PRY, SHE SUFFERS FROM HYPOGLYCEMIA OF THE HERNIA. AND I SHOULD HOPE YOU WOULDN'T DISCRIMINATE AGAINST HER FOR THAT.
YES, JUST GIVE HER TEN MINUTES AND SHE'LL BE FLYING LIKE THE CONCORDE!
TELL YOU WHAT -- I'LL TAKE HER BAG TOO FOR NOW, AND COVER HA-CHAN'S TERRITORY. THAT'S GONNA BE A-OK WITH YOU, RIGHT, COACH?
WELL... I SUPPOSE... AS LONG AS YOU FEEL THIS ISN'T ANYTHING SERIOUS...
"Coach?"
HERE I GO!
SHE IS ONE TO GET IN YOUR FACE.

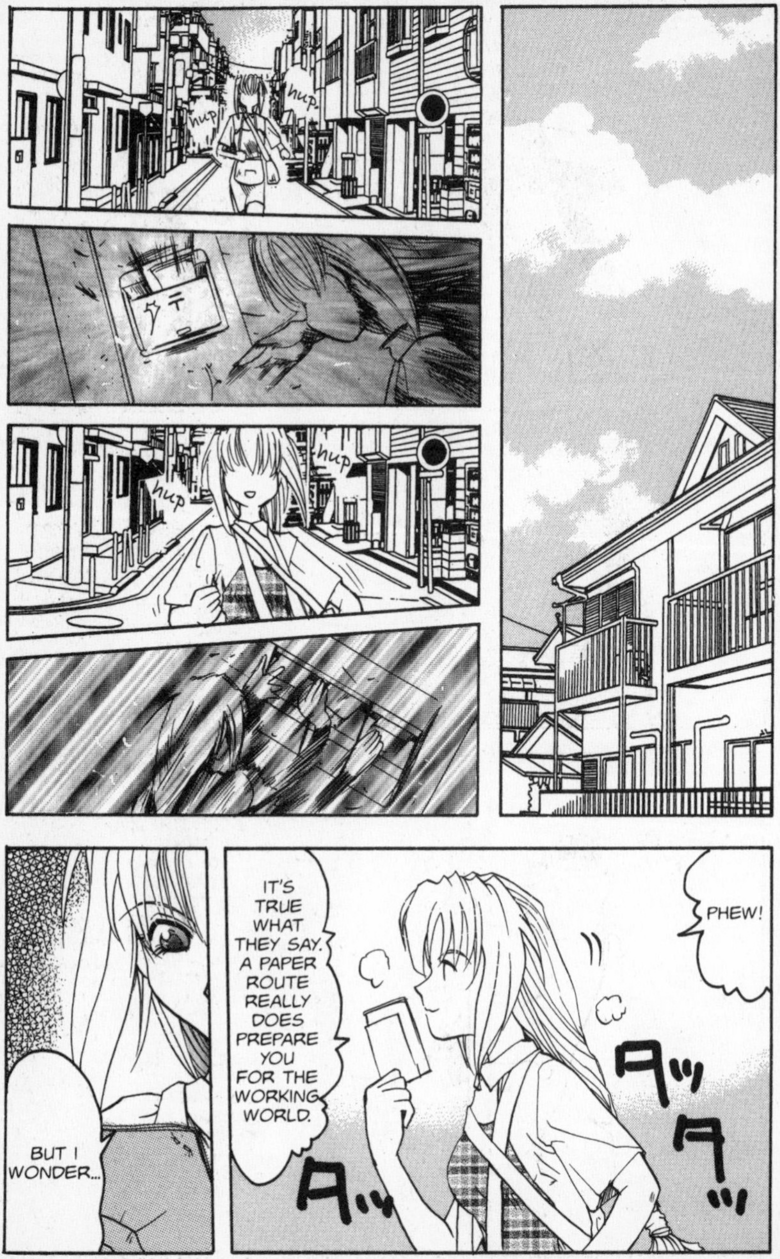
hup
hup
hup
hup
PHEW!
タッ
タッ
IT'S TRUE WHAT THEY SAY. A PAPER ROUTE REALLY DOES PREPARE YOU FOR THE WORKING WORLD.
タッ
BUT I WONDER...

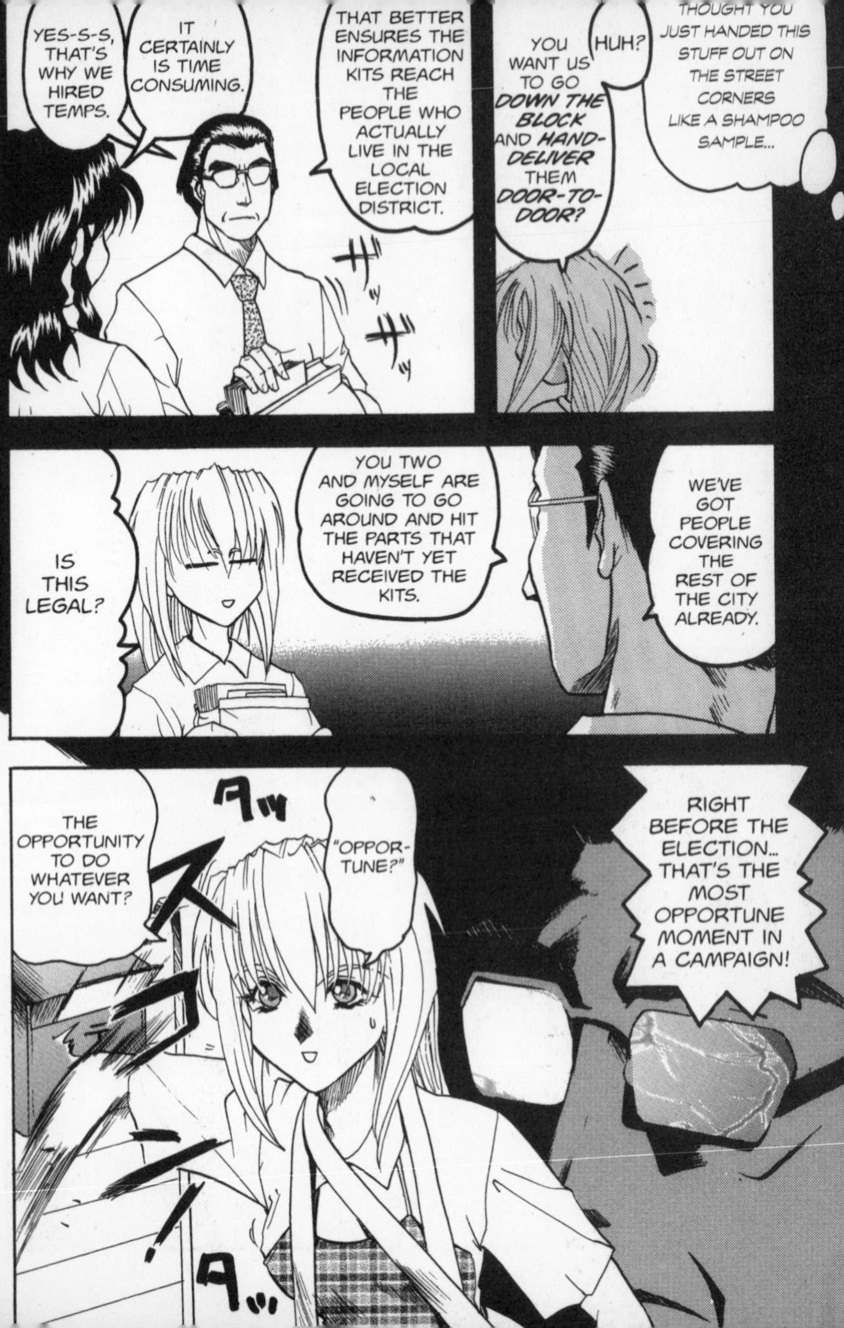
THOUGHT YOU JUST HANDED THIS STUFF OUT ON THE STREET CORNERS LIKE A SHAMPOO SAMPLE...
HUH?
YOU WANT US TO GO DOWN THE BLOCK AND HAND-DELIVER THEM DOOR-TO-DOOR?
THAT BETTER ENSURES THE INFORMATION KITS REACH THE PEOPLE WHO ACTUALLY LIVE IN THE LOCAL ELECTION DISTRICT.
IT CERTAINLY IS TIME CONSUMING.
YES-S-S, THAT'S WHY WE HIRED TEMPS.
WE'VE GOT PEOPLE COVERING THE REST OF THE CITY ALREADY.
YOU TWO AND MYSELF ARE GOING TO GO AROUND AND HIT THE PARTS THAT HAVEN'T YET RECEIVED THE KITS.
IS THIS LEGAL?
RIGHT BEFORE THE ELECTION... THAT'S THE MOST OPPORTUNE MOMENT IN A CAMPAIGN!
"OPPOR-TUNE?"
THE OPPORTUNITY TO DO WHATEVER YOU WANT?

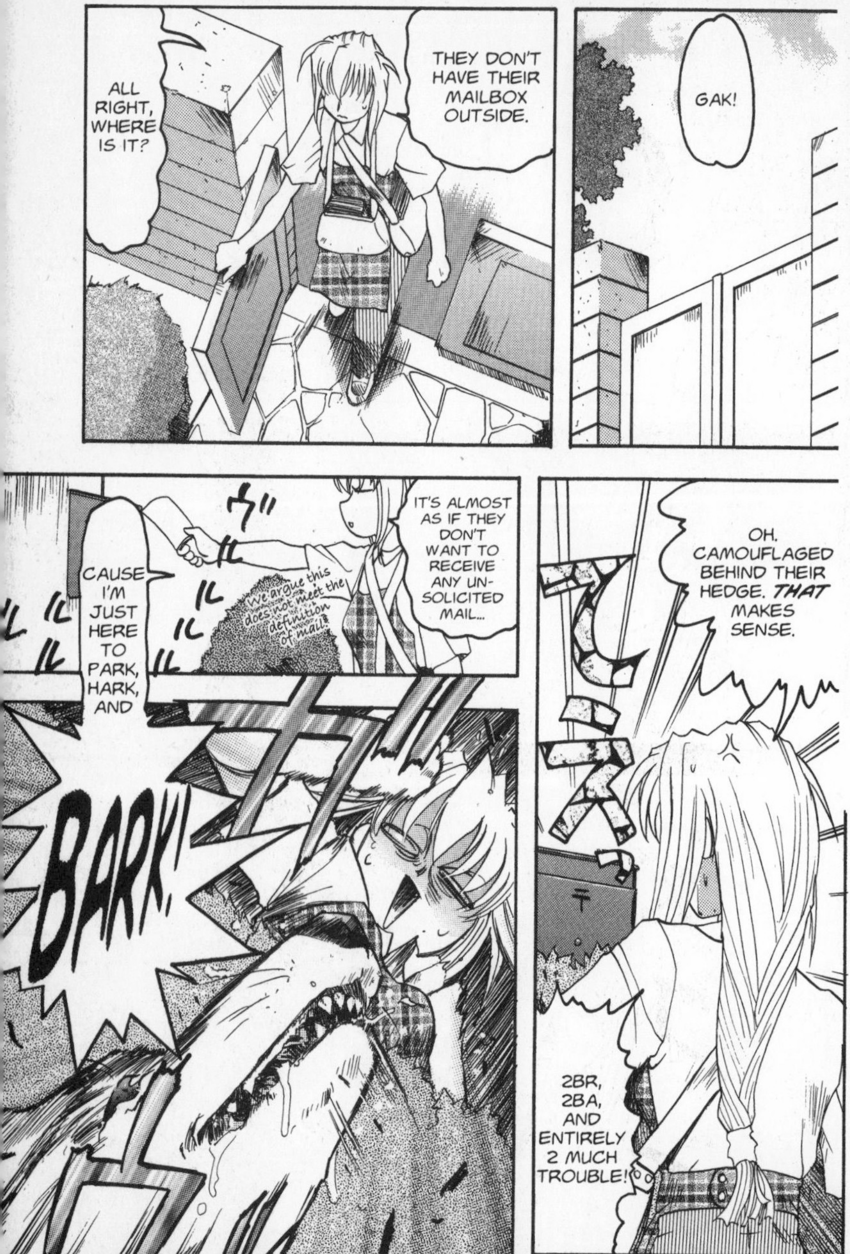
GAK!
THEY DON'T HAVE THEIR MAILBOX OUTSIDE.
ALL RIGHT, WHERE IS IT?
OH. CAMOUFLAGED BEHIND THEIR HEDGE. *THAT* MAKES SENSE.
2BR, 2BA, AND ENTIRELY 2 MUCH TROUBLE!
IT'S ALMOST AS IF THEY DON'T WANT TO RECEIVE ANY UN-SOLICITED MAIL...
We argue this does not meet the definition of mail!
CAUSE I'M JUST HERE TO PARK, HARK, AND
BARK!

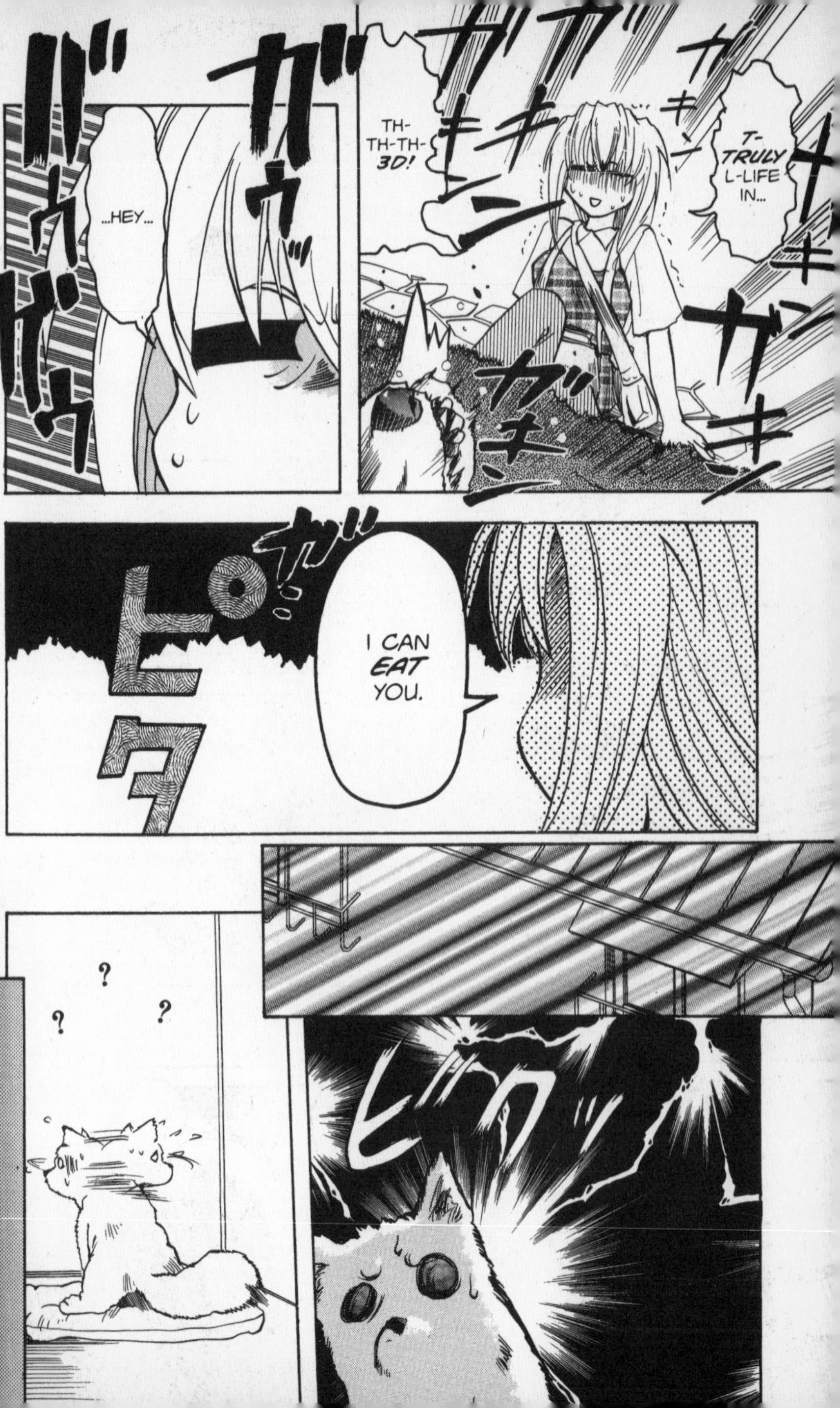
T-TRULY L-LIFE IN...
TH-TH-TH-3D!
...HEY...
I CAN EAT YOU.

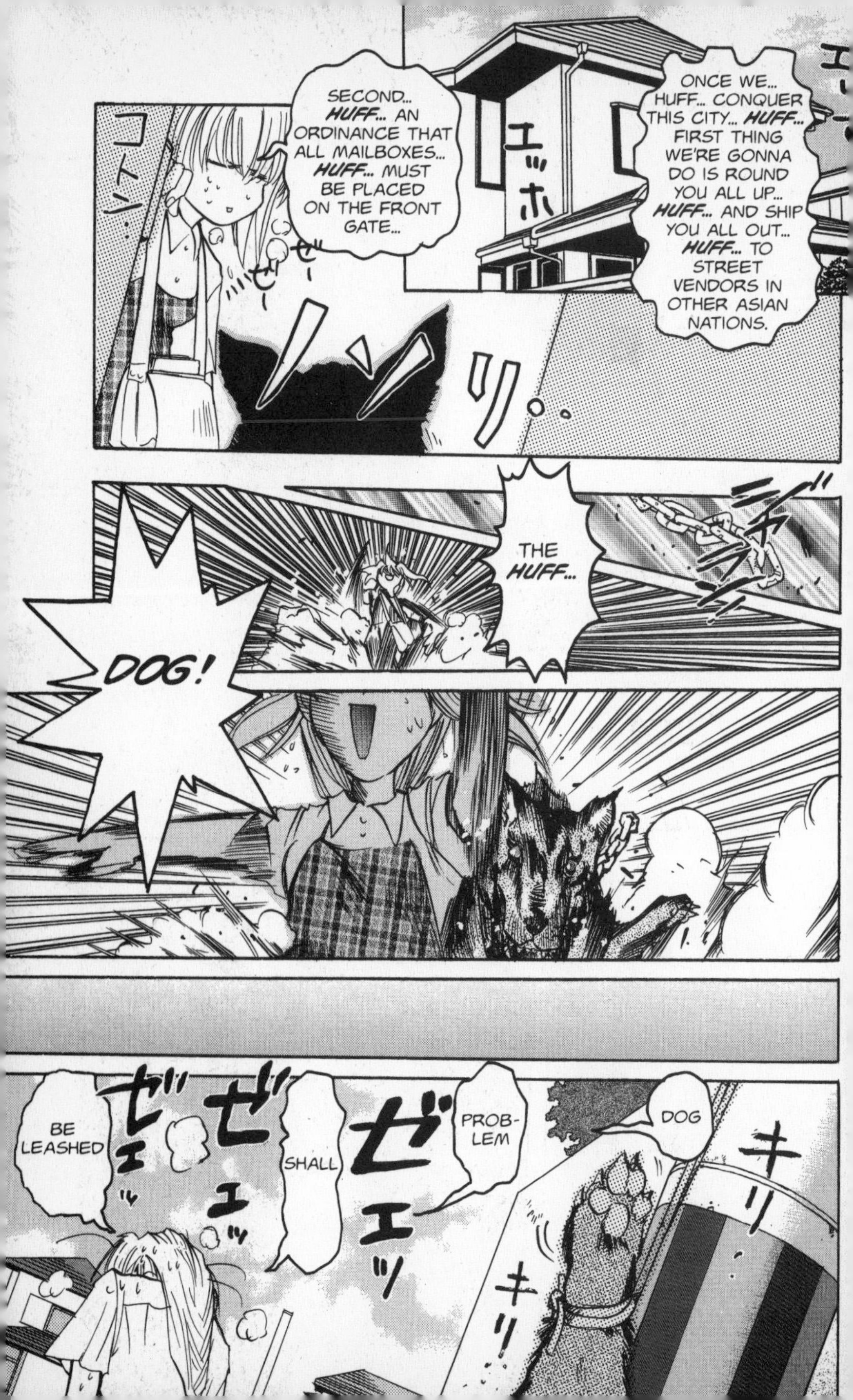
ONCE WE... HUFF... CONQUER THIS CITY... HUFF... FIRST THING WE'RE GONNA DO IS ROUND YOU ALL UP... HUFF... AND SHIP YOU ALL OUT... HUFF... TO STREET VENDORS IN OTHER ASIAN NATIONS.
エッホ
SECOND... HUFF... AN ORDINANCE THAT ALL MAILBOXES... HUFF... MUST BE PLACED ON THE FRONT GATE...
THE HUFF...
DOG!
DOG
PROB-LEM
SHALL
BE LEASHED

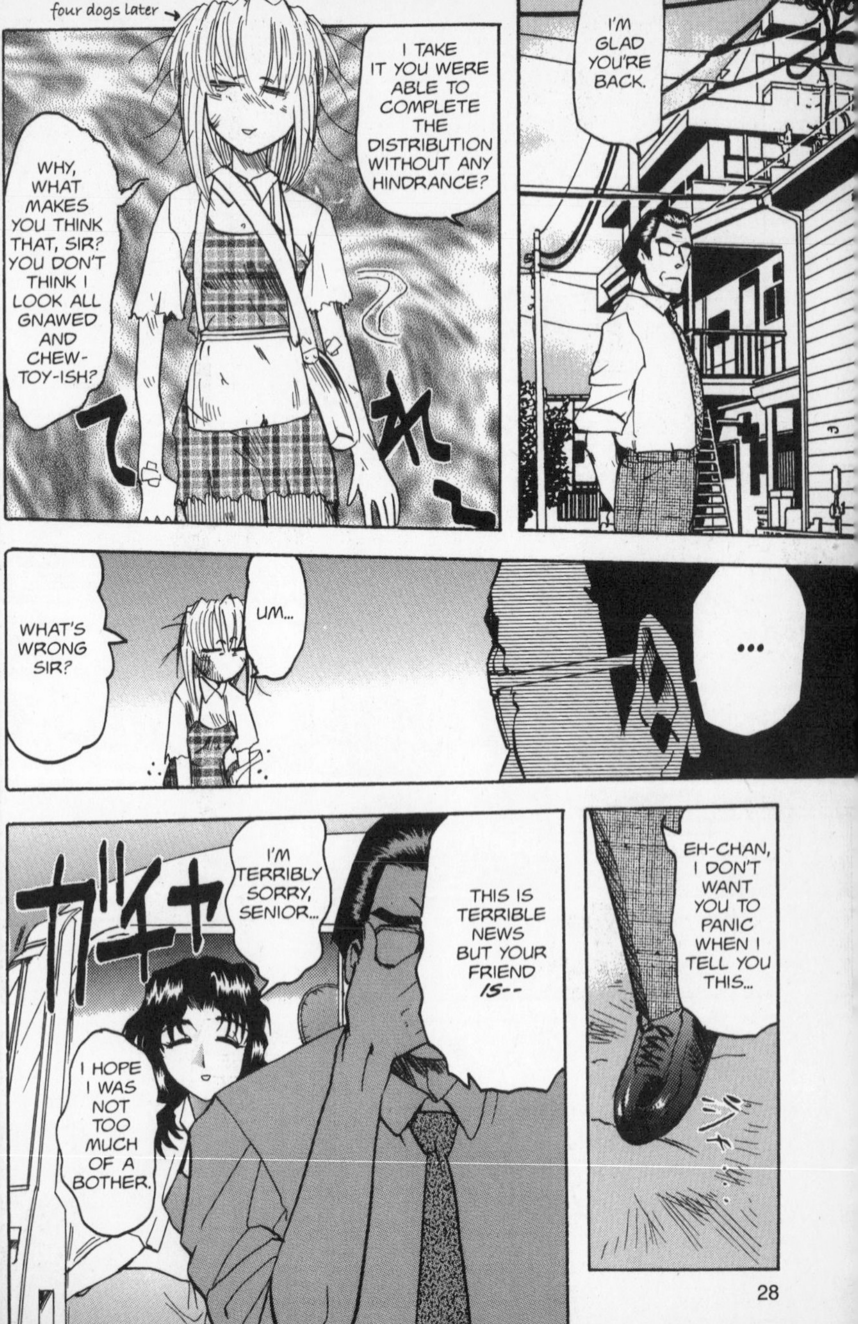
I'M GLAD YOU'RE BACK.
four dogs later
I TAKE IT YOU WERE ABLE TO COMPLETE THE DISTRIBUTION WITHOUT ANY HINDRANCE?
WHY, WHAT MAKES YOU THINK THAT, SIR? YOU DON'T THINK I LOOK ALL GNAWED AND CHEW-TOY-ISH?
てれ〜
...
UM...
WHAT'S WRONG SIR?
EH-CHAN, I DON'T WANT YOU TO PANIC WHEN I TELL YOU THIS...
THIS IS TERRIBLE NEWS BUT YOUR FRIEND *IS--*
I'M TERRIBLY SORRY, SENIOR...
I HOPE I WAS NOT TOO MUCH OF A BOTHER.

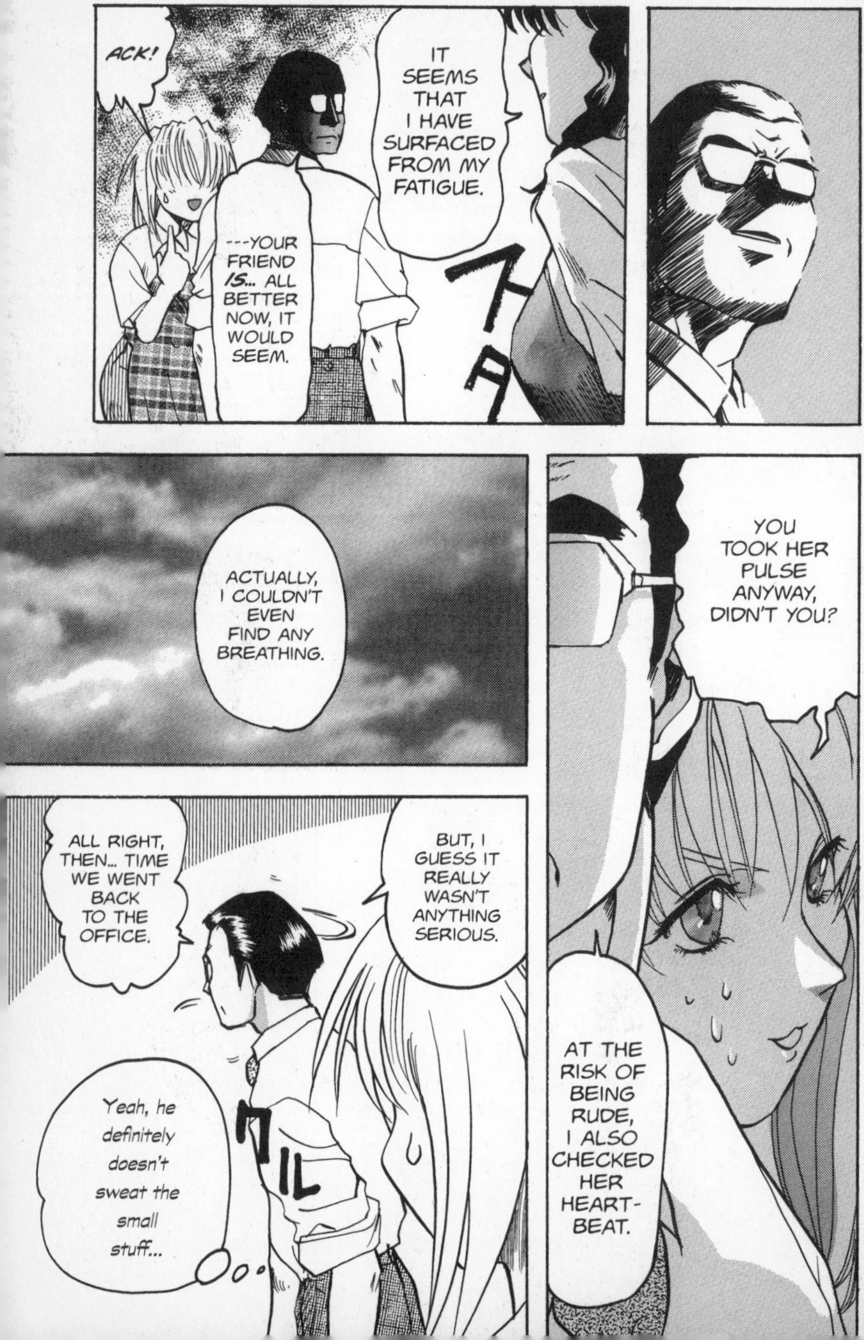
IT SEEMS THAT I HAVE SURFACED FROM MY FATIGUE.
ACK!
---YOUR FRIEND *IS*... ALL BETTER NOW, IT WOULD SEEM.
YOU TOOK HER PULSE ANYWAY, DIDN'T YOU?
AT THE RISK OF BEING RUDE, I ALSO CHECKED HER HEART-BEAT.
ACTUALLY, I COULDN'T EVEN FIND ANY BREATHING.
BUT, I GUESS IT REALLY WASN'T ANYTHING SERIOUS.
ALL RIGHT, THEN... TIME WE WENT BACK TO THE OFFICE.
Yeah, he definitely doesn't sweat the small stuff...

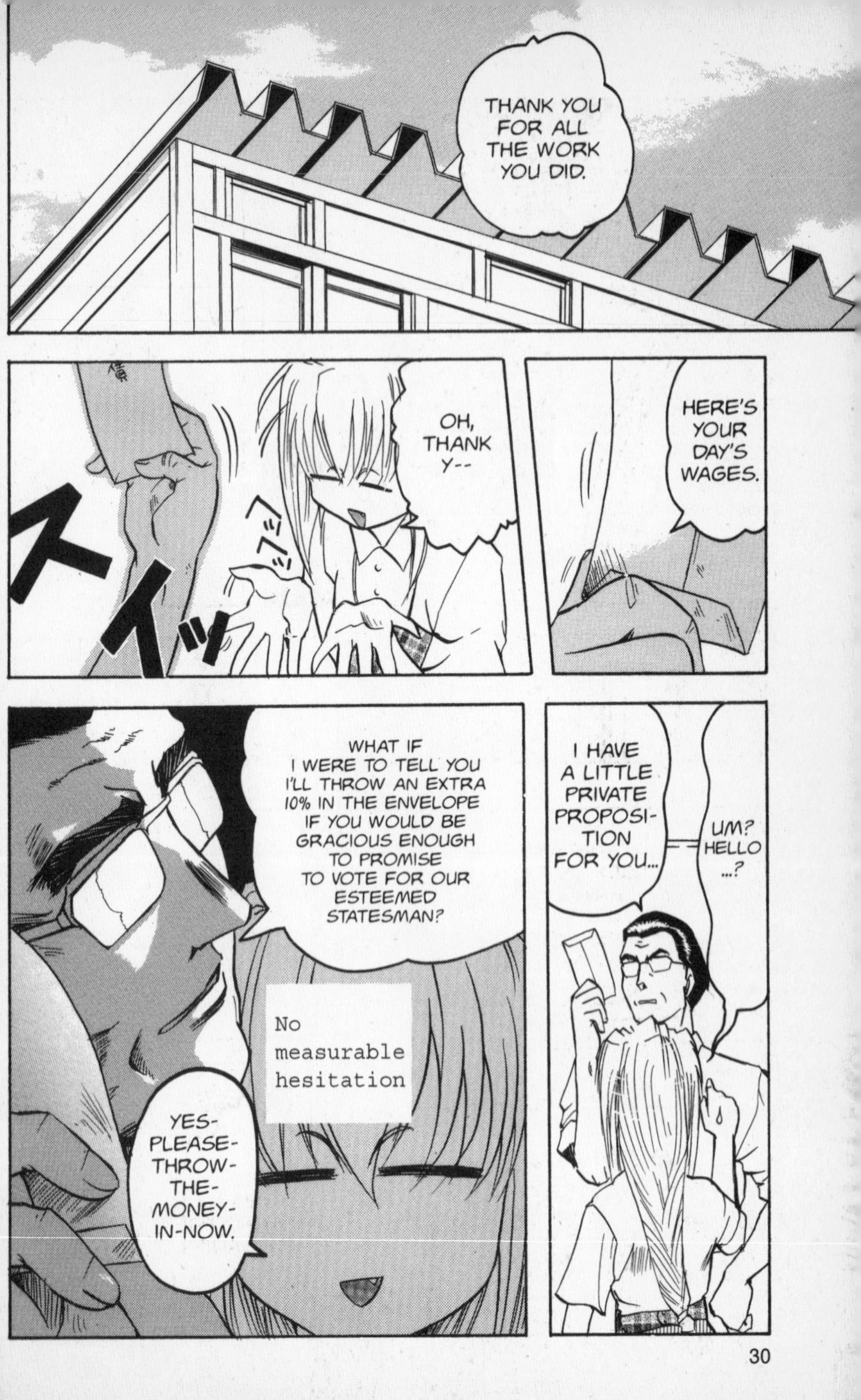
THANK YOU FOR ALL THE WORK YOU DID.
HERE'S YOUR DAY'S WAGES.
OH, THANK Y--
I HAVE A LITTLE PRIVATE PROPOSITION FOR YOU...
UM? HELLO ...?
WHAT IF I WERE TO TELL YOU I'LL THROW AN EXTRA 10% IN THE ENVELOPE IF YOU WOULD BE GRACIOUS ENOUGH TO PROMISE TO VOTE FOR OUR ESTEEMED STATESMAN?
No measurable hesitation
YES-PLEASE-THROW-THE-MONEY-IN-NOW.

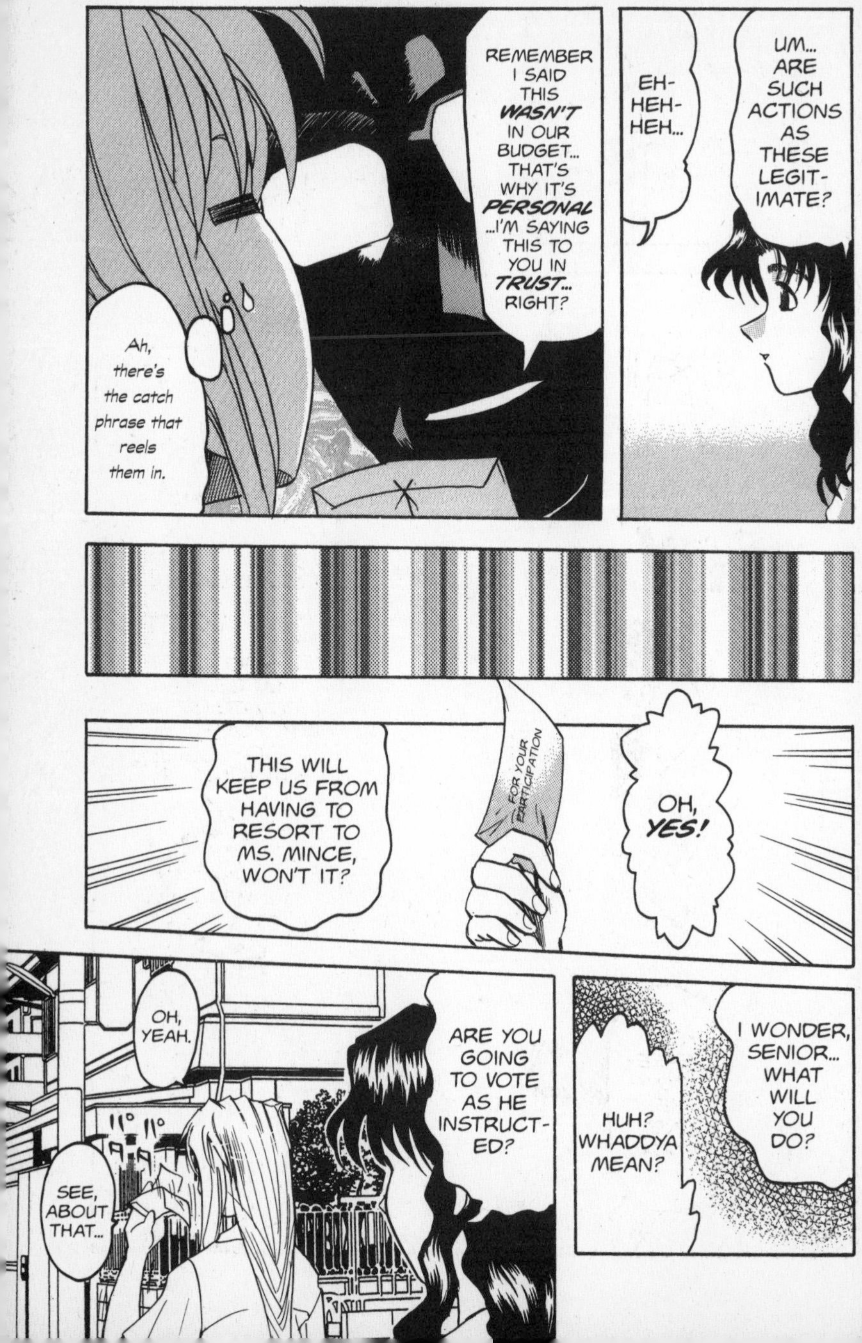
UM... ARE SUCH ACTIONS AS THESE LEGIT-IMATE?
EH-HEH-HEH...
REMEMBER I SAID THIS **WASN'T** IN OUR BUDGET... THAT'S WHY IT'S **PERSONAL** ...I'M SAYING THIS TO YOU IN **TRUST**... RIGHT?
Ah, there's the catch phrase that reels them in.
OH, **YES!**
FOR YOUR PARTICIPATION
THIS WILL KEEP US FROM HAVING TO RESORT TO MS. MINCE, WON'T IT?
I WONDER, SENIOR... WHAT WILL YOU DO?
HUH? WHADDYA MEAN?
ARE YOU GOING TO VOTE AS HE INSTRUCT-ED?
OH, YEAH.
SEE, ABOUT THAT...

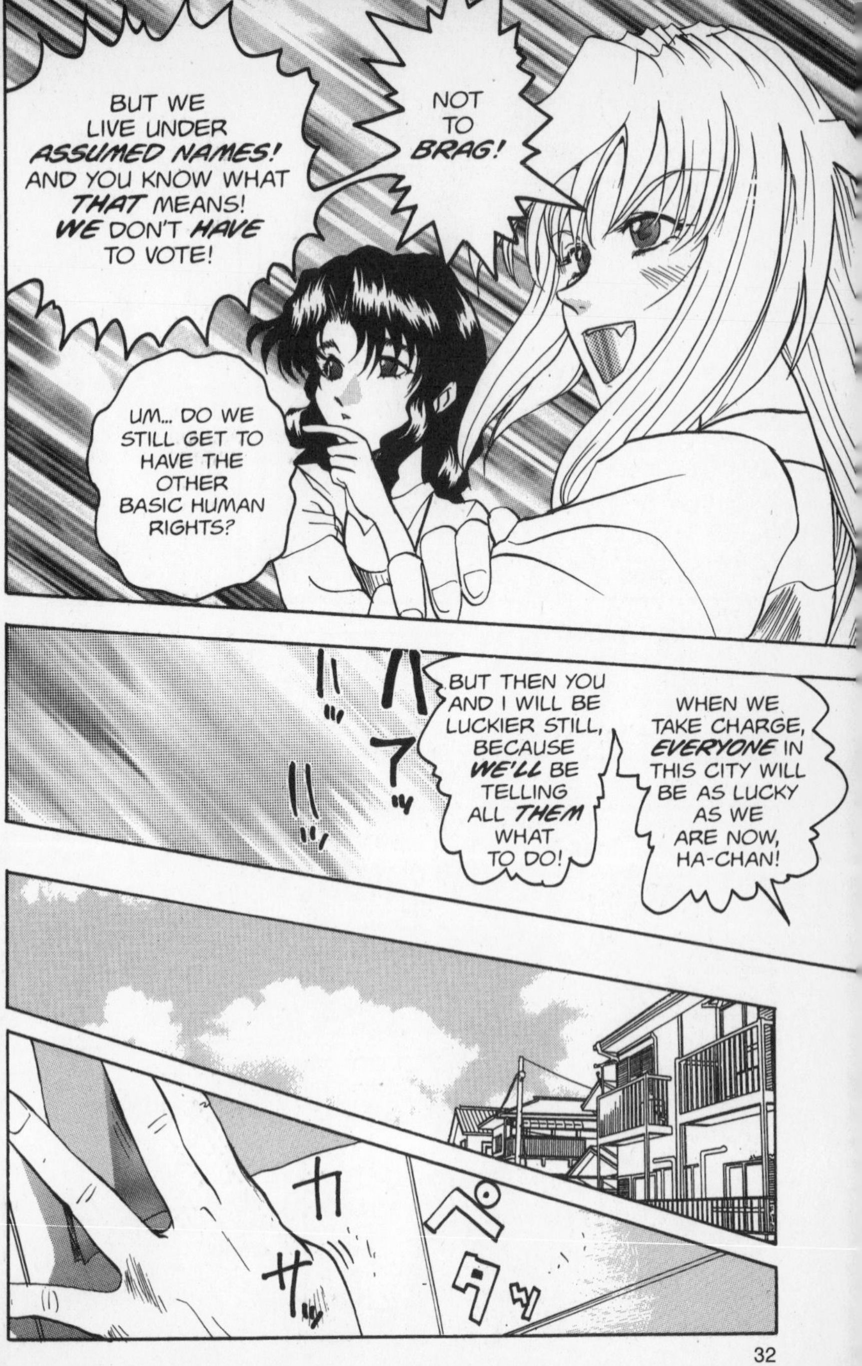
NOT TO *BRAG!*
BUT WE LIVE UNDER *ASSUMED NAMES!* AND YOU KNOW WHAT *THAT* MEANS! *WE* DON'T *HAVE* TO VOTE!
UM... DO WE STILL GET TO HAVE THE OTHER BASIC HUMAN RIGHTS?
WHEN WE TAKE CHARGE, *EVERYONE* IN THIS CITY WILL BE AS LUCKY AS WE ARE NOW, HA-CHAN!
BUT THEN YOU AND I WILL BE LUCKIER STILL, BECAUSE *WE'LL* BE TELLING ALL *THEM* WHAT TO DO!

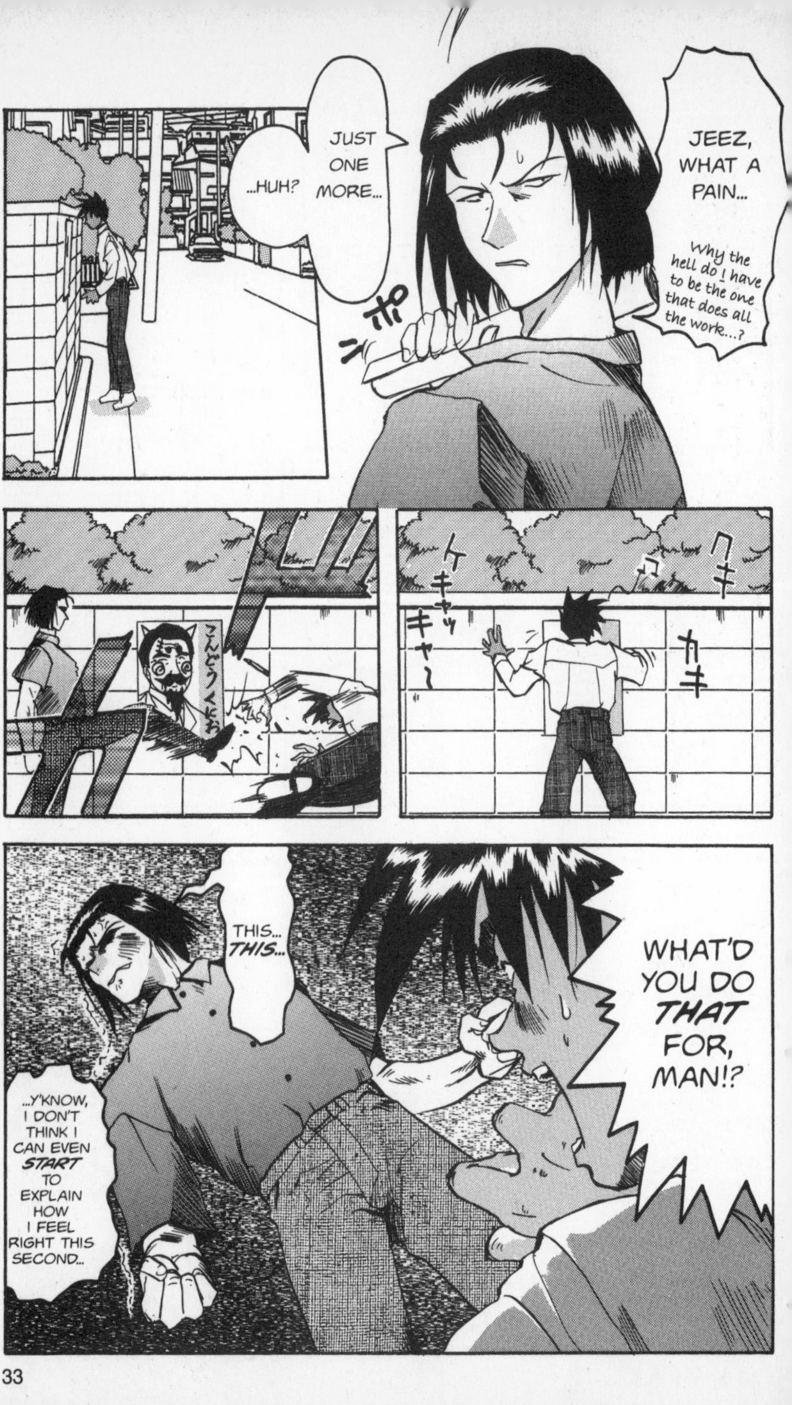
JEEZ, WHAT A PAIN...
Why the hell do I have to be the one that does all the work...?
ポン
JUST ONE MORE...
...HUH?
カキ
カキ
ケキャッキャ~
こんどうくにお
WHAT'D YOU DO *THAT* FOR, MAN!?
THIS... *THIS*...
...Y'KNOW, I DON'T THINK I CAN EVEN *START* TO EXPLAIN HOW I FEEL RIGHT THIS SECOND...

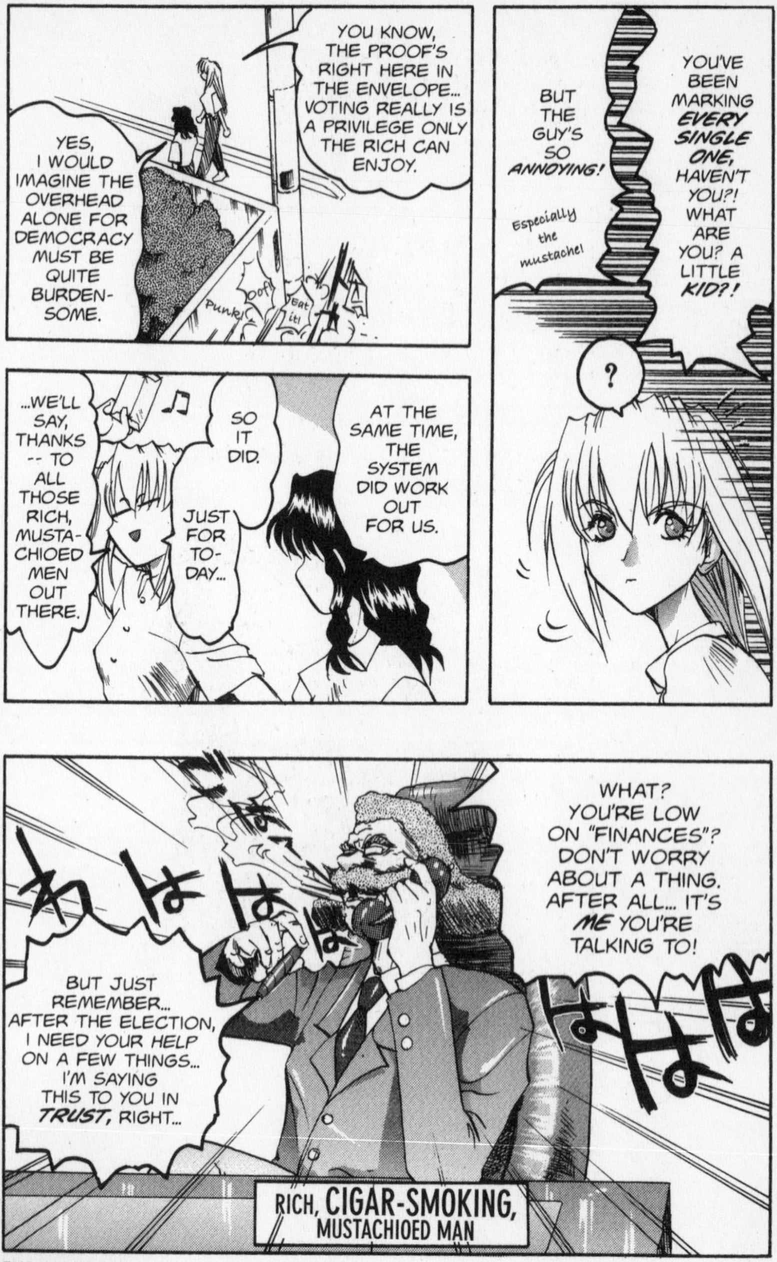
YOU'VE BEEN MARKING *EVERY SINGLE ONE,* HAVEN'T YOU?! WHAT ARE YOU? A LITTLE *KID?!*
BUT THE GUY'S SO *ANNOYING!*
Especially the mustache!
?
YOU KNOW, THE PROOF'S RIGHT HERE IN THE ENVELOPE... VOTING REALLY IS A PRIVILEGE ONLY THE RICH CAN ENJOY.
YES, I WOULD IMAGINE THE OVERHEAD ALONE FOR DEMOCRACY MUST BE QUITE BURDEN-SOME.
Eat it!
Oof!
Punk!
AT THE SAME TIME, THE SYSTEM DID WORK OUT FOR US.
SO IT DID.
JUST FOR TO-DAY...
...WE'LL SAY, THANKS -- TO ALL THOSE RICH, MUSTA-CHIOED MEN OUT THERE.
WHAT? YOU'RE LOW ON "FINANCES"? DON'T WORRY ABOUT A THING. AFTER ALL... IT'S *ME* YOU'RE TALKING TO!
わははは
ははは
BUT JUST REMEMBER... AFTER THE ELECTION, I NEED YOUR HELP ON A FEW THINGS... I'M SAYING THIS TO YOU IN *TRUST,* RIGHT...
RICH, CIGAR-SMOKING, MUSTACHIOED MAN

END MISSION 1

EXCEL SAGA

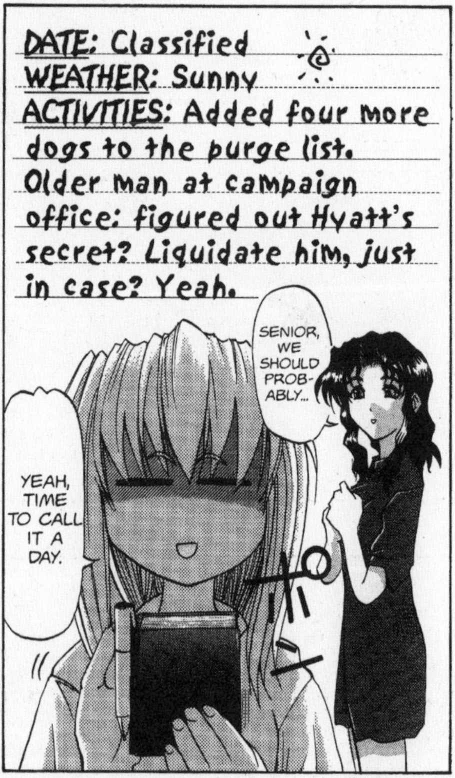
DATE: Classified
WEATHER: Sunny
ACTIVITIES: Added four more dogs to the purge list. Older man at campaign office: figured out Hyatt's secret? Liquidate him, just in case? Yeah.
SENIOR, WE SHOULD PROBABLY...
YEAH, TIME TO CALL IT A DAY.

EXCEL SAGA

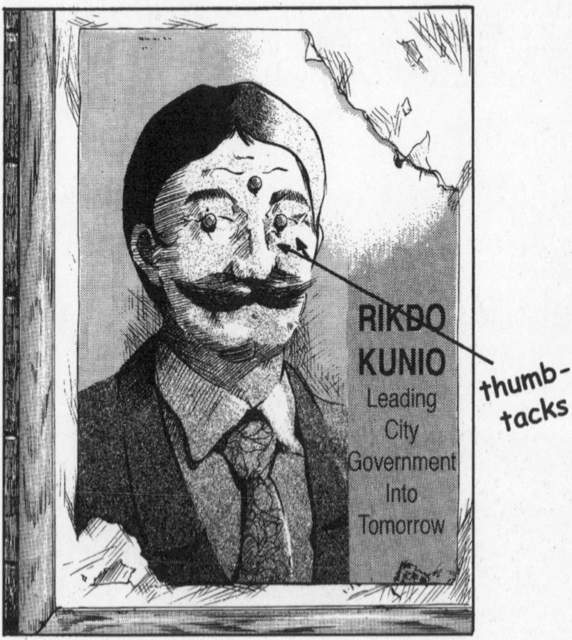
RIKDO KUNIO
Leading City Government Into Tomorrow
thumb-tacks

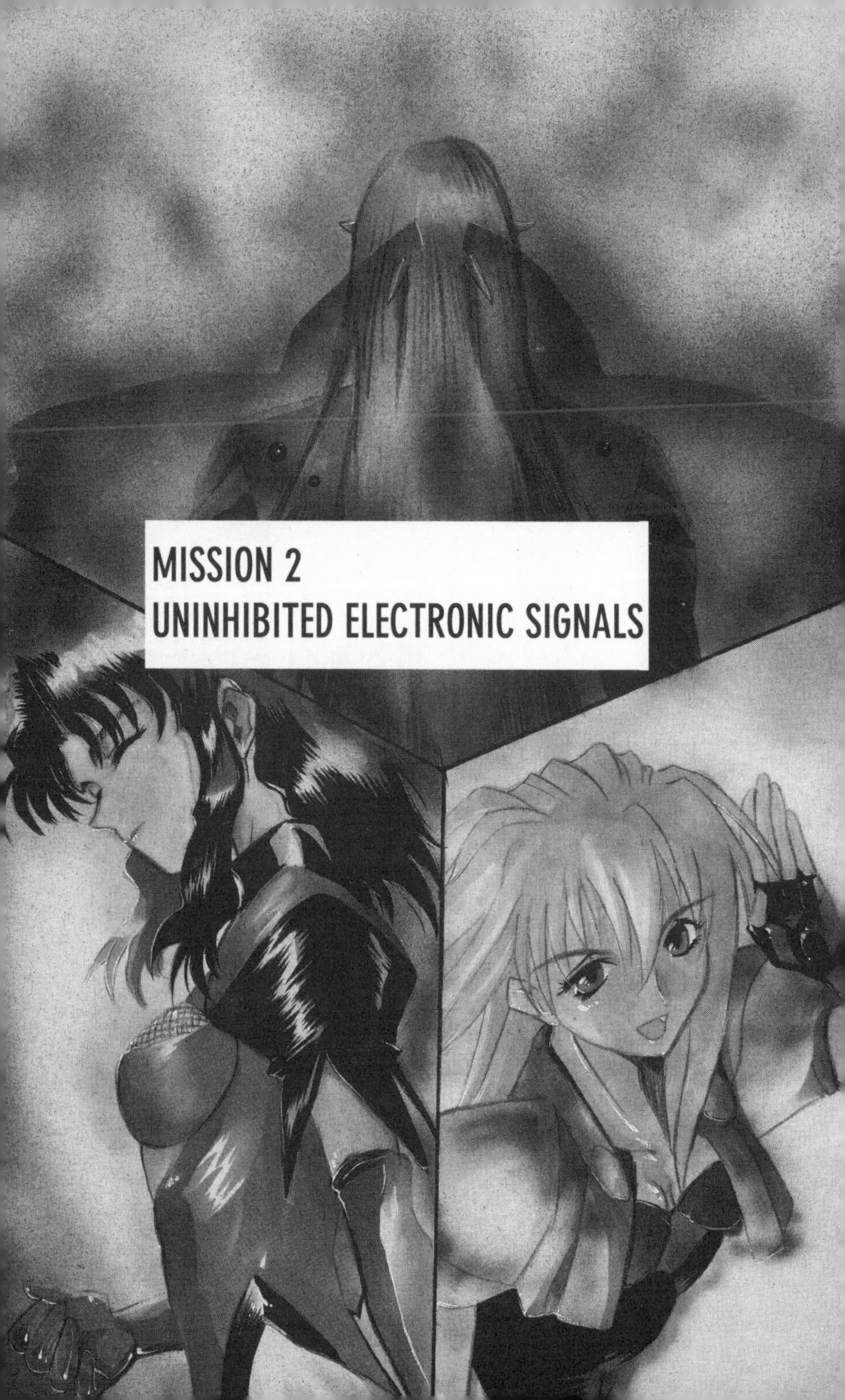
MISSION 2
UNINHIBITED ELECTRONIC SIGNALS

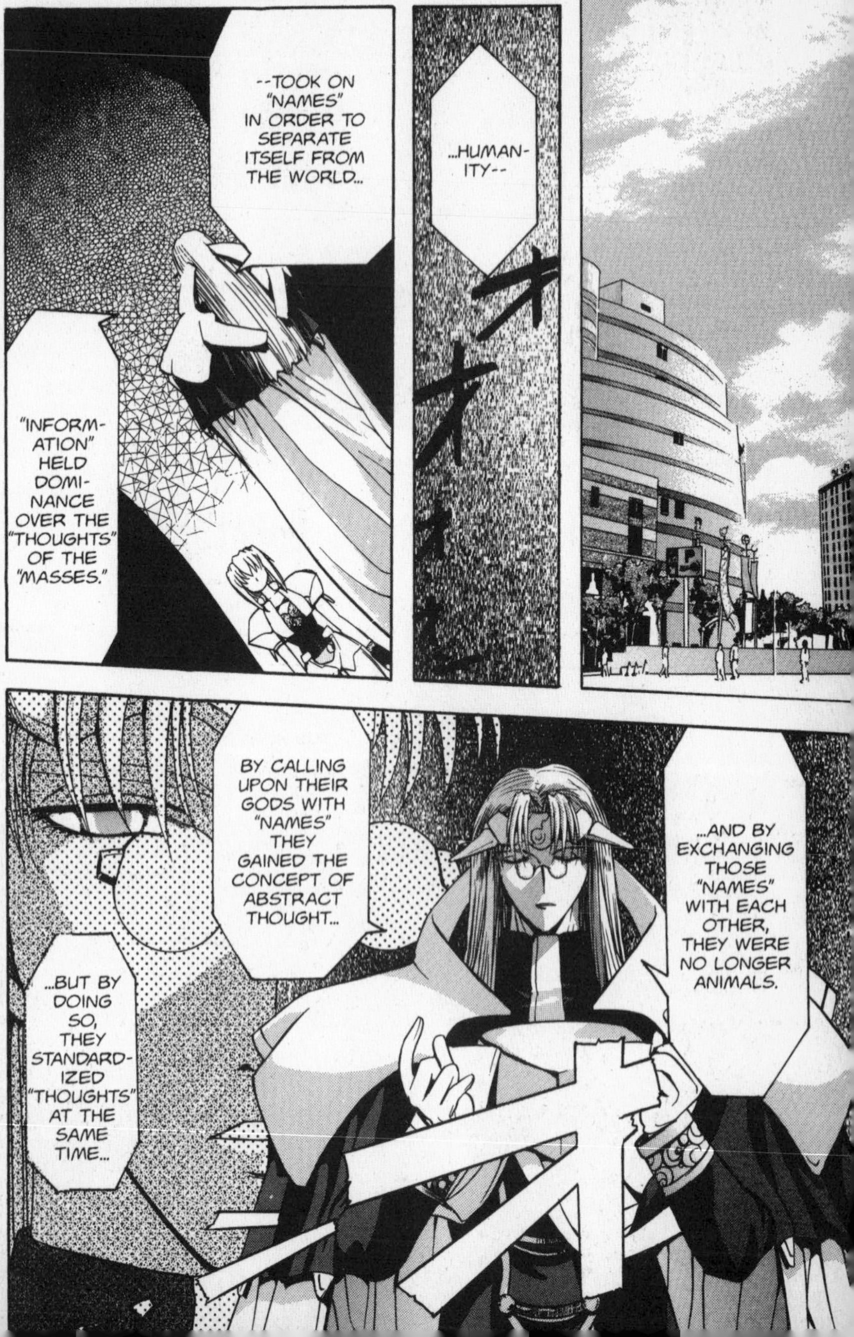
...HUMAN-ITY--
--TOOK ON "NAMES" IN ORDER TO SEPARATE ITSELF FROM THE WORLD...
"INFORM-ATION" HELD DOMI-NANCE OVER THE "THOUGHTS" OF THE "MASSES."
...AND BY EXCHANGING THOSE "NAMES" WITH EACH OTHER, THEY WERE NO LONGER ANIMALS.
BY CALLING UPON THEIR GODS WITH "NAMES" THEY GAINED THE CONCEPT OF ABSTRACT THOUGHT...
...BUT BY DOING SO, THEY STANDARD-IZED "THOUGHTS" AT THE SAME TIME...

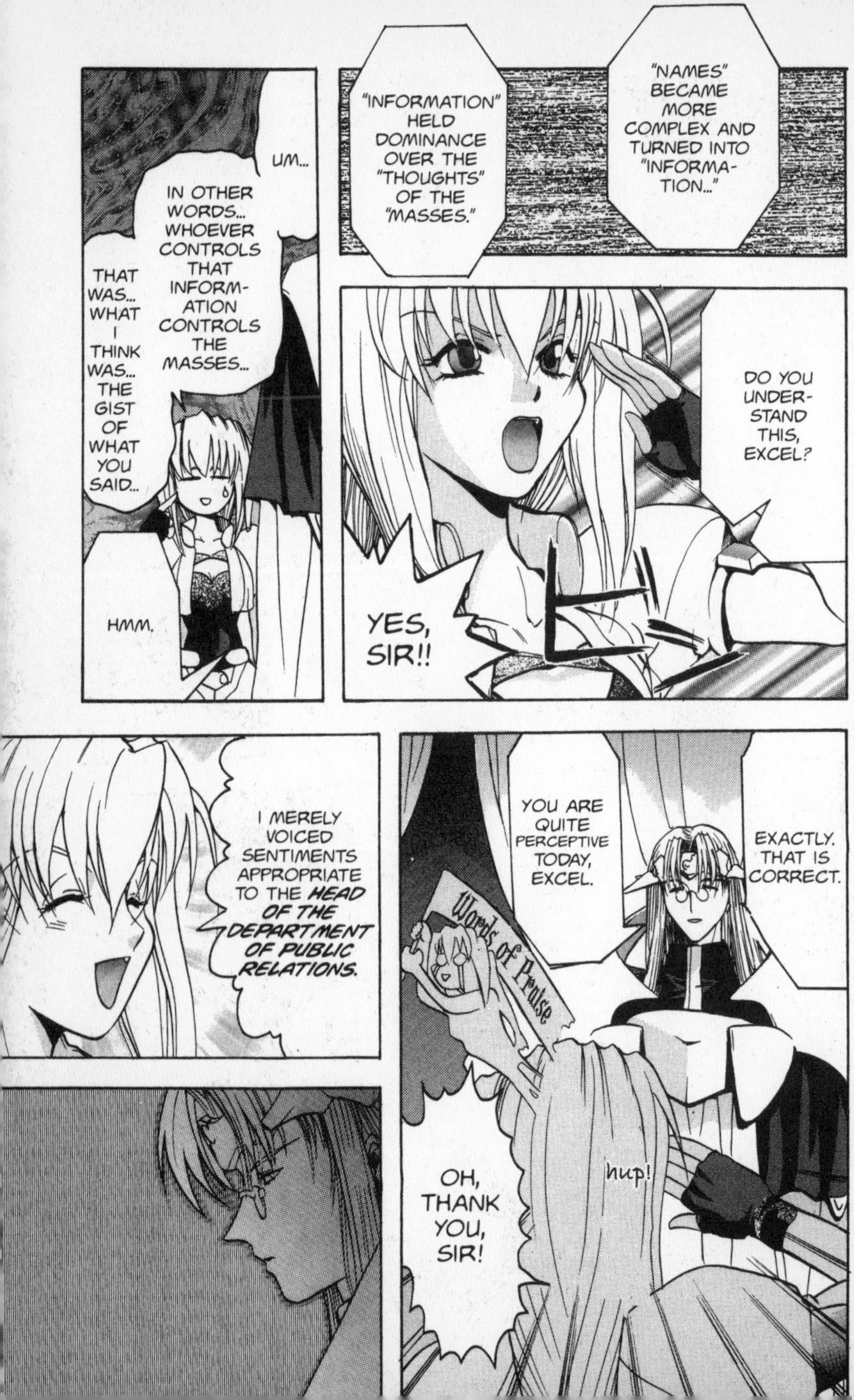
"NAMES" BECAME MORE COMPLEX AND TURNED INTO "INFORMATION..."
"INFORMATION" HELD DOMINANCE OVER THE "THOUGHTS" OF THE "MASSES."
DO YOU UNDERSTAND THIS, EXCEL?
YES, SIR!!
UM...
IN OTHER WORDS... WHOEVER CONTROLS THAT INFORMATION CONTROLS THE MASSES...
THAT WAS... WHAT I THINK WAS... THE GIST OF WHAT YOU SAID...
HMM.
EXACTLY. THAT IS CORRECT.
YOU ARE QUITE PERCEPTIVE TODAY, EXCEL.
Words of Praise
hup!
OH, THANK YOU, SIR!
I MERELY VOICED SENTIMENTS APPROPRIATE TO THE *HEAD OF THE DEPARTMENT OF PUBLIC RELATIONS.*

EXCEL SAGA

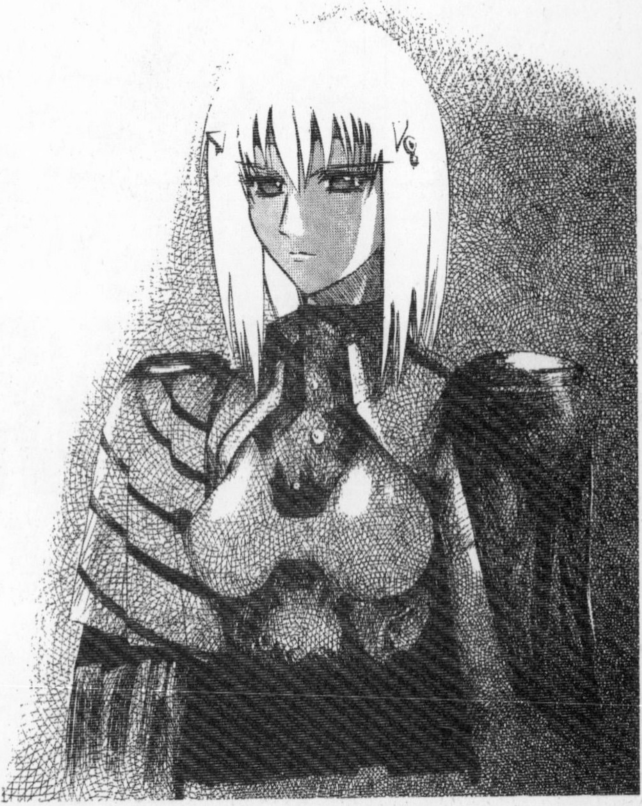

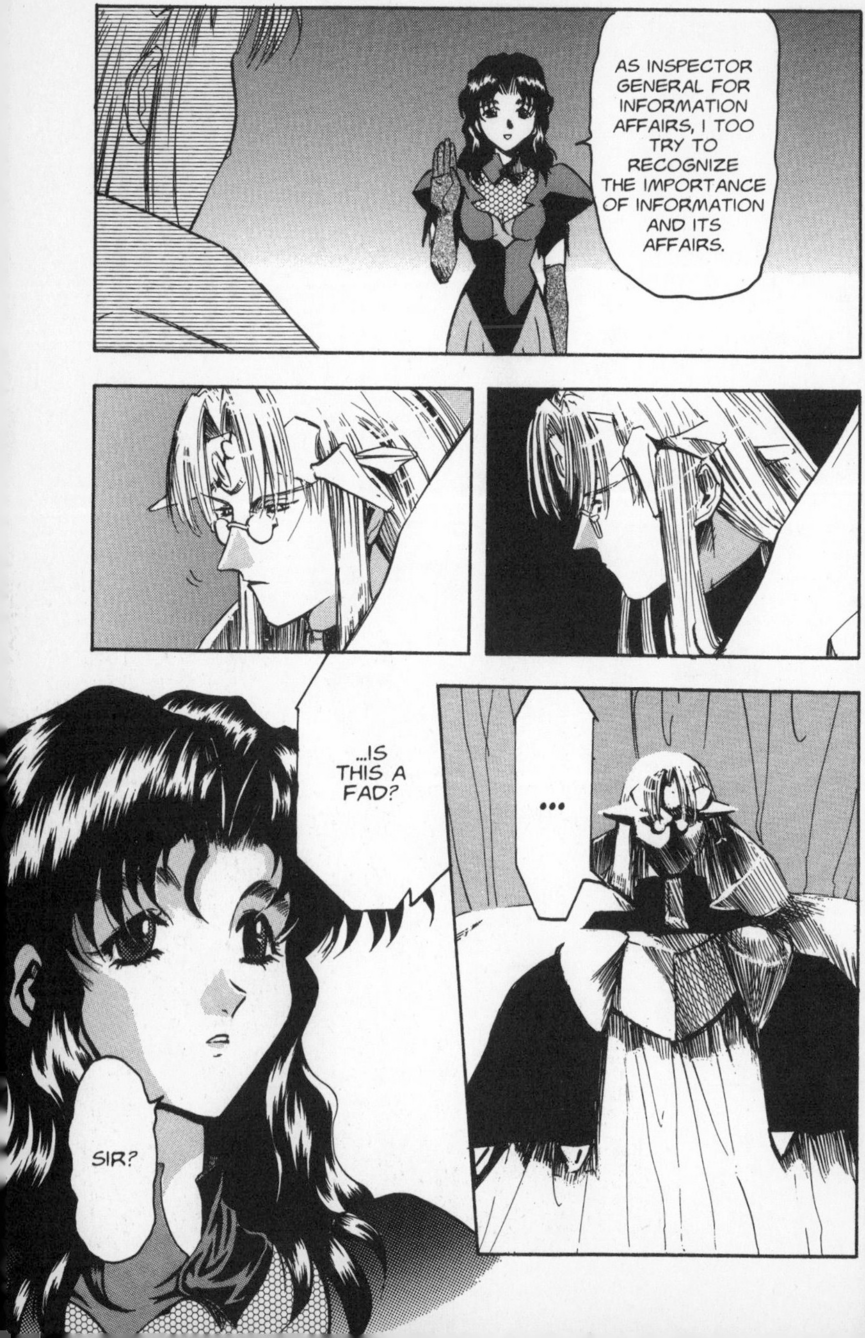
AS INSPECTOR GENERAL FOR INFORMATION AFFAIRS, I TOO TRY TO RECOGNIZE THE IMPORTANCE OF INFORMATION AND ITS AFFAIRS.
...
...IS THIS A FAD?
SIR?

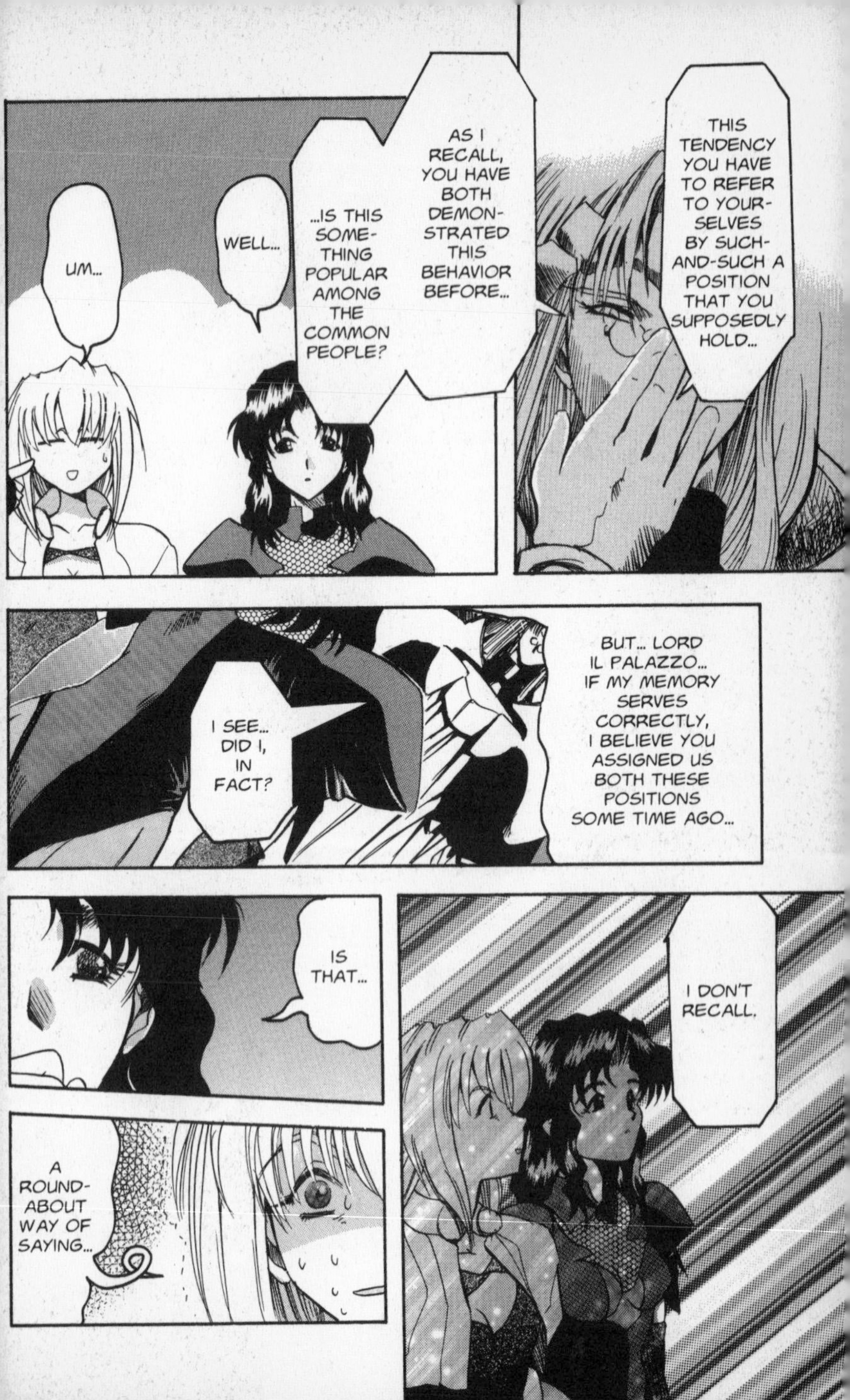
THIS TENDENCY YOU HAVE TO REFER TO YOURSELVES BY SUCH-AND-SUCH A POSITION THAT YOU SUPPOSEDLY HOLD...
AS I RECALL, YOU HAVE BOTH DEMONSTRATED THIS BEHAVIOR BEFORE...
...IS THIS SOMETHING POPULAR AMONG THE COMMON PEOPLE?
WELL...
UM...
BUT... LORD IL PALAZZO... IF MY MEMORY SERVES CORRECTLY, I BELIEVE YOU ASSIGNED US BOTH THESE POSITIONS SOME TIME AGO...
I SEE... DID I, IN FACT?
I DON'T RECALL.
IS THAT...
A ROUND-ABOUT WAY OF SAYING...

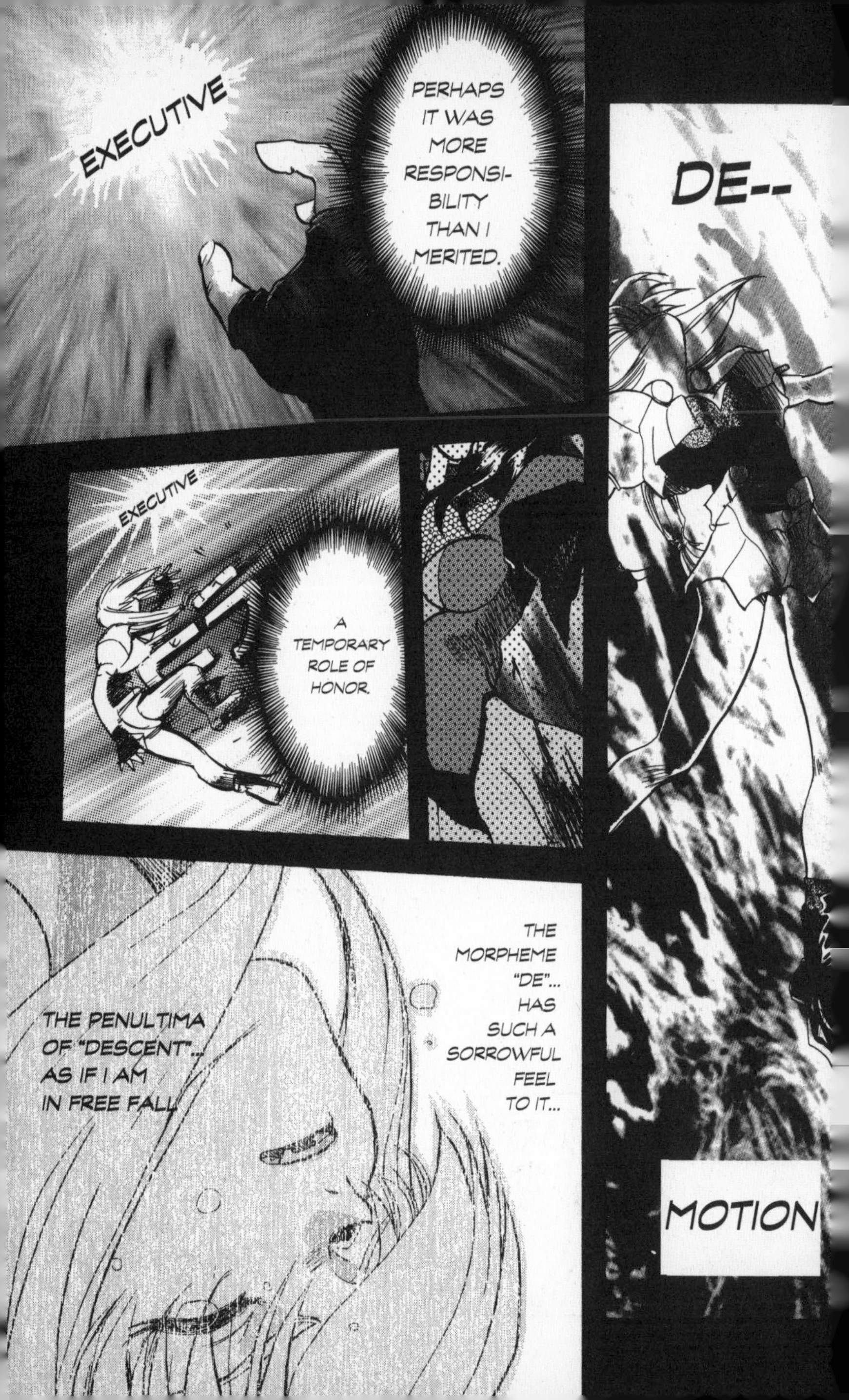
DE--
MOTION
EXECUTIVE
PERHAPS IT WAS MORE RESPONSIBILITY THAN I MERITED.
EXECUTIVE
A TEMPORARY ROLE OF HONOR.
THE MORPHEME "DE"... HAS SUCH A SORROWFUL FEEL TO IT...
THE PENULTIMA OF "DESCENT"... AS IF I AM IN FREE FALL

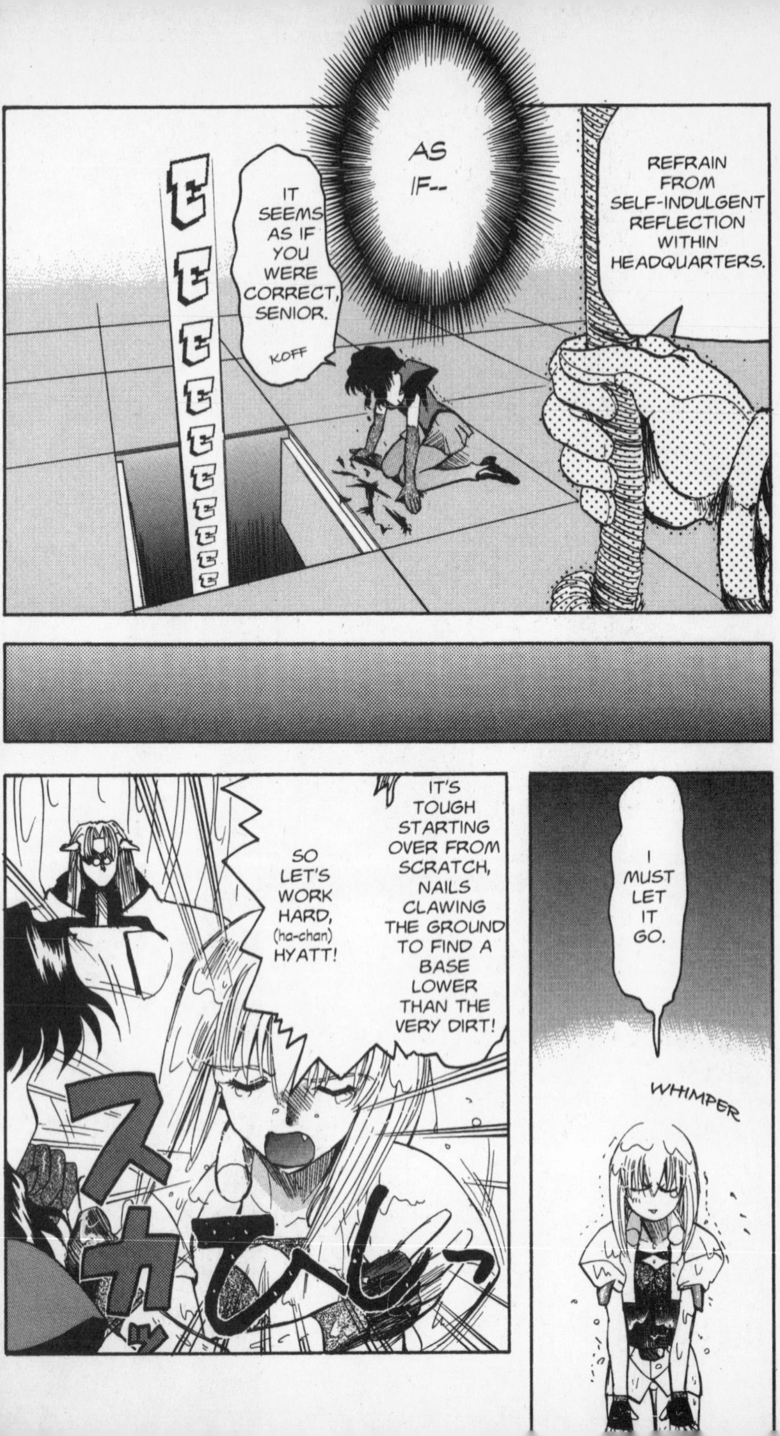
REFRAIN FROM SELF-INDULGENT REFLECTION WITHIN HEADQUARTERS.
AS IF--
IT SEEMS AS IF YOU WERE CORRECT, SENIOR.
KOFF
EEEEEEEEEEE
I MUST LET IT GO.
WHIMPER
IT'S TOUGH STARTING OVER FROM SCRATCH, NAILS CLAWING THE GROUND TO FIND A BASE LOWER THAN THE VERY DIRT!
SO LET'S WORK HARD, (ha-chan) HYATT!

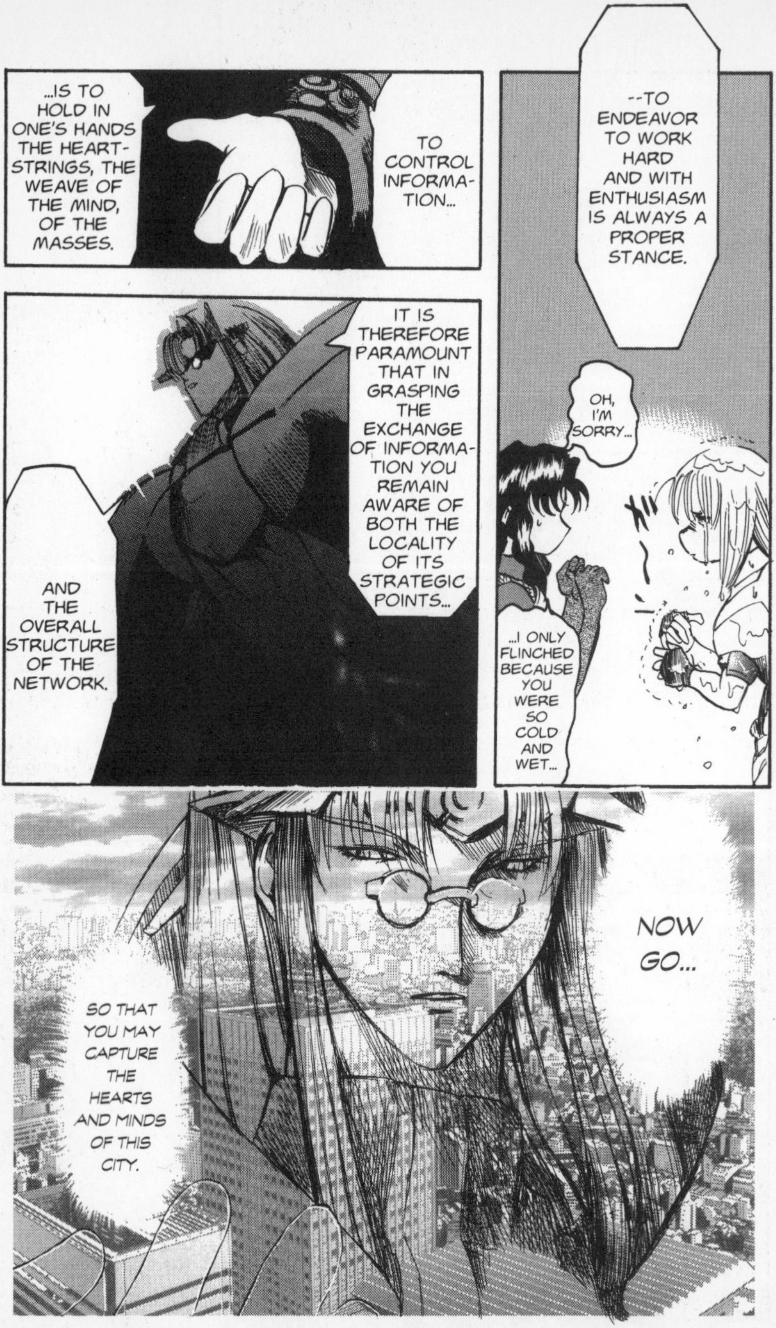
--TO ENDEAVOR TO WORK HARD AND WITH ENTHUSIASM IS ALWAYS A PROPER STANCE.
OH, I'M SORRY...
...I ONLY FLINCHED BECAUSE YOU WERE SO COLD AND WET...
TO CONTROL INFORMATION...
...IS TO HOLD IN ONE'S HANDS THE HEART-STRINGS, THE WEAVE OF THE MIND, OF THE MASSES.
IT IS THEREFORE PARAMOUNT THAT IN GRASPING THE EXCHANGE OF INFORMATION YOU REMAIN AWARE OF BOTH THE LOCALITY OF ITS STRATEGIC POINTS...
AND THE OVERALL STRUCTURE OF THE NETWORK.
NOW GO...
SO THAT YOU MAY CAPTURE THE HEARTS AND MINDS OF THIS CITY.

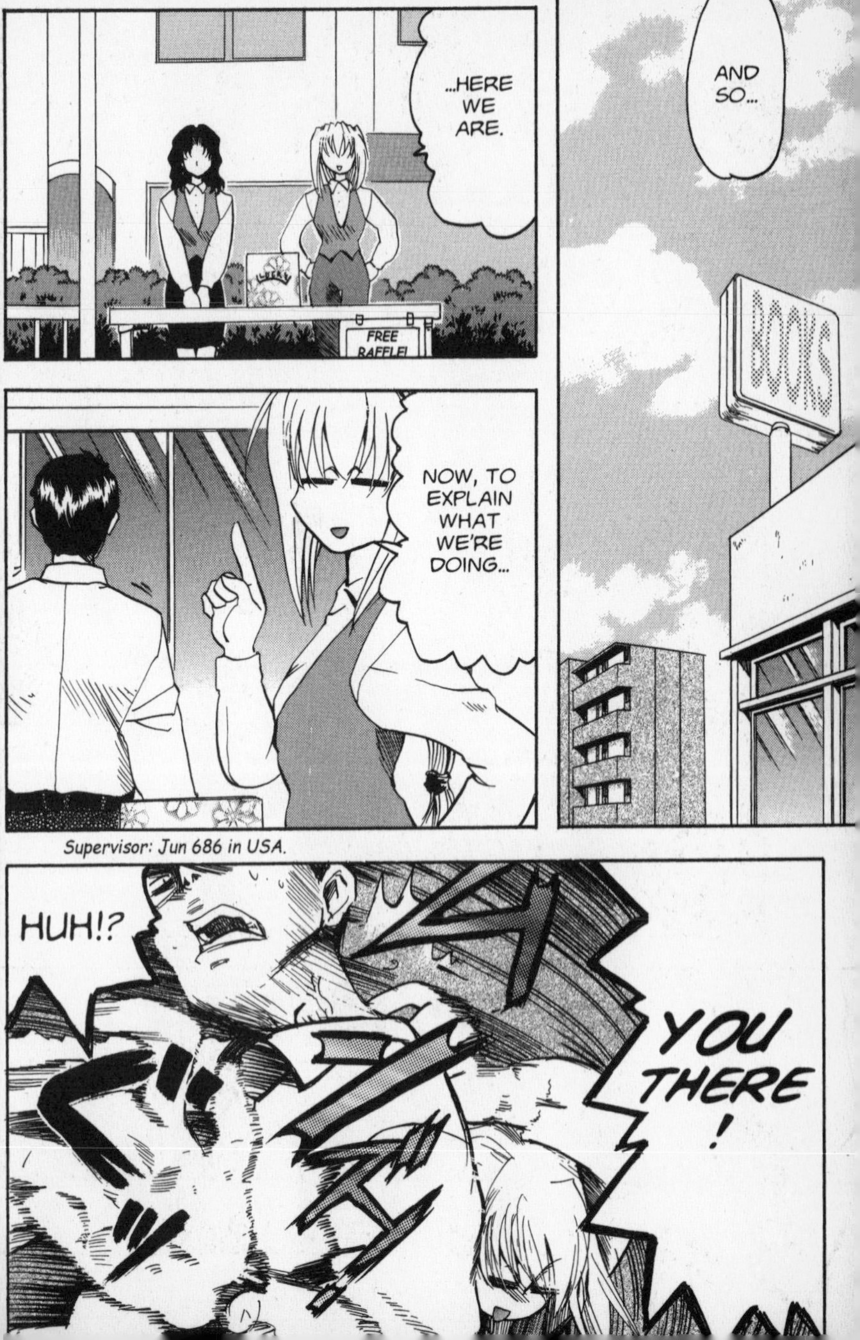
AND SO...
BOOKS
...HERE WE ARE.
FREE RAFFLE!
NOW, TO EXPLAIN WHAT WE'RE DOING...
YOU THERE!
HUH!?

Supervisor: Jun 686 in USA.

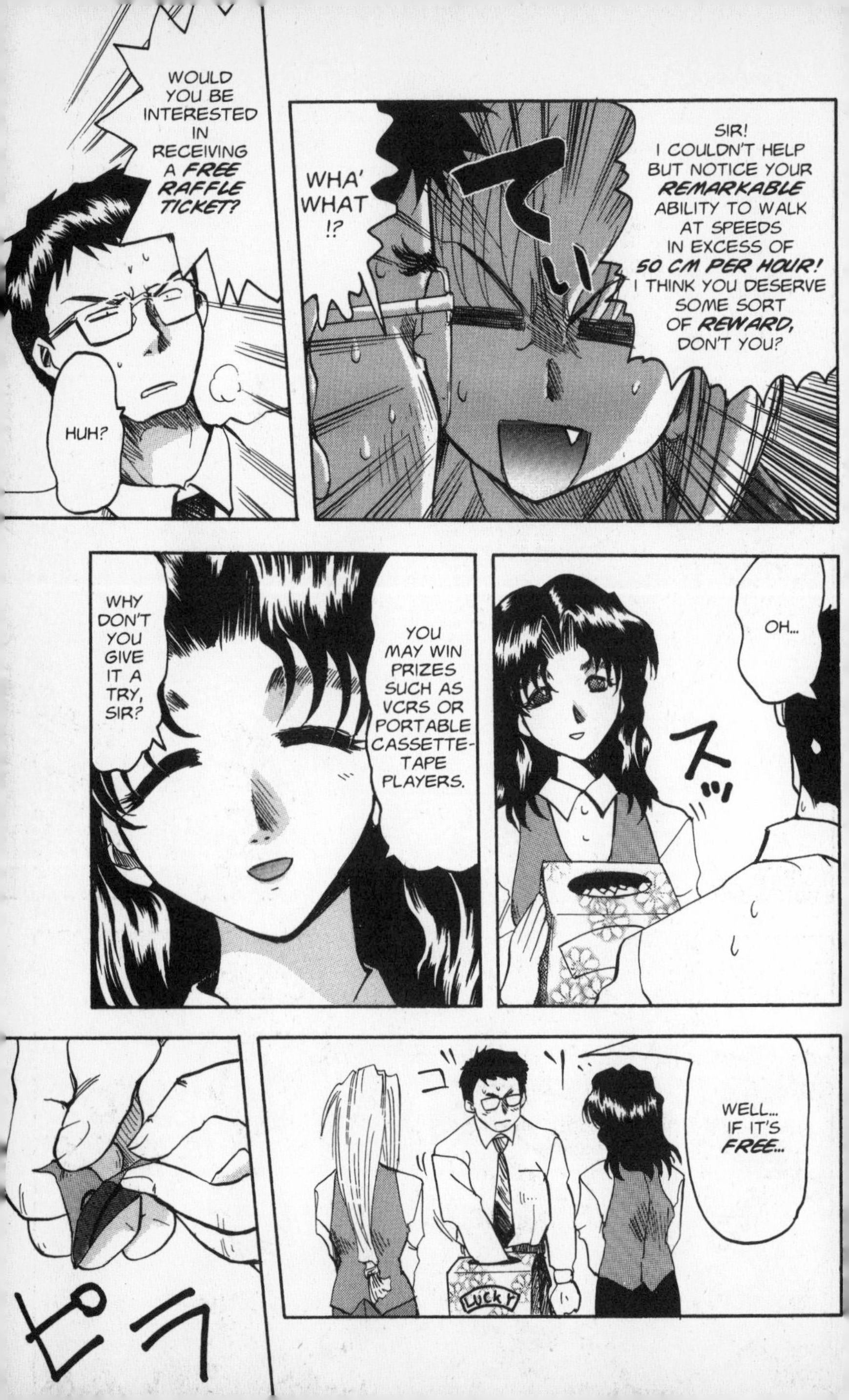

SIR! I COULDN'T HELP BUT NOTICE YOUR ***REMARKABLE*** ABILITY TO WALK AT SPEEDS IN EXCESS OF ***50 CM PER HOUR!*** I THINK YOU DESERVE SOME SORT OF ***REWARD,*** DON'T YOU?
WHA' WHAT !?
WOULD YOU BE INTERESTED IN RECEIVING A ***FREE RAFFLE TICKET?***
HUH?
OH...
スッ
YOU MAY WIN PRIZES SUCH AS VCRS OR PORTABLE CASSETTE-TAPE PLAYERS.
WHY DON'T YOU GIVE IT A TRY, SIR?
WELL... IF IT'S ***FREE...***
LUCKY
ピラ

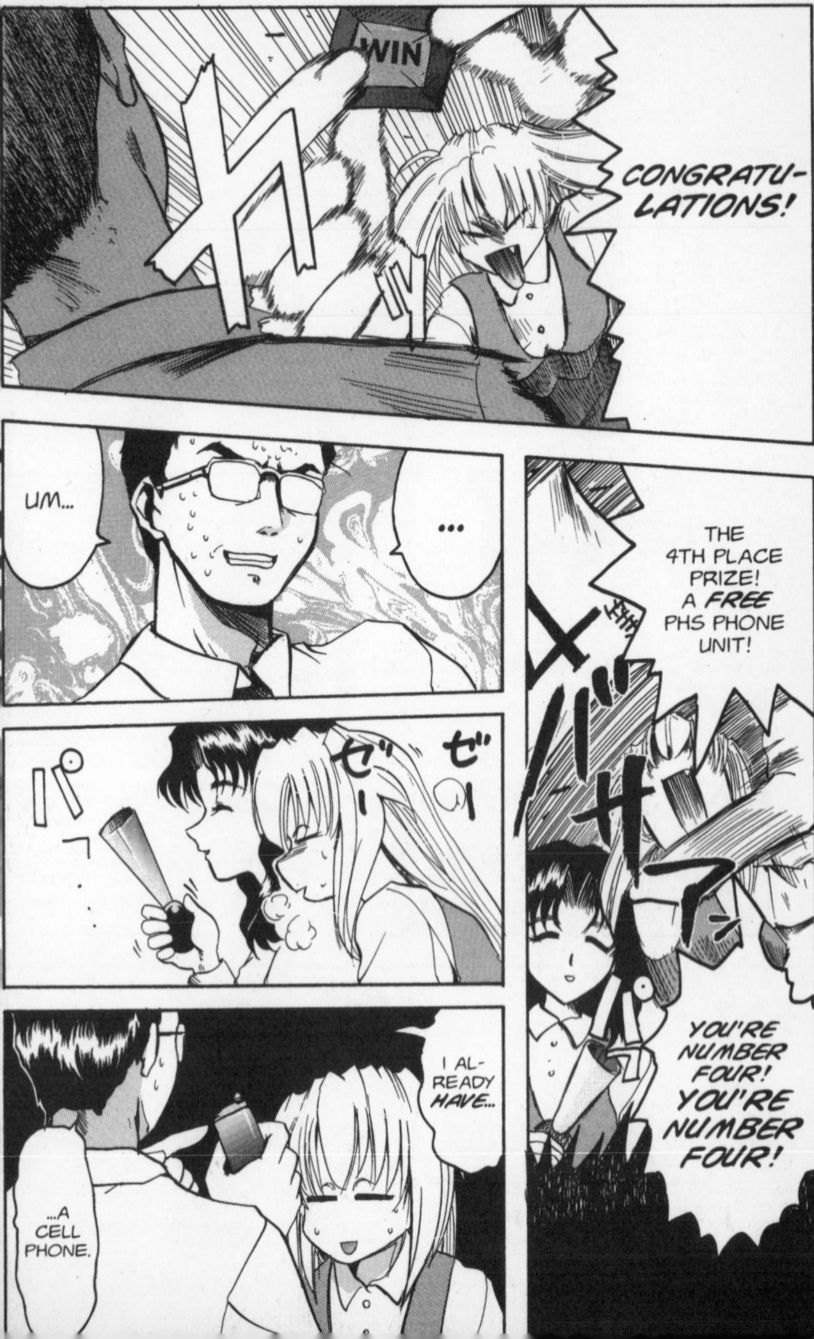
CONGRATU-
LATIONS!
THE 4TH PLACE PRIZE! A *FREE* PHS PHONE UNIT!
YOU'RE NUMBER FOUR! YOU'RE NUMBER FOUR!
...
UM...
I AL-READY *HAVE*...
...A CELL PHONE.

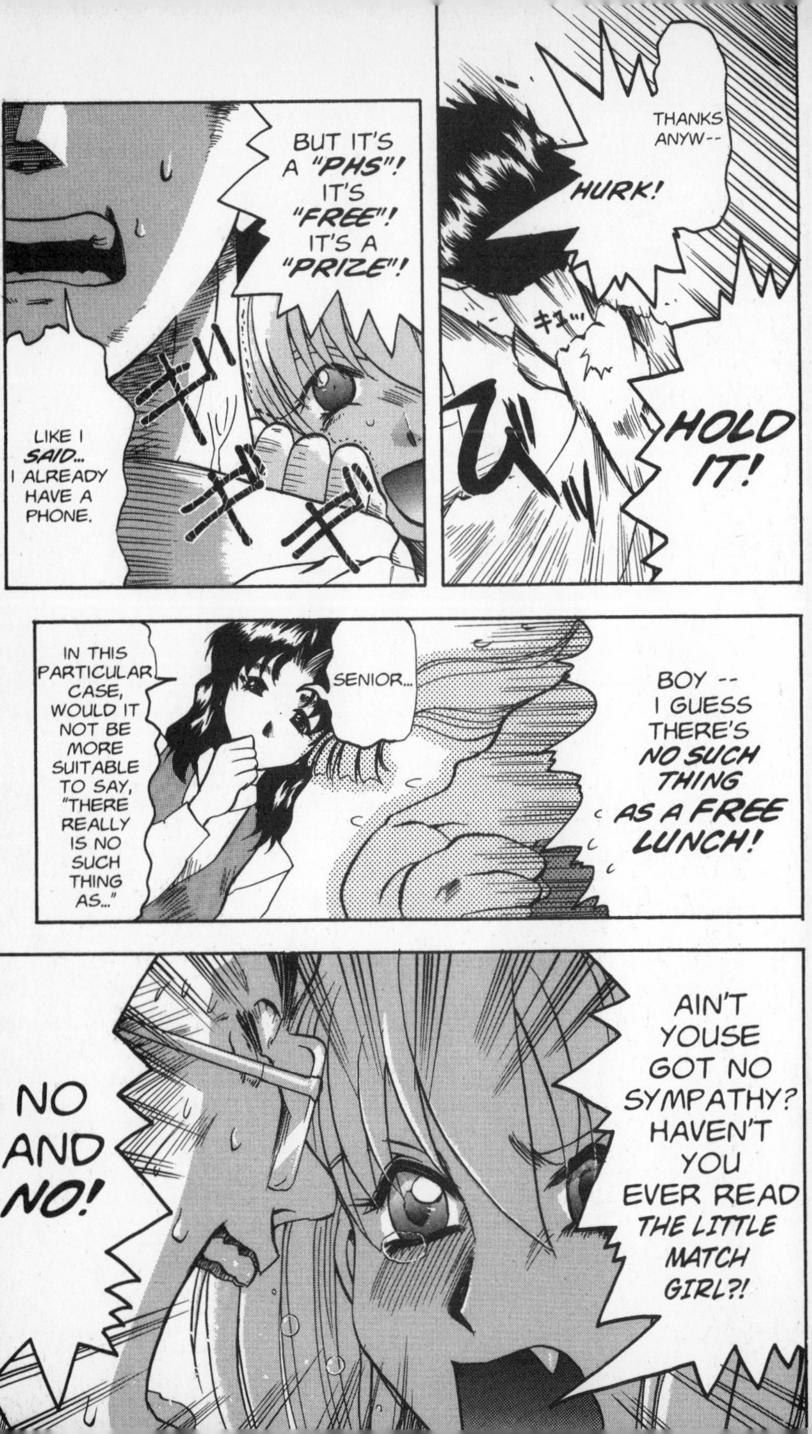
THANKS ANYW--
HURK!
HOLD IT!
BUT IT'S A "PHS"! IT'S "FREE"! IT'S A "PRIZE"!
LIKE I SAID... I ALREADY HAVE A PHONE.
BOY -- I GUESS THERE'S NO SUCH THING AS A FREE LUNCH!
SENIOR...
IN THIS PARTICULAR CASE, WOULD IT NOT BE MORE SUITABLE TO SAY, "THERE REALLY IS NO SUCH THING AS..."
AIN'T YOUSE GOT NO SYMPATHY? HAVEN'T YOU EVER READ THE LITTLE MATCH GIRL?!
NO AND NO!

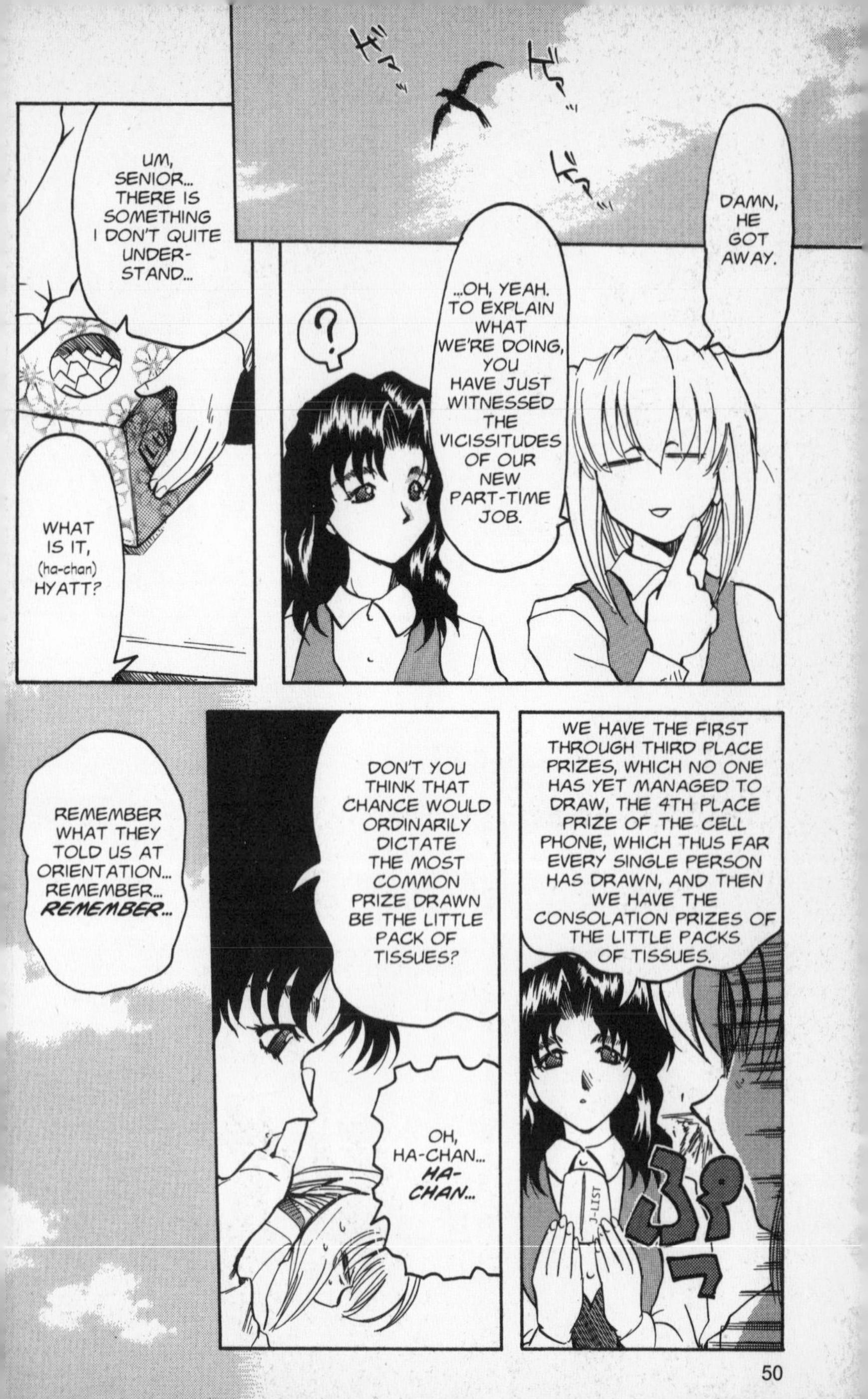
DAMN, HE GOT AWAY.
...OH, YEAH. TO EXPLAIN WHAT WE'RE DOING, YOU HAVE JUST WITNESSED THE VICISSITUDES OF OUR NEW PART-TIME JOB.
?
UM, SENIOR... THERE IS SOMETHING I DON'T QUITE UNDER-STAND...
WHAT IS IT, (ha-chan) HYATT?
WE HAVE THE FIRST THROUGH THIRD PLACE PRIZES, WHICH NO ONE HAS YET MANAGED TO DRAW, THE 4TH PLACE PRIZE OF THE CELL PHONE, WHICH THUS FAR EVERY SINGLE PERSON HAS DRAWN, AND THEN WE HAVE THE CONSOLATION PRIZES OF THE LITTLE PACKS OF TISSUES.
J-LIST
DON'T YOU THINK THAT CHANCE WOULD ORDINARILY DICTATE THE MOST COMMON PRIZE DRAWN BE THE LITTLE PACK OF TISSUES?
OH, HA-CHAN... *HA-CHAN...*
REMEMBER WHAT THEY TOLD US AT ORIENTATION... REMEMBER... *REMEMBER...*

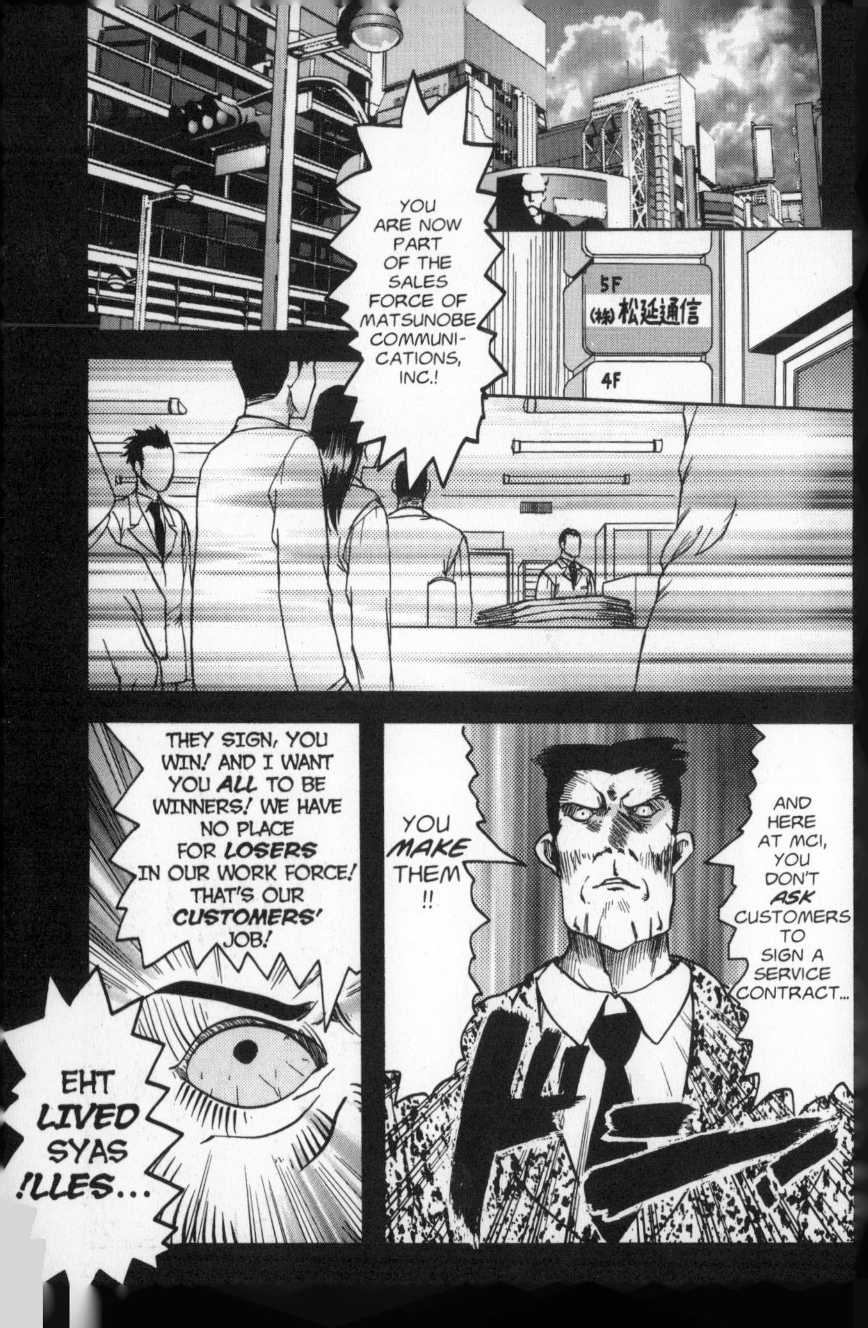
YOU ARE NOW PART OF THE SALES FORCE OF MATSUNOBE COMMUNI-CATIONS, INC.!
5F
(株)松延通信
4F
AND HERE AT MCI, YOU DON'T ASK CUSTOMERS TO SIGN A SERVICE CONTRACT...
YOU MAKE THEM !!
THEY SIGN, YOU WIN! AND I WANT YOU ALL TO BE WINNERS! WE HAVE NO PLACE FOR LOSERS IN OUR WORK FORCE! THAT'S OUR CUSTOMERS' JOB!
EHT LIVED SYAS !LLES...

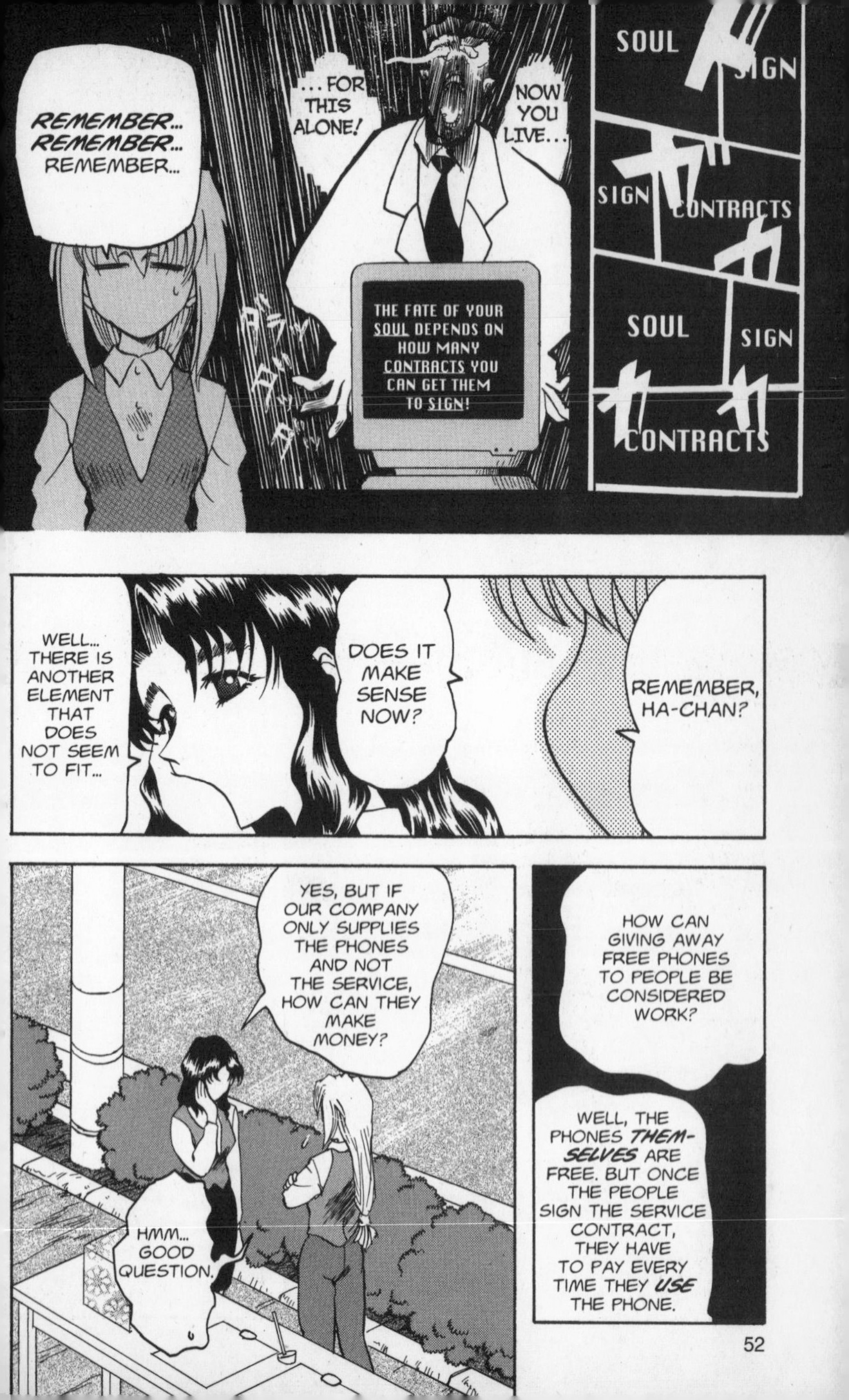
SOUL SIGN
SIGN CONTRACTS
SOUL SIGN
CONTRACTS
NOW YOU LIVE...
...FOR THIS ALONE!
THE FATE OF YOUR SOUL DEPENDS ON HOW MANY CONTRACTS YOU CAN GET THEM TO SIGN!
REMEMBER... REMEMBER... REMEMBER...
REMEMBER, HA-CHAN?
DOES IT MAKE SENSE NOW?
WELL... THERE IS ANOTHER ELEMENT THAT DOES NOT SEEM TO FIT...
HOW CAN GIVING AWAY FREE PHONES TO PEOPLE BE CONSIDERED WORK?
WELL, THE PHONES ***THEMSELVES*** ARE FREE. BUT ONCE THE PEOPLE SIGN THE SERVICE CONTRACT, THEY HAVE TO PAY EVERY TIME THEY ***USE*** THE PHONE.
YES, BUT IF OUR COMPANY ONLY SUPPLIES THE PHONES AND NOT THE SERVICE, HOW CAN THEY MAKE MONEY?
HMM... GOOD QUESTION.

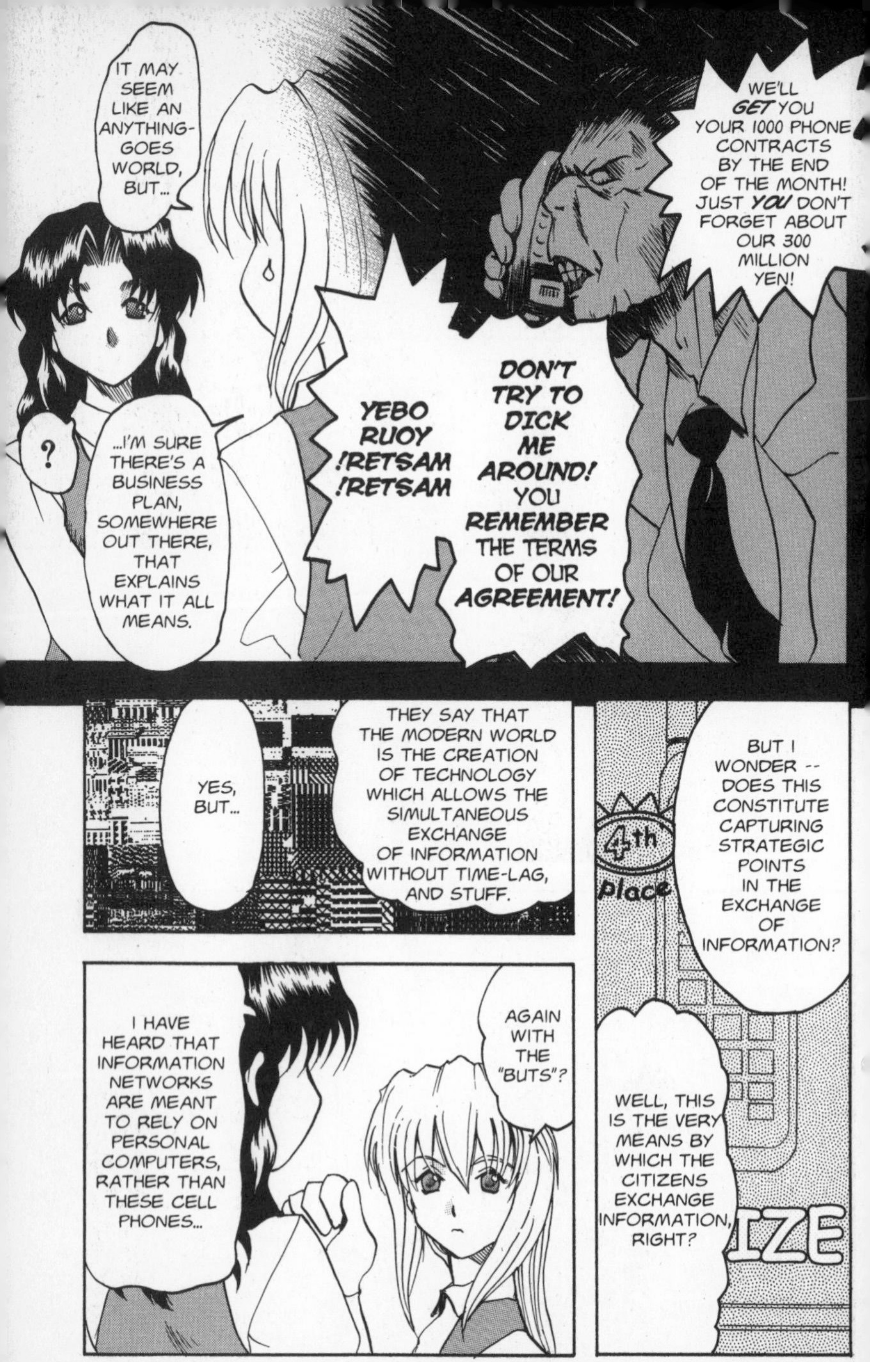
WE'LL GET YOU YOUR 1000 PHONE CONTRACTS BY THE END OF THE MONTH! JUST YOU DON'T FORGET ABOUT OUR 300 MILLION YEN!
DON'T TRY TO DICK ME AROUND! YOU REMEMBER THE TERMS OF OUR AGREEMENT!
YEBO RUOY !RETSAM !RETSAM
IT MAY SEEM LIKE AN ANYTHING-GOES WORLD, BUT...
?
...I'M SURE THERE'S A BUSINESS PLAN, SOMEWHERE OUT THERE, THAT EXPLAINS WHAT IT ALL MEANS.
4th place
BUT I WONDER -- DOES THIS CONSTITUTE CAPTURING STRATEGIC POINTS IN THE EXCHANGE OF INFORMATION?
WELL, THIS IS THE VERY MEANS BY WHICH THE CITIZENS EXCHANGE INFORMATION, RIGHT?
IZE
THEY SAY THAT THE MODERN WORLD IS THE CREATION OF TECHNOLOGY WHICH ALLOWS THE SIMULTANEOUS EXCHANGE OF INFORMATION WITHOUT TIME-LAG, AND STUFF.
YES, BUT...
AGAIN WITH THE "BUTS"?
I HAVE HEARD THAT INFORMATION NETWORKS ARE MEANT TO RELY ON PERSONAL COMPUTERS, RATHER THAN THESE CELL PHONES...

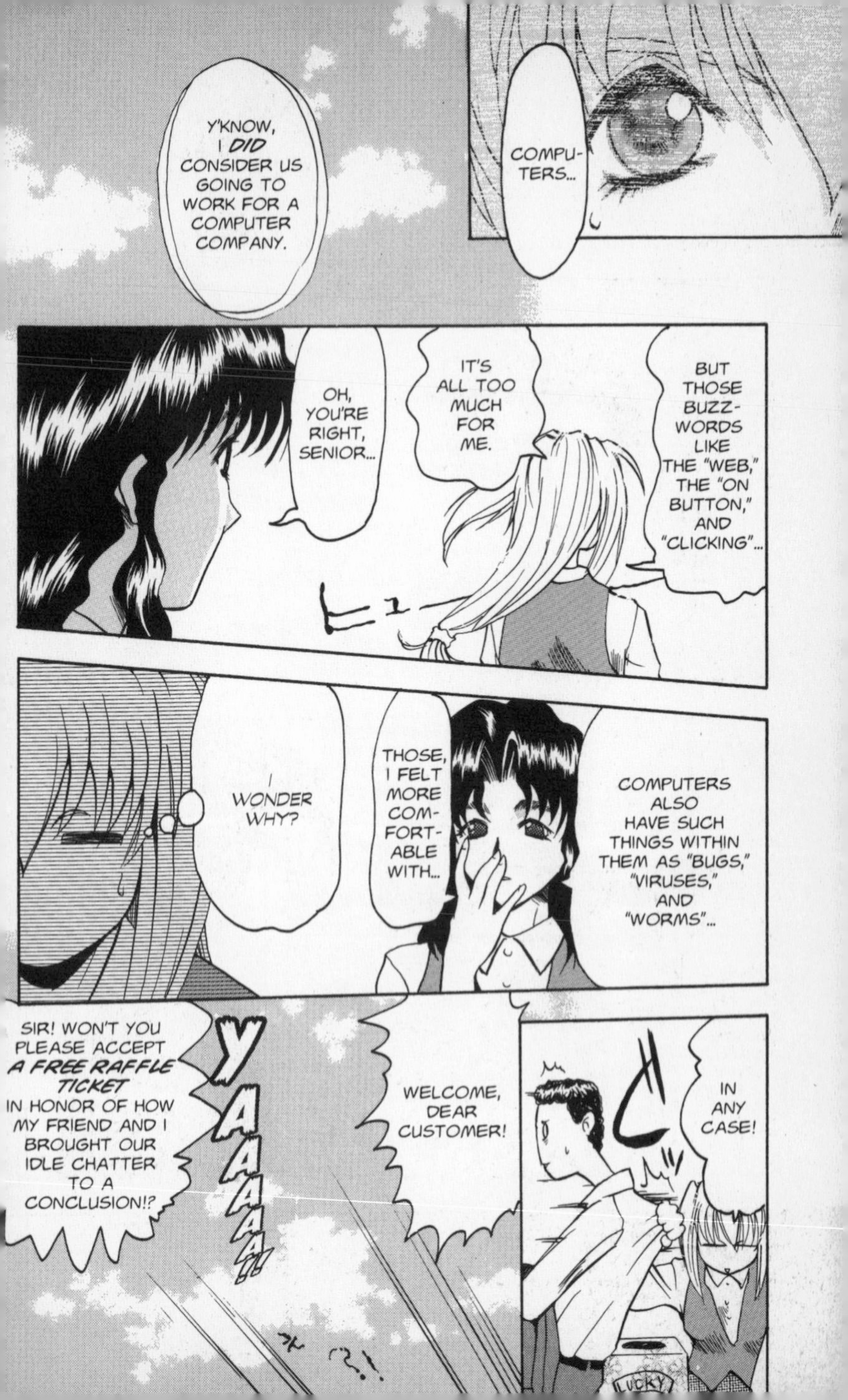
COMPU-TERS...
Y'KNOW, I *DID* CONSIDER US GOING TO WORK FOR A COMPUTER COMPANY.
BUT THOSE BUZZ-WORDS LIKE THE "WEB," THE "ON BUTTON," AND "CLICKING"...
IT'S ALL TOO MUCH FOR ME.
OH, YOU'RE RIGHT, SENIOR...
COMPUTERS ALSO HAVE SUCH THINGS WITHIN THEM AS "BUGS," "VIRUSES," AND "WORMS"...
THOSE, I FELT MORE COM-FORT-ABLE WITH...
I WONDER WHY?
IN ANY CASE!
WELCOME, DEAR CUSTOMER!
YAAAAA!!
SIR! WON'T YOU PLEASE ACCEPT ***A FREE RAFFLE TICKET*** IN HONOR OF HOW MY FRIEND AND I BROUGHT OUR IDLE CHATTER TO A CONCLUSION!?
LUCKY

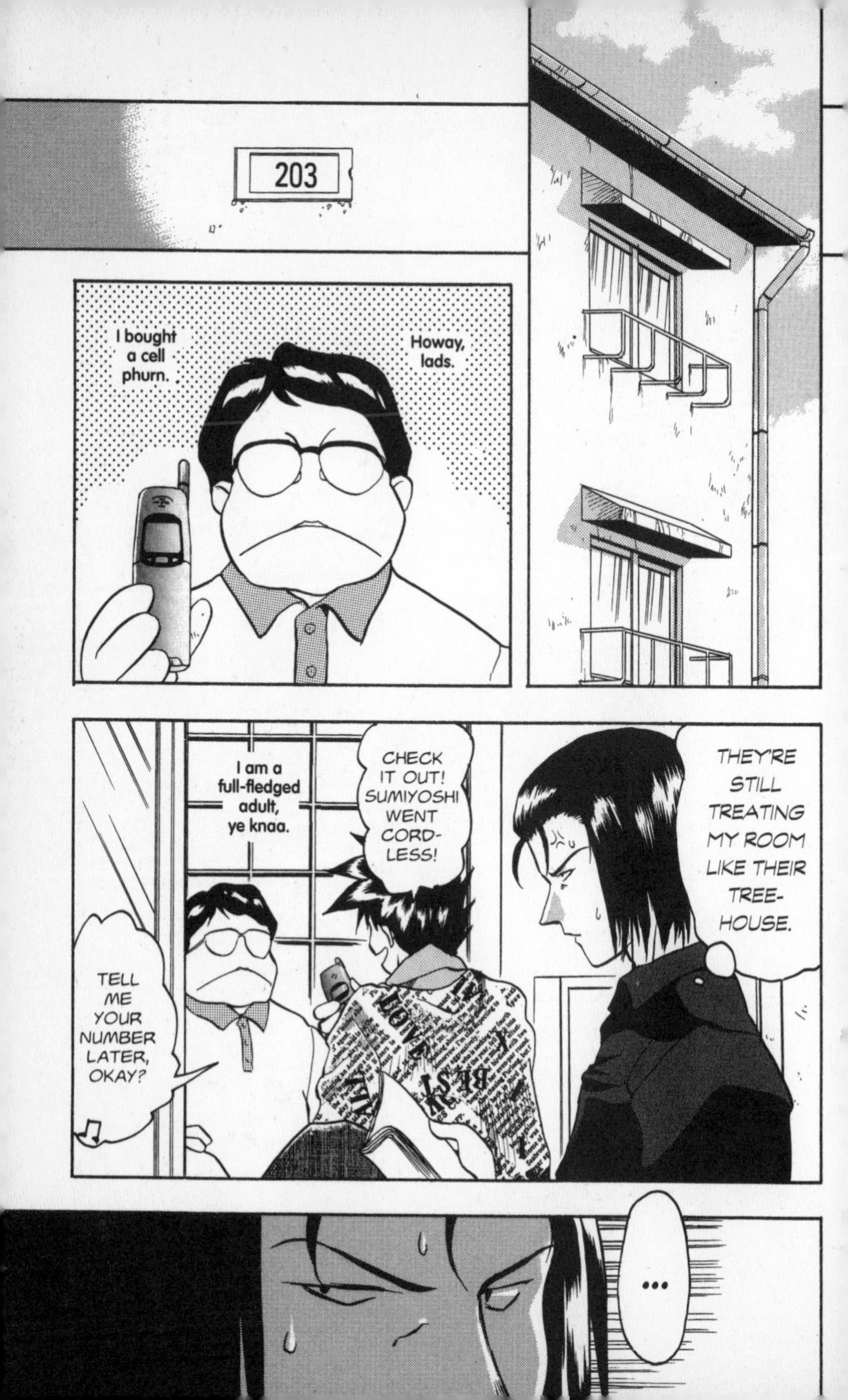
203
Howay, lads.
I bought a cell phurn.
THEY'RE STILL TREATING MY ROOM LIKE THEIR TREE-HOUSE.
CHECK IT OUT! SUMIYOSHI WENT CORDLESS!
I am a full-fledged adult, ye knaa.
TELL ME YOUR NUMBER LATER, OKAY?
...

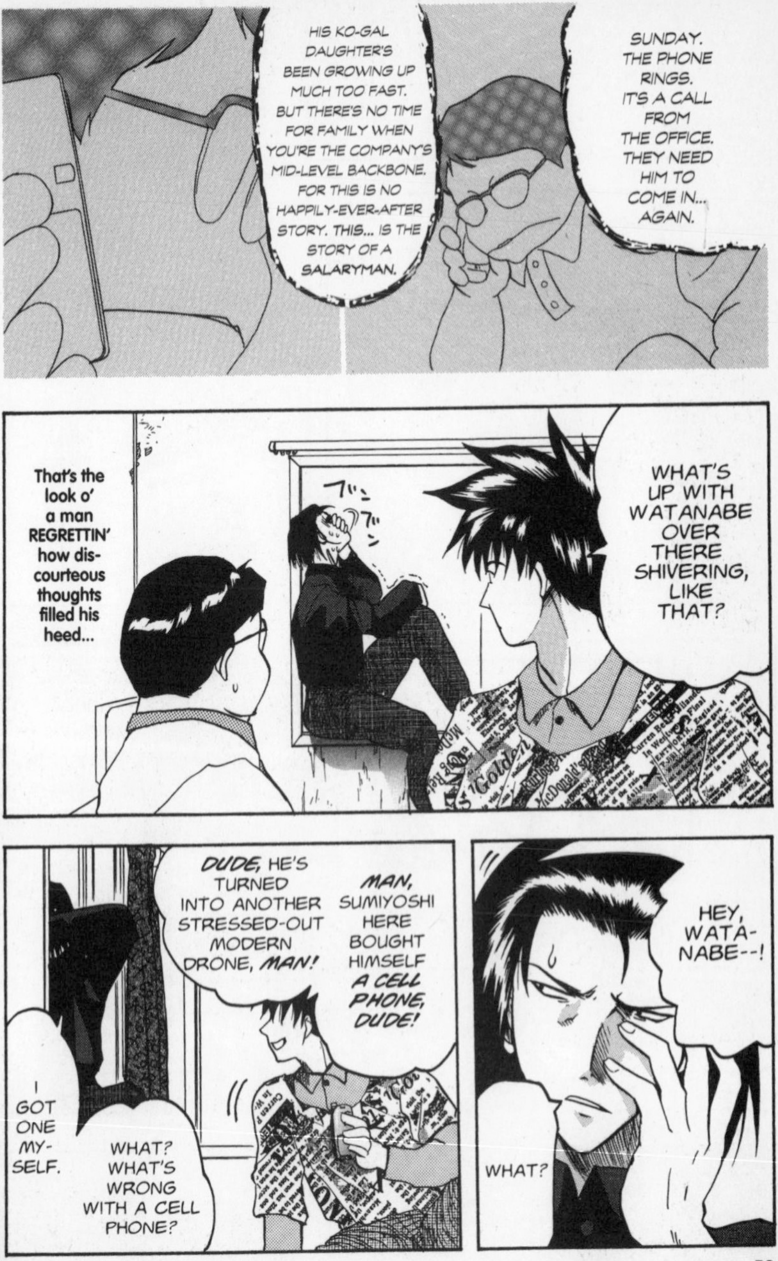
SUNDAY. THE PHONE RINGS. IT'S A CALL FROM THE OFFICE. THEY NEED HIM TO COME IN... AGAIN.
HIS KO-GAL DAUGHTER'S BEEN GROWING UP MUCH TOO FAST. BUT THERE'S NO TIME FOR FAMILY WHEN YOU'RE THE COMPANY'S MID-LEVEL BACKBONE. FOR THIS IS NO HAPPILY-EVER-AFTER STORY. THIS... IS THE STORY OF A SALARYMAN.
WHAT'S UP WITH WATANABE OVER THERE SHIVERING, LIKE THAT?
That's the look o' a man REGRETTIN' how dis-courteous thoughts filled his heed...
HEY, WATA-NABE--!
WHAT?
MAN, SUMIYOSHI HERE BOUGHT HIMSELF A CELL PHONE, DUDE!
DUDE, HE'S TURNED INTO ANOTHER STRESSED-OUT MODERN DRONE, MAN!
WHAT? WHAT'S WRONG WITH A CELL PHONE?
I GOT ONE MY-SELF.

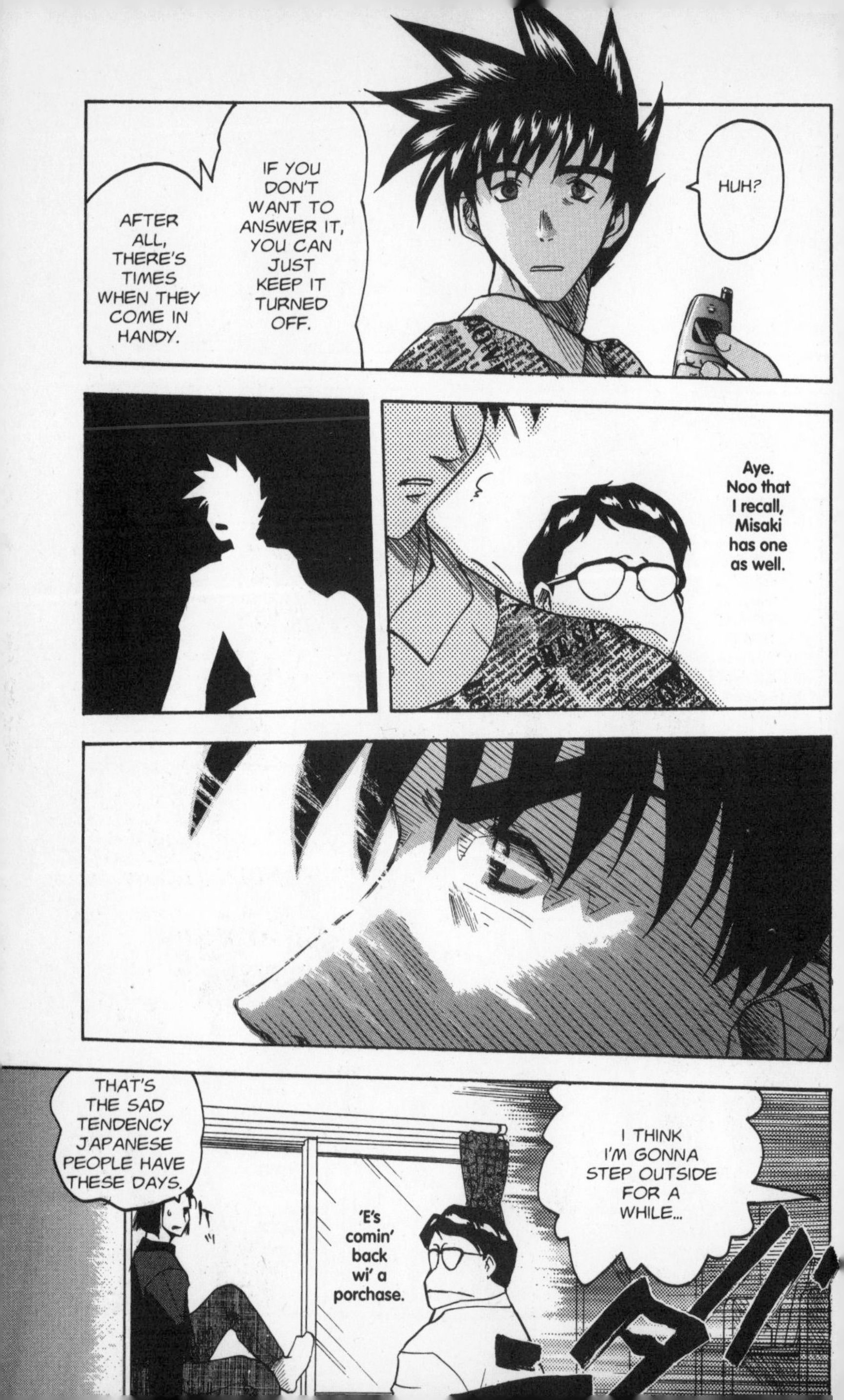
HUH?
IF YOU DON'T WANT TO ANSWER IT, YOU CAN JUST KEEP IT TURNED OFF.
AFTER ALL, THERE'S TIMES WHEN THEY COME IN HANDY.
Aye. Noo that I recall, Misaki has one as well.
I THINK I'M GONNA STEP OUTSIDE FOR A WHILE...
'E's comin' back wi' a porchase.
THAT'S THE SAD TENDENCY JAPANESE PEOPLE HAVE THESE DAYS.

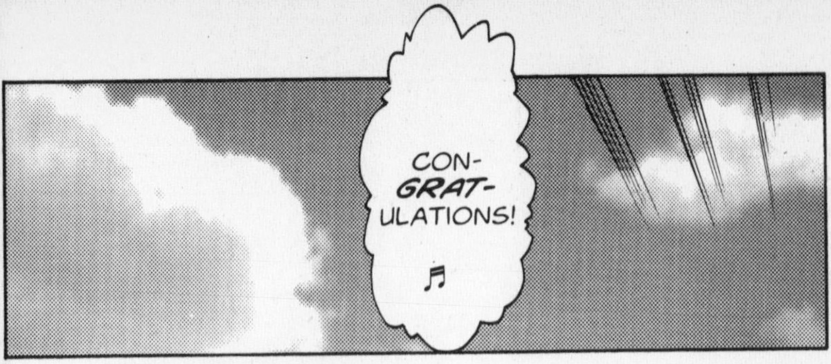
CON-GRAT-ULATIONS! ♬

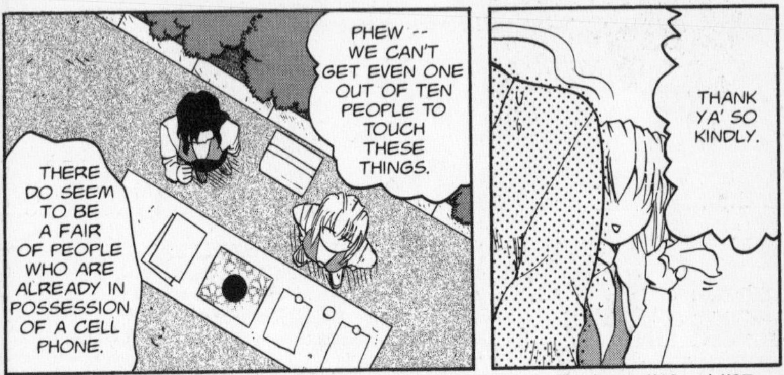
THANK YA' SO KINDLY.
PHEW -- WE CAN'T GET EVEN ONE OUT OF TEN PEOPLE TO TOUCH THESE THINGS.
THERE DO SEEM TO BE A FAIR OF PEOPLE WHO ARE ALREADY IN POSSESSION OF A CELL PHONE.

Thanks to: #69 and #87.

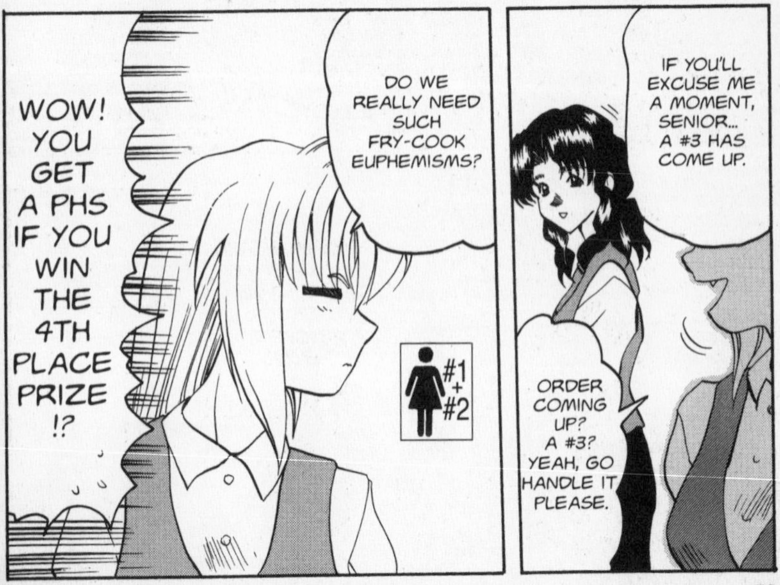
IF YOU'LL EXCUSE ME A MOMENT, SENIOR... A #3 HAS COME UP.
ORDER COMING UP? A #3? YEAH, GO HANDLE IT PLEASE.
DO WE REALLY NEED SUCH FRY-COOK EUPHEMISMS?
#1 + #2
WOW! YOU GET A PHS IF YOU WIN THE 4TH PLACE PRIZE !?

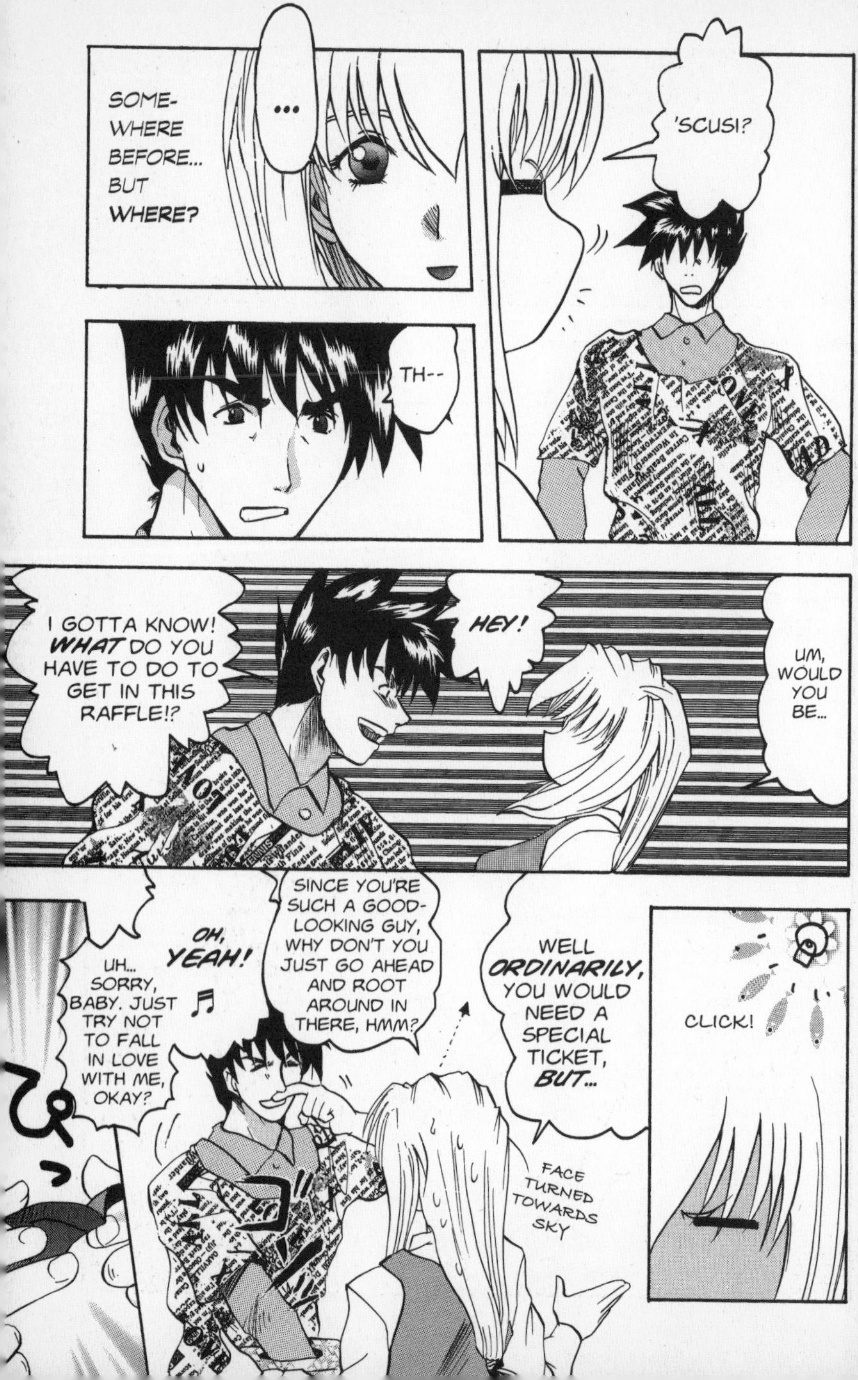
'SCUSI?
...
SOME-WHERE BEFORE... BUT WHERE?
TH--
UM, WOULD YOU BE...
HEY!
I GOTTA KNOW! WHAT DO YOU HAVE TO DO TO GET IN THIS RAFFLE!?
CLICK!
WELL ORDINARILY, YOU WOULD NEED A SPECIAL TICKET, BUT...
FACE TURNED TOWARDS SKY
SINCE YOU'RE SUCH A GOOD-LOOKING GUY, WHY DON'T YOU JUST GO AHEAD AND ROOT AROUND IN THERE, HMM?
OH, YEAH! ♫
UH... SORRY, BABY. JUST TRY NOT TO FALL IN LOVE WITH ME, OKAY?

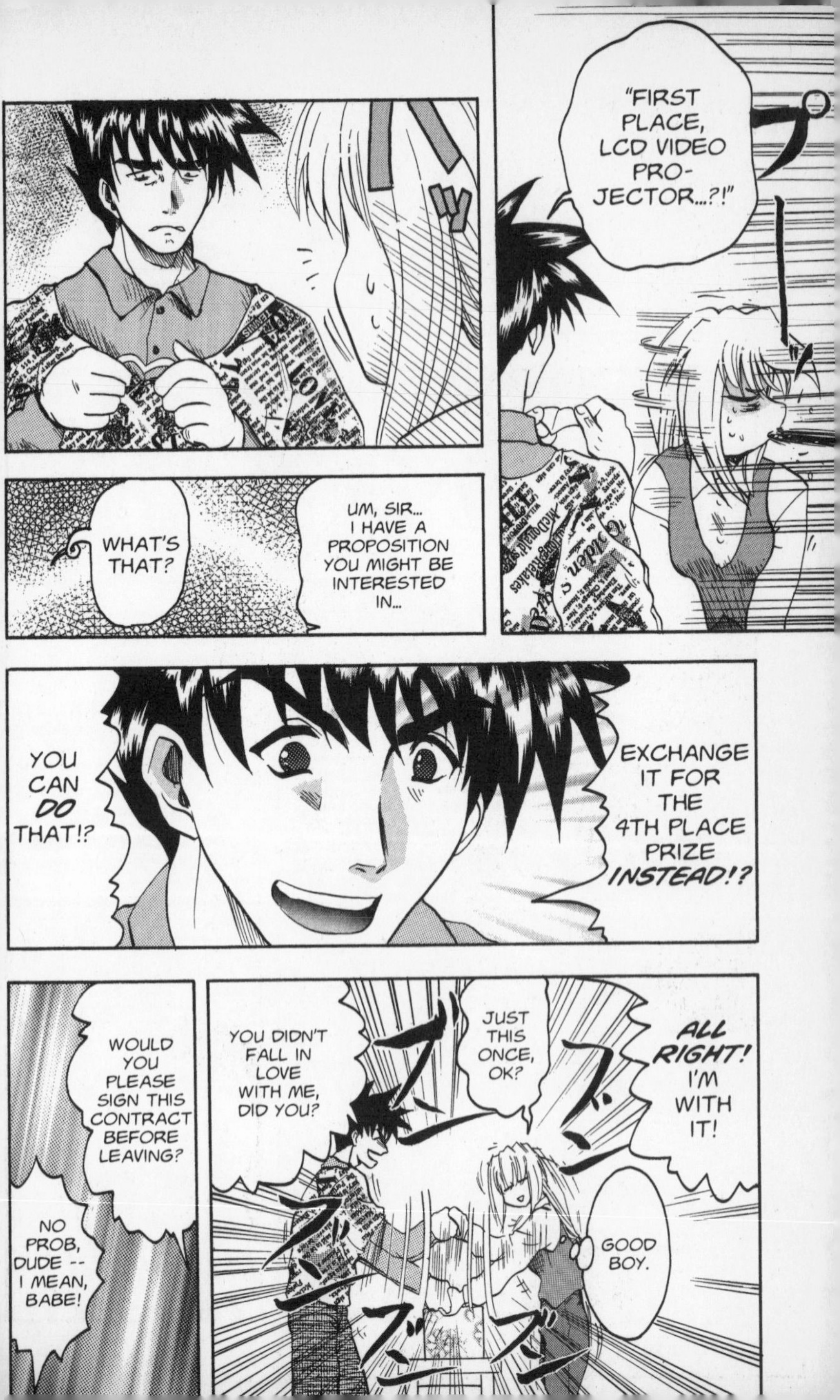
"FIRST PLACE, LCD VIDEO PRO- JECTOR...?!"
UM, SIR... I HAVE A PROPOSITION YOU MIGHT BE INTERESTED IN...
WHAT'S THAT?
EXCHANGE IT FOR THE 4TH PLACE PRIZE *INSTEAD!?*
YOU CAN *DO* THAT!?
ALL RIGHT! I'M WITH IT!
JUST THIS ONCE, OK?
YOU DIDN'T FALL IN LOVE WITH ME, DID YOU?
GOOD BOY.
WOULD YOU PLEASE SIGN THIS CONTRACT BEFORE LEAVING?
NO PROB, DUDE -- I MEAN, BABE!

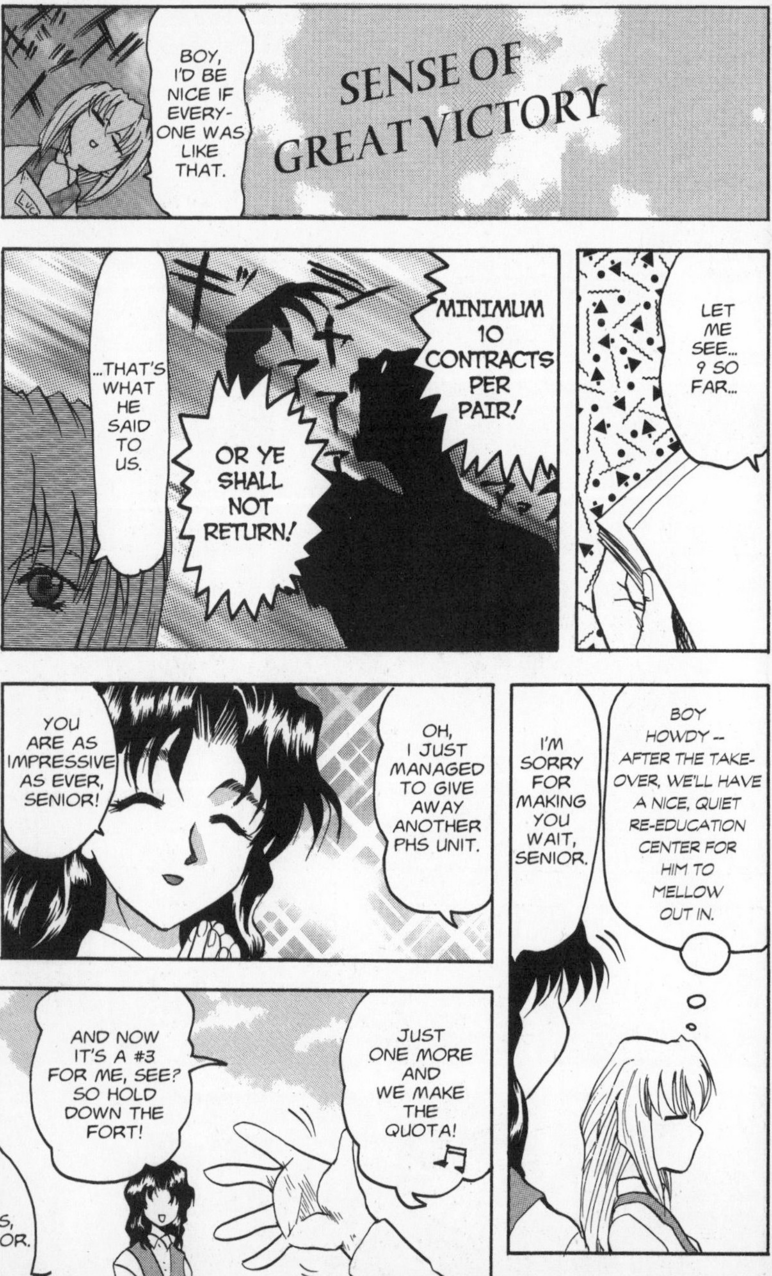
SENSE OF GREAT VICTORY
BOY, I'D BE NICE IF EVERY-ONE WAS LIKE THAT.
LET ME SEE... 9 SO FAR...
MINIMUM 10 CONTRACTS PER PAIR!
OR YE SHALL NOT RETURN!
...THAT'S WHAT HE SAID TO US.
BOY HOWDY -- AFTER THE TAKE-OVER, WE'LL HAVE A NICE, QUIET RE-EDUCATION CENTER FOR HIM TO MELLOW OUT IN.
I'M SORRY FOR MAKING YOU WAIT, SENIOR.
OH, I JUST MANAGED TO GIVE AWAY ANOTHER PHS UNIT.
YOU ARE AS IMPRESSIVE AS EVER, SENIOR!
JUST ONE MORE AND WE MAKE THE QUOTA!
AND NOW IT'S A #3 FOR ME, SEE? SO HOLD DOWN THE FORT!
YES, SENIOR.

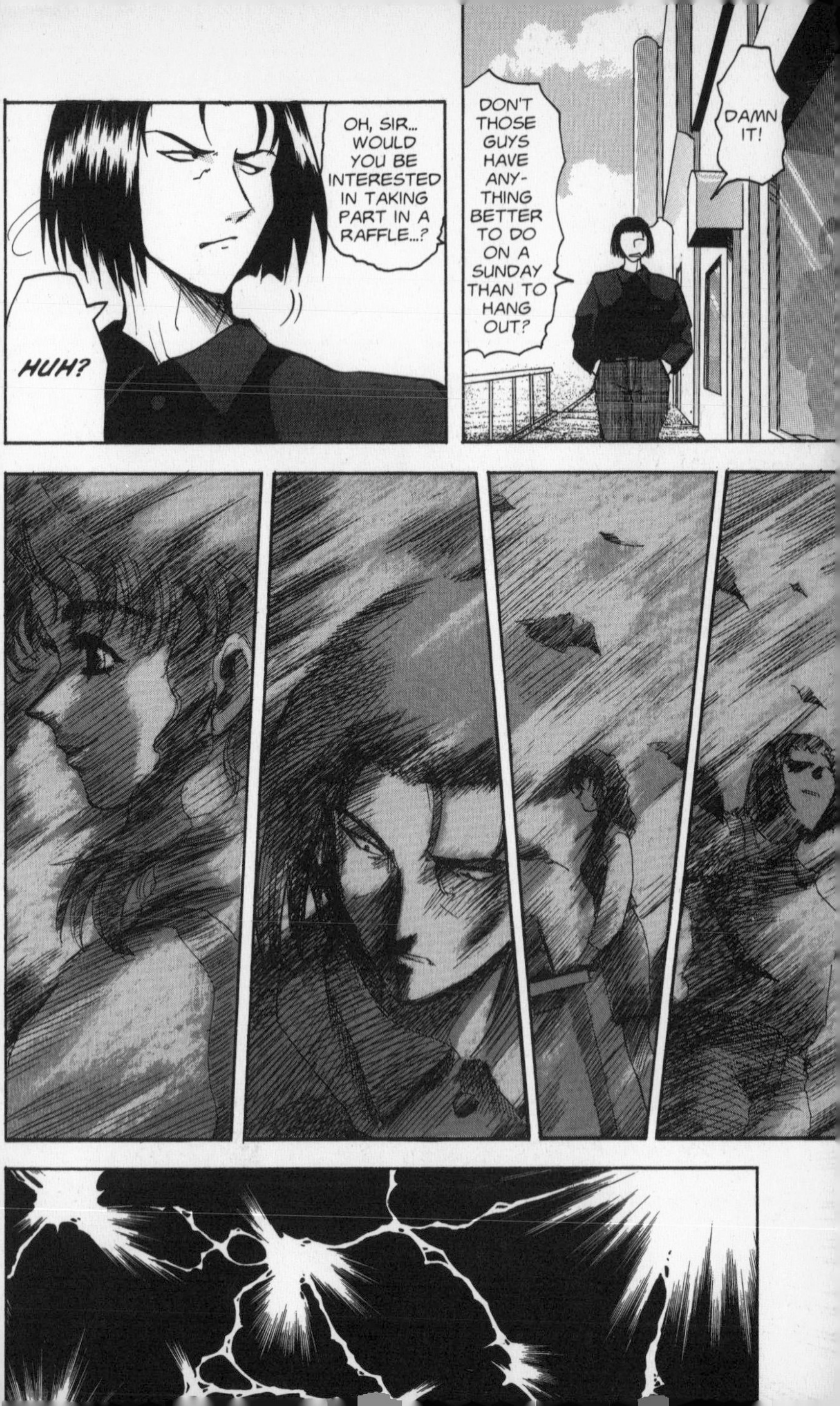
DAMN IT!
DON'T THOSE GUYS HAVE ANY-THING BETTER TO DO ON A SUNDAY THAN TO HANG OUT?
OH, SIR... WOULD YOU BE INTERESTED IN TAKING PART IN A RAFFLE...?
HUH?

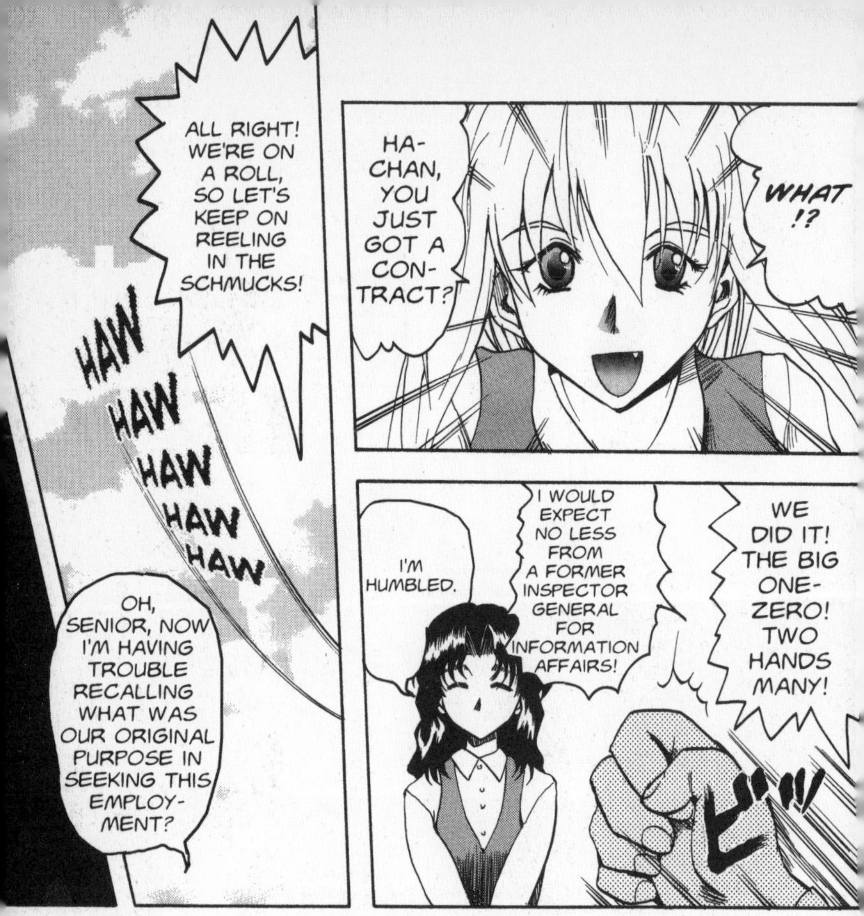
HA-CHAN, YOU JUST GOT A CONTRACT?
WHAT!?
WE DID IT! THE BIG ONE-ZERO! TWO HANDS MANY!
I WOULD EXPECT NO LESS FROM A FORMER INSPECTOR GENERAL FOR INFORMATION AFFAIRS!
I'M HUMBLED.
ALL RIGHT! WE'RE ON A ROLL, SO LET'S KEEP ON REELING IN THE SCHMUCKS!
HAW HAW HAW HAW HAW
OH, SENIOR, NOW I'M HAVING TROUBLE RECALLING WHAT WAS OUR ORIGINAL PURPOSE IN SEEKING THIS EMPLOYMENT?

A few days later

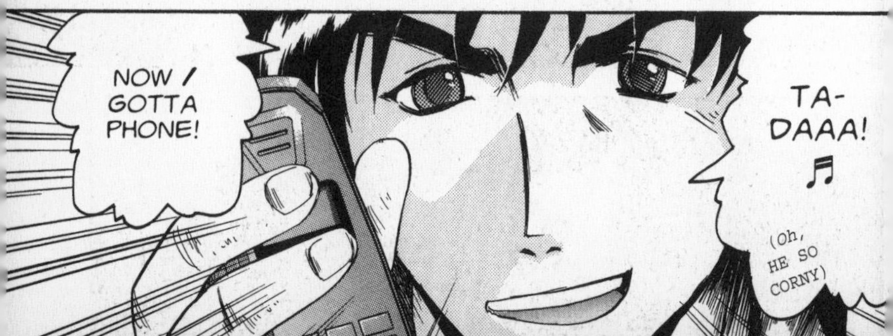
TA-DAAA! ♬
(Oh, HE SO CORNY)
NOW I GOTTA PHONE!

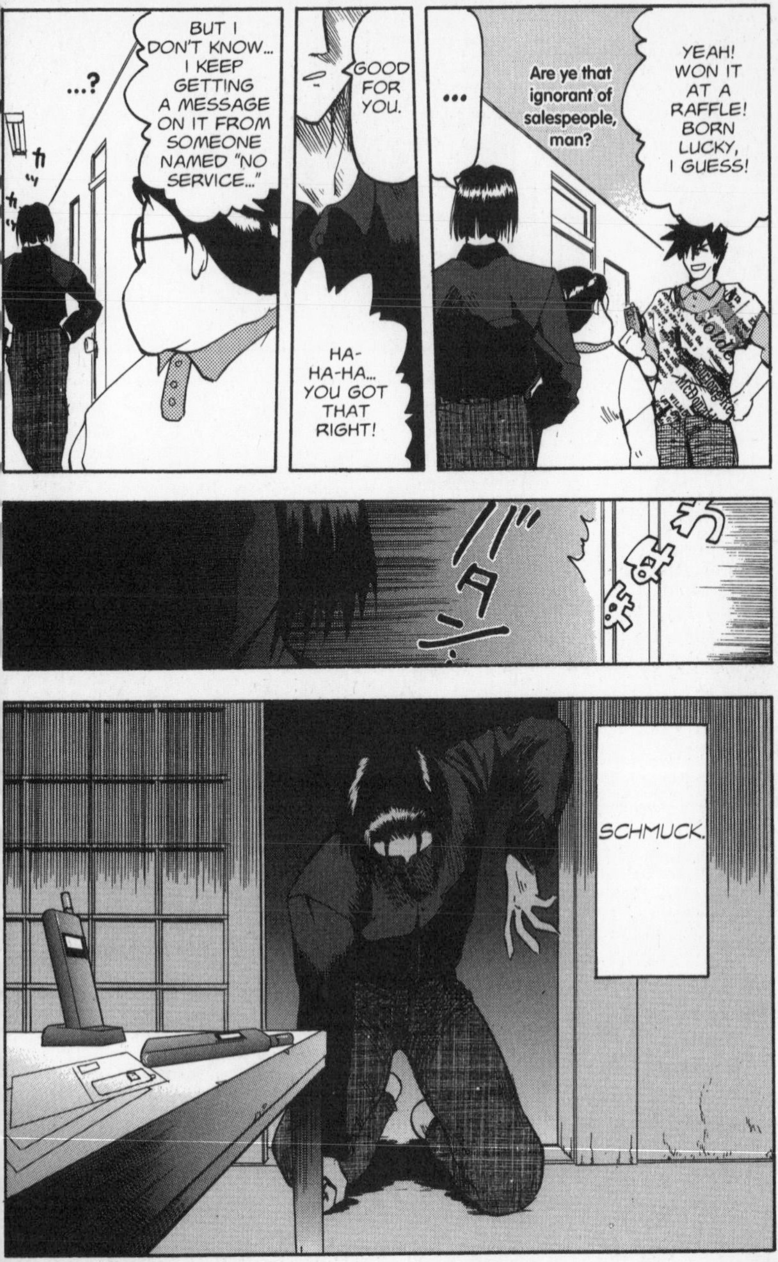
YEAH! WON IT AT A RAFFLE! BORN LUCKY, I GUESS!
Are ye that ignorant of salespeople, man?
...
GOOD FOR YOU.
HA-HA-HA... YOU GOT THAT RIGHT!
BUT I DON'T KNOW... I KEEP GETTING A MESSAGE ON IT FROM SOMEONE NAMED "NO SERVICE..."
...?
バタン
SCHMUCK.

END MISSION 2

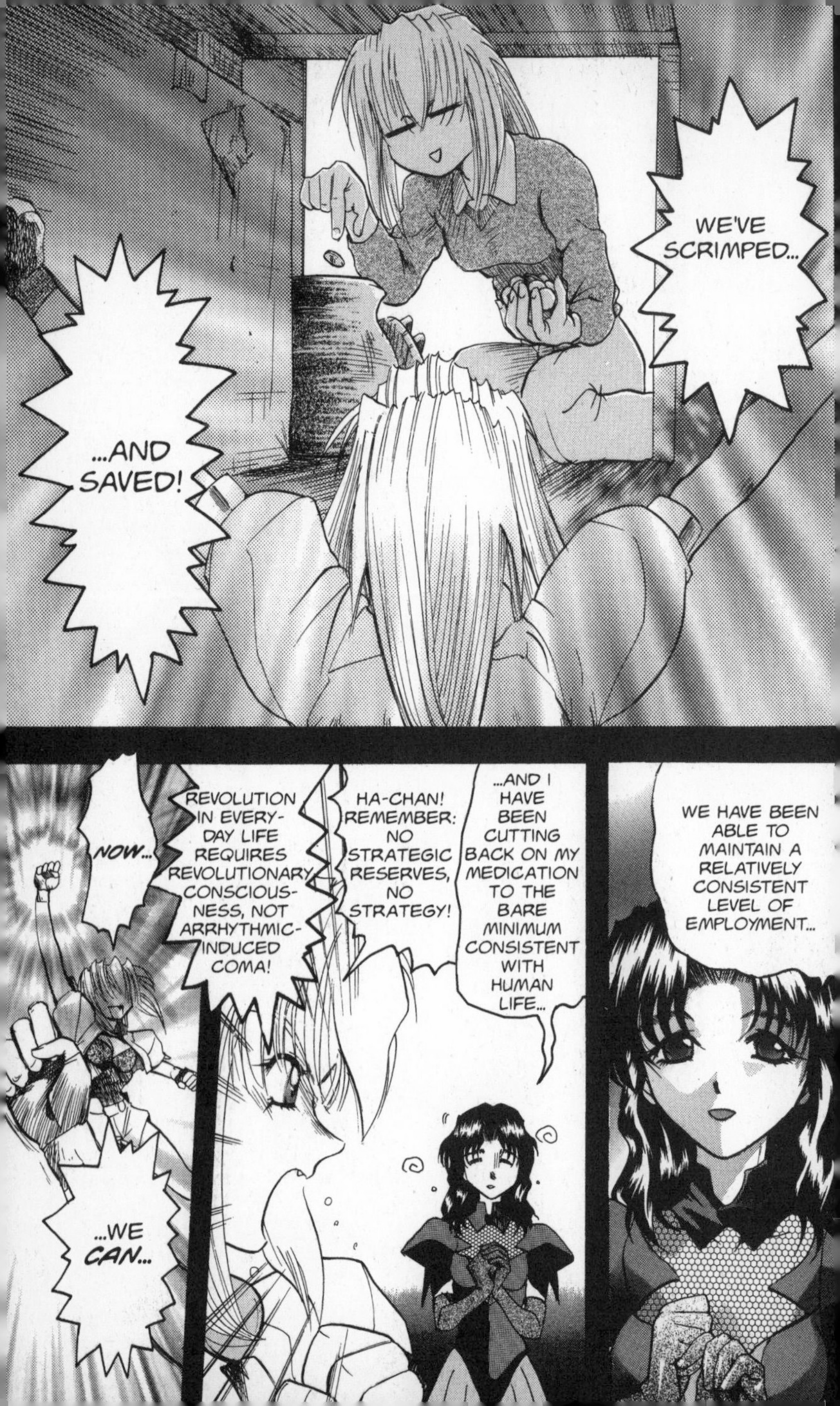
WE'VE SCRIMPED...
...AND SAVED!
WE HAVE BEEN ABLE TO MAINTAIN A RELATIVELY CONSISTENT LEVEL OF EMPLOYMENT...
...AND I HAVE BEEN CUTTING BACK ON MY MEDICATION TO THE BARE MINIMUM CONSISTENT WITH HUMAN LIFE...
HA-CHAN! REMEMBER: NO STRATEGIC RESERVES, NO STRATEGY!
REVOLUTION IN EVERYDAY LIFE REQUIRES REVOLUTIONARY CONSCIOUSNESS, NOT ARRHYTHMIC-INDUCED COMA!
NOW...
...WE CAN...

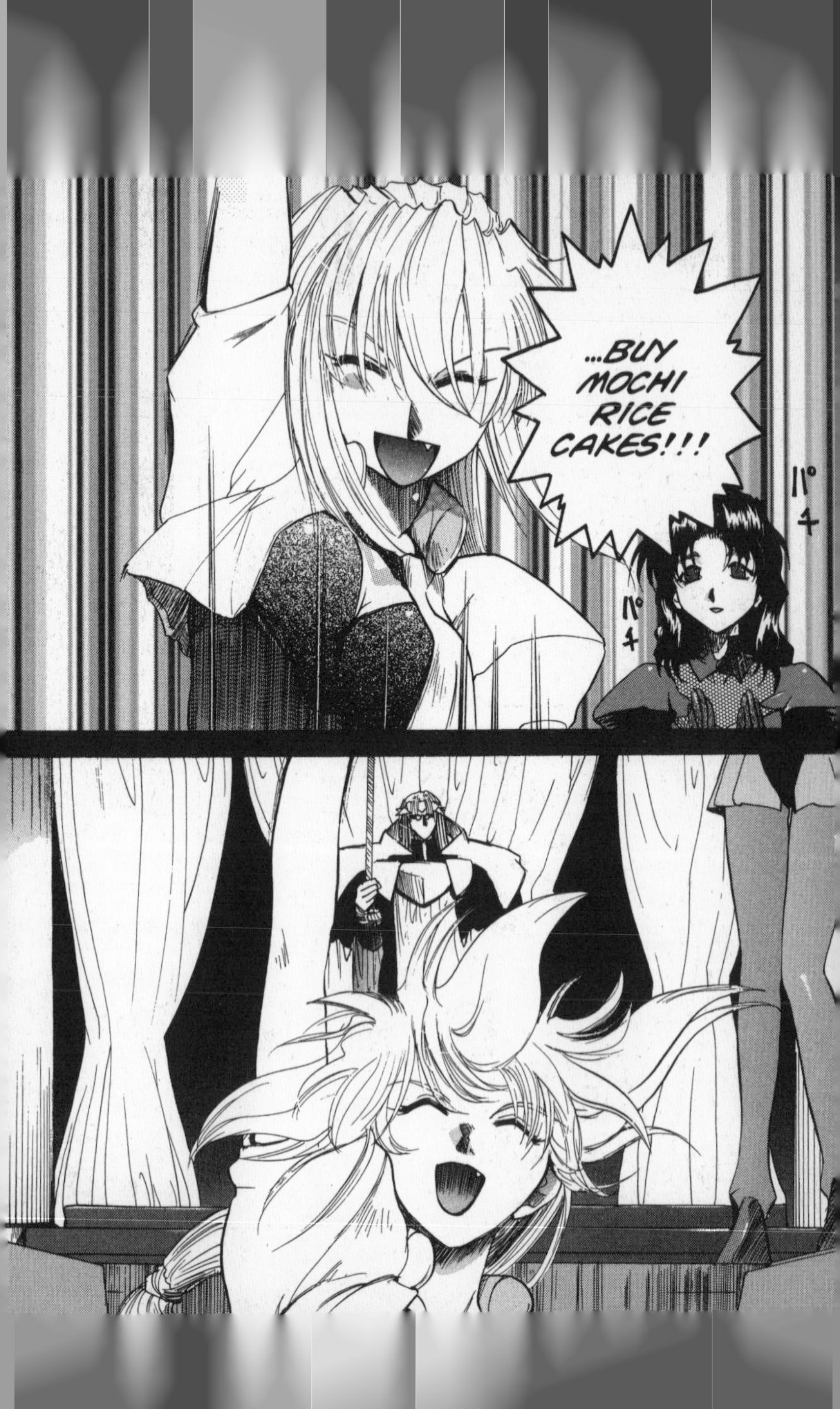
...BUY MOCHI RICE CAKES!!!
パチ
パチ

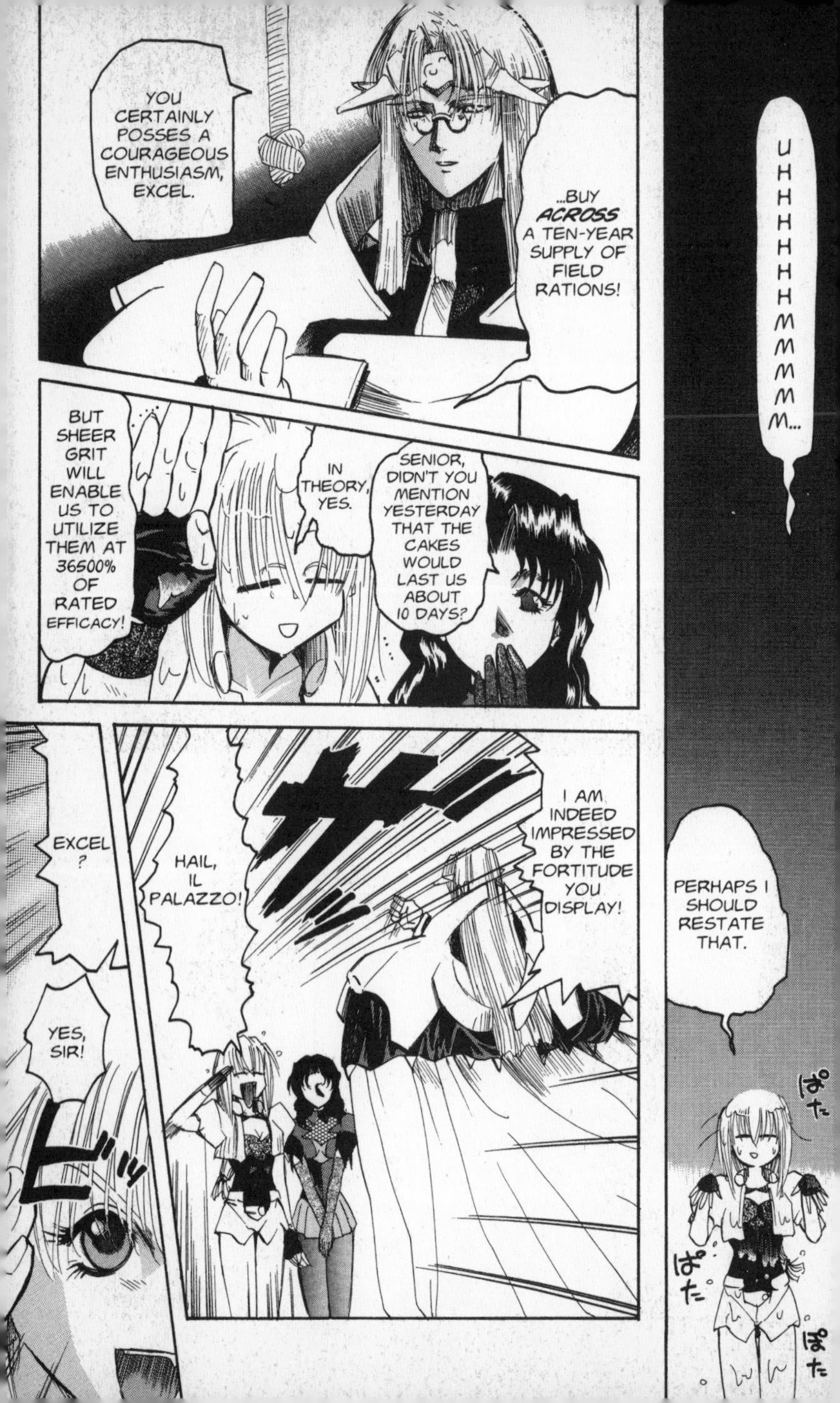

...BUY **ACROSS** A TEN-YEAR SUPPLY OF FIELD RATIONS!
UHHHHHHHMMMMMM...
YOU CERTAINLY POSSES A COURAGEOUS ENTHUSIASM, EXCEL.
SENIOR, DIDN'T YOU MENTION YESTERDAY THAT THE CAKES WOULD LAST US ABOUT 10 DAYS?
IN THEORY, YES.
BUT SHEER GRIT WILL ENABLE US TO UTILIZE THEM AT 36500% OF RATED EFFICACY!
PERHAPS I SHOULD RESTATE THAT.
ぽた ぽた ぽた
I AM INDEED IMPRESSED BY THE FORTITUDE YOU DISPLAY!
HAIL, IL PALAZZO!
EXCEL ?
YES, SIR!

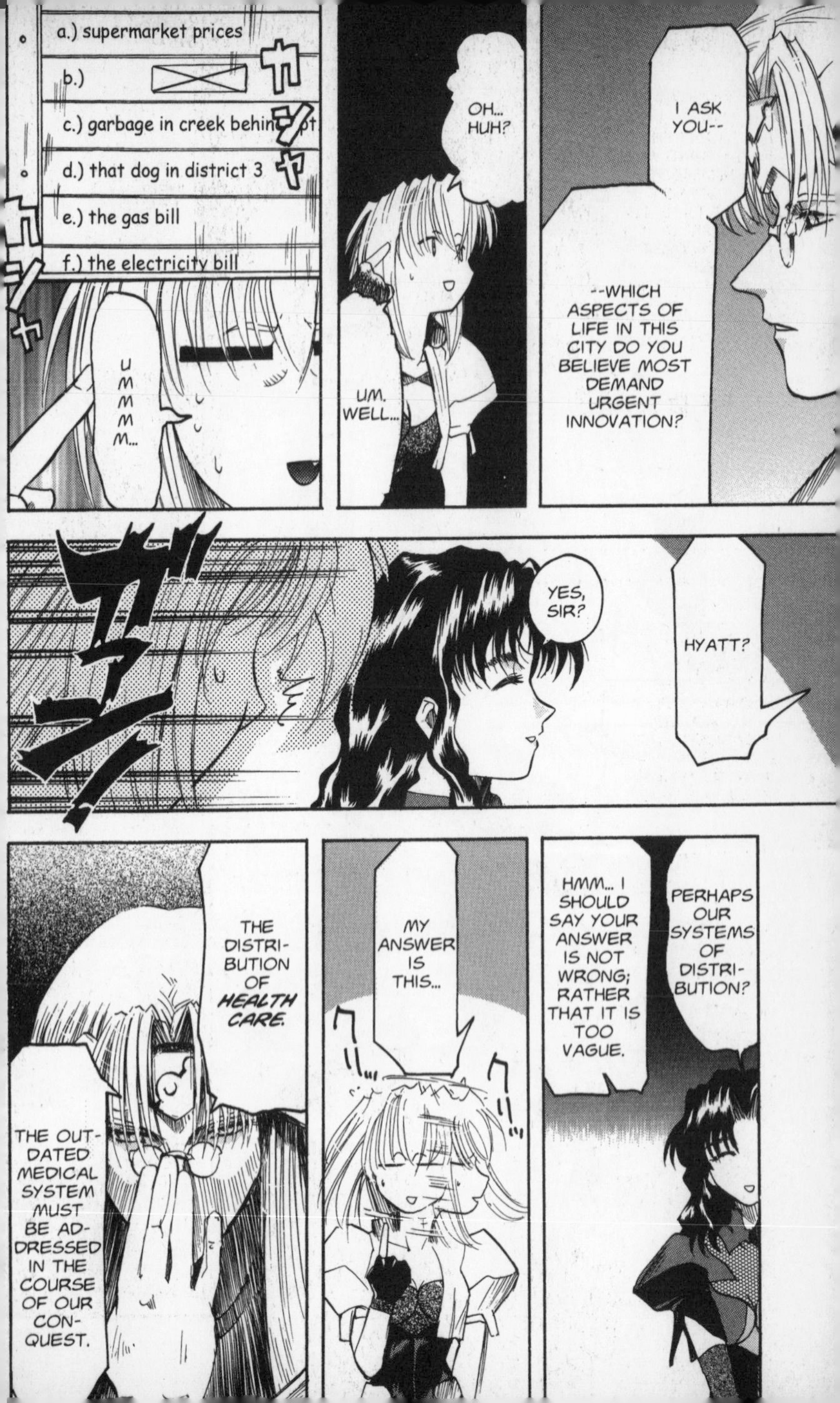

I ASK YOU--
--WHICH ASPECTS OF LIFE IN THIS CITY DO YOU BELIEVE MOST DEMAND URGENT INNOVATION?
OH... HUH?
UM. WELL...
a.) supermarket prices
b.)
c.) garbage in creek behin
d.) that dog in district 3
e.) the gas bill
f.) the electricity bill
UMMMM...
HYATT?
YES, SIR?
PERHAPS OUR SYSTEMS OF DISTRIBUTION?
HMM... I SHOULD SAY YOUR ANSWER IS NOT WRONG; RATHER THAT IT IS TOO VAGUE.
MY ANSWER IS THIS...
THE DISTRIBUTION OF *HEALTH CARE.*
THE OUTDATED MEDICAL SYSTEM MUST BE ADDRESSED IN THE COURSE OF OUR CONQUEST.

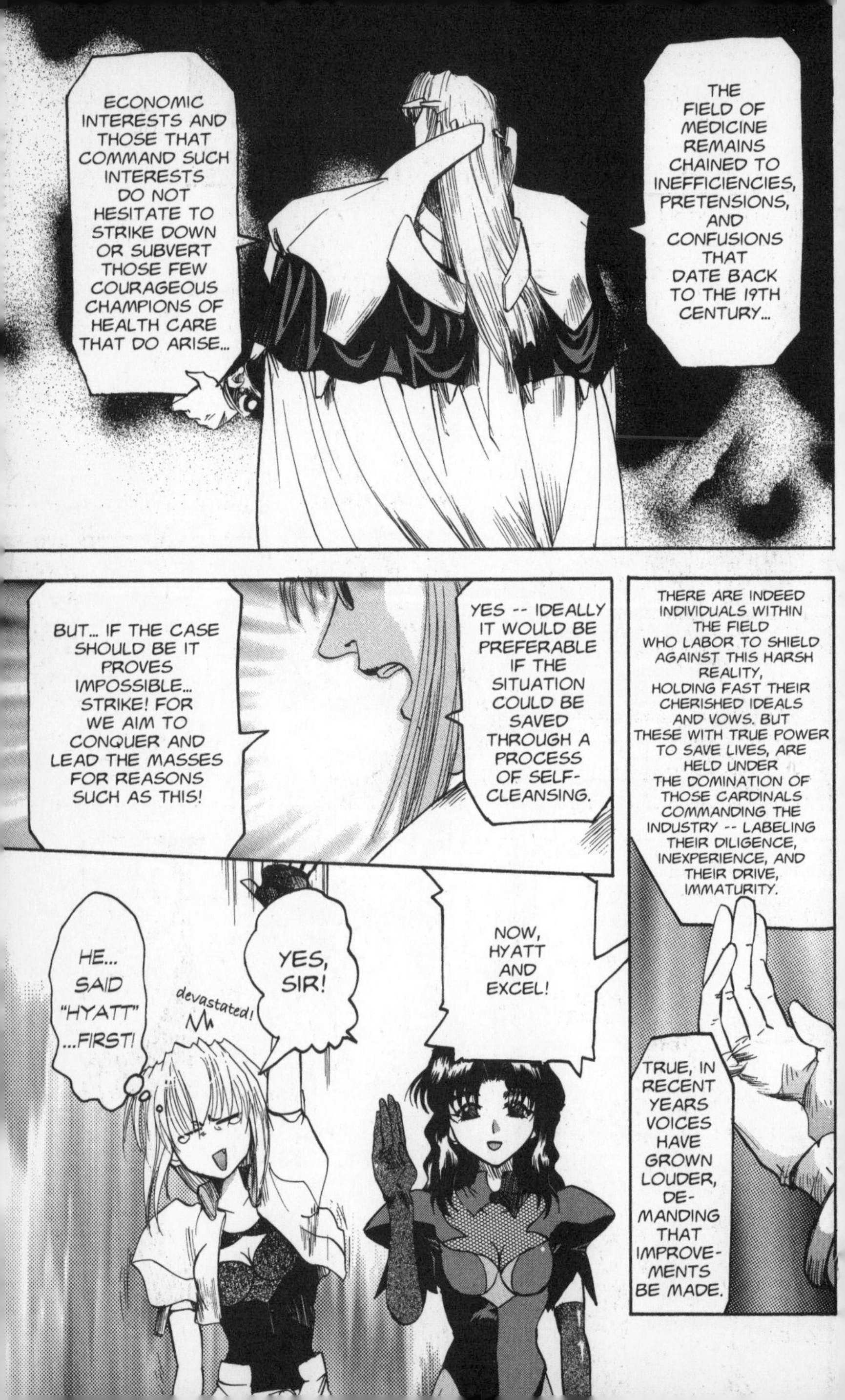
THE FIELD OF MEDICINE REMAINS CHAINED TO INEFFICIENCIES, PRETENSIONS, AND CONFUSIONS THAT DATE BACK TO THE 19TH CENTURY...
ECONOMIC INTERESTS AND THOSE THAT COMMAND SUCH INTERESTS DO NOT HESITATE TO STRIKE DOWN OR SUBVERT THOSE FEW COURAGEOUS CHAMPIONS OF HEALTH CARE THAT DO ARISE...
THERE ARE INDEED INDIVIDUALS WITHIN THE FIELD WHO LABOR TO SHIELD AGAINST THIS HARSH REALITY, HOLDING FAST THEIR CHERISHED IDEALS AND VOWS. BUT THESE WITH TRUE POWER TO SAVE LIVES, ARE HELD UNDER THE DOMINATION OF THOSE CARDINALS COMMANDING THE INDUSTRY -- LABELING THEIR DILIGENCE, INEXPERIENCE, AND THEIR DRIVE, IMMATURITY.
TRUE, IN RECENT YEARS VOICES HAVE GROWN LOUDER, DE-MANDING THAT IMPROVE-MENTS BE MADE.
YES -- IDEALLY IT WOULD BE PREFERABLE IF THE SITUATION COULD BE SAVED THROUGH A PROCESS OF SELF-CLEANSING.
BUT... IF THE CASE SHOULD BE IT PROVES IMPOSSIBLE... STRIKE! FOR WE AIM TO CONQUER AND LEAD THE MASSES FOR REASONS SUCH AS THIS!
NOW, HYATT AND EXCEL!
YES, SIR!
devastated!
HE... SAID "HYATT" ...FIRST!

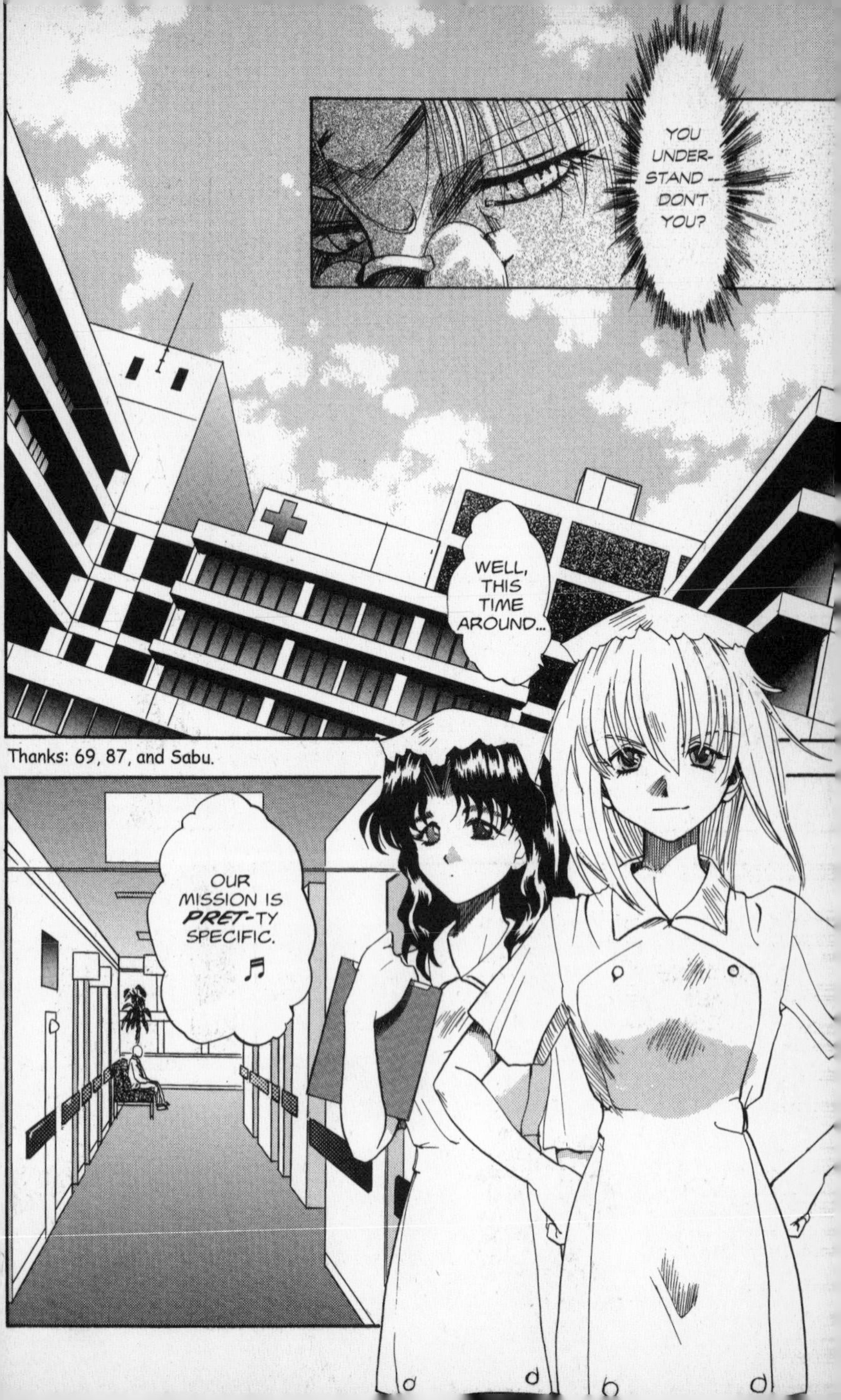
YOU UNDER-STAND -- DON'T YOU?
WELL, THIS TIME AROUND...
OUR MISSION IS PRET-TY SPECIFIC. ♪

Thanks: 69, 87, and Sabu.

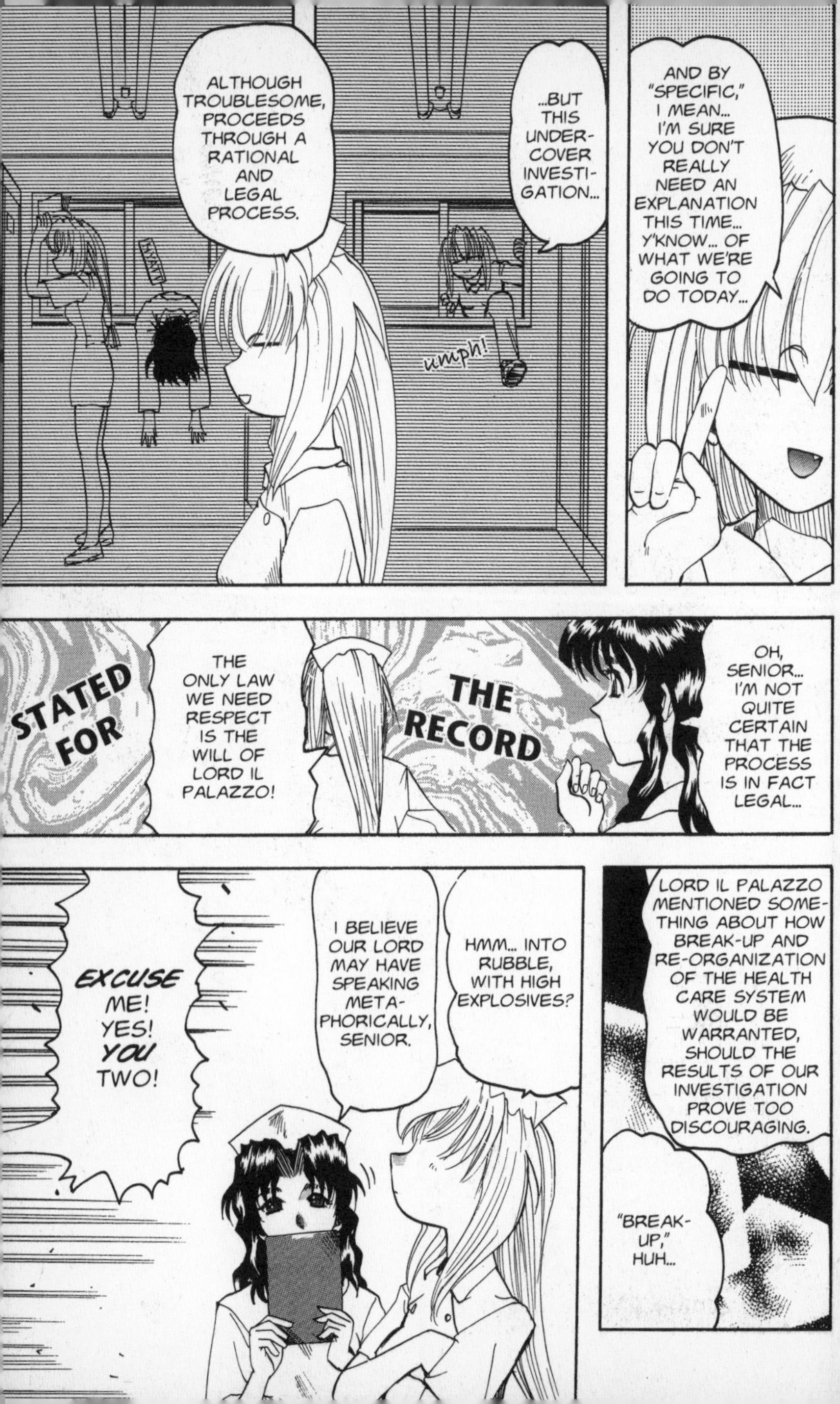
AND BY "SPECIFIC," I MEAN... I'M SURE YOU DON'T REALLY NEED AN EXPLANATION THIS TIME... Y'KNOW... OF WHAT WE'RE GOING TO DO TODAY...
...BUT THIS UNDER-COVER INVESTI-GATION...
ALTHOUGH TROUBLESOME, PROCEEDS THROUGH A RATIONAL AND LEGAL PROCESS.
umph!
OH, SENIOR... I'M NOT QUITE CERTAIN THAT THE PROCESS IS IN FACT LEGAL...
THE ONLY LAW WE NEED RESPECT IS THE WILL OF LORD IL PALAZZO!
STATED FOR THE RECORD
LORD IL PALAZZO MENTIONED SOME-THING ABOUT HOW BREAK-UP AND RE-ORGANIZATION OF THE HEALTH CARE SYSTEM WOULD BE WARRANTED, SHOULD THE RESULTS OF OUR INVESTIGATION PROVE TOO DISCOURAGING.
"BREAK-UP," HUH...
HMM... INTO RUBBLE, WITH HIGH EXPLOSIVES?
I BELIEVE OUR LORD MAY HAVE SPEAKING META-PHORICALLY, SENIOR.
EXCUSE ME! YES! YOU TWO!

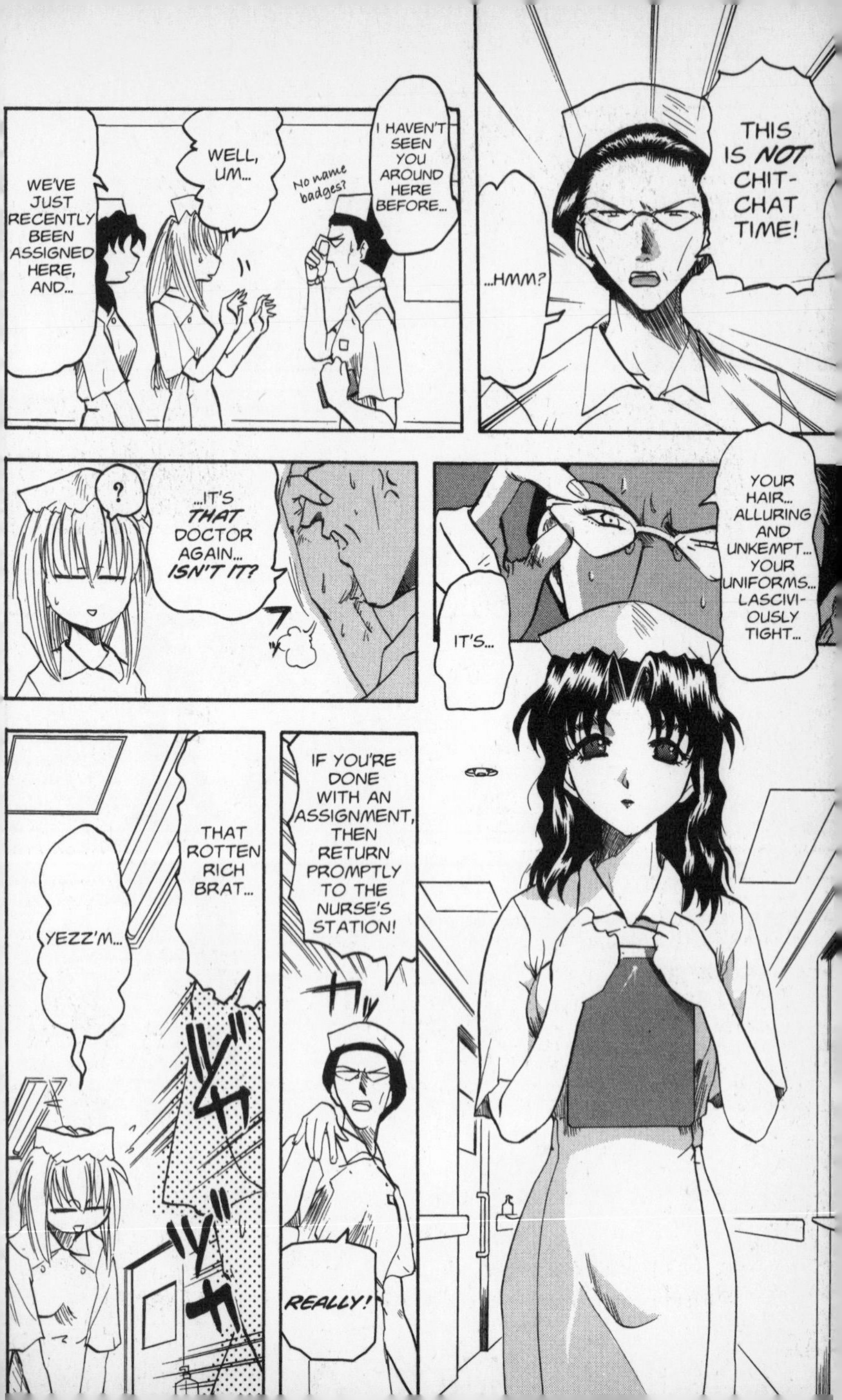
THIS IS *NOT* CHIT-CHAT TIME!
...HMM?
I HAVEN'T SEEN YOU AROUND HERE BEFORE...
No name badges?
WELL, UM...
WE'VE JUST RECENTLY BEEN ASSIGNED HERE, AND...
YOUR HAIR... ALLURING AND UNKEMPT... YOUR UNIFORMS... LASCIVIOUSLY TIGHT...
IT'S...
...IT'S *THAT* DOCTOR AGAIN... *ISN'T IT?*
?
IF YOU'RE DONE WITH AN ASSIGNMENT, THEN RETURN PROMPTLY TO THE NURSE'S STATION!
REALLY!
THAT ROTTEN RICH BRAT...
YEZZ'M...

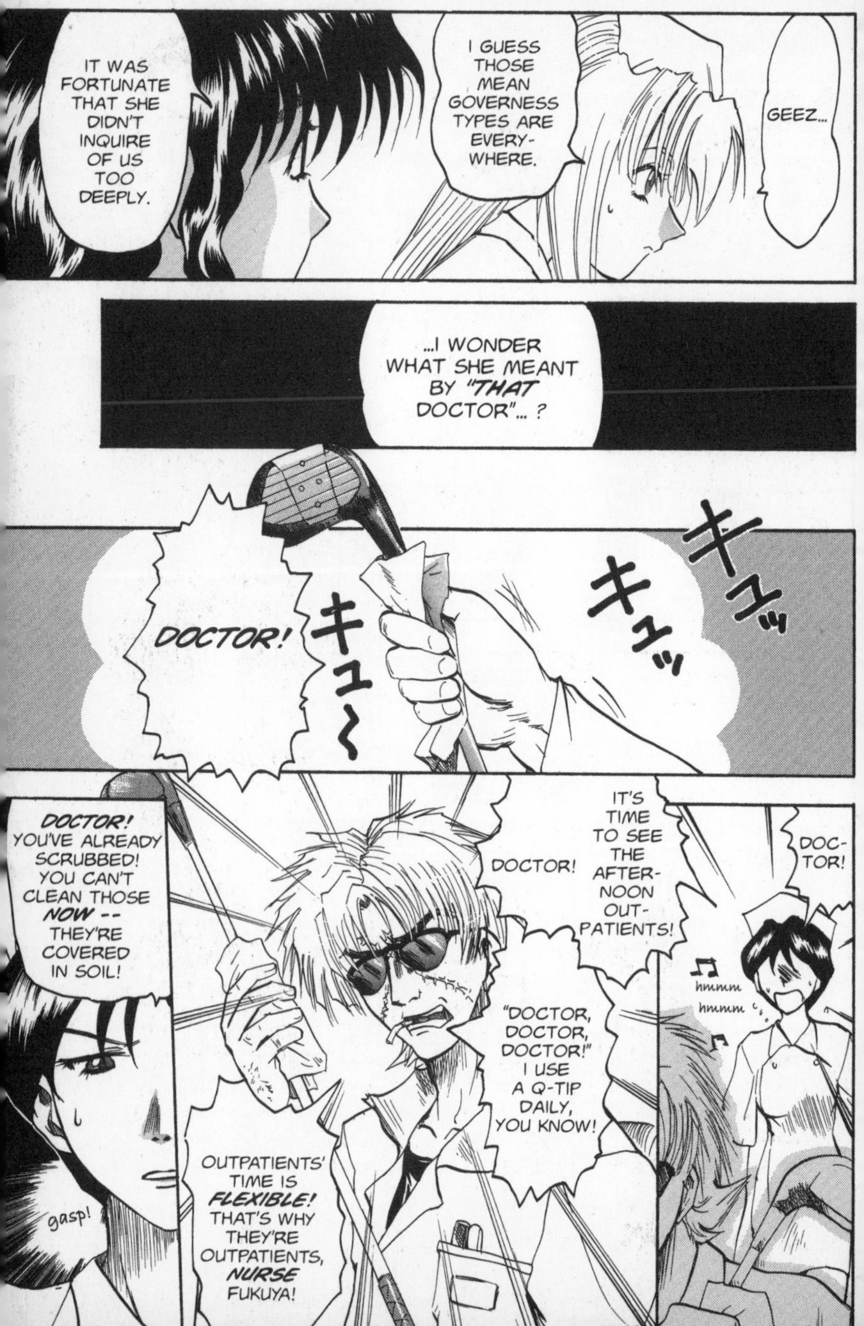

GEEZ...
I GUESS THOSE MEAN GOVERNESS TYPES ARE EVERYWHERE.
IT WAS FORTUNATE THAT SHE DIDN'T INQUIRE OF US TOO DEEPLY.
...I WONDER WHAT SHE MEANT BY "*THAT* DOCTOR"... ?
キュッ
キュッ
キュ〜
DOCTOR!
DOC-TOR!
IT'S TIME TO SEE THE AFTERNOON OUTPATIENTS!
DOCTOR!
hmmm hmmm
DOCTOR! YOU'VE ALREADY SCRUBBED! YOU CAN'T CLEAN THOSE ***NOW*** -- THEY'RE COVERED IN SOIL!
"DOCTOR, DOCTOR, DOCTOR!" I USE A Q-TIP DAILY, YOU KNOW!
OUTPATIENTS' TIME IS ***FLEXIBLE!*** THAT'S WHY THEY'RE OUTPATIENTS, ***NURSE*** FUKUYA!
gasp!

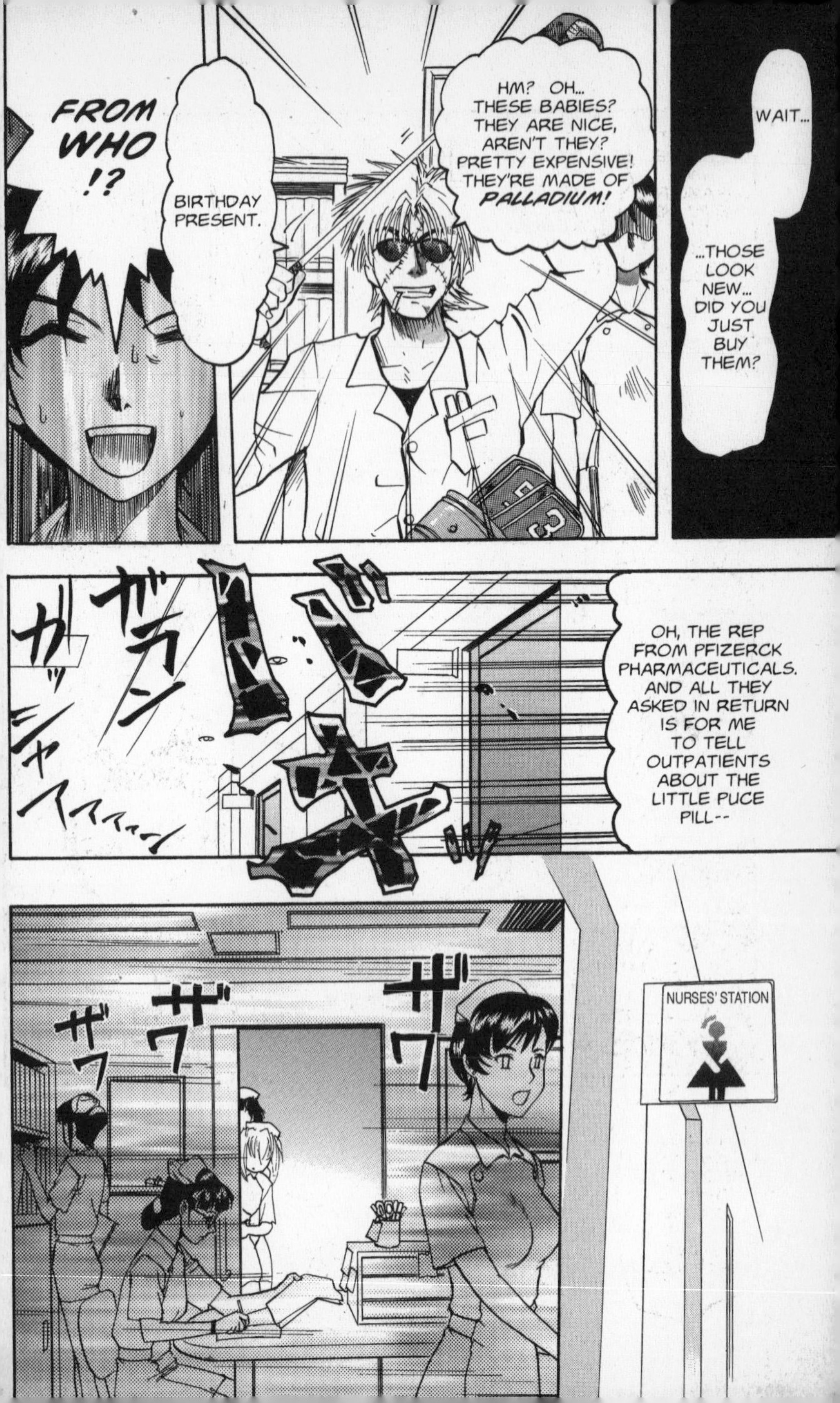
WAIT...
...THOSE LOOK NEW... DID YOU JUST BUY THEM?
HM? OH... THESE BABIES? THEY ARE NICE, AREN'T THEY? PRETTY EXPENSIVE! THEY'RE MADE OF *PALLADIUM!*
BIRTHDAY PRESENT.
FROM WHO!?
OH, THE REP FROM PFIZERCK PHARMACEUTICALS. AND ALL THEY ASKED IN RETURN IS FOR ME TO TELL OUTPATIENTS ABOUT THE LITTLE PUCE PILL--
ガラン
NURSES' STATION
ザワ
ザワ

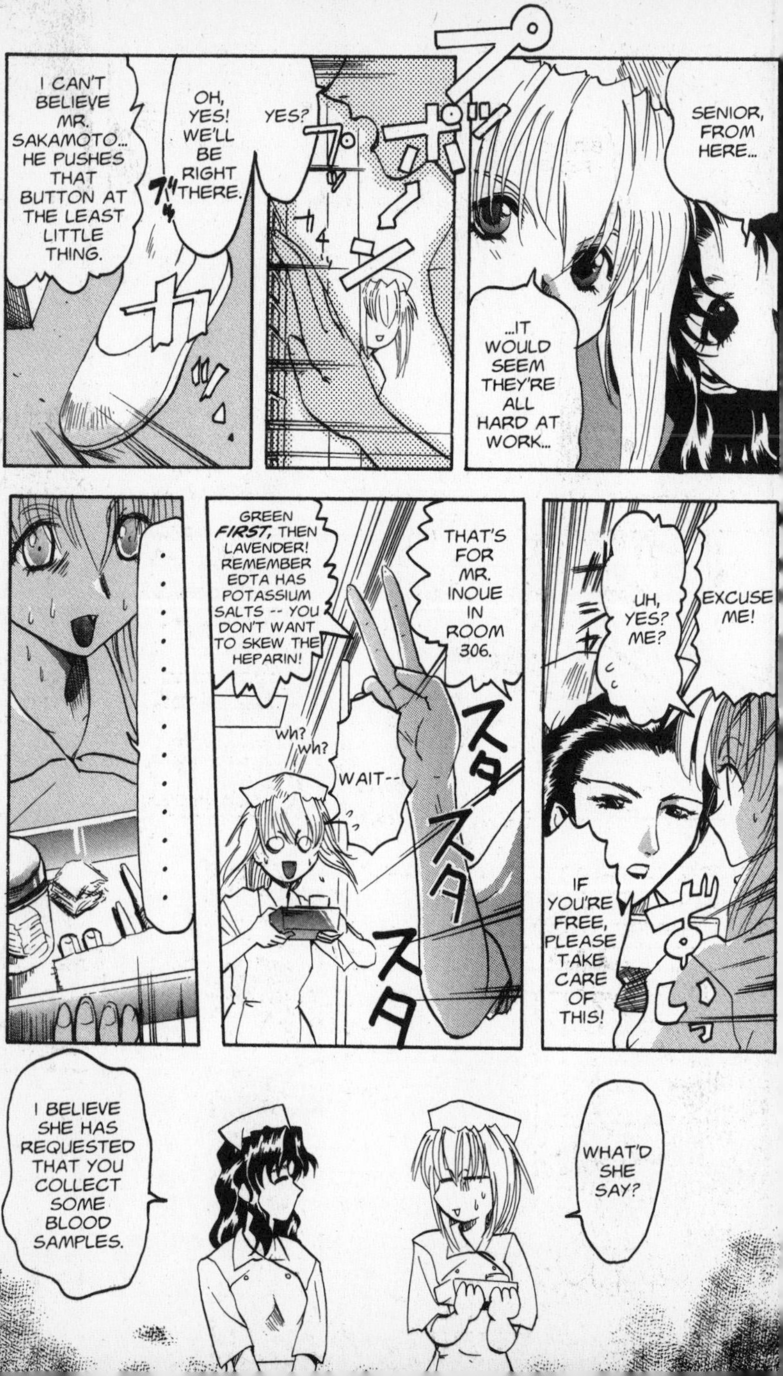
SENIOR, FROM HERE...
...IT WOULD SEEM THEY'RE ALL HARD AT WORK...
YES?
OH, YES! WE'LL BE RIGHT THERE.
I CAN'T BELIEVE MR. SAKAMOTO... HE PUSHES THAT BUTTON AT THE LEAST LITTLE THING.
EXCUSE ME!
UH, YES? ME?
IF YOU'RE FREE, PLEASE TAKE CARE OF THIS!
THAT'S FOR MR. INOUE IN ROOM 306.
GREEN FIRST, THEN LAVENDER! REMEMBER EDTA HAS POTASSIUM SALTS -- YOU DON'T WANT TO SKEW THE HEPARIN!
WAIT--
wh? wh?
....
WHAT'D SHE SAY?
I BELIEVE SHE HAS REQUESTED THAT YOU COLLECT SOME BLOOD SAMPLES.

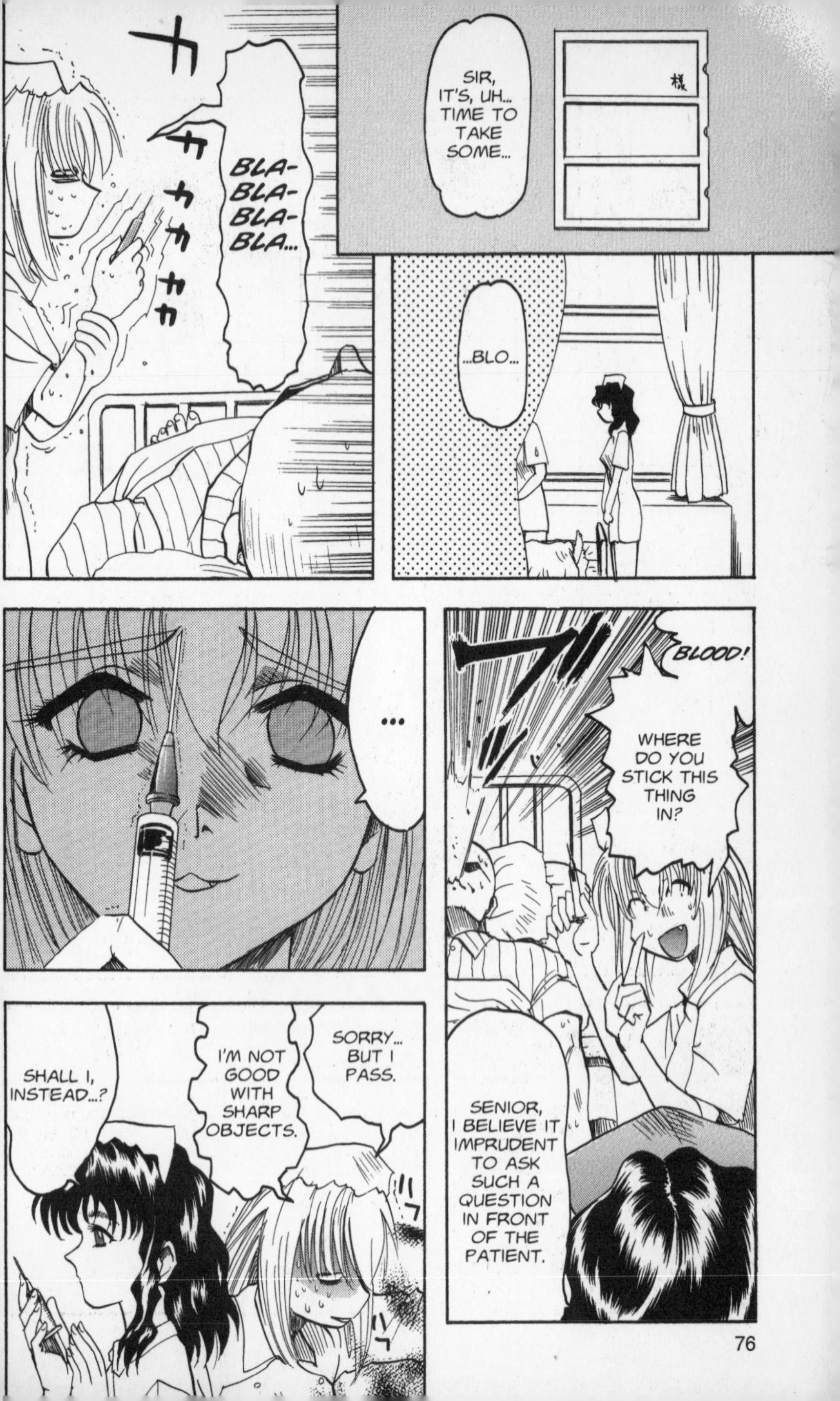

SIR, IT'S, UH... TIME TO TAKE SOME...
様
...BLO...
BLA-BLA-BLA-BLA...
BLOOD!
WHERE DO YOU STICK THIS THING IN?
SENIOR, I BELIEVE IT IMPRUDENT TO ASK SUCH A QUESTION IN FRONT OF THE PATIENT.
...
SORRY... BUT I PASS.
I'M NOT GOOD WITH SHARP OBJECTS.
SHALL I, INSTEAD...?

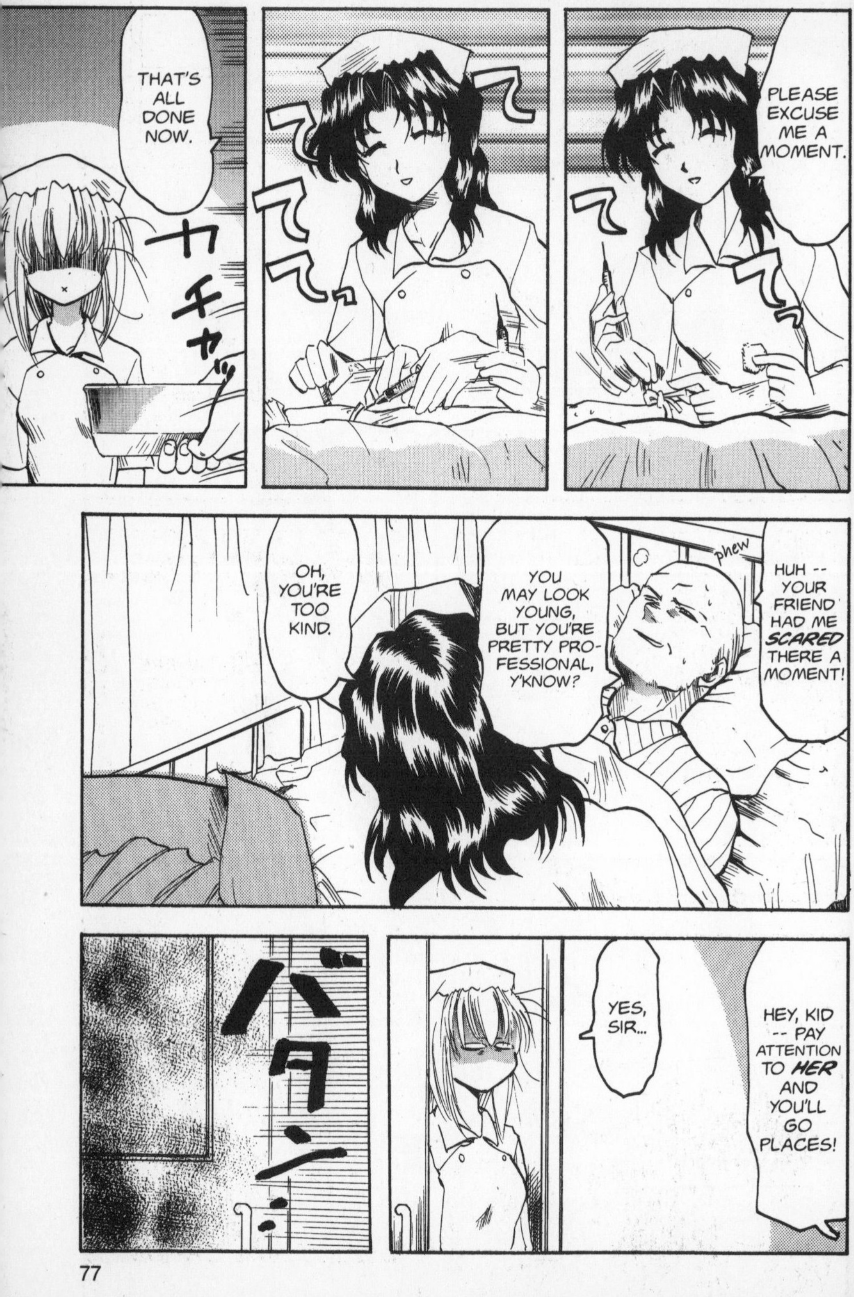
PLEASE EXCUSE ME A MOMENT.
THAT'S ALL DONE NOW.
カチャ
HUH -- YOUR FRIEND HAD ME SCARED THERE A MOMENT!
phew
YOU MAY LOOK YOUNG, BUT YOU'RE PRETTY PRO-FESSIONAL, Y'KNOW?
OH, YOU'RE TOO KIND.
HEY, KID -- PAY ATTENTION TO HER AND YOU'LL GO PLACES!
YES, SIR...
バタン…

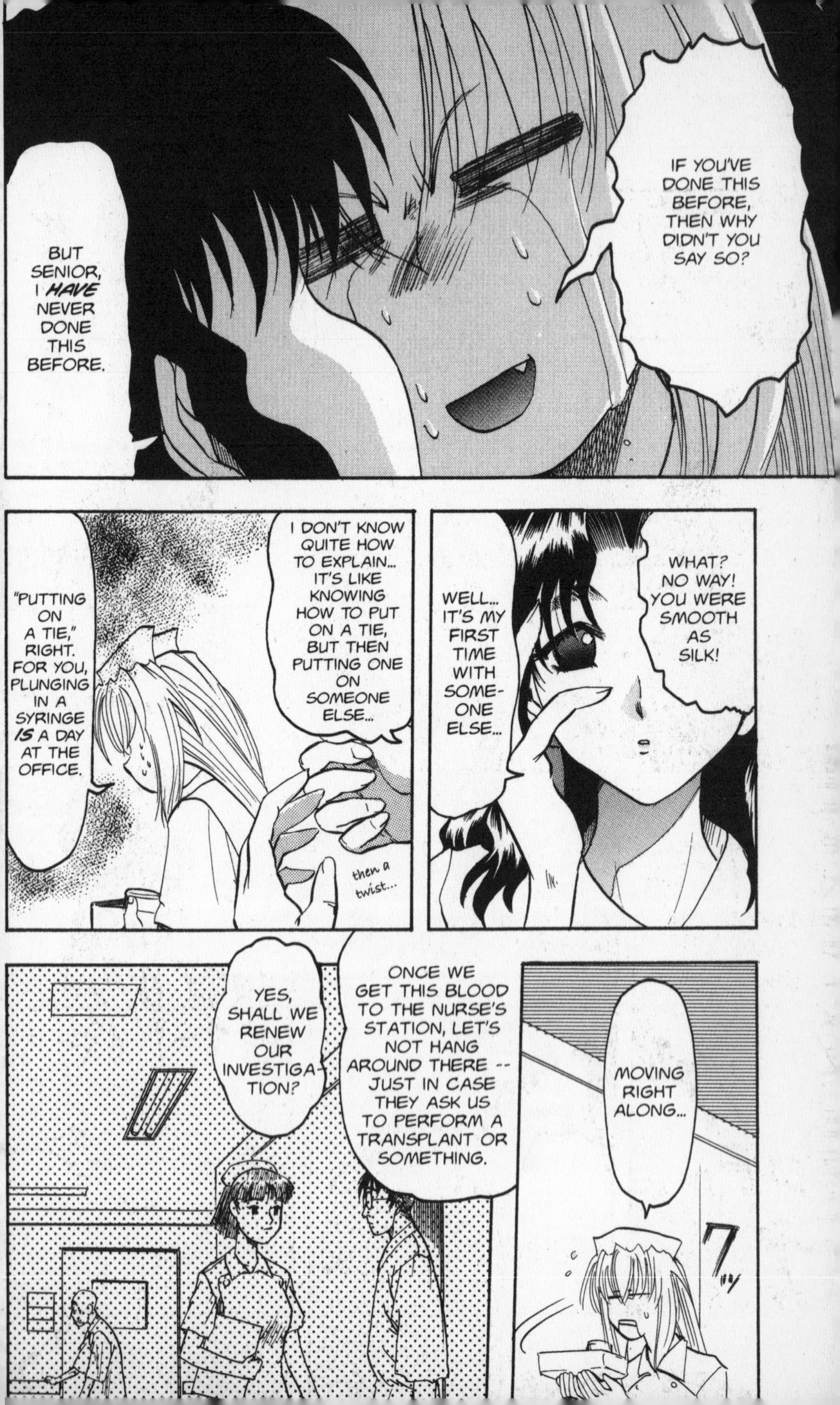
IF YOU'VE DONE THIS BEFORE, THEN WHY DIDN'T YOU SAY SO?
BUT SENIOR, I *HAVE* NEVER DONE THIS BEFORE.
WHAT? NO WAY! YOU WERE SMOOTH AS SILK!
WELL... IT'S MY FIRST TIME WITH SOME-ONE ELSE...
I DON'T KNOW QUITE HOW TO EXPLAIN... IT'S LIKE KNOWING HOW TO PUT ON A TIE, BUT THEN PUTTING ONE ON SOMEONE ELSE...
then a twist...
"PUTTING ON A TIE," RIGHT. FOR YOU, PLUNGING IN A SYRINGE *IS* A DAY AT THE OFFICE.
MOVING RIGHT ALONG...
ONCE WE GET THIS BLOOD TO THE NURSE'S STATION, LET'S NOT HANG AROUND THERE -- JUST IN CASE THEY ASK US TO PERFORM A TRANSPLANT OR SOMETHING.
YES, SHALL WE RENEW OUR INVESTIGA-TION?

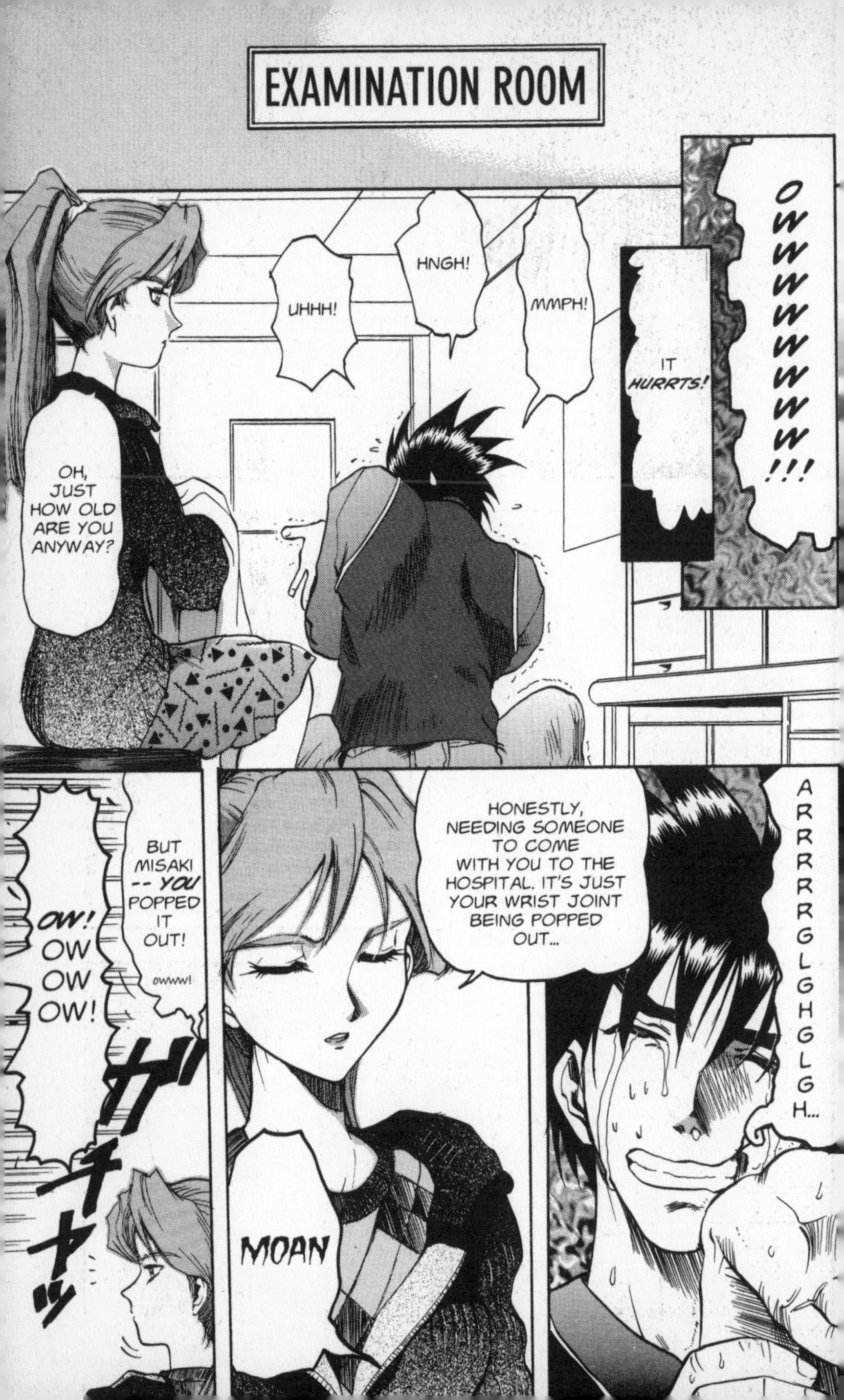
EXAMINATION ROOM
OWWWWWWWWW!!!
IT HURRTS!
MMPH!
HNGH!
UHHH!
OH, JUST HOW OLD ARE YOU ANYWAY?
ARRRRRGLGHGLGH...
HONESTLY, NEEDING SOMEONE TO COME WITH YOU TO THE HOSPITAL. IT'S JUST YOUR WRIST JOINT BEING POPPED OUT...
MOAN
BUT MISAKI -- YOU POPPED IT OUT!
owww!
OW! OW OW OW!
ガチャッ

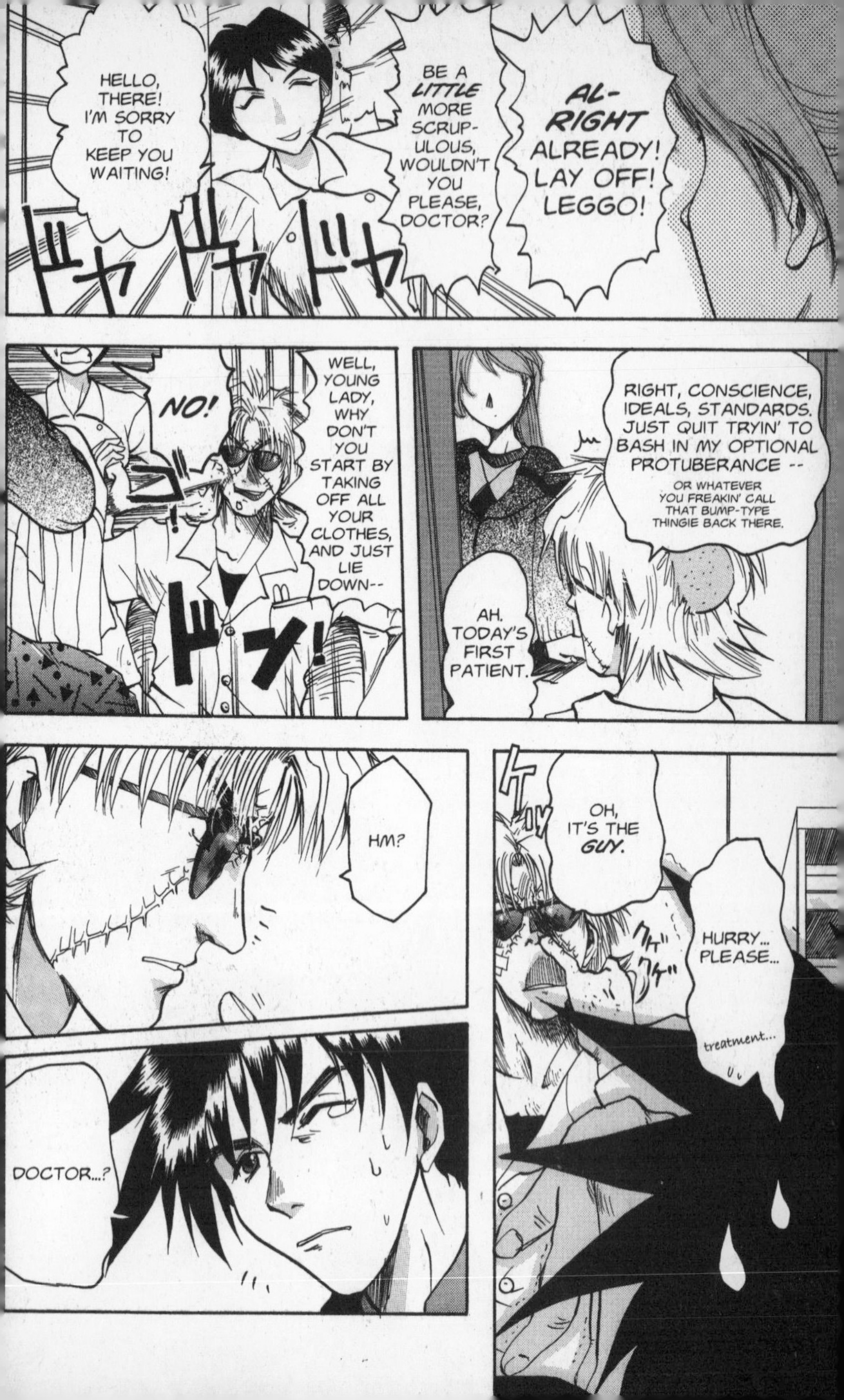
AL-RIGHT ALREADY! LAY OFF! LEGGO!
BE A LITTLE MORE SCRUPULOUS, WOULDN'T YOU PLEASE, DOCTOR?
HELLO, THERE! I'M SORRY TO KEEP YOU WAITING!
RIGHT, CONSCIENCE, IDEALS, STANDARDS. JUST QUIT TRYIN' TO BASH IN MY OPTIONAL PROTUBERANCE --
OR WHATEVER YOU FREAKIN' CALL THAT BUMP-TYPE THINGIE BACK THERE.
AH. TODAY'S FIRST PATIENT.
WELL, YOUNG LADY, WHY DON'T YOU START BY TAKING OFF ALL YOUR CLOTHES, AND JUST LIE DOWN--
NO!
OH, IT'S THE GUY.
HURRY... PLEASE...
treatment...
HM?
DOCTOR...?

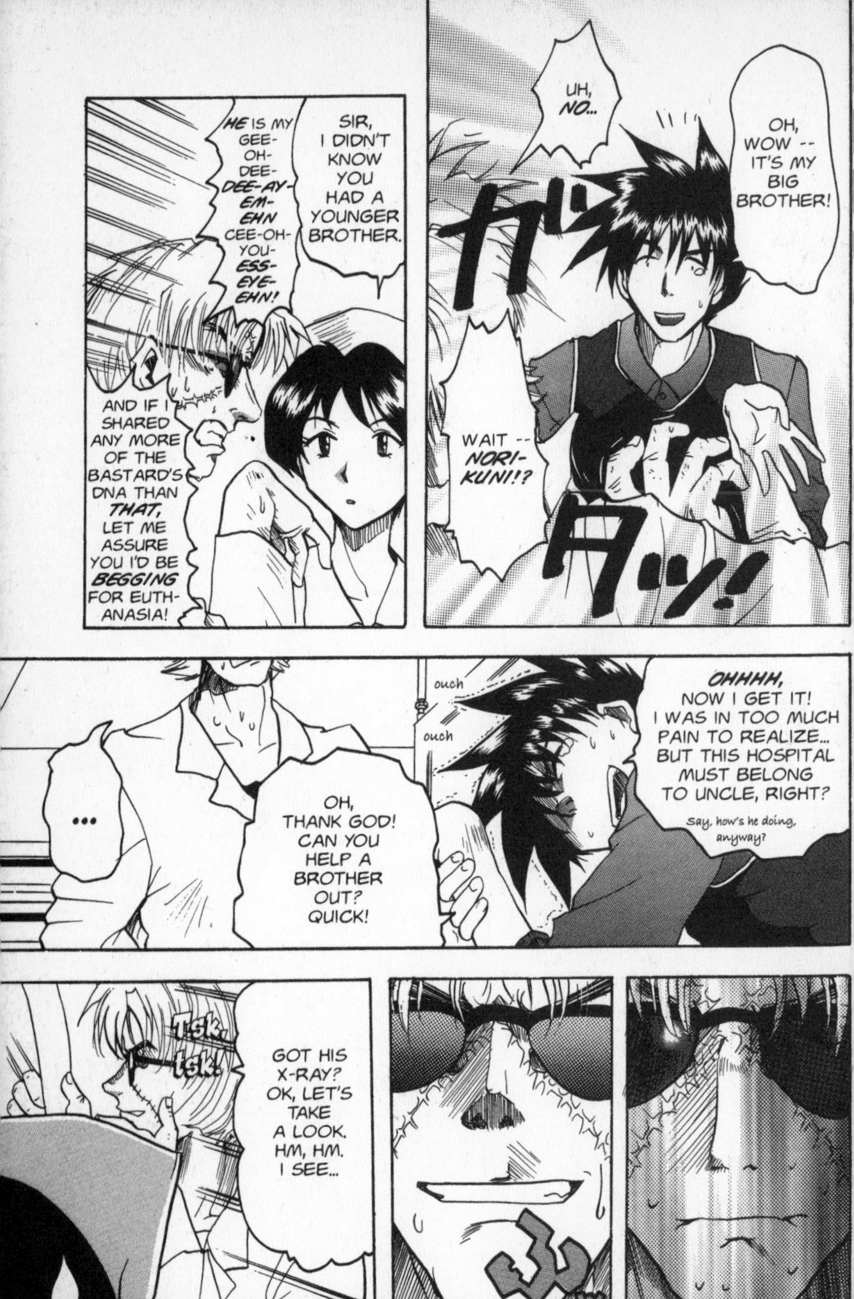
OH, WOW -- IT'S MY BIG BROTHER!
UH, NO...
ガッ
WAIT -- NORI-KUNI!?
タッ!
SIR, I DIDN'T KNOW YOU HAD A YOUNGER BROTHER.
HE IS MY GEE-OH-DEE-DEE-AY-EM-EHN CEE-OH-YOU-ESS-EYE-EHN!
AND IF I SHARED ANY MORE OF THE BASTARD'S DNA THAN THAT, LET ME ASSURE YOU I'D BE BEGGING FOR EUTH-ANASIA!
OHHHH, NOW I GET IT! I WAS IN TOO MUCH PAIN TO REALIZE... BUT THIS HOSPITAL MUST BELONG TO UNCLE, RIGHT?
Say, how's he doing, anyway?
ouch
ouch
OH, THANK GOD! CAN YOU HELP A BROTHER OUT? QUICK!
...
GOT HIS X-RAY? OK, LET'S TAKE A LOOK. HM, HM. I SEE...
Tsk. tsk!

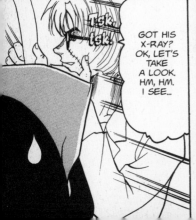

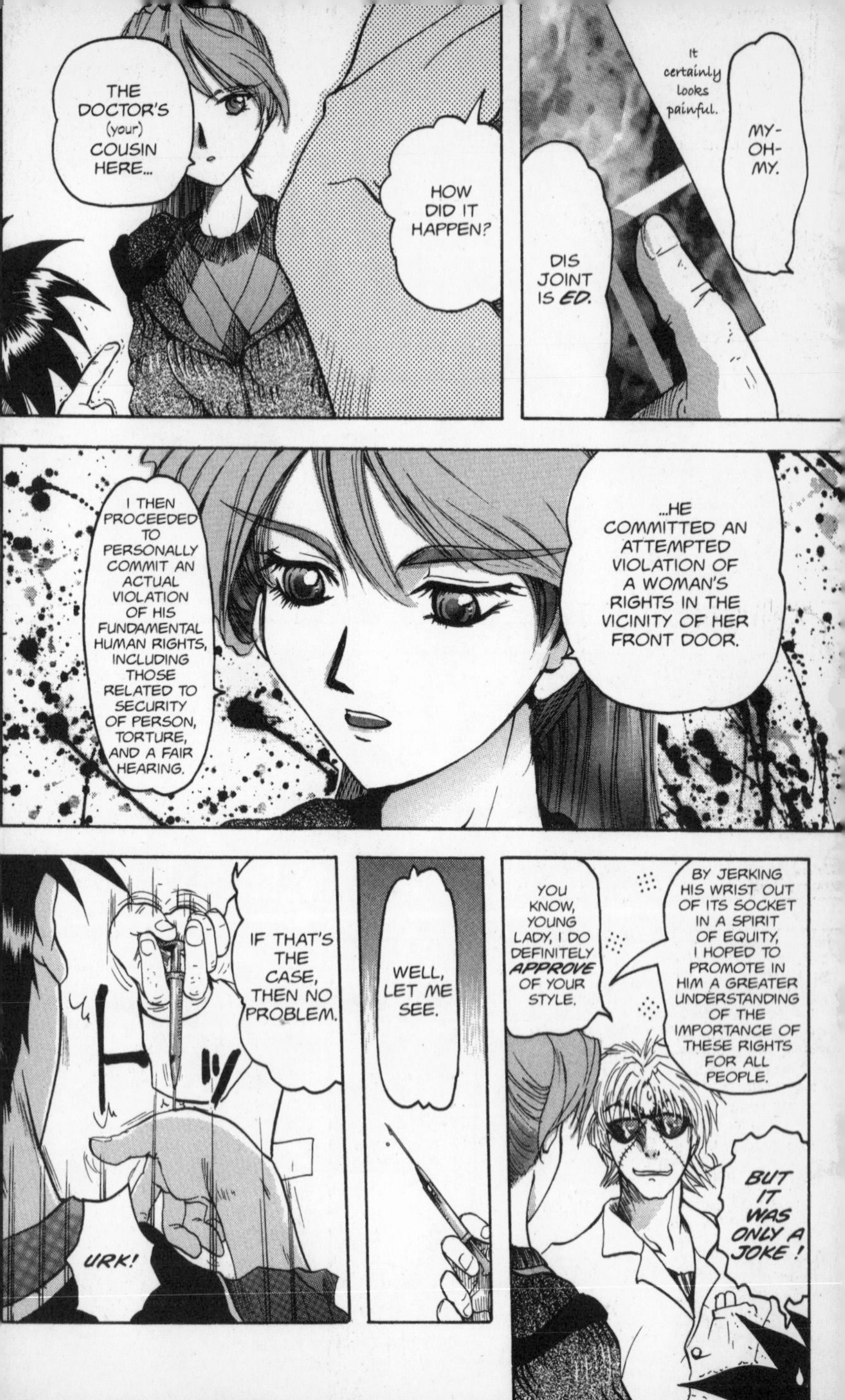
MY-OH-MY.
It certainly looks painful.
DIS JOINT IS *ED.*
HOW DID IT HAPPEN?
THE DOCTOR'S (your) COUSIN HERE...
...HE COMMITTED AN ATTEMPTED VIOLATION OF A WOMAN'S RIGHTS IN THE VICINITY OF HER FRONT DOOR.
I THEN PROCEEDED TO PERSONALLY COMMIT AN ACTUAL VIOLATION OF HIS FUNDAMENTAL HUMAN RIGHTS, INCLUDING THOSE RELATED TO SECURITY OF PERSON, TORTURE, AND A FAIR HEARING.
BY JERKING HIS WRIST OUT OF ITS SOCKET IN A SPIRIT OF EQUITY, I HOPED TO PROMOTE IN HIM A GREATER UNDERSTANDING OF THE IMPORTANCE OF THESE RIGHTS FOR ALL PEOPLE.
YOU KNOW, YOUNG LADY, I DO DEFINITELY *APPROVE* OF YOUR STYLE.
BUT IT WAS ONLY A JOKE!
WELL, LET ME SEE.
IF THAT'S THE CASE, THEN NO PROBLEM.
URK!

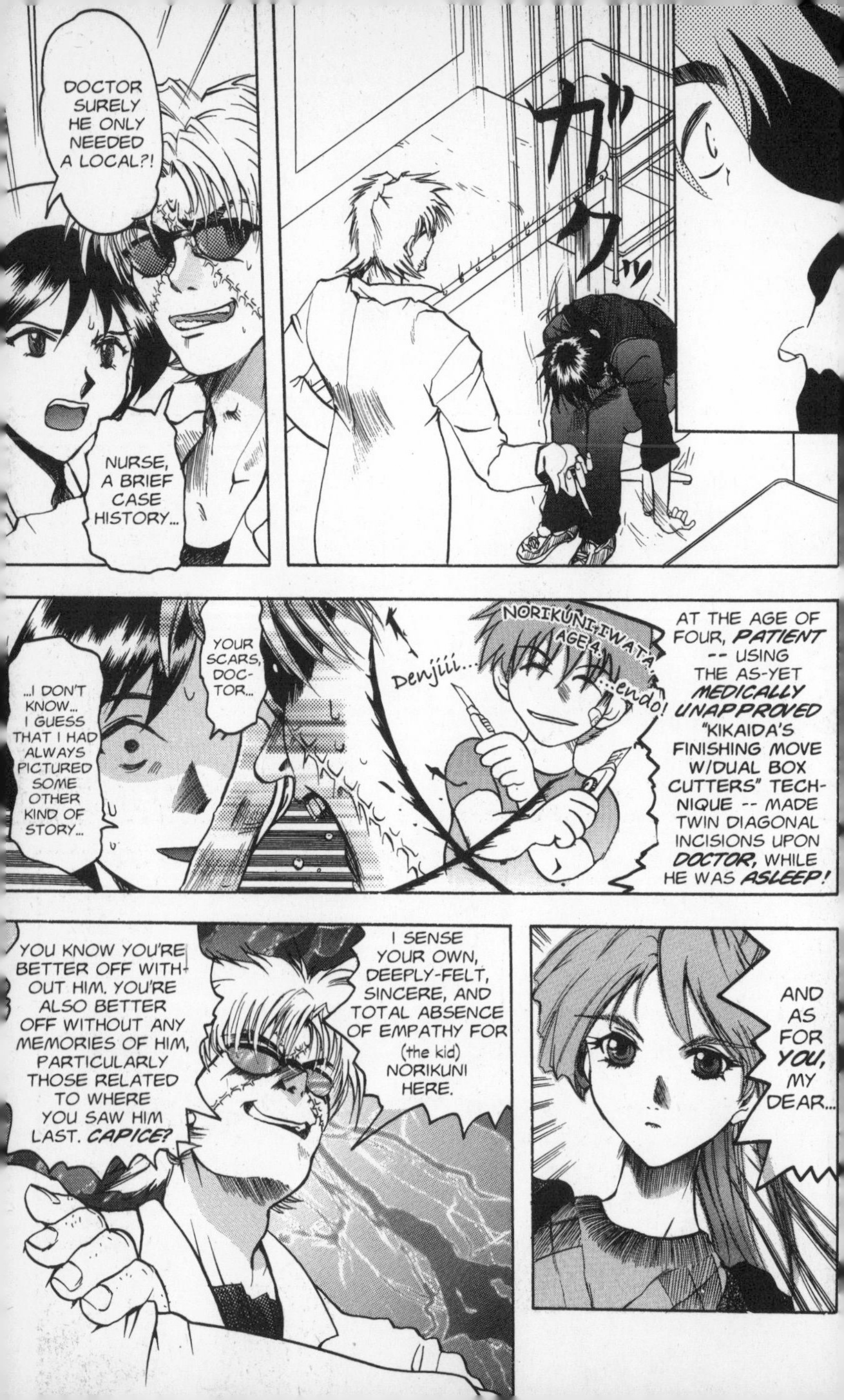
DOCTOR SURELY HE ONLY NEEDED A LOCAL?!
NURSE, A BRIEF CASE HISTORY...
AT THE AGE OF FOUR, *PATIENT* -- USING THE AS-YET *MEDICALLY UNAPPROVED* "KIKAIDA'S FINISHING MOVE W/DUAL BOX CUTTERS" TECHNIQUE -- MADE TWIN DIAGONAL INCISIONS UPON *DOCTOR,* WHILE HE WAS *ASLEEP!*
NORIKUNI IWATA AGE 4
Denjiii... ...endo!
YOUR SCARS, DOCTOR...
...I DON'T KNOW... I GUESS THAT I HAD ALWAYS PICTURED SOME OTHER KIND OF STORY...
AND AS FOR *YOU,* MY DEAR...
I SENSE YOUR OWN, DEEPLY-FELT, SINCERE, AND TOTAL ABSENCE OF EMPATHY FOR (the kid) NORIKUNI HERE.
YOU KNOW YOU'RE BETTER OFF WITHOUT HIM. YOU'RE ALSO BETTER OFF WITHOUT ANY MEMORIES OF HIM, PARTICULARLY THOSE RELATED TO WHERE YOU SAW HIM LAST. *CAPICE?*

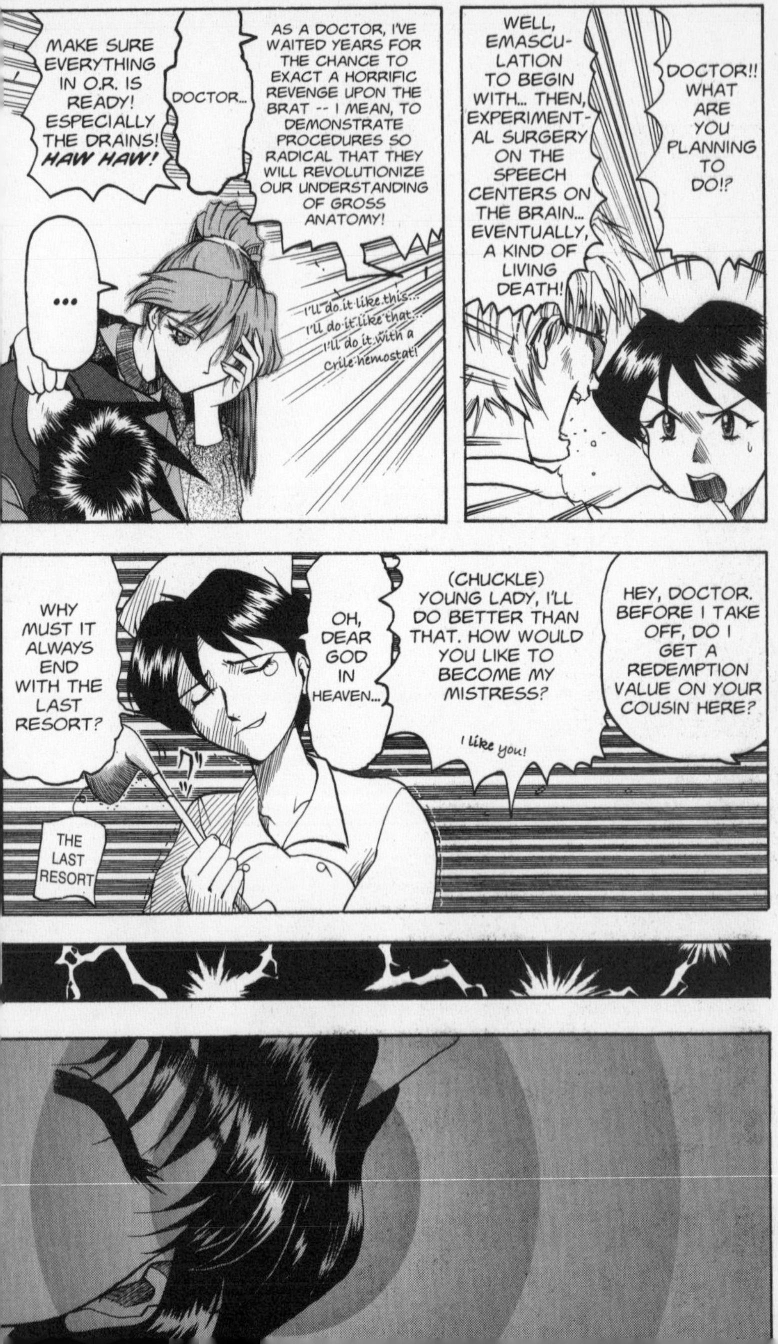
DOCTOR!! WHAT ARE YOU PLANNING TO DO!?
WELL, EMASCULATION TO BEGIN WITH... THEN, EXPERIMENTAL SURGERY ON THE SPEECH CENTERS ON THE BRAIN... EVENTUALLY, A KIND OF LIVING DEATH!
AS A DOCTOR, I'VE WAITED YEARS FOR THE CHANCE TO EXACT A HORRIFIC REVENGE UPON THE BRAT -- I MEAN, TO DEMONSTRATE PROCEDURES SO RADICAL THAT THEY WILL REVOLUTIONIZE OUR UNDERSTANDING OF GROSS ANATOMY!
DOCTOR...
MAKE SURE EVERYTHING IN O.R. IS READY! ESPECIALLY THE DRAINS! ***HAW HAW!***
I'll do it like this... I'll do it like that... I'll do it with a Crile hemostat!
...
HEY, DOCTOR. BEFORE I TAKE OFF, DO I GET A REDEMPTION VALUE ON YOUR COUSIN HERE?
(CHUCKLE) YOUNG LADY, I'LL DO BETTER THAN THAT. HOW WOULD YOU LIKE TO BECOME MY MISTRESS?
OH, DEAR GOD IN HEAVEN...
I like you!
WHY MUST IT ALWAYS END WITH THE LAST RESORT?
THE LAST RESORT

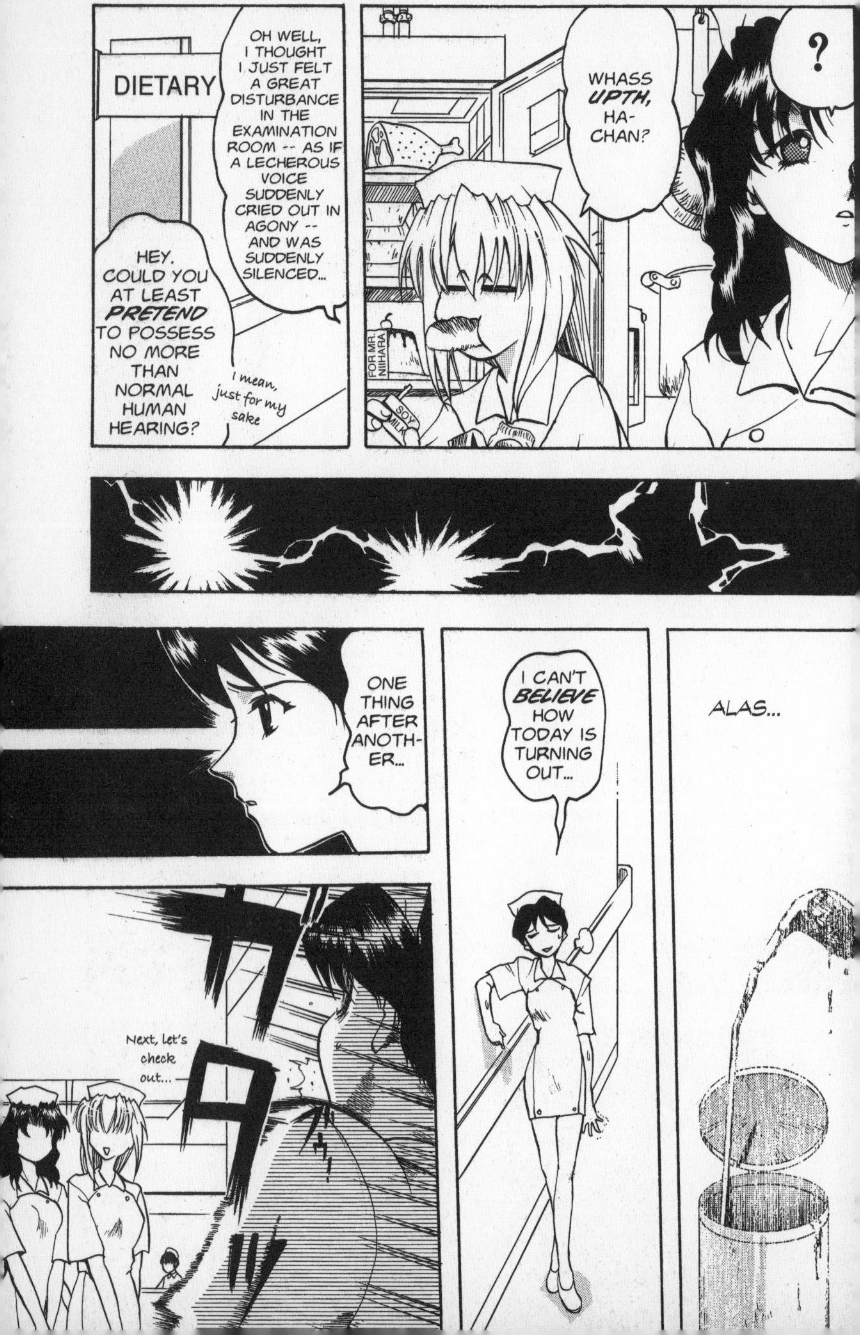
?
WHASS *UPTH,* HA-CHAN?
FOR MR. NIIHARA
SOY MILK
DIETARY
OH WELL, I THOUGHT I JUST FELT A GREAT DISTURBANCE IN THE EXAMINATION ROOM -- AS IF A LECHEROUS VOICE SUDDENLY CRIED OUT IN AGONY -- AND WAS SUDDENLY SILENCED...
HEY. COULD YOU AT LEAST *PRETEND* TO POSSESS NO MORE THAN NORMAL HUMAN HEARING?
I mean, just for my sake
ALAS...
I CAN'T *BELIEVE* HOW TODAY IS TURNING OUT...
ONE THING AFTER ANOTHER...
Next, let's check out...

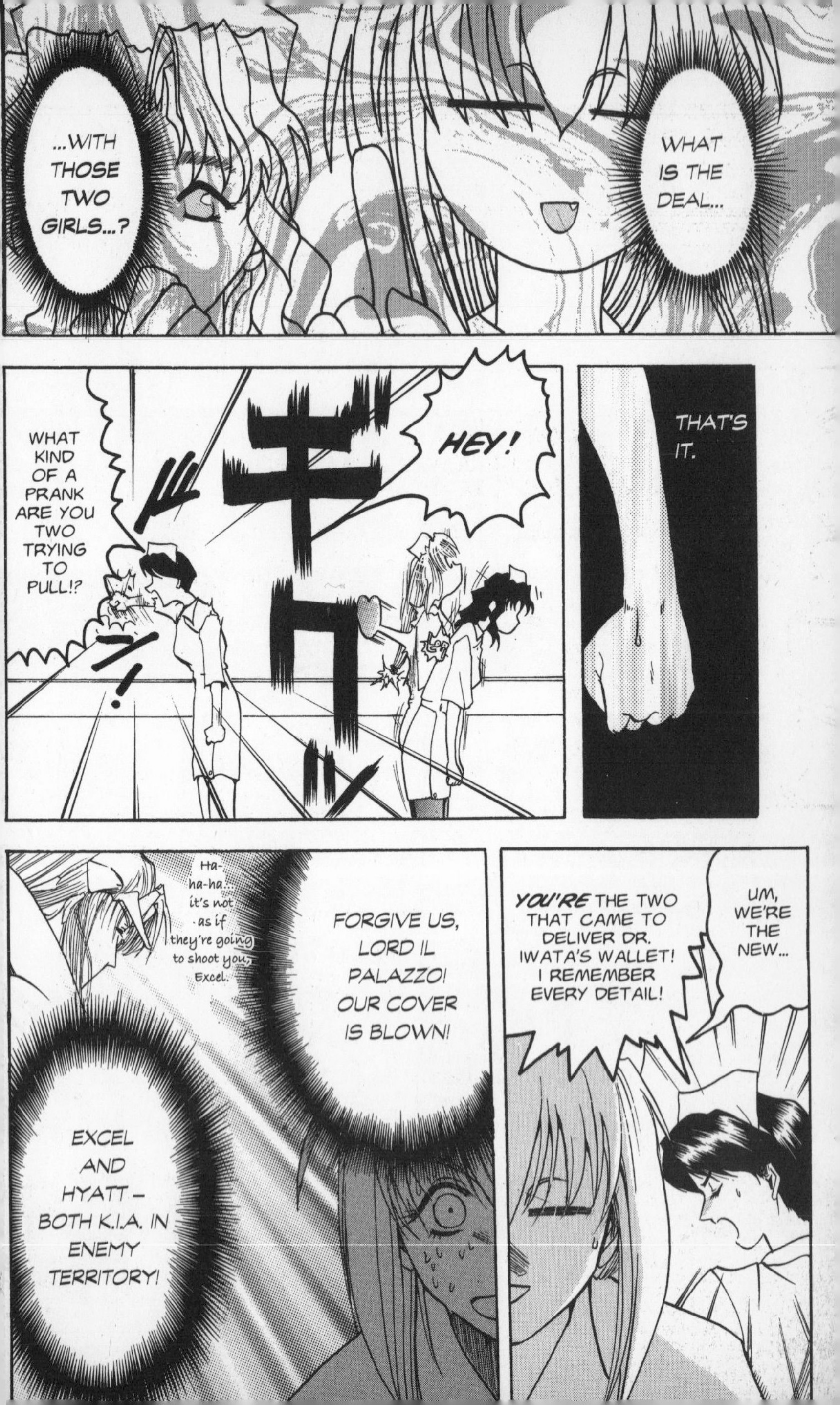
WHAT IS THE DEAL...
...WITH THOSE TWO GIRLS...?
THAT'S IT.
HEY!
ギク
WHAT KIND OF A PRANK ARE YOU TWO TRYING TO PULL!?
UM, WE'RE THE NEW...
YOU'RE THE TWO THAT CAME TO DELIVER DR. IWATA'S WALLET! I REMEMBER EVERY DETAIL!
FORGIVE US, LORD IL PALAZZO! OUR COVER IS BLOWN!
EXCEL AND HYATT – BOTH K.I.A. IN ENEMY TERRITORY!
Ha-ha-ha... it's not as if they're going to shoot you, Excel.

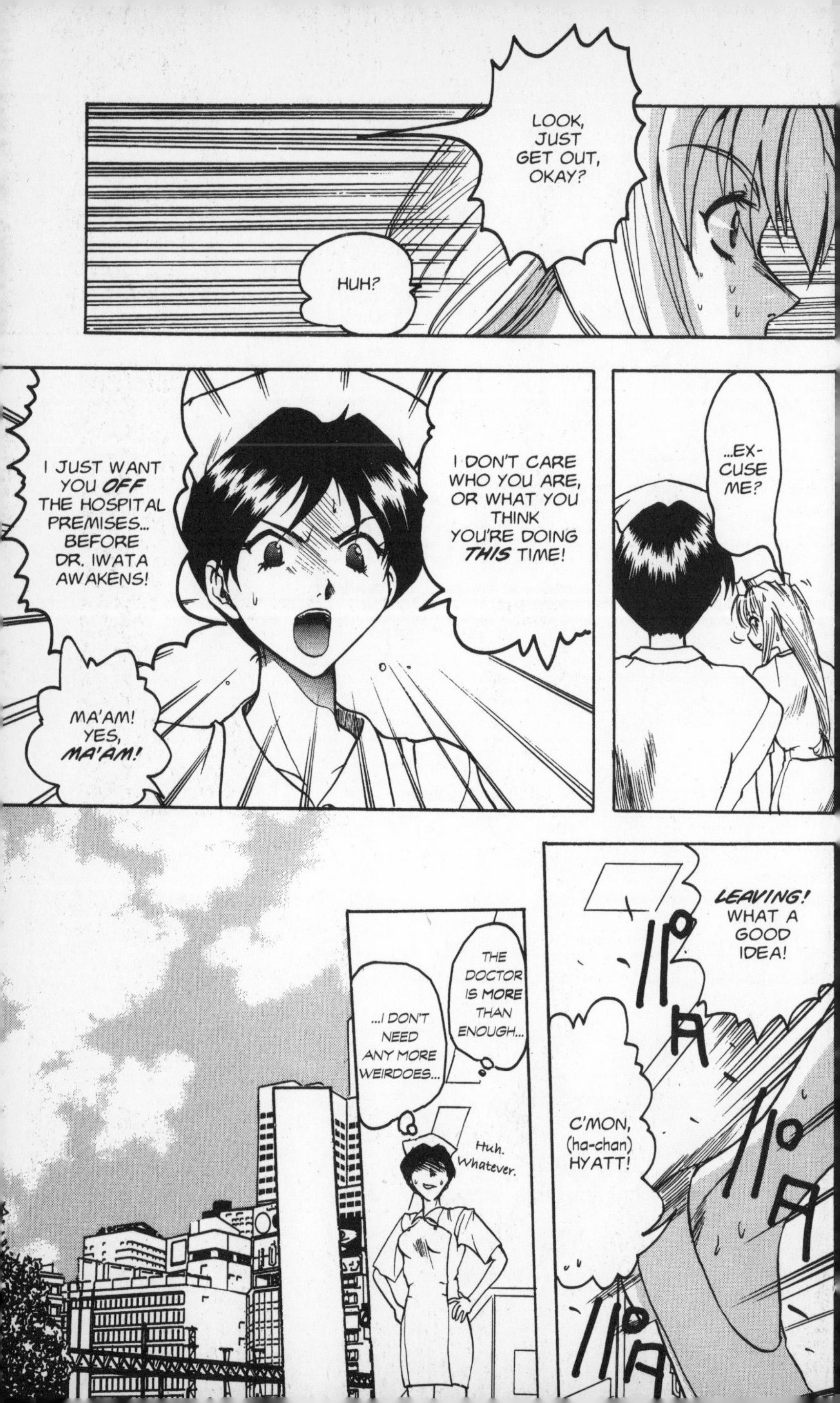

LOOK, JUST GET OUT, OKAY?
HUH?
...EX-CUSE ME?
I DON'T CARE WHO YOU ARE, OR WHAT YOU THINK YOU'RE DOING *THIS* TIME!
I JUST WANT YOU *OFF* THE HOSPITAL PREMISES... BEFORE DR. IWATA AWAKENS!
MA'AM! YES, *MA'AM!*
LEAVING! WHAT A GOOD IDEA!
パタ
C'MON, (ha-chan) HYATT!
パタ
パタ
THE DOCTOR IS MORE THAN ENOUGH...
...I DON'T NEED ANY MORE WEIRDOES...
Huh. Whatever.

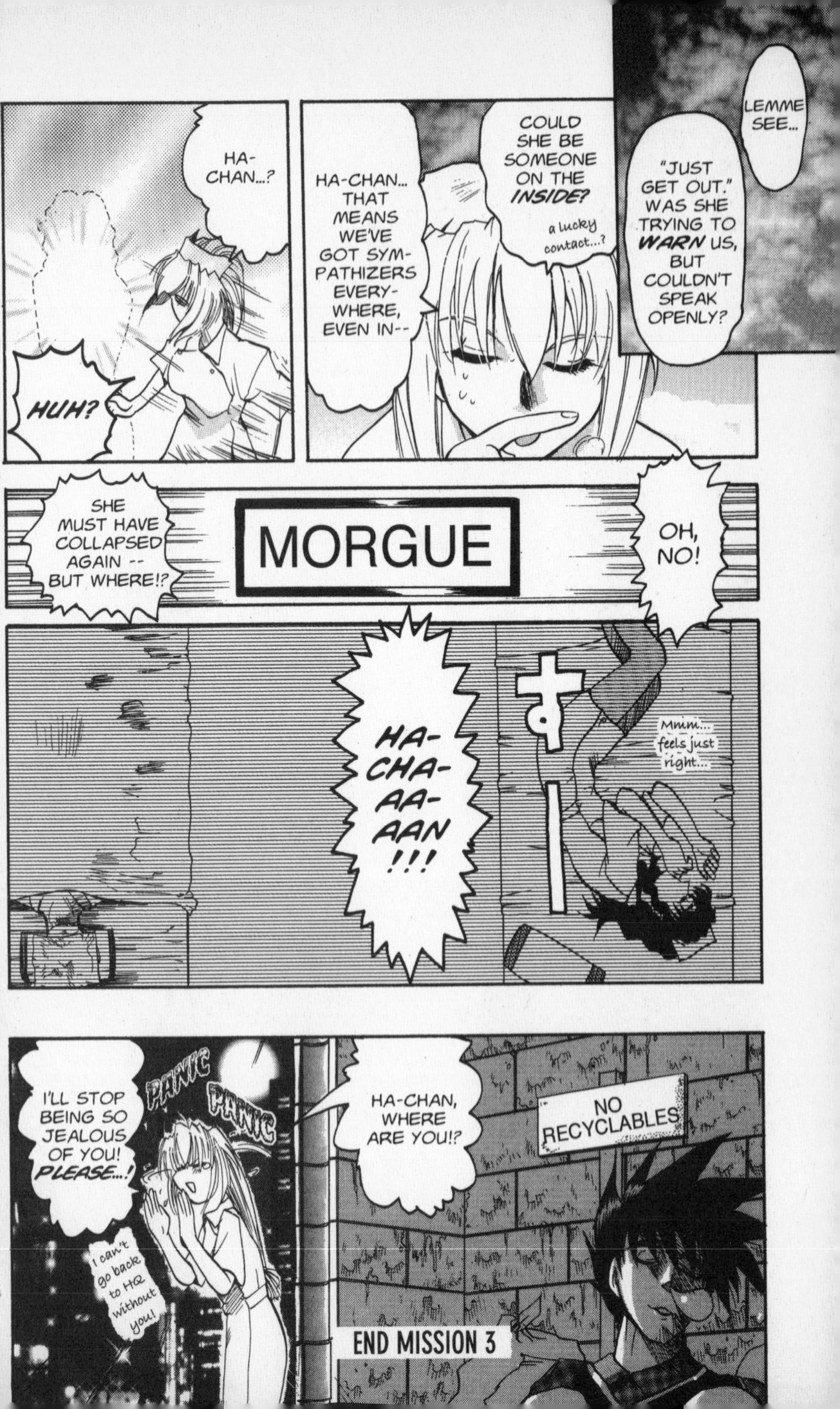
LEMME SEE...
"JUST GET OUT." WAS SHE TRYING TO *WARN* US, BUT COULDN'T SPEAK OPENLY?
COULD SHE BE SOMEONE ON THE *INSIDE?*
a lucky contact...?
HA-CHAN... THAT MEANS WE'VE GOT SYM-PATHIZERS EVERY-WHERE, EVEN IN--
HA-CHAN...?
HUH?
OH, NO!
MORGUE
SHE MUST HAVE COLLAPSED AGAIN -- BUT WHERE!?
Mmm... feels just right...
HA-CHA-AA-AAN!!!
NO RECYCLABLES
HA-CHAN, WHERE ARE YOU!?
END MISSION 3
PANIC
PANIC
I'LL STOP BEING SO JEALOUS OF YOU! *PLEASE...!*
I can't go back to HQ without you!

EXCEL SAGA

HEY! SO WHAT EVER HAPPENED TO IWATA?
CAN'T SAY. DID HIS WRIST POP BACK?
She put him oot of joint, then?

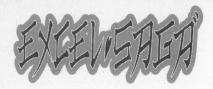

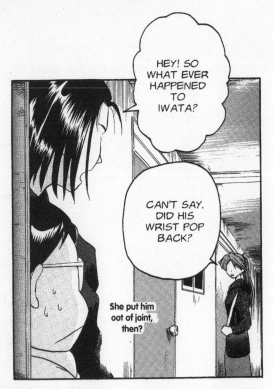

FEATURED CHARACTER # (WHOLE LOT) + 3

THE DOCTOR AND THE NURSE

■ Think of the health-care system as a vast jungle ecology. These two people are like winged, parasitic insects who might alight anywhere.

■ The Doctor is a third-generation practitioner in a family that runs an entire hospital network. He trusts in this elite background to Teflon™-coat his license, no matter what stunts, hi-jinks, or gross and willful negligence he should commit.

■ The Nurse was attached to the Doctor as part of a will left behind by his father—not unlike those electronic ankle cuffs worn by parolees. Her job is to monitor him constantly.

■ The Doctor is a cousin of the same guy named "Iwata" who lives in Excel and Hyatt's apartment building.

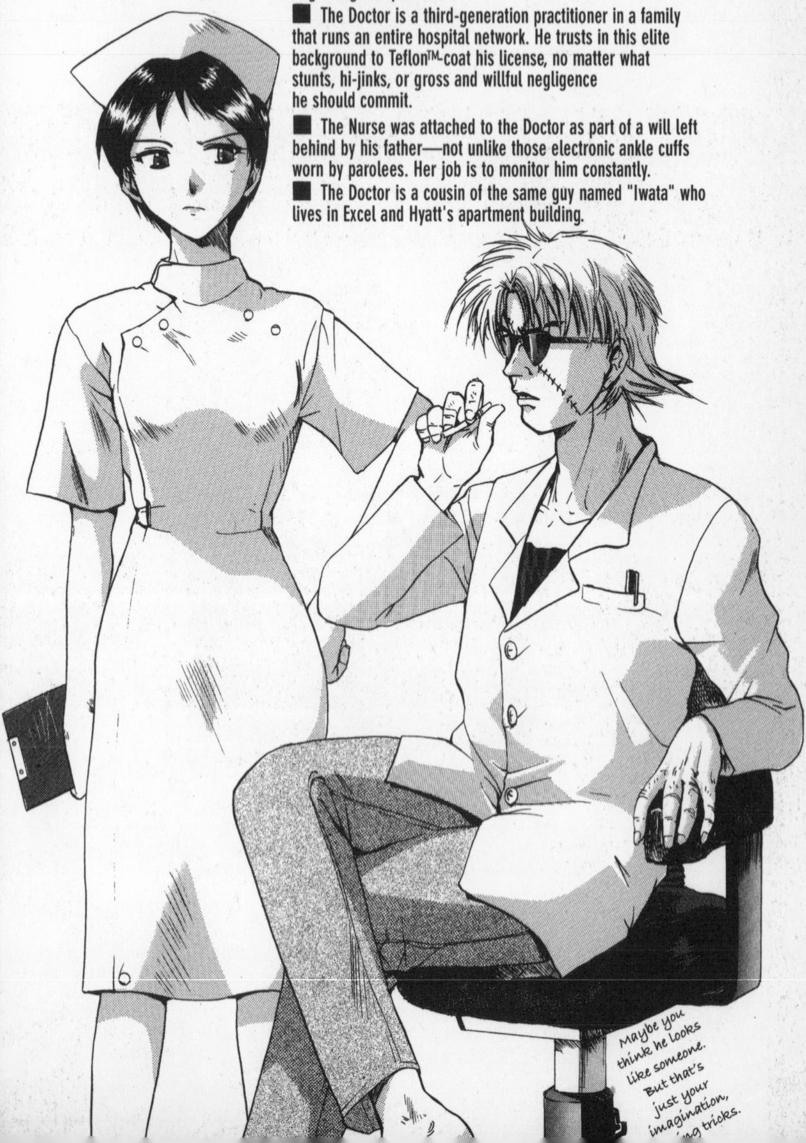
Maybe you think he looks like someone. But that's just your imagination,
tricks.

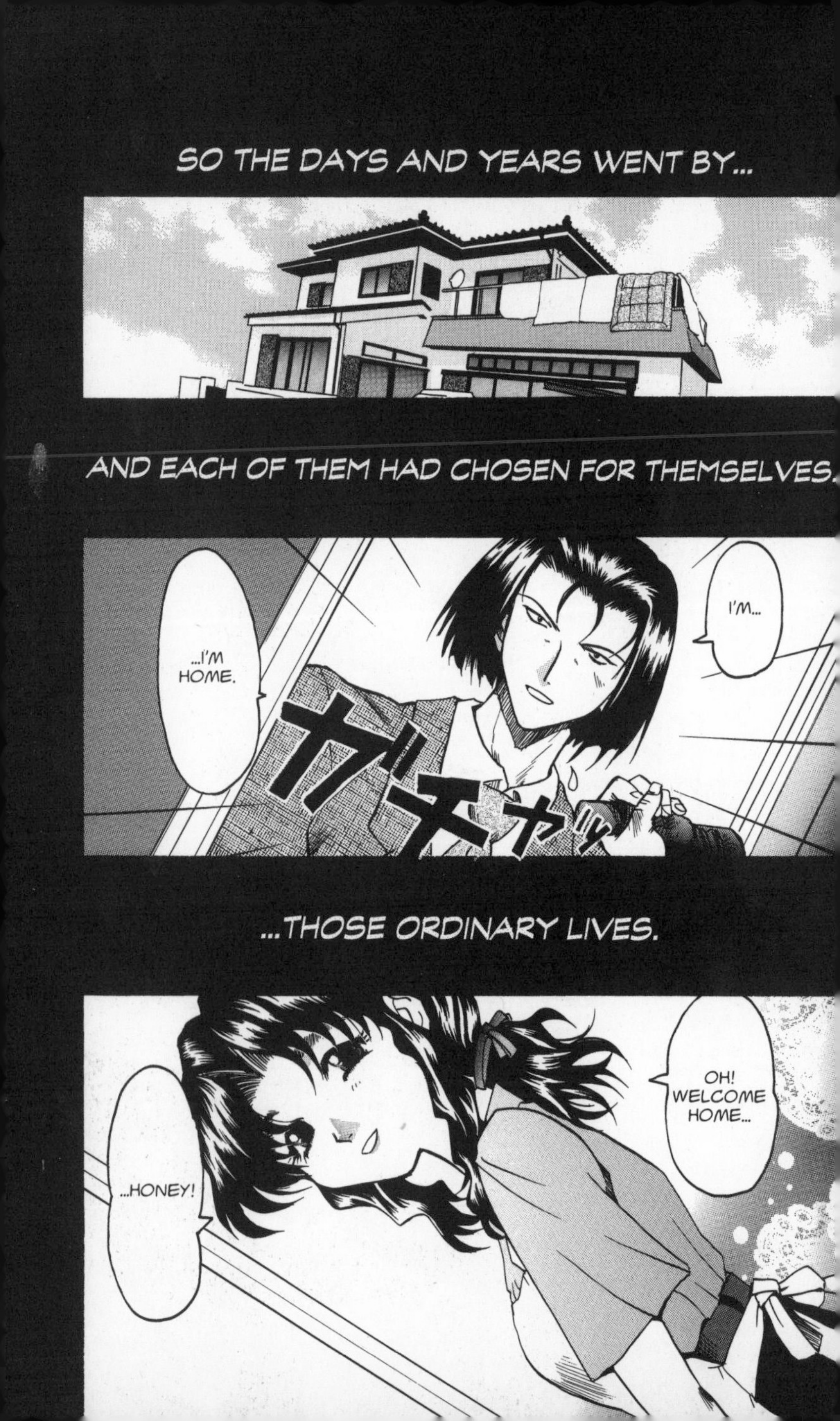
SO THE DAYS AND YEARS WENT BY...
AND EACH OF THEM HAD CHOSEN FOR THEMSELVES...
I'M...
...I'M HOME.
ガチャッ
...THOSE ORDINARY LIVES.
OH! WELCOME HOME...
...HONEY!

MISSION 4
THE LOOKING GLASS OF DELICATE BUBBLES

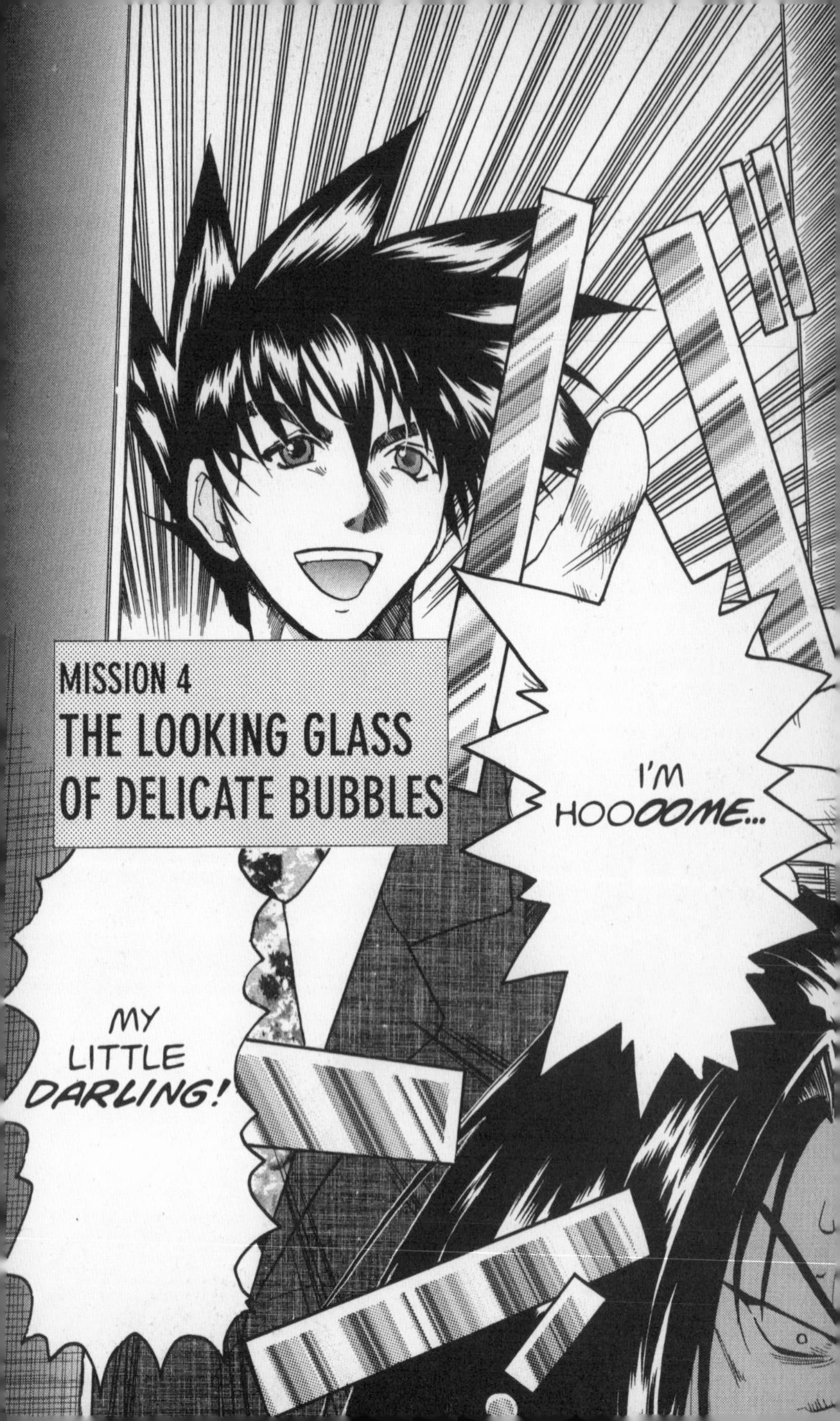
I'M HOOOOOME...
MY LITTLE DARLING!

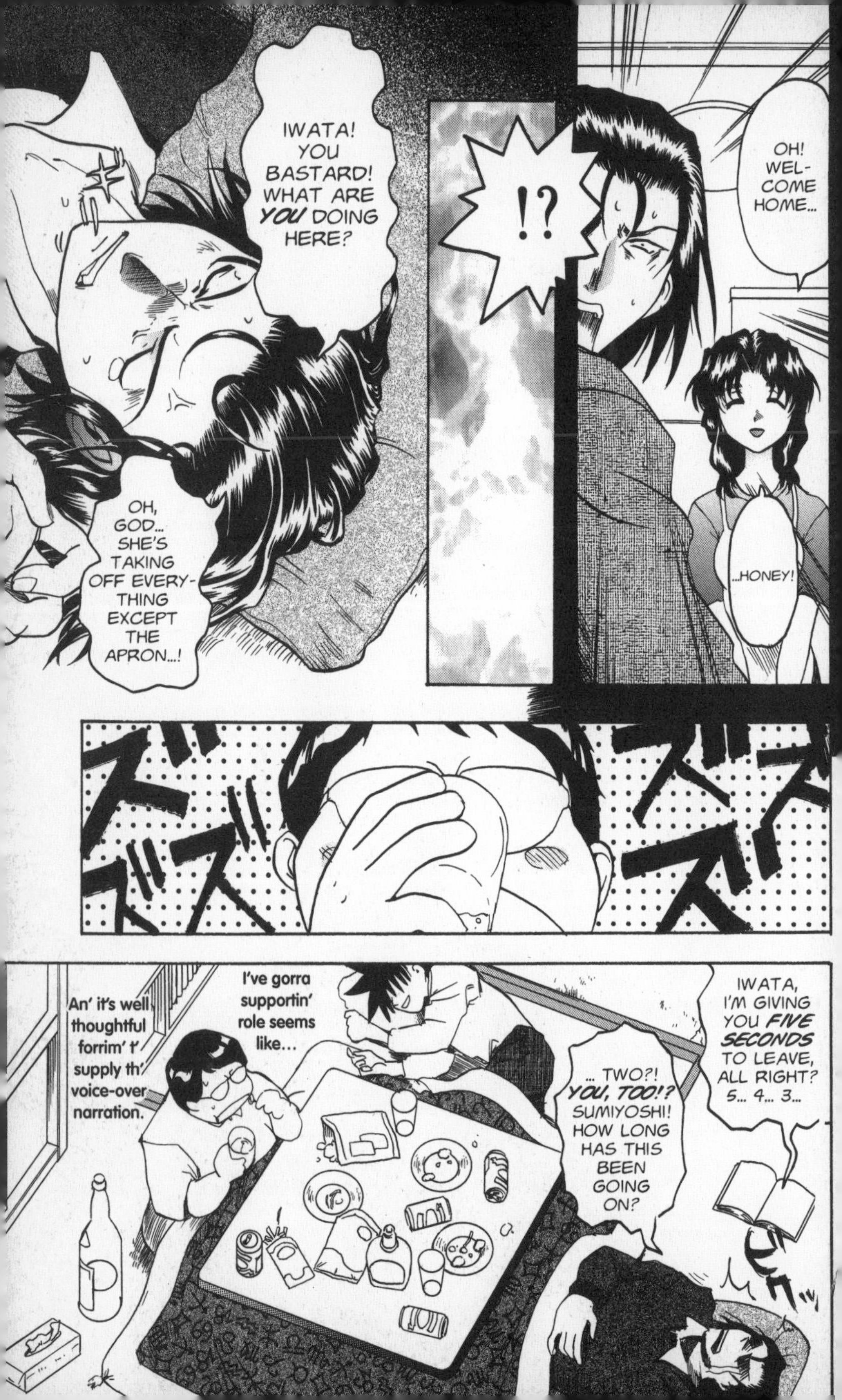
OH! WEL- COME HOME...
...HONEY!
!?
IWATA! YOU BASTARD! WHAT ARE YOU DOING HERE?
OH, GOD... SHE'S TAKING OFF EVERY- THING EXCEPT THE APRON...!
IWATA, I'M GIVING YOU FIVE SECONDS TO LEAVE, ALL RIGHT? 5... 4... 3...
... TWO?! YOU, TOO!? SUMIYOSHI! HOW LONG HAS THIS BEEN GOING ON?
I've gorra supportin' role seems like...
An' it's well thoughtful forrim' t' supply th' voice-over narration.

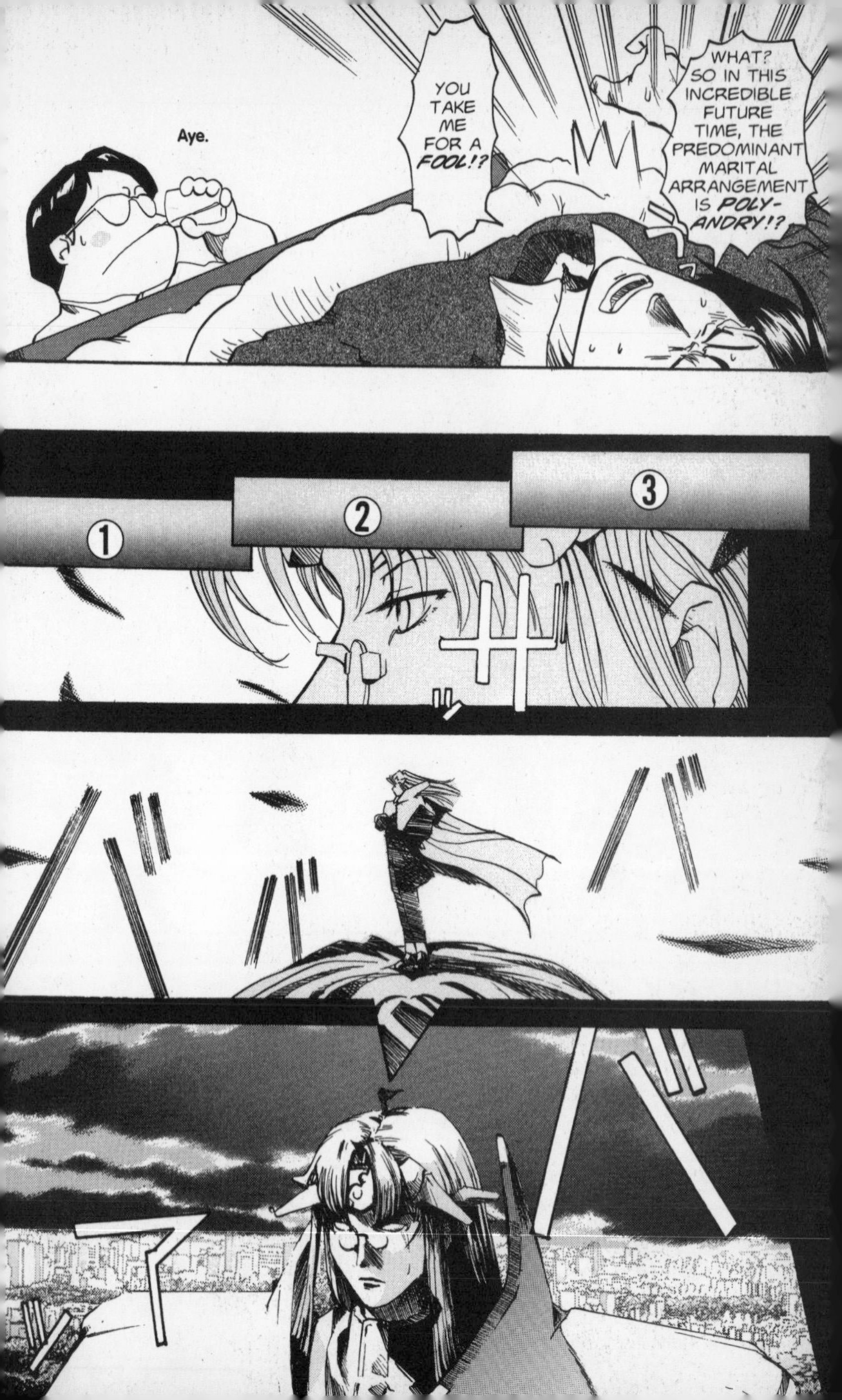

WHAT? SO IN THIS INCREDIBLE FUTURE TIME, THE PREDOMINANT MARITAL ARRANGEMENT IS POLY-ANDRY!?
YOU TAKE ME FOR A FOOL!?
Aye.
③
②
①

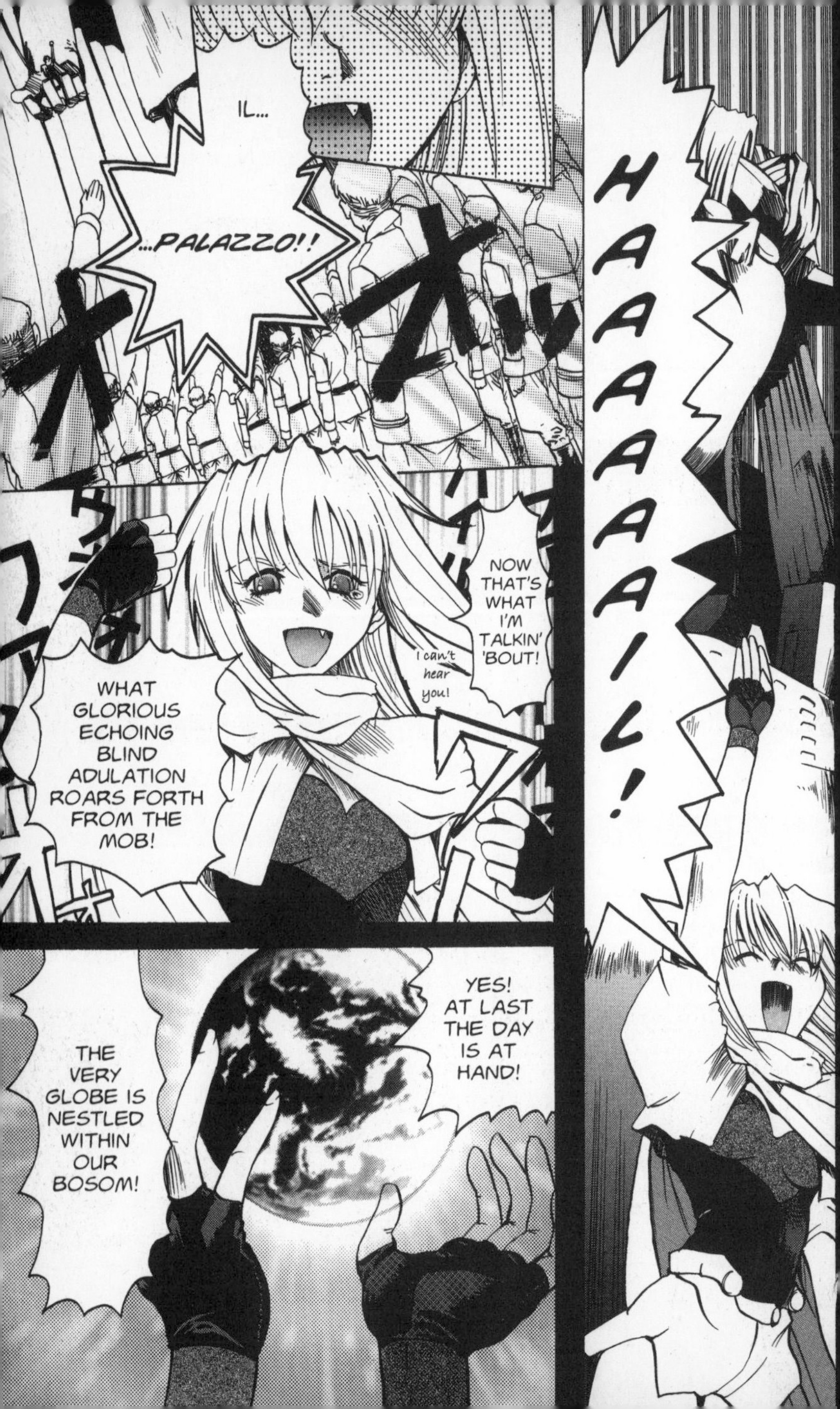
HAAAAAAIL!
IL...
...PALAZZO!!
NOW THAT'S WHAT I'M TALKIN' 'BOUT!
I can't hear you!
WHAT GLORIOUS ECHOING BLIND ADULATION ROARS FORTH FROM THE MOB!
YES! AT LAST THE DAY IS AT HAND!
THE VERY GLOBE IS NESTLED WITHIN OUR BOSOM!

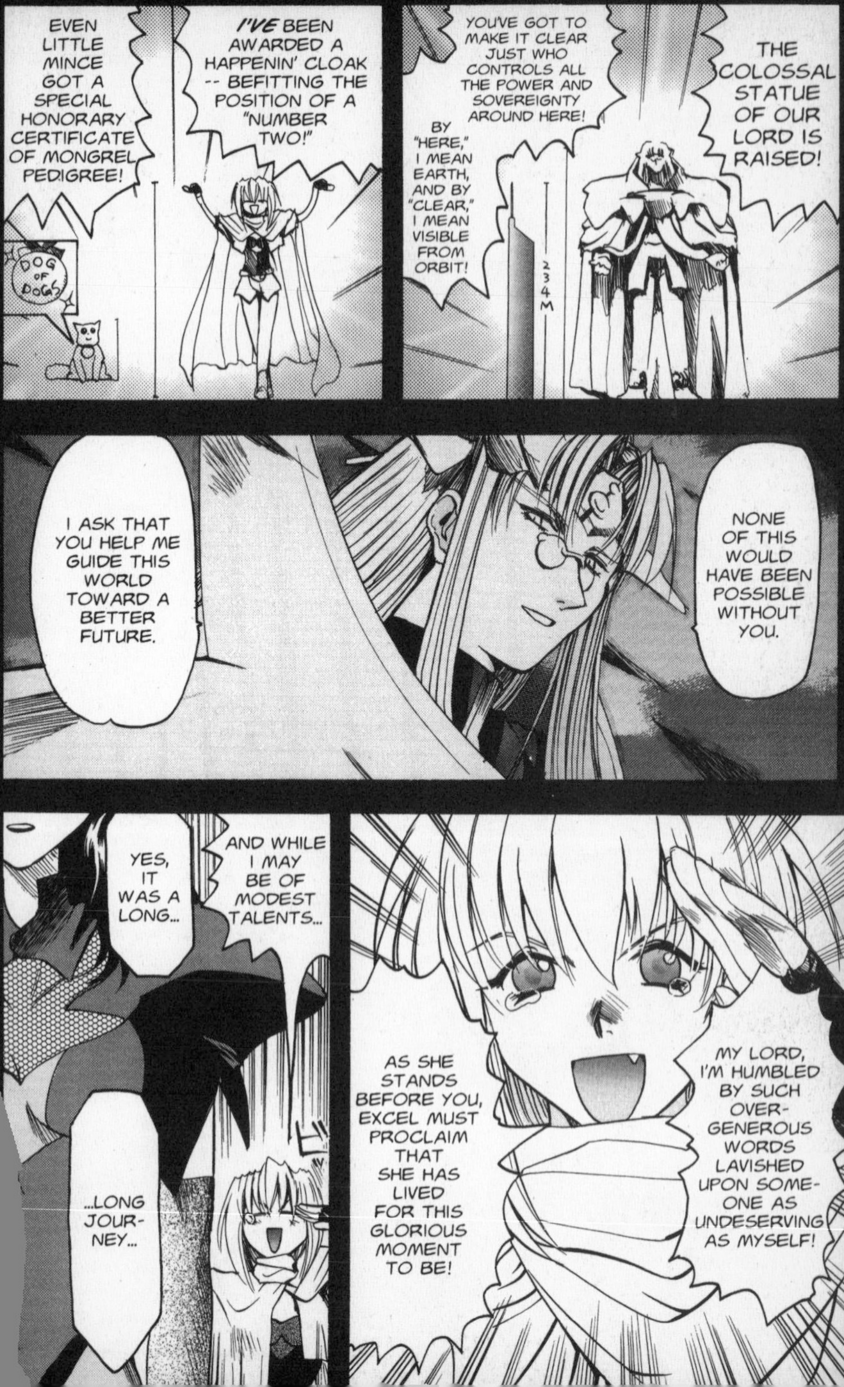
THE COLOSSAL STATUE OF OUR LORD IS RAISED!
YOU'VE GOT TO MAKE IT CLEAR JUST WHO CONTROLS ALL THE POWER AND SOVEREIGNTY AROUND HERE!
BY "HERE," I MEAN EARTH, AND BY "CLEAR," I MEAN VISIBLE FROM ORBIT!
234M
I'VE BEEN AWARDED A HAPPENIN' CLOAK -- BEFITTING THE POSITION OF A "NUMBER TWO!"
EVEN LITTLE MINCE GOT A SPECIAL HONORARY CERTIFICATE OF MONGREL PEDIGREE!
DOG OF DOGS
NONE OF THIS WOULD HAVE BEEN POSSIBLE WITHOUT YOU.
I ASK THAT YOU HELP ME GUIDE THIS WORLD TOWARD A BETTER FUTURE.
MY LORD, I'M HUMBLED BY SUCH OVER-GENEROUS WORDS LAVISHED UPON SOME-ONE AS UNDESERVING AS MYSELF!
AS SHE STANDS BEFORE YOU, EXCEL MUST PROCLAIM THAT SHE HAS LIVED FOR THIS GLORIOUS MOMENT TO BE!
AND WHILE I MAY BE OF MODEST TALENTS...
YES, IT WAS A LONG...
...LONG JOURNEY...

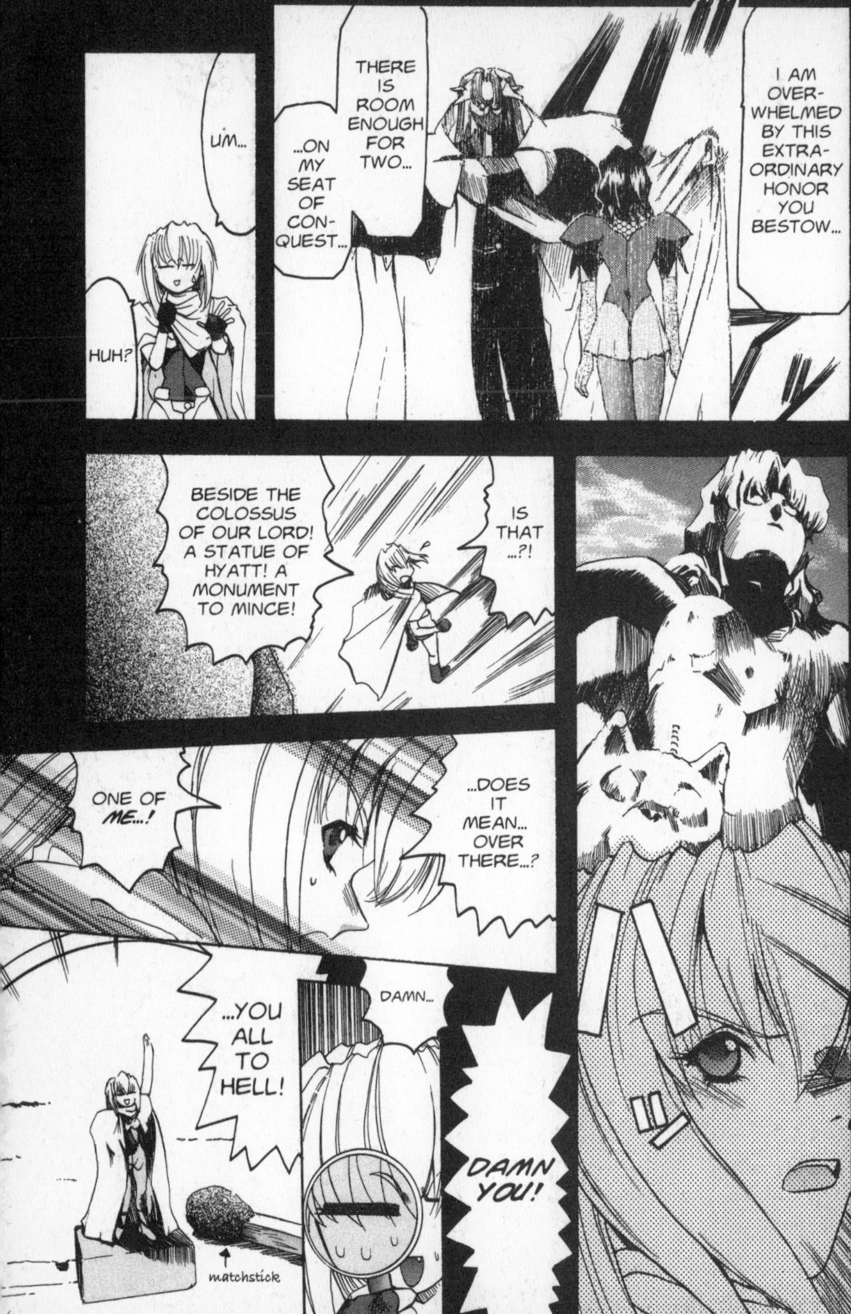
I AM OVERWHELMED BY THIS EXTRAORDINARY HONOR YOU BESTOW...
THERE IS ROOM ENOUGH FOR TWO...
...ON MY SEAT OF CONQUEST...
UM...
HUH?
DAMN YOU!
IS THAT ...?!
BESIDE THE COLOSSUS OF OUR LORD! A STATUE OF HYATT! A MONUMENT TO MINCE!
...DOES IT MEAN... OVER THERE...?
ONE OF *ME*...!
DAMN...
...YOU ALL TO HELL!
matchstick

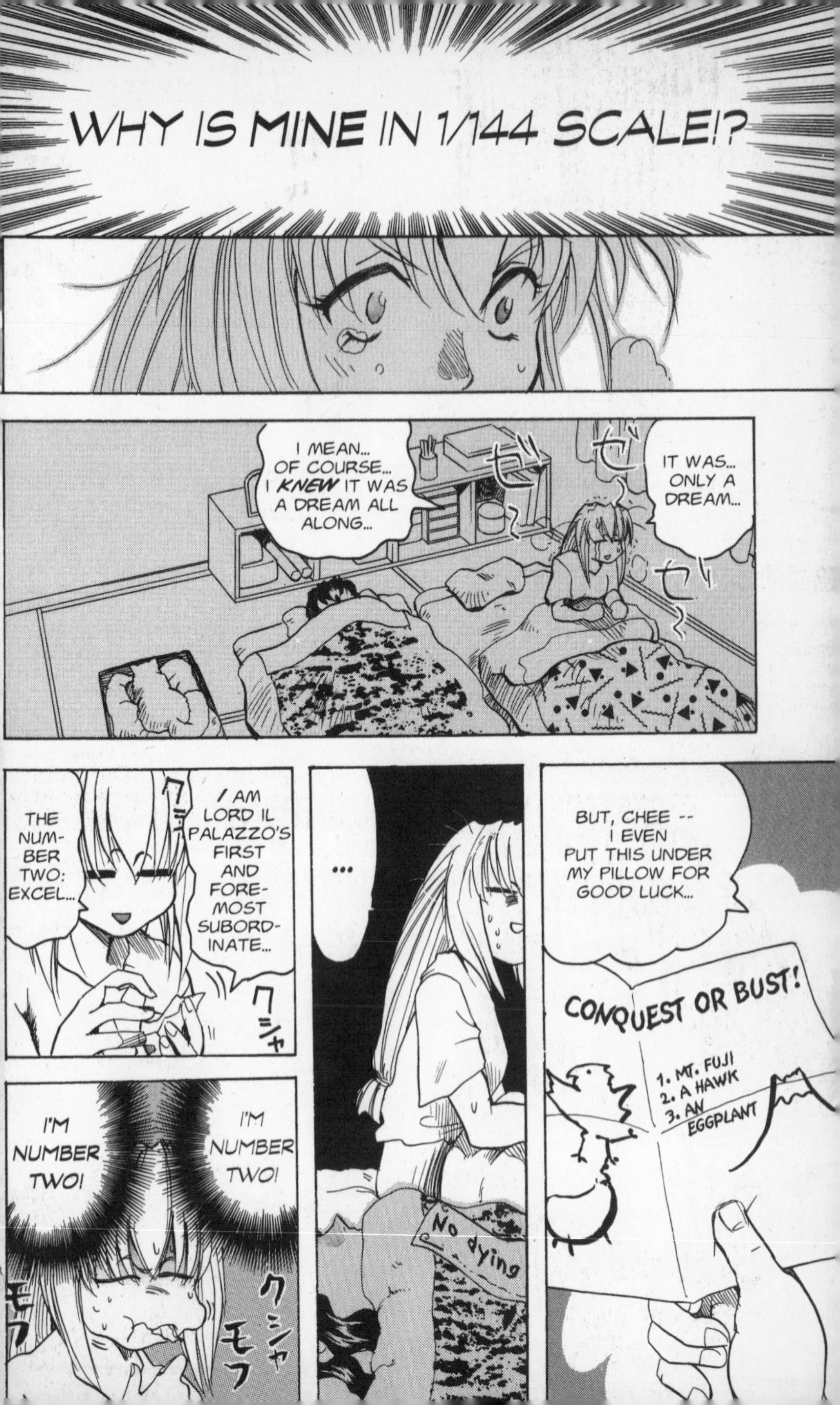
WHY IS MINE IN 1/144 SCALE!?
IT WAS... ONLY A DREAM...
I MEAN... OF COURSE... I *KNEW* IT WAS A DREAM ALL ALONG...
BUT, CHEE -- I EVEN PUT THIS UNDER MY PILLOW FOR GOOD LUCK...
CONQUEST OR BUST!
1. MT. FUJI
2. A HAWK
3. AN EGGPLANT
...
No dying
I AM LORD IL PALAZZO'S FIRST AND FOREMOST SUBORDINATE...
THE NUMBER TWO: EXCEL...
クシャ
I'M NUMBER TWO!
I'M NUMBER TWO!
クシャ
モフ

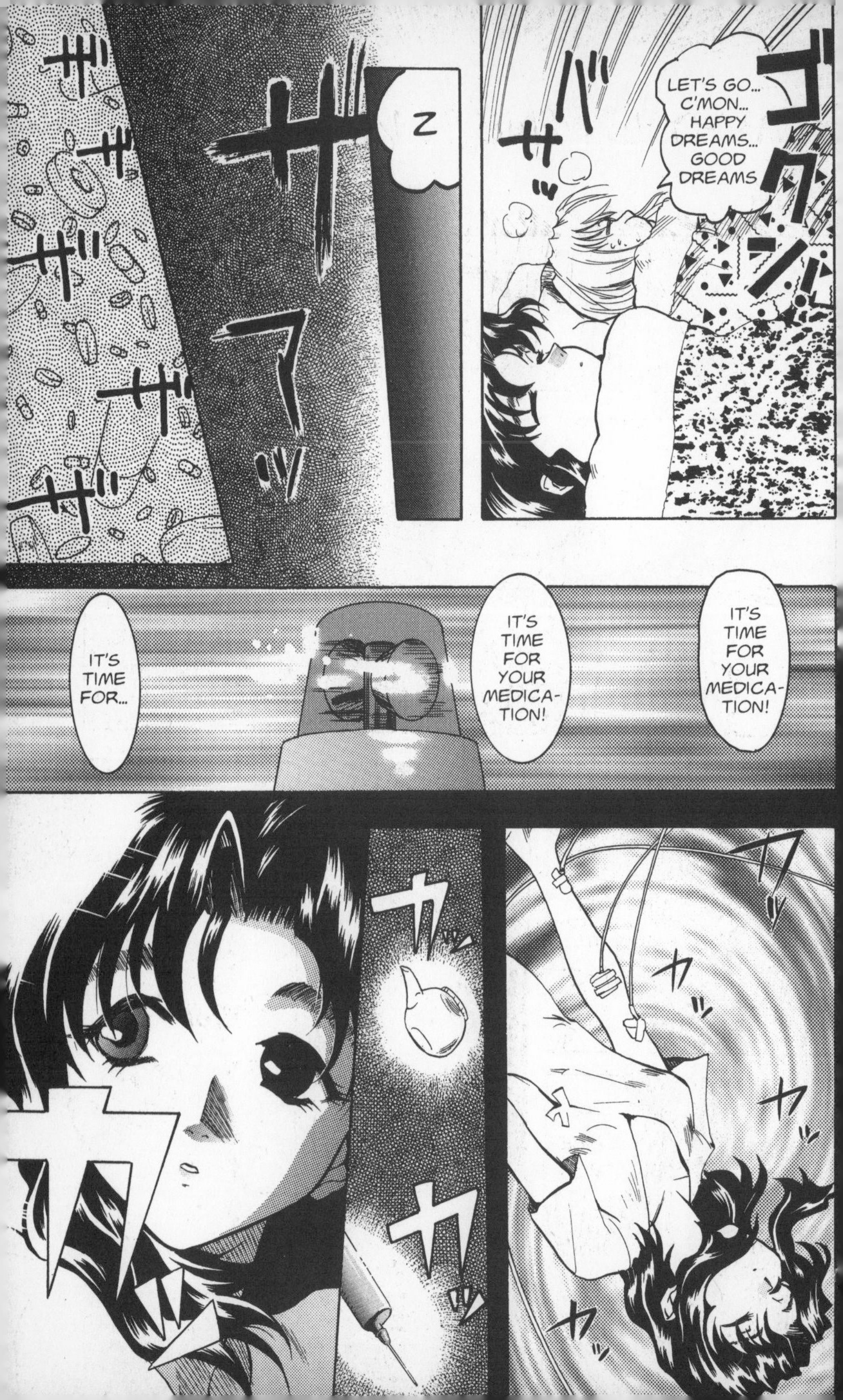
LET'S GO... C'MON... HAPPY DREAMS... GOOD DREAMS
Z
IT'S TIME FOR YOUR MEDICA-TION!
IT'S TIME FOR YOUR MEDICA-TION!
IT'S TIME FOR...

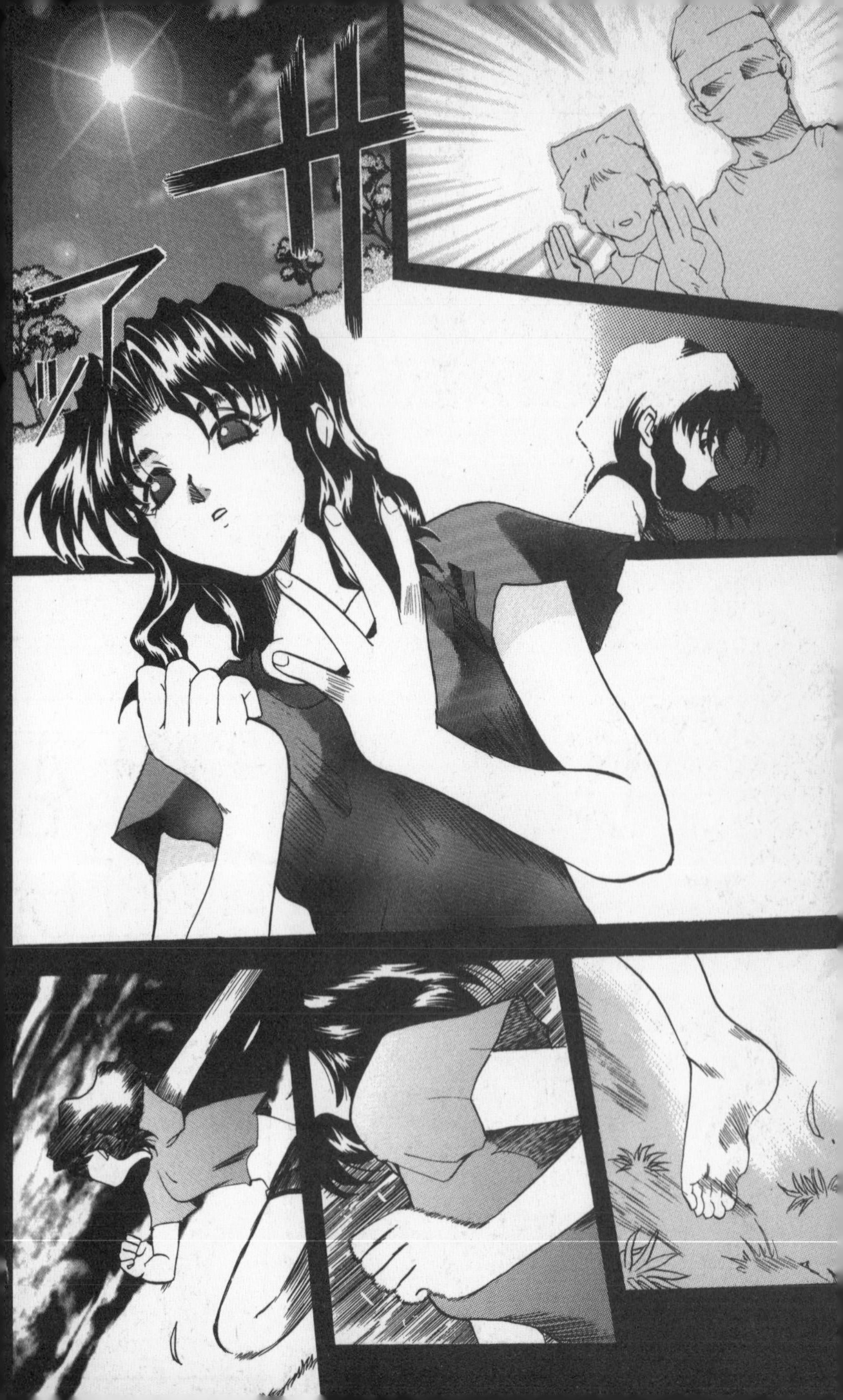

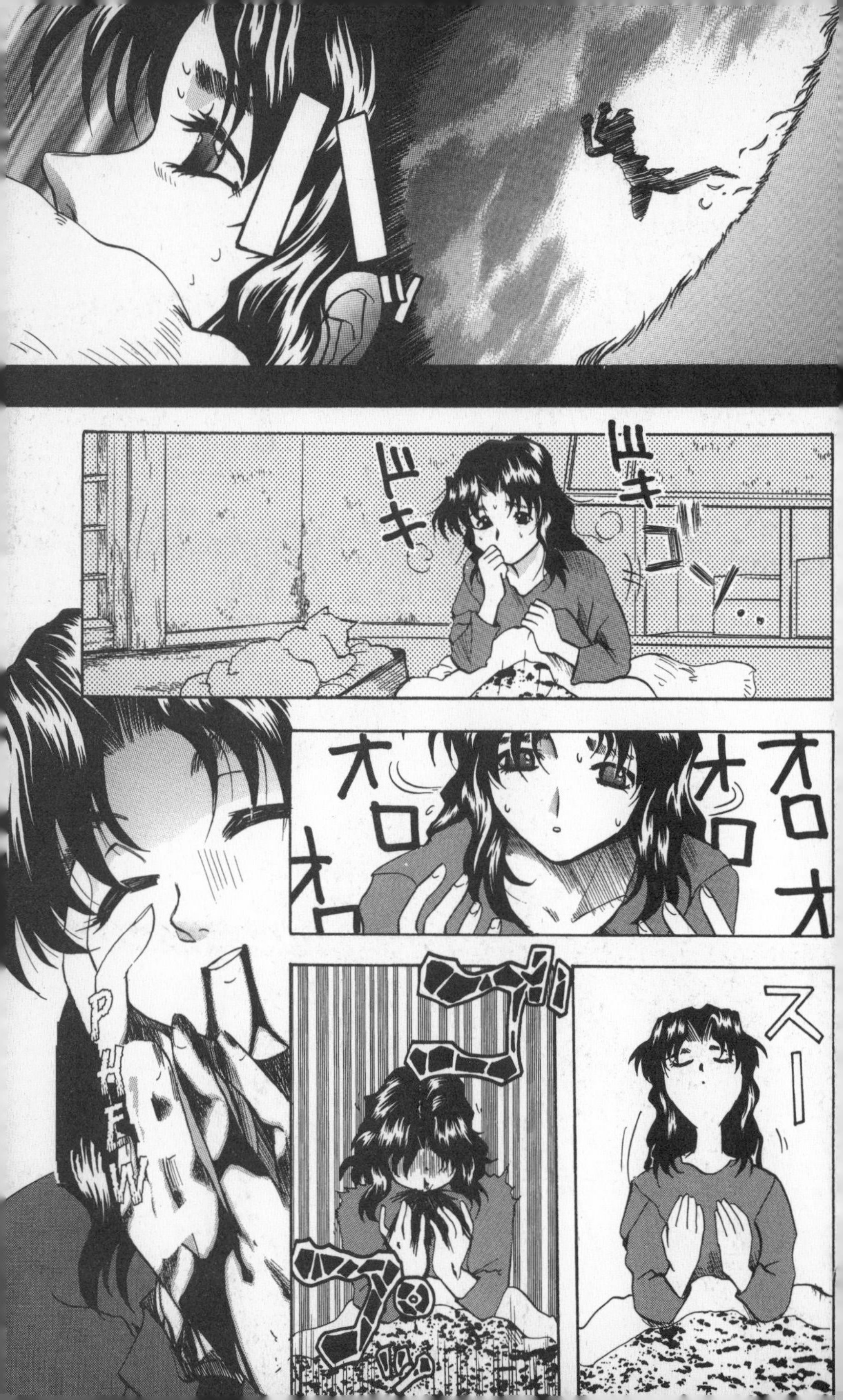

ドキ
ドキ
ゴン
オロオロ
オロオロ
スー
PHEW

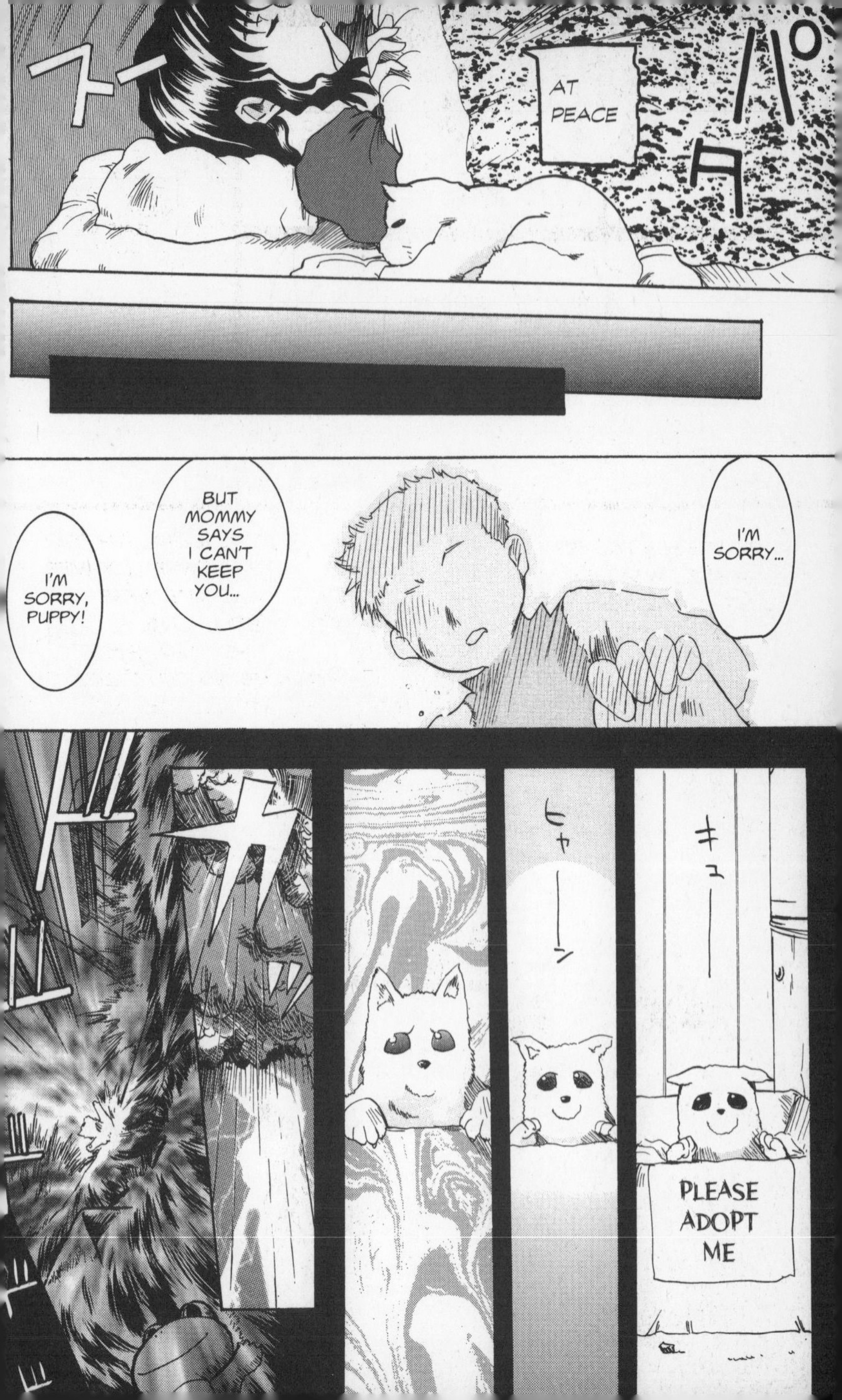
AT PEACE
I'M SORRY...
BUT MOMMY SAYS I CAN'T KEEP YOU...
I'M SORRY, PUPPY!
キュー
PLEASE ADOPT ME
ヒャーン

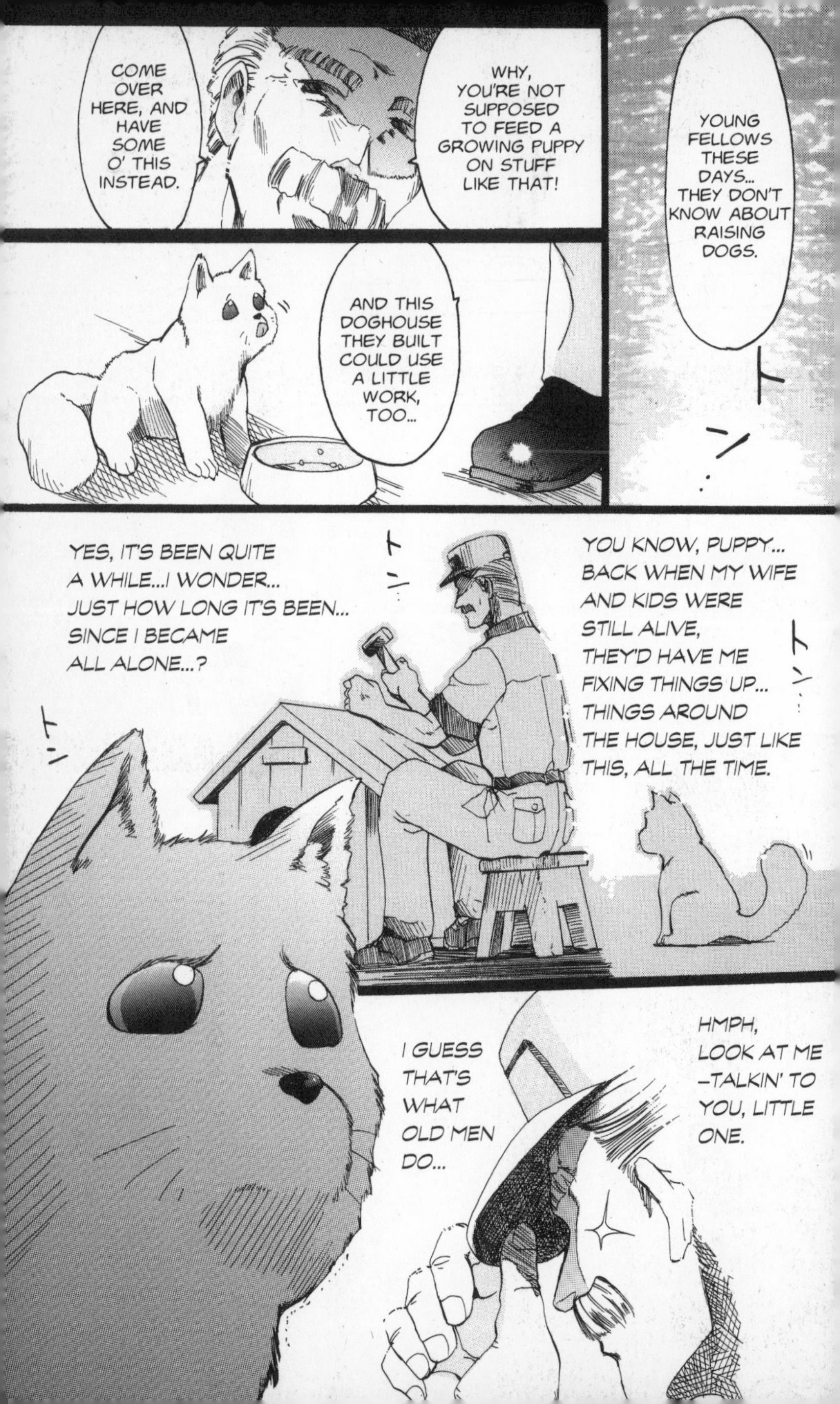

YOUNG FELLOWS THESE DAYS... THEY DON'T KNOW ABOUT RAISING DOGS.
WHY, YOU'RE NOT SUPPOSED TO FEED A GROWING PUPPY ON STUFF LIKE THAT!
COME OVER HERE, AND HAVE SOME O' THIS INSTEAD.
AND THIS DOGHOUSE THEY BUILT COULD USE A LITTLE WORK, TOO...
YOU KNOW, PUPPY... BACK WHEN MY WIFE AND KIDS WERE STILL ALIVE, THEY'D HAVE ME FIXING THINGS UP... THINGS AROUND THE HOUSE, JUST LIKE THIS, ALL THE TIME.
YES, IT'S BEEN QUITE A WHILE...I WONDER... JUST HOW LONG IT'S BEEN... SINCE I BECAME ALL ALONE...?
HMPH, LOOK AT ME —TALKIN' TO YOU, LITTLE ONE.
I GUESS THAT'S WHAT OLD MEN DO...

MINCE
!!!

MINCE
TASTES
GOOOOOOD.

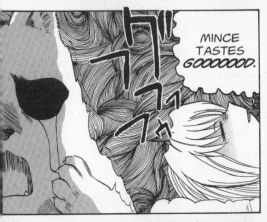

104

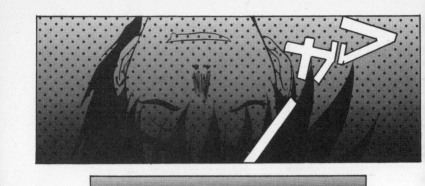

I'M A CRUEL AND CUNNING SPY!

I'VE JUST ESCAPED OUT OF A SECRET LABORATORY (ERECTED IN A GEOGRAPHICALLY PRECARIOUS SPOT) THAT I HAD INFILTRATED!

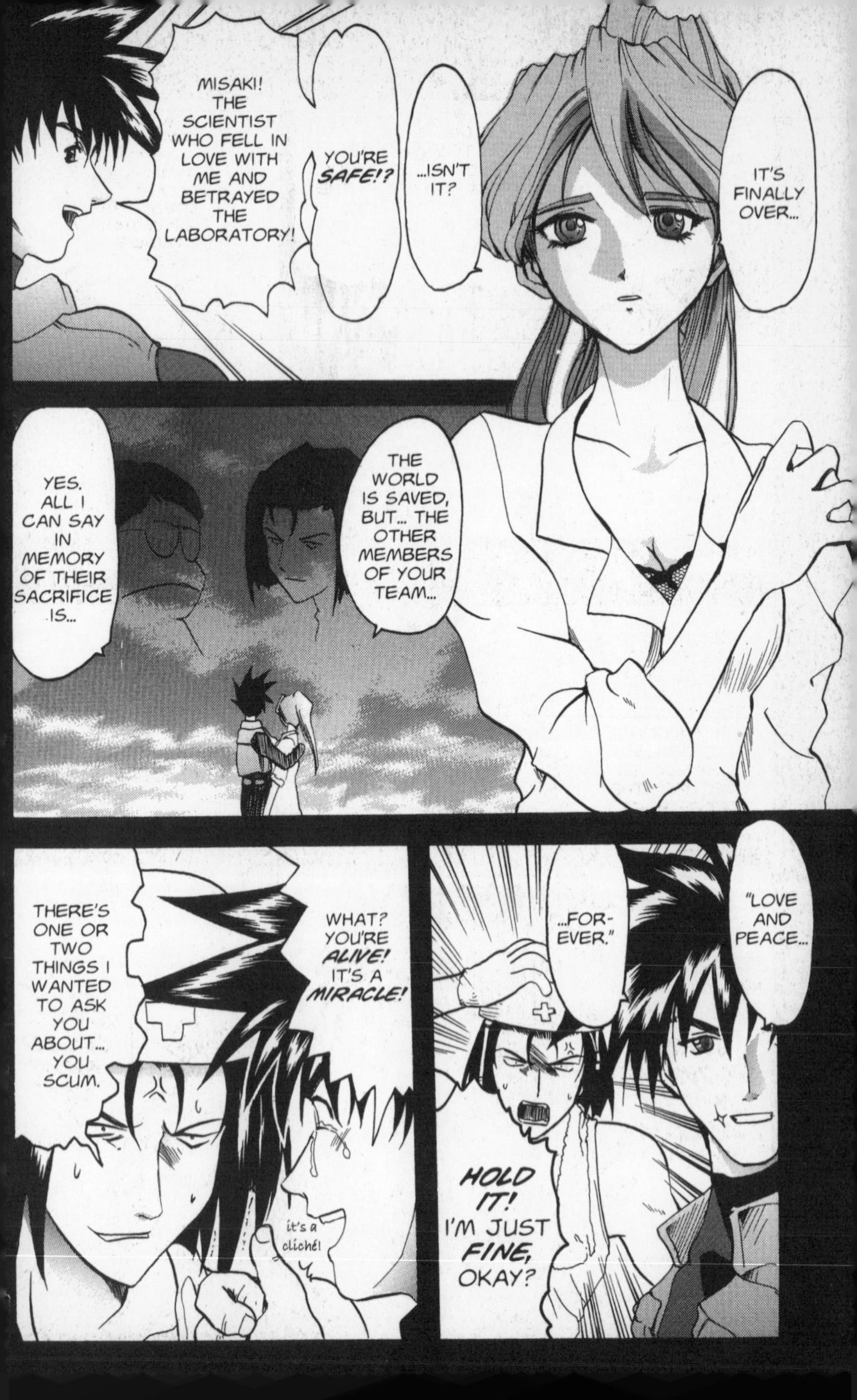
IT'S FINALLY OVER...
...ISN'T IT?
YOU'RE SAFE!?
MISAKI! THE SCIENTIST WHO FELL IN LOVE WITH ME AND BETRAYED THE LABORATORY!
THE WORLD IS SAVED, BUT... THE OTHER MEMBERS OF YOUR TEAM...
YES. ALL I CAN SAY IN MEMORY OF THEIR SACRIFICE IS...
"LOVE AND PEACE...
...FOR-EVER."
HOLD IT! I'M JUST FINE, OKAY?
WHAT? YOU'RE ALIVE! IT'S A MIRACLE!
it's a cliché!
THERE'S ONE OR TWO THINGS I WANTED TO ASK YOU ABOUT... YOU SCUM.

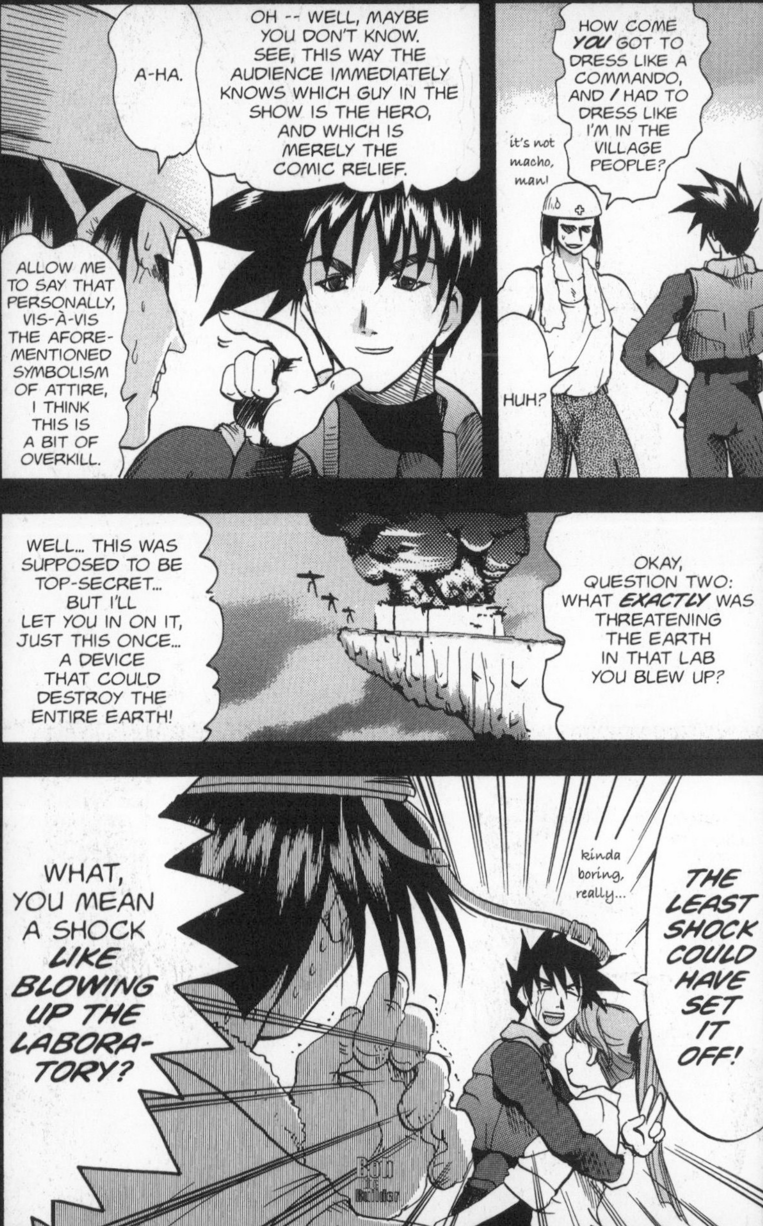
HOW COME *YOU* GOT TO DRESS LIKE A COMMANDO, AND *I* HAD TO DRESS LIKE I'M IN THE VILLAGE PEOPLE?
it's not macho, man!
HUH?
OH -- WELL, MAYBE YOU DON'T KNOW. SEE, THIS WAY THE AUDIENCE IMMEDIATELY KNOWS WHICH GUY IN THE SHOW IS THE HERO, AND WHICH IS MERELY THE COMIC RELIEF.
A-HA.
ALLOW ME TO SAY THAT PERSONALLY, VIS-À-VIS THE AFORE-MENTIONED SYMBOLISM OF ATTIRE, I THINK THIS IS A BIT OF OVERKILL.
OKAY, QUESTION TWO: WHAT *EXACTLY* WAS THREATENING THE EARTH IN THAT LAB YOU BLEW UP?
WELL... THIS WAS SUPPOSED TO BE TOP-SECRET... BUT I'LL LET YOU IN ON IT, JUST THIS ONCE... A DEVICE THAT COULD DESTROY THE ENTIRE EARTH!
THE LEAST SHOCK COULD HAVE SET IT OFF!
kinda boring, really...
WHAT, YOU MEAN A SHOCK *LIKE BLOWING UP THE LABORA-TORY?*

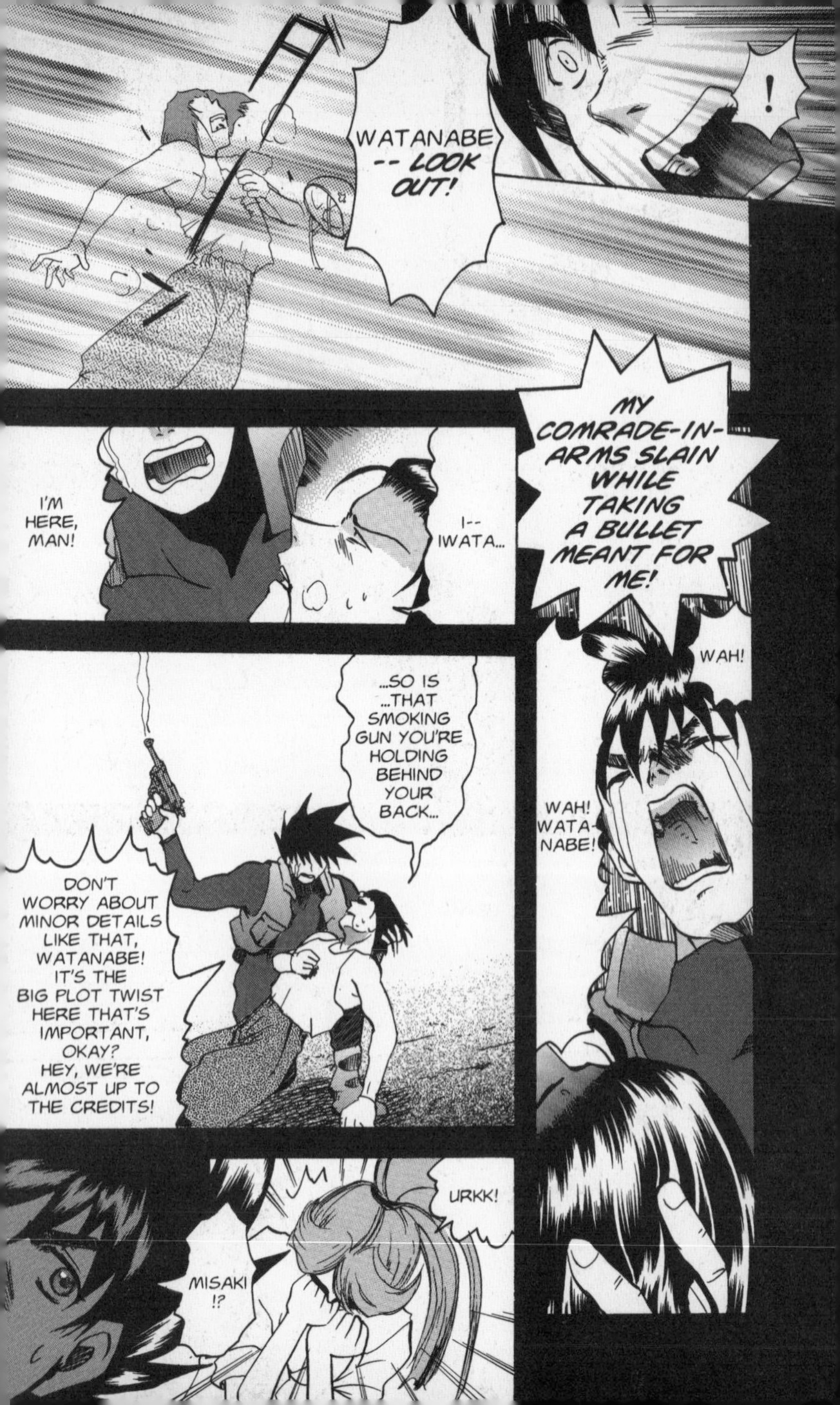
!
WATANABE -- LOOK OUT!
MY COMRADE-IN-ARMS SLAIN WHILE TAKING A BULLET MEANT FOR ME!
WAH!
WAH! WATANABE!
I-- IWATA...
I'M HERE, MAN!
...SO IS ...THAT SMOKING GUN YOU'RE HOLDING BEHIND YOUR BACK...
DON'T WORRY ABOUT MINOR DETAILS LIKE THAT, WATANABE! IT'S THE BIG PLOT TWIST HERE THAT'S IMPORTANT, OKAY? HEY, WE'RE ALMOST UP TO THE CREDITS!
URKK!
MISAKI !?

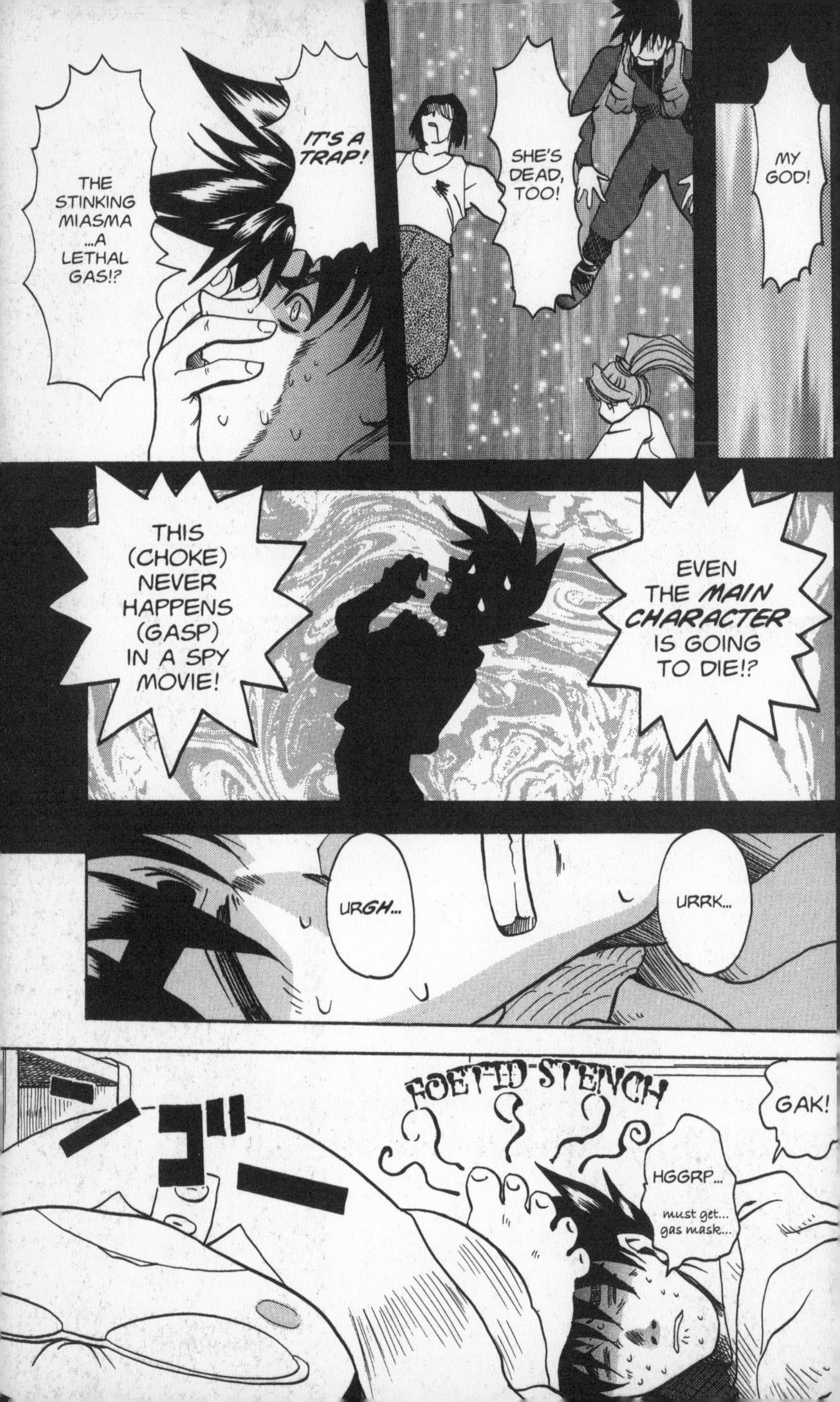
MY GOD!
SHE'S DEAD, TOO!
IT'S A TRAP!
THE STINKING MIASMA ...A LETHAL GAS!?
EVEN THE MAIN CHARACTER IS GOING TO DIE!?
THIS (CHOKE) NEVER HAPPENS (GASP) IN A SPY MOVIE!
URRK...
URGH...
GAK!
FOETID STENCH
HGGRP...
must get... gas mask...

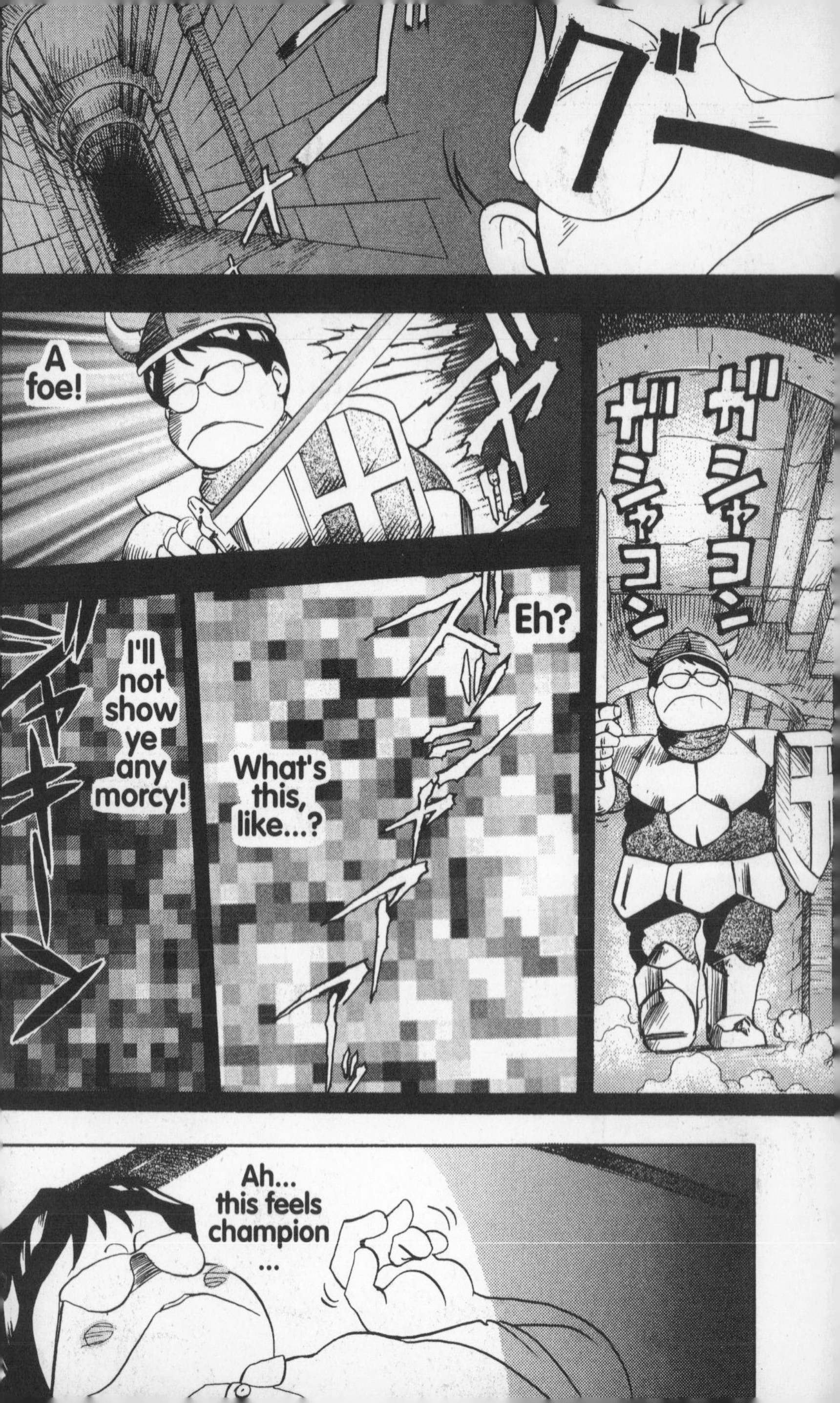
グー
ガシャコン
ガシャコン
A foe!
Eh?
What's this, like...?
I'll not show ye any morcy!
Ah... this feels champion ...

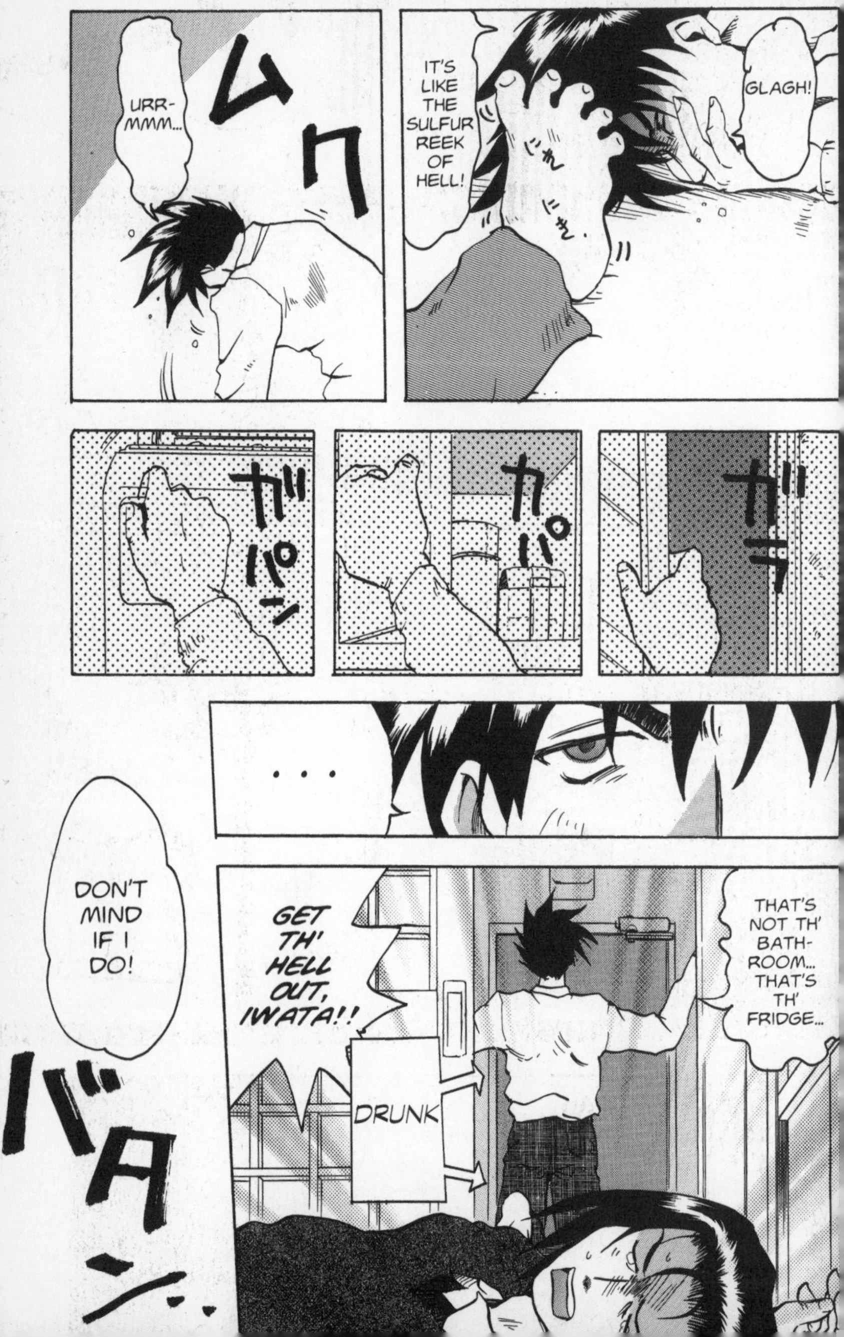
GLAGH!
IT'S LIKE THE SULFUR REEK OF HELL!
URR-MMM...
. . .
THAT'S NOT TH' BATHROOM... THAT'S TH' FRIDGE...
GET TH' HELL OUT, IWATA!!
DRUNK
DON'T MIND IF I DO!

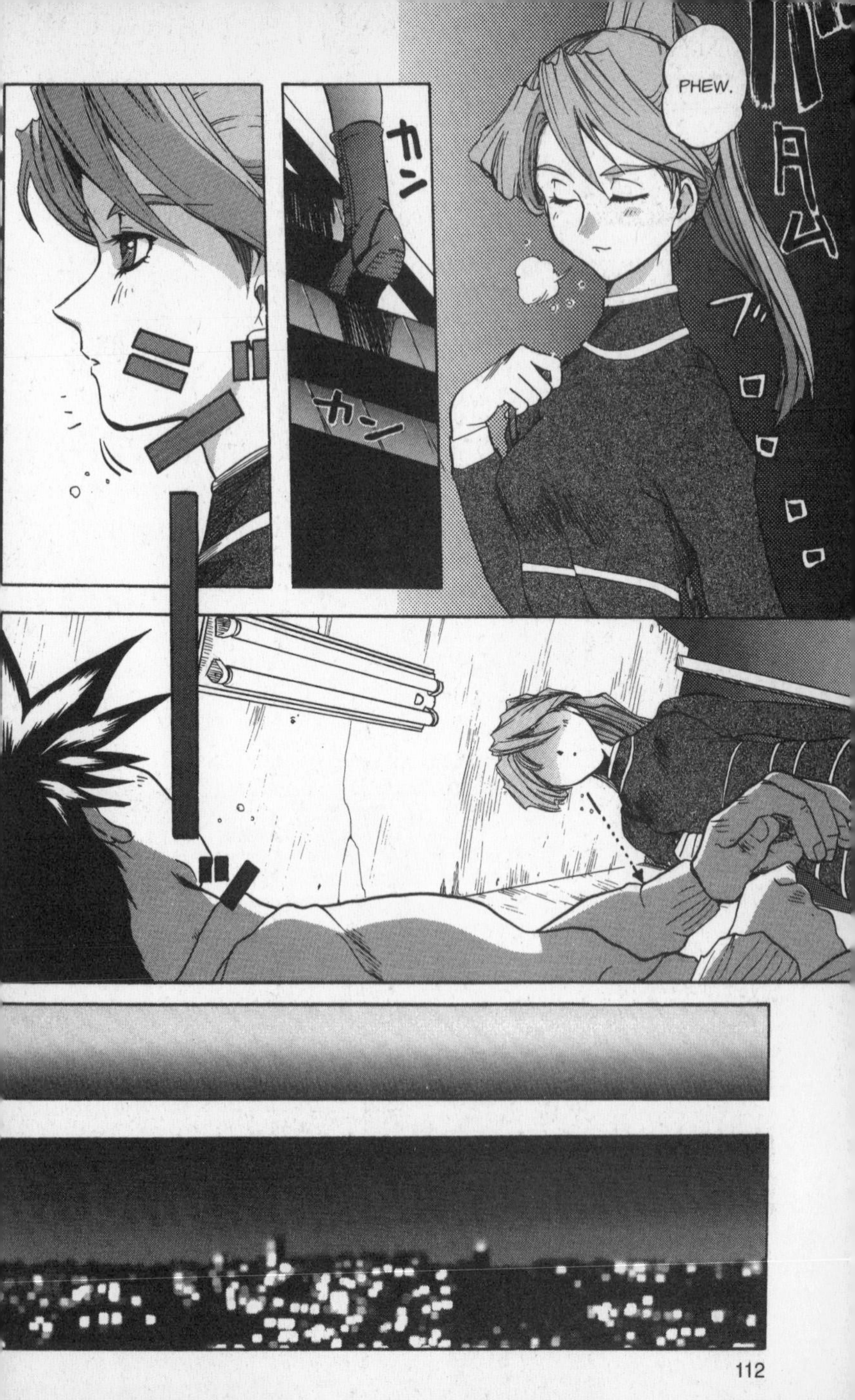
PHEW.
ブロロロロロ
カン
カン

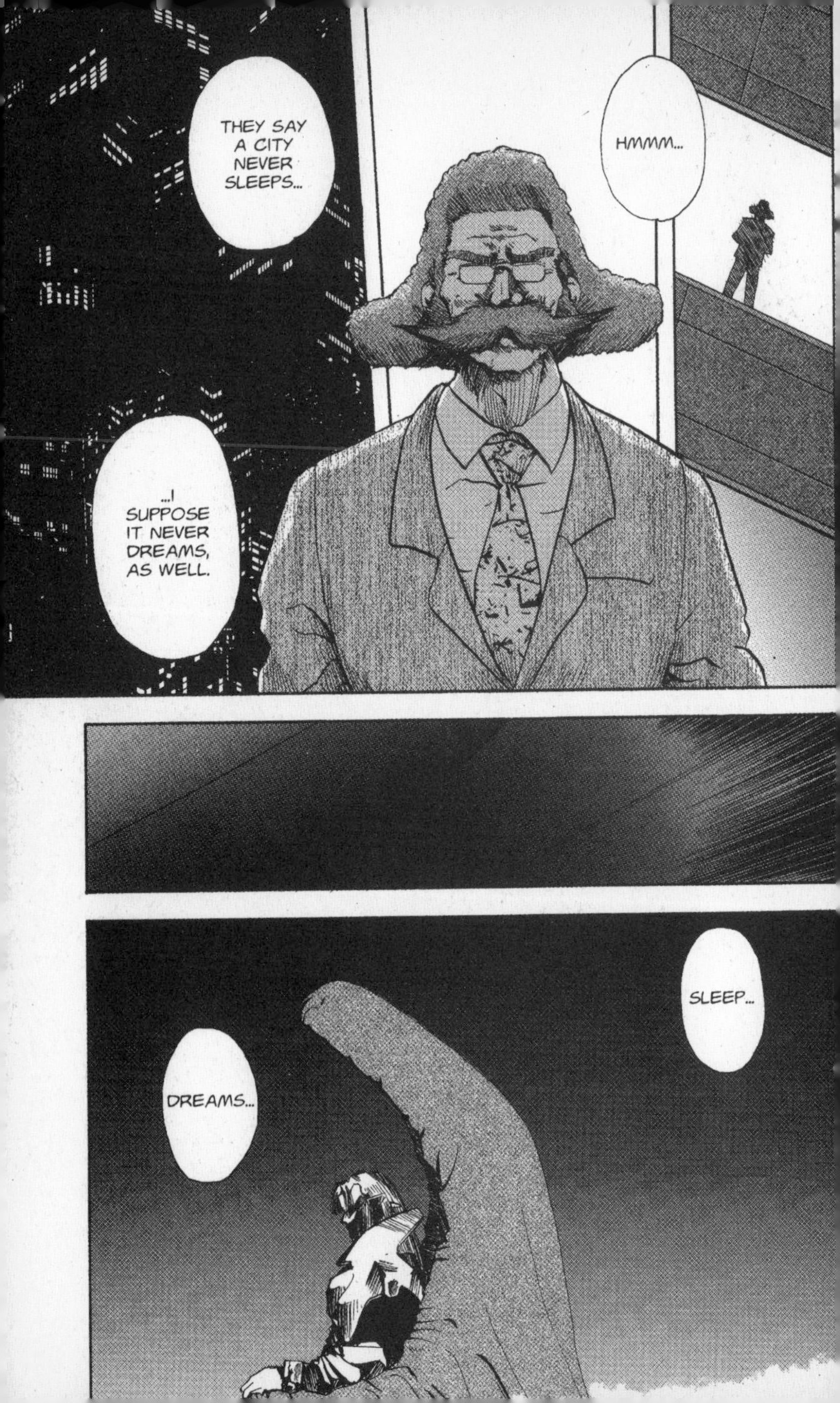
HMMM...
THEY SAY A CITY NEVER SLEEPS...
...I SUPPOSE IT NEVER DREAMS, AS WELL.
SLEEP...
DREAMS...

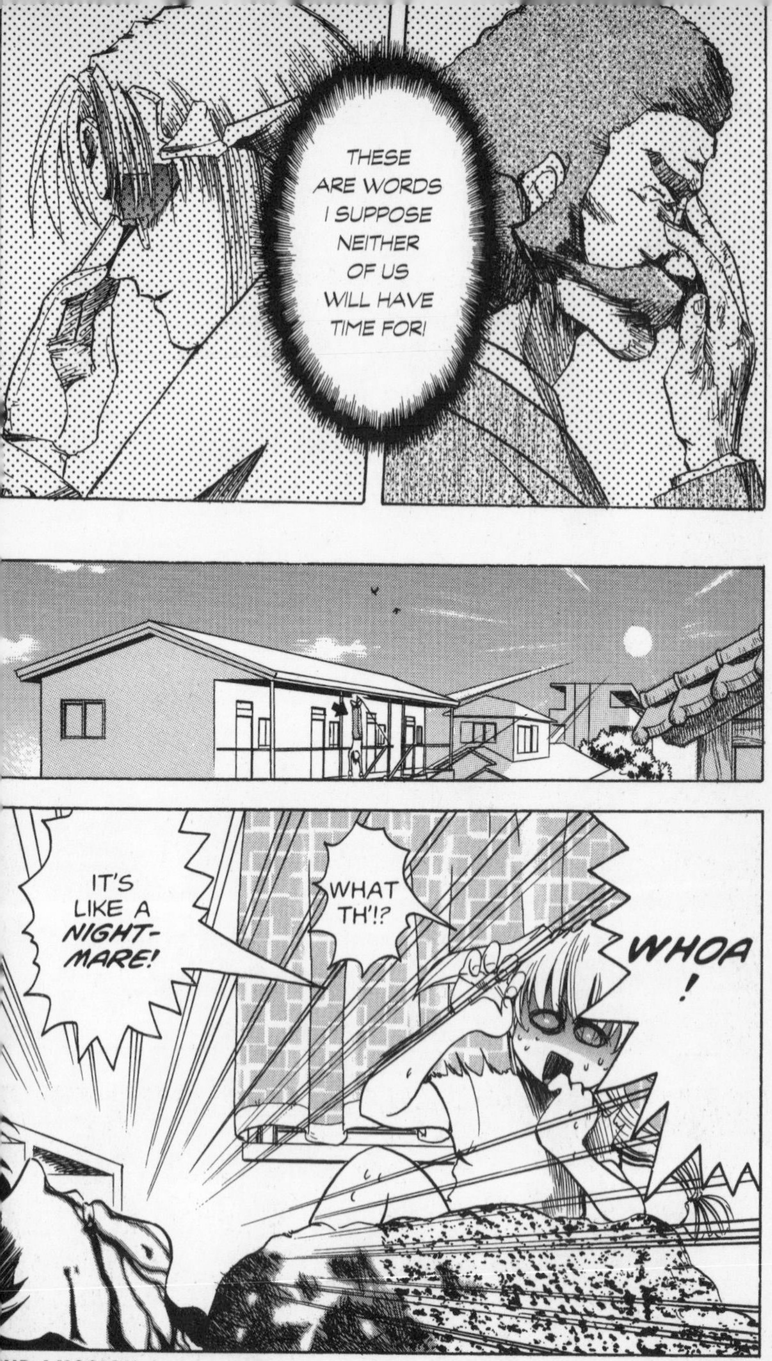
THESE ARE WORDS I SUPPOSE NEITHER OF US WILL HAVE TIME FOR!
WHOA!
WHAT TH'!?
IT'S LIKE A NIGHT-MARE!

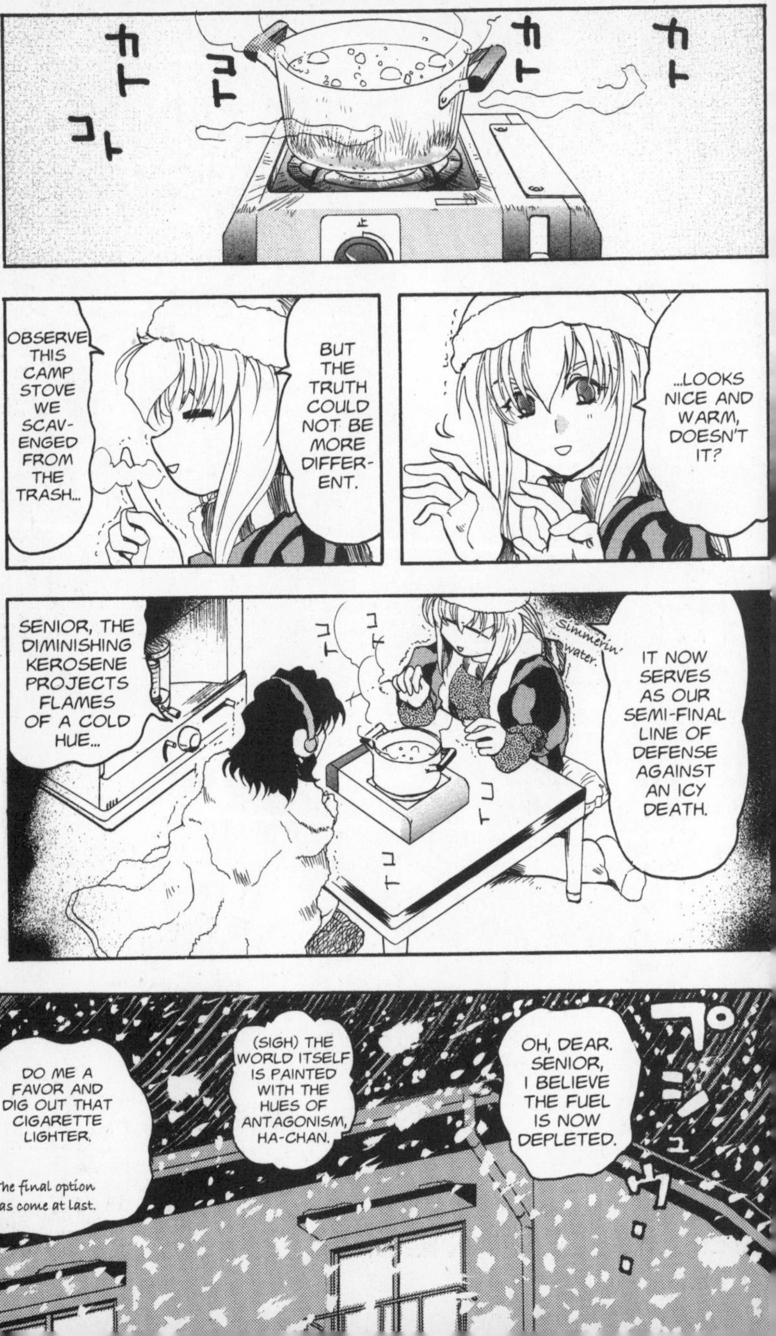
カト
カト
コト
カト
コト
...LOOKS NICE AND WARM, DOESN'T IT?
BUT THE TRUTH COULD NOT BE MORE DIFFERENT.
OBSERVE THIS CAMP STOVE WE SCAVENGED FROM THE TRASH...
IT NOW SERVES AS OUR SEMI-FINAL LINE OF DEFENSE AGAINST AN ICY DEATH.
Simmerin' water.
コト
コト
コト
SENIOR, THE DIMINISHING KEROSENE PROJECTS FLAMES OF A COLD HUE...
OH, DEAR. SENIOR, I BELIEVE THE FUEL IS NOW DEPLETED.
(SIGH) THE WORLD ITSELF IS PAINTED WITH THE HUES OF ANTAGONISM, HA-CHAN.
DO ME A FAVOR AND DIG OUT THAT CIGARETTE LIGHTER.
The final option has come at last.

MISSION 5
THAT WHICH SCATTERS ABOUT IN THE WHITE SKIES

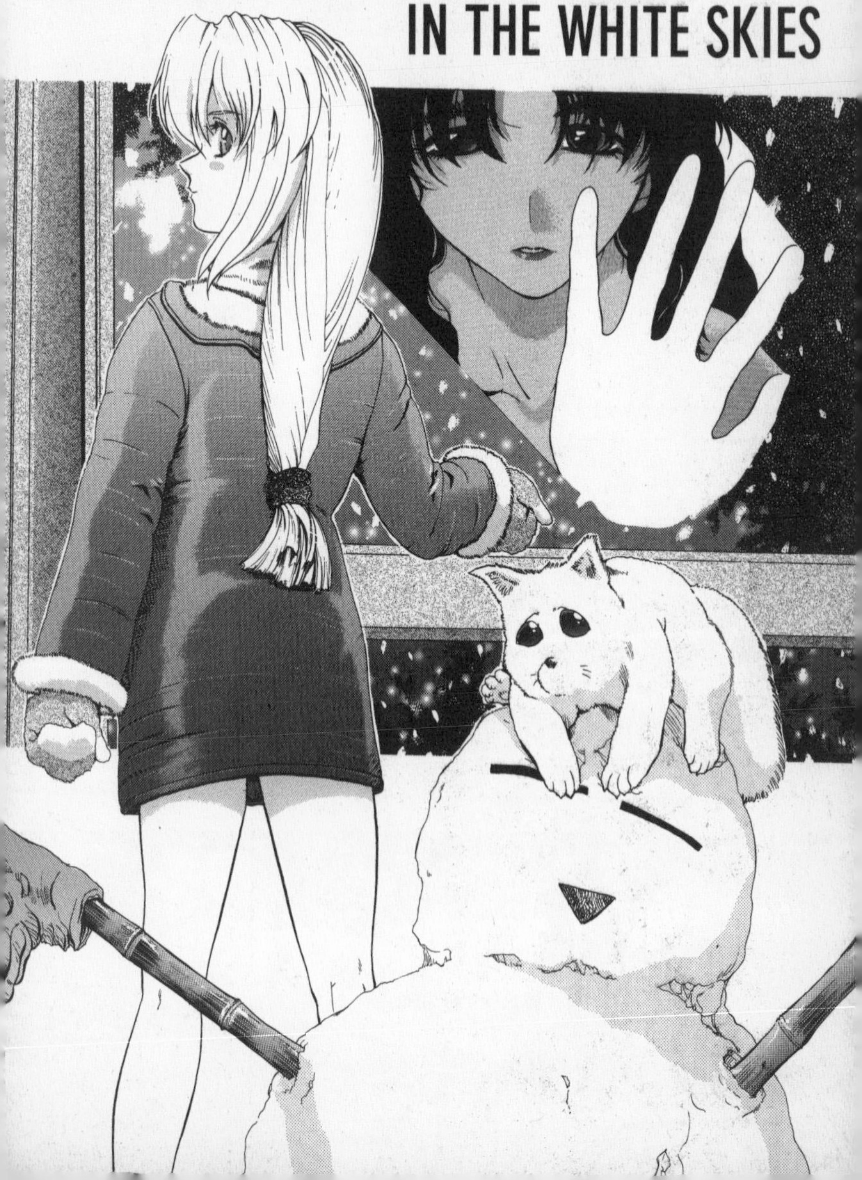

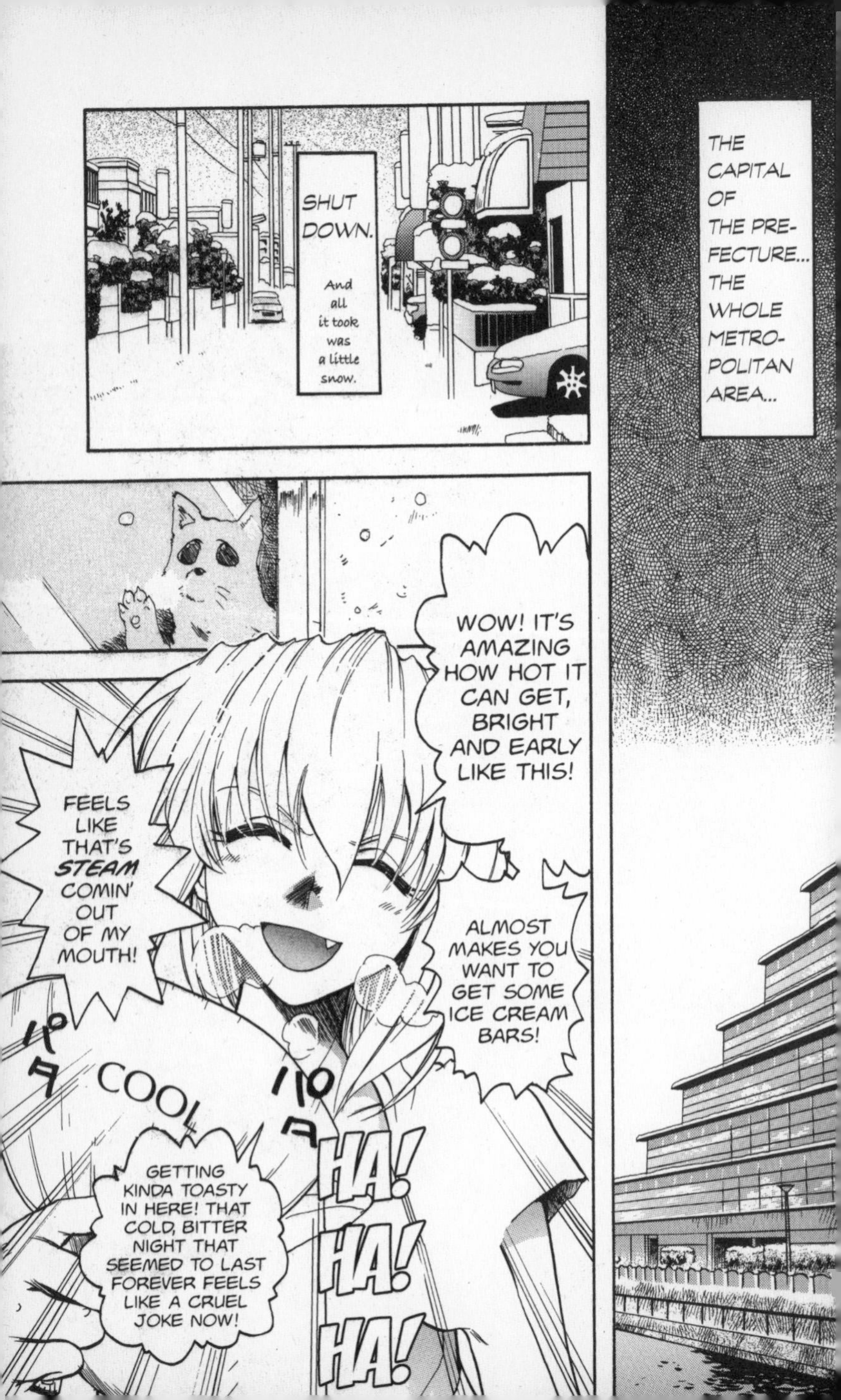
THE CAPITAL OF THE PRE-FECTURE... THE WHOLE METRO-POLITAN AREA...
SHUT DOWN.
And all it took was a little snow.
WOW! IT'S AMAZING HOW HOT IT CAN GET, BRIGHT AND EARLY LIKE THIS!
ALMOST MAKES YOU WANT TO GET SOME ICE CREAM BARS!
FEELS LIKE THAT'S *STEAM* COMIN' OUT OF MY MOUTH!
パタ
COOL
パタ
HA! HA! HA!
GETTING KINDA TOASTY IN HERE! THAT COLD, BITTER NIGHT THAT SEEMED TO LAST FOREVER FEELS LIKE A CRUEL JOKE NOW!

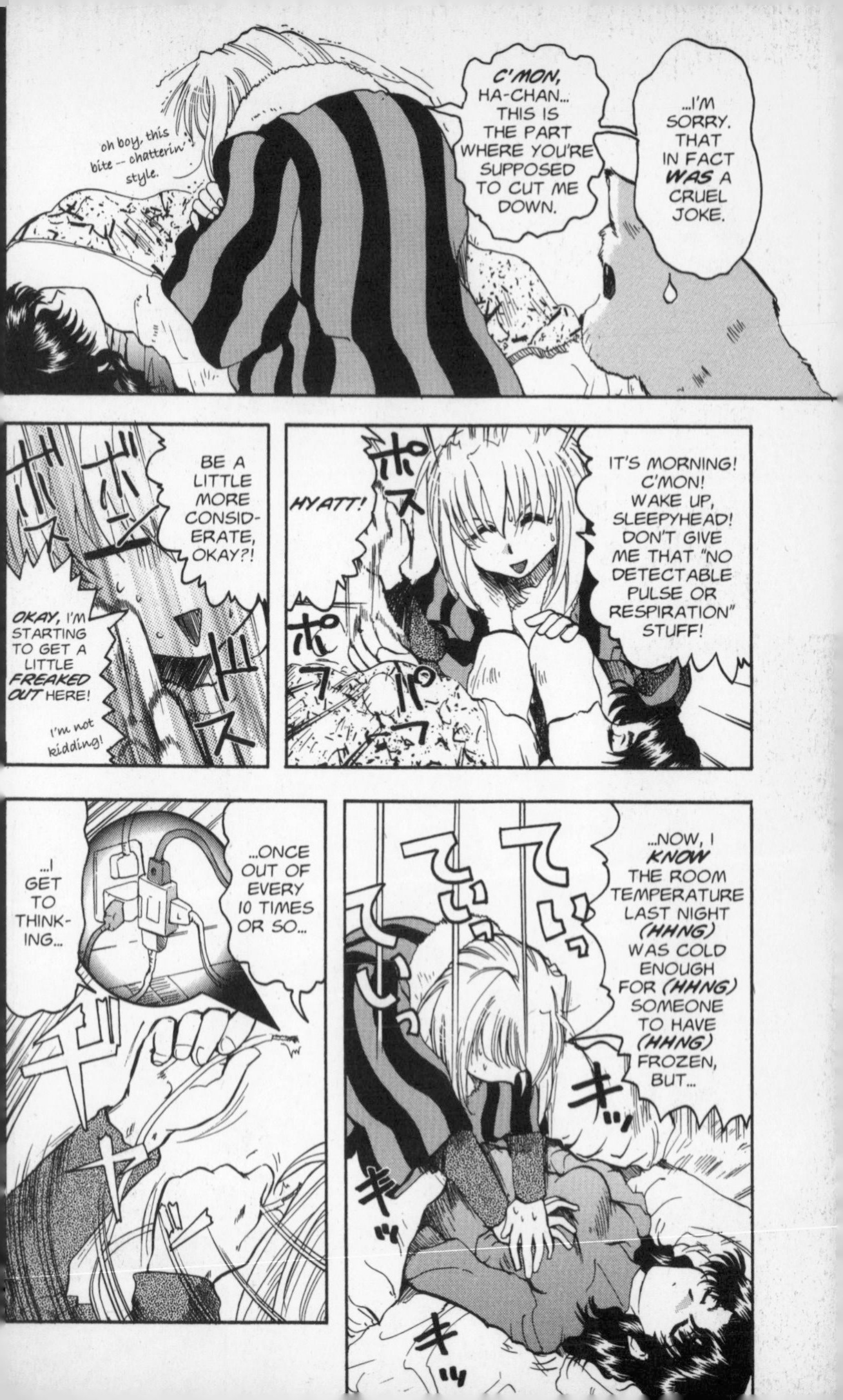
...I'M SORRY. THAT IN FACT WAS A CRUEL JOKE.
C'MON, HA-CHAN... THIS IS THE PART WHERE YOU'RE SUPPOSED TO CUT ME DOWN.
oh boy, this bite -- chatterin' style.
IT'S MORNING! C'MON! WAKE UP, SLEEPYHEAD! DON'T GIVE ME THAT "NO DETECTABLE PULSE OR RESPIRATION" STUFF!
HYATT!
BE A LITTLE MORE CONSID-ERATE, OKAY?!
OKAY, I'M STARTING TO GET A LITTLE FREAKED OUT HERE!
I'm not kidding!
...NOW, I KNOW THE ROOM TEMPERATURE LAST NIGHT (HHNG) WAS COLD ENOUGH FOR (HHNG) SOMEONE TO HAVE (HHNG) FROZEN, BUT...
...ONCE OUT OF EVERY 10 TIMES OR SO...
...I GET TO THINK-ING...

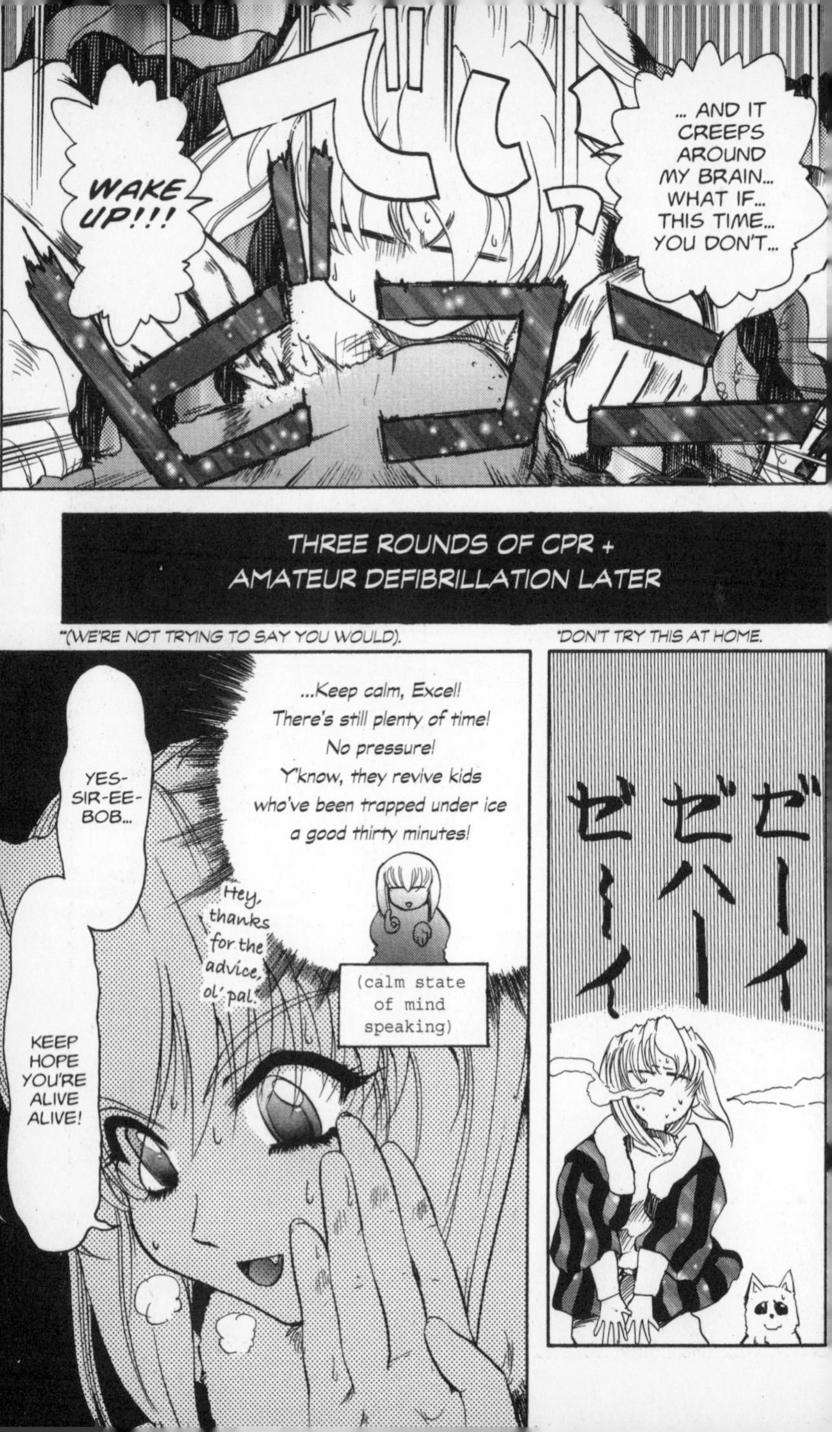
... AND IT CREEPS AROUND MY BRAIN... WHAT IF... THIS TIME... YOU DON'T...
WAKE UP!!!
THREE ROUNDS OF CPR + AMATEUR DEFIBRILLATION LATER
*DON'T TRY THIS AT HOME.
**(WE'RE NOT TRYING TO SAY YOU WOULD).
ゼーイ ゼハー ゼーイ
...Keep calm, Excel! There's still plenty of time! No pressure! Y'know, they revive kids who've been trapped under ice a good thirty minutes!
(calm state of mind speaking)
Hey, thanks for the advice, ol' pal.
YES-SIR-EE-BOB...
KEEP HOPE YOU'RE ALIVE ALIVE!

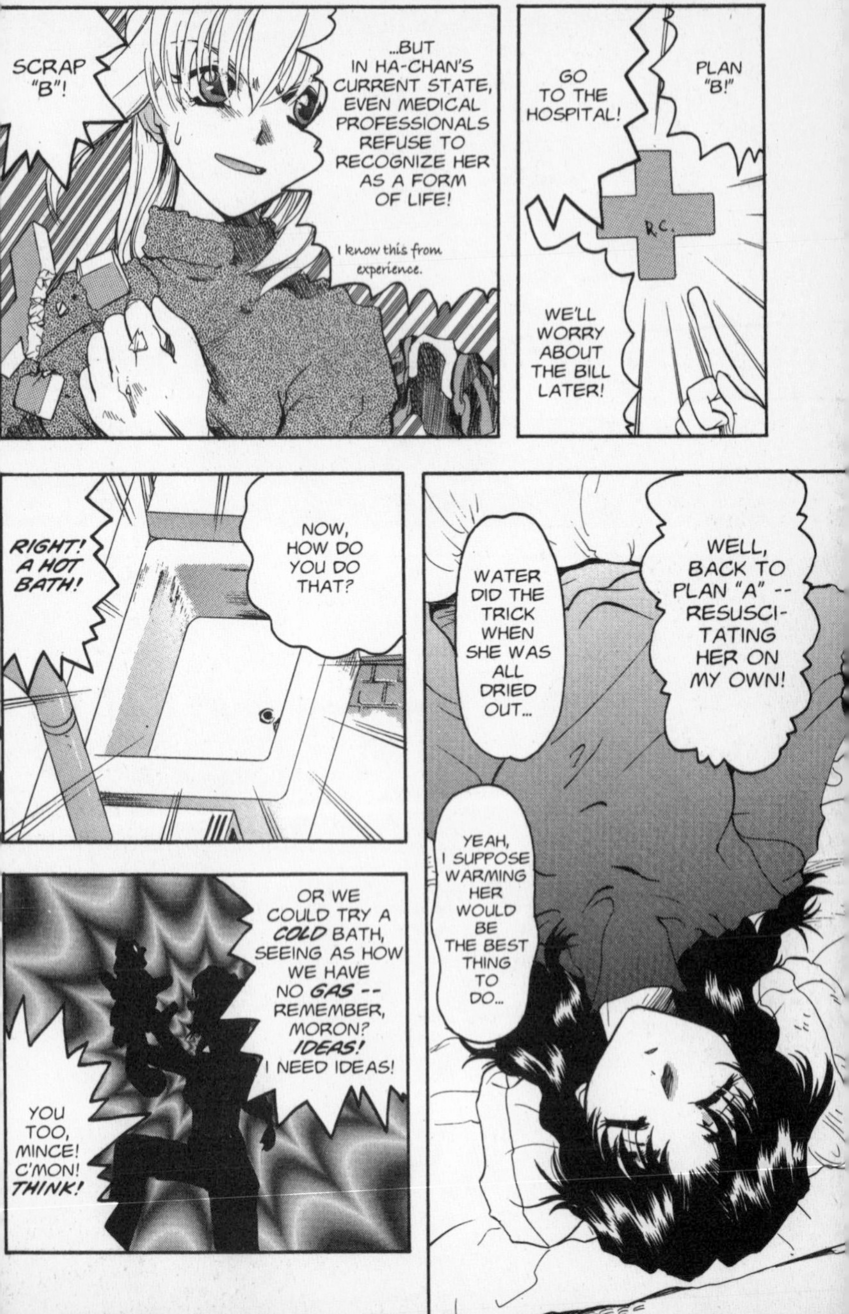
PLAN "B!"
GO TO THE HOSPITAL!
WE'LL WORRY ABOUT THE BILL LATER!
R.C.
...BUT IN HA-CHAN'S CURRENT STATE, EVEN MEDICAL PROFESSIONALS REFUSE TO RECOGNIZE HER AS A FORM OF LIFE!
SCRAP "B"!
I know this from experience.
WELL, BACK TO PLAN "A" -- RESUSCI-TATING HER ON MY OWN!
WATER DID THE TRICK WHEN SHE WAS ALL DRIED OUT...
YEAH, I SUPPOSE WARMING HER WOULD BE THE BEST THING TO DO...
RIGHT! A HOT BATH!
NOW, HOW DO YOU DO THAT?
OR WE COULD TRY A COLD BATH, SEEING AS HOW WE HAVE NO GAS -- REMEMBER, MORON? IDEAS! I NEED IDEAS!
YOU TOO, MINCE! C'MON! THINK!

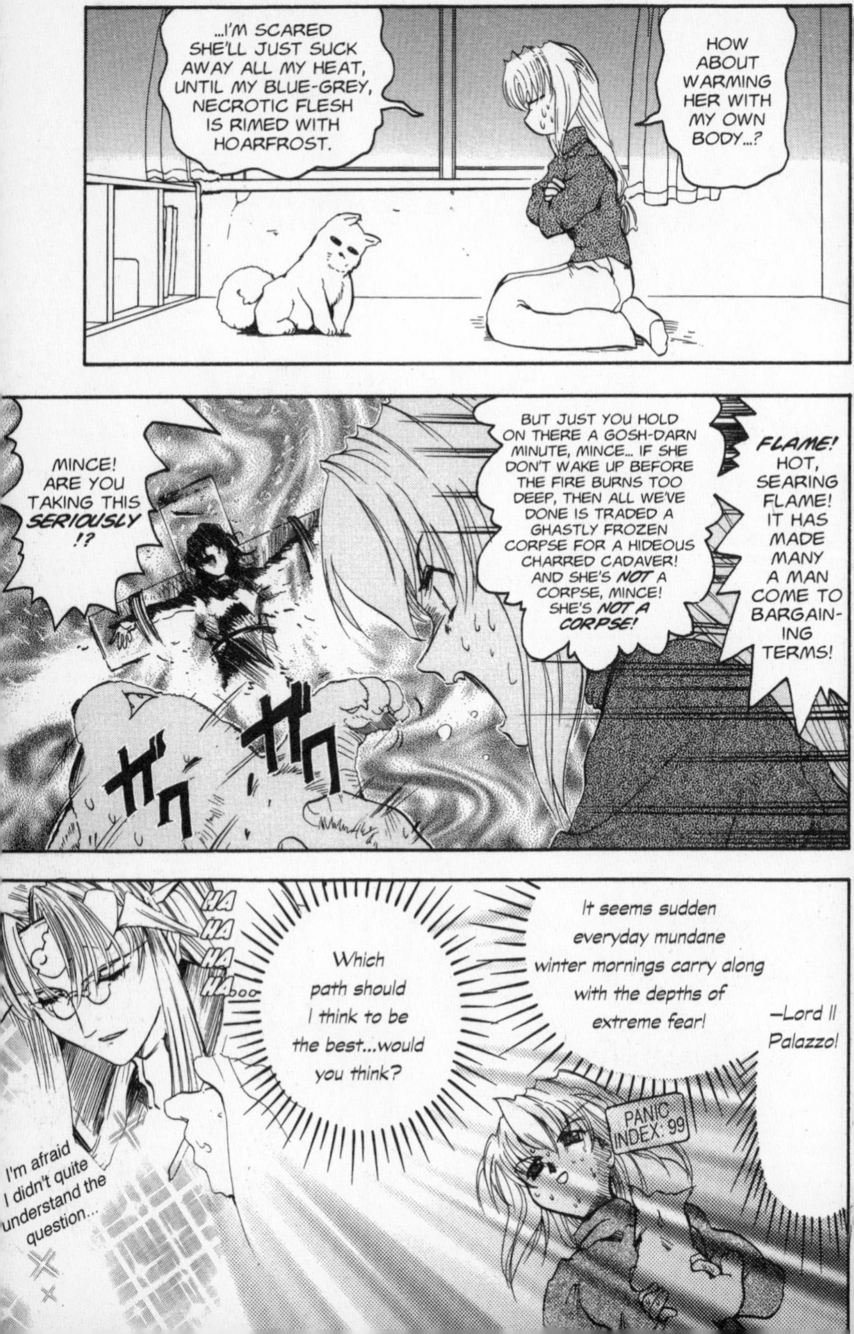
HOW ABOUT WARMING HER WITH MY OWN BODY...?
...I'M SCARED SHE'LL JUST SUCK AWAY ALL MY HEAT, UNTIL MY BLUE-GREY, NECROTIC FLESH IS RIMED WITH HOARFROST.
FLAME! HOT, SEARING FLAME! IT HAS MADE MANY A MAN COME TO BARGAIN-ING TERMS!
BUT JUST YOU HOLD ON THERE A GOSH-DARN MINUTE, MINCE... IF SHE DON'T WAKE UP BEFORE THE FIRE BURNS TOO DEEP, THEN ALL WE'VE DONE IS TRADED A GHASTLY FROZEN CORPSE FOR A HIDEOUS CHARRED CADAVER! AND SHE'S *NOT* A CORPSE, MINCE! SHE'S *NOT A CORPSE!*
MINCE! ARE YOU TAKING THIS *SERIOUSLY* !?
ザク ザク
—Lord Il Palazzo!
It seems sudden everyday mundane winter mornings carry along with the depths of extreme fear!
Which path should I think to be the best...would you think?
HA HA HA HA HAooo
PANIC INDEX: 99
I'm afraid I didn't quite understand the question...

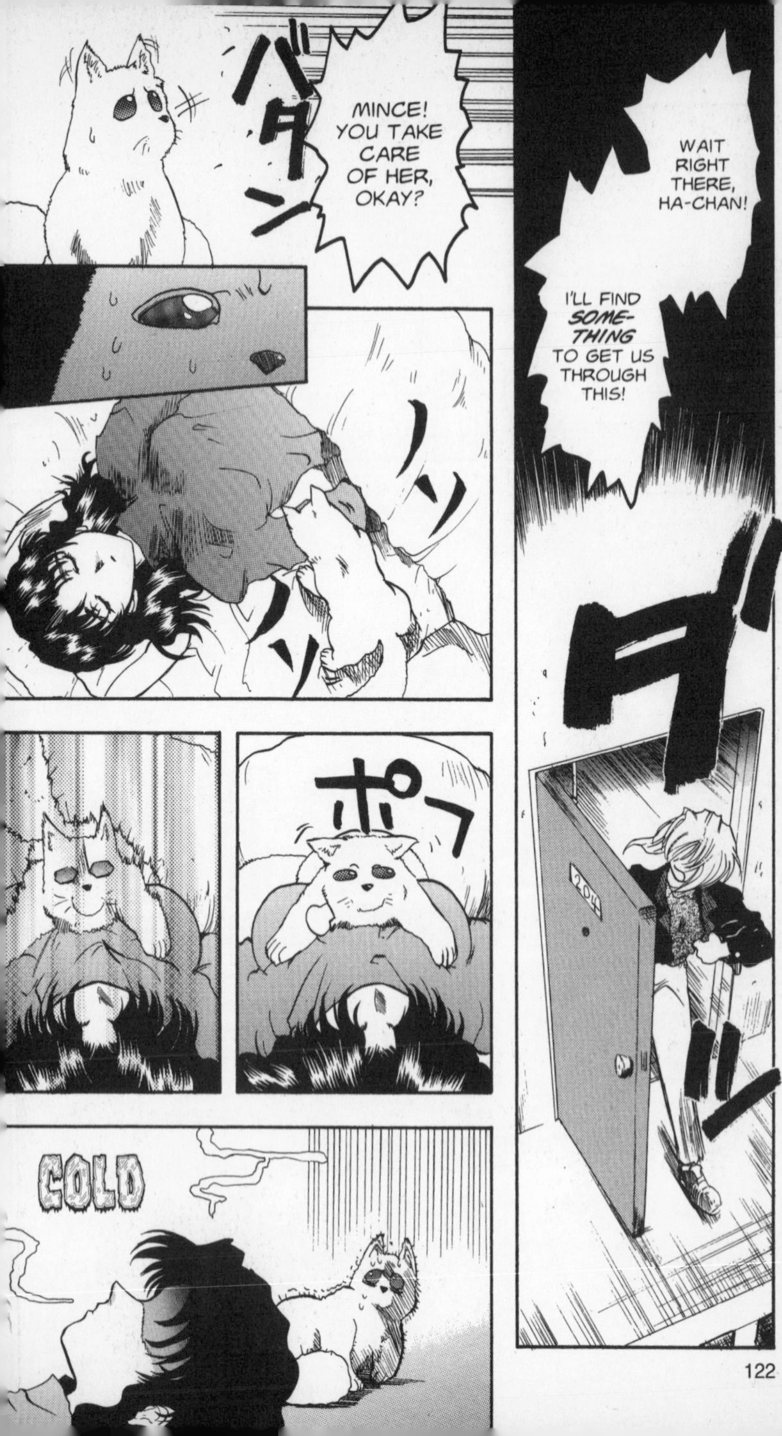
WAIT RIGHT THERE, HA-CHAN!
I'LL FIND *SOME-THING* TO GET US THROUGH THIS!
204
バタン
MINCE! YOU TAKE CARE OF HER, OKAY?
ポフ
COLD

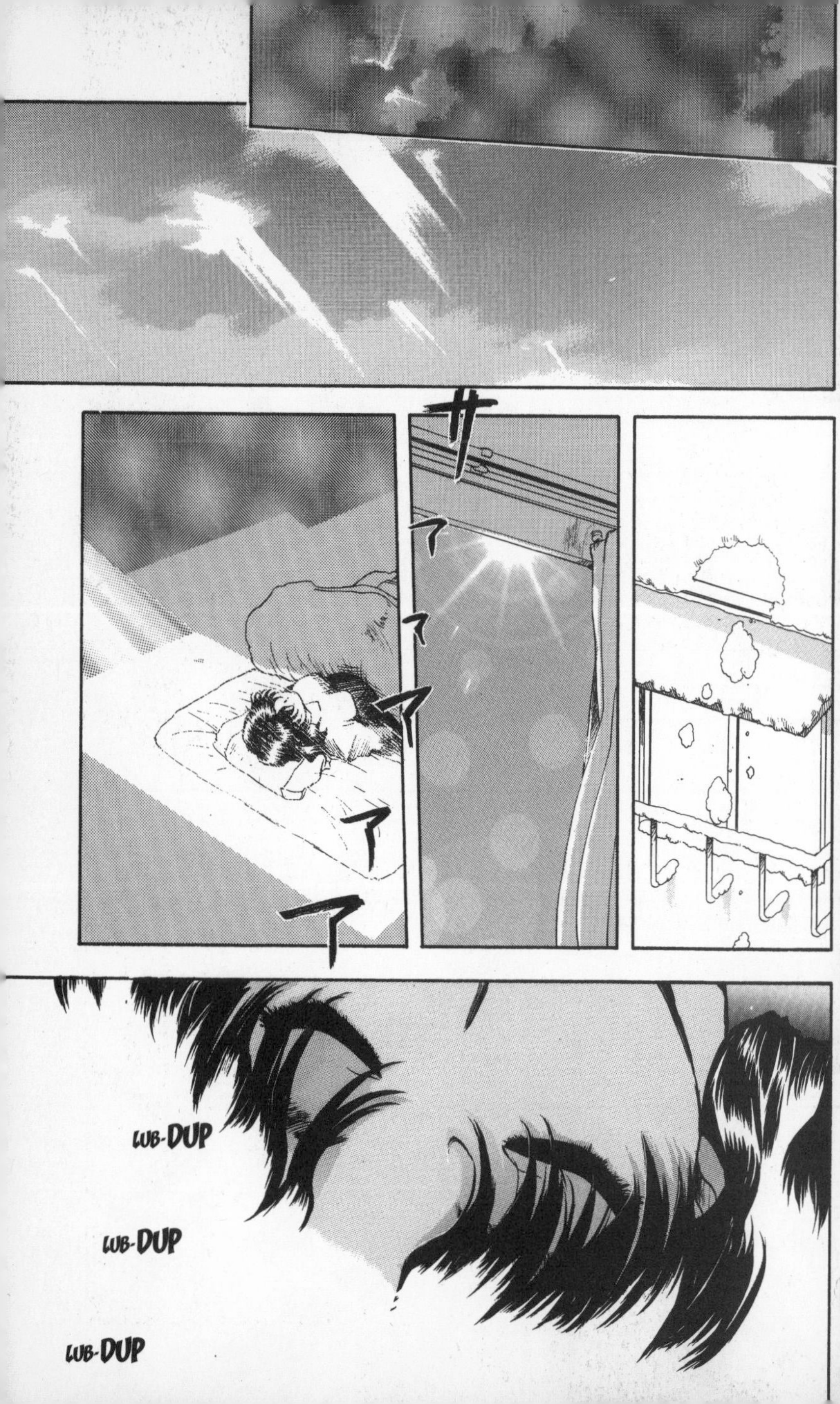
サァァァァァ
LUB-DUP
LUB-DUP
LUB-DUP

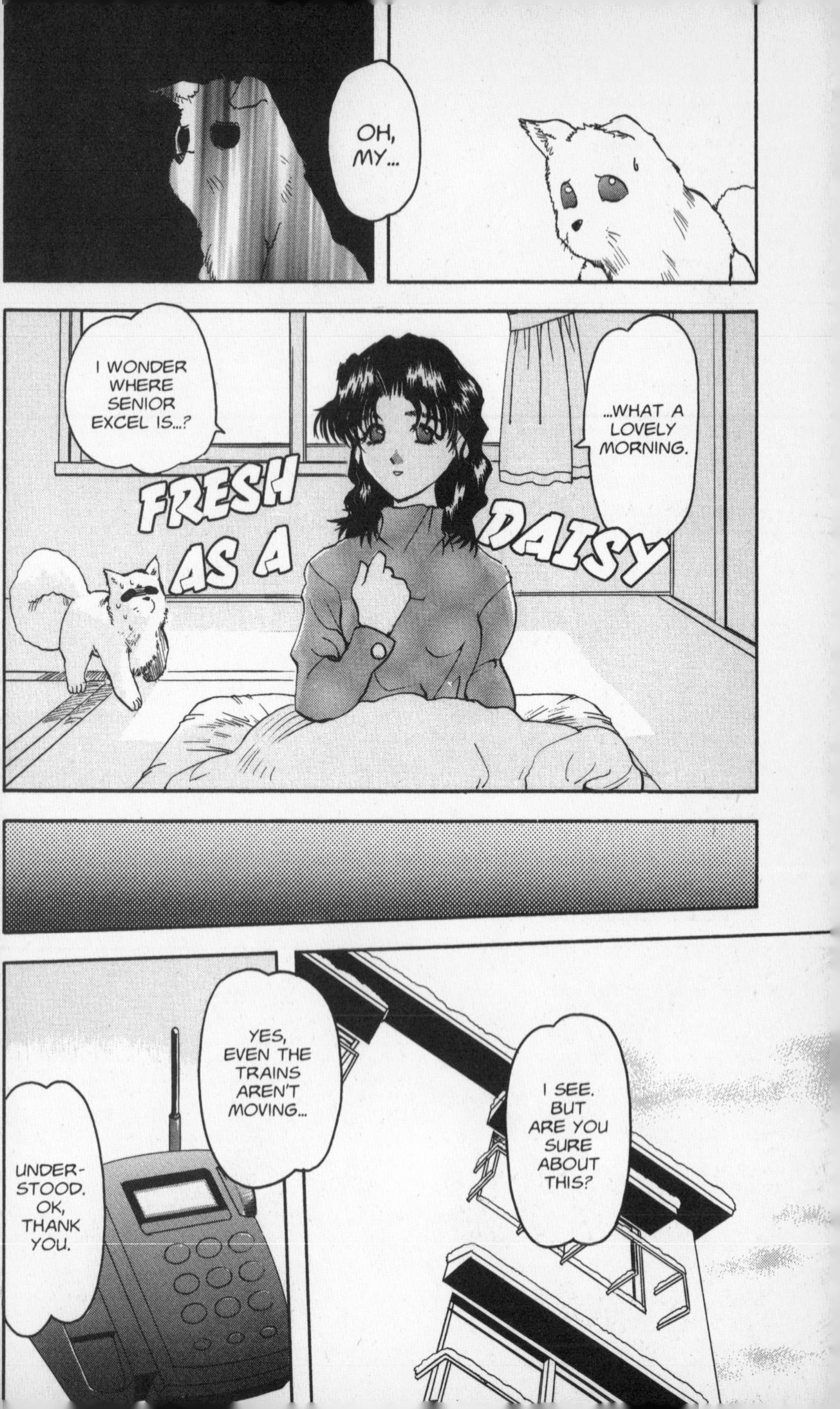
OH, MY...
...WHAT A LOVELY MORNING.
FRESH AS A DAISY
I WONDER WHERE SENIOR EXCEL IS...?
I SEE. BUT ARE YOU SURE ABOUT THIS?
YES, EVEN THE TRAINS AREN'T MOVING...
UNDER-STOOD. OK, THANK YOU.

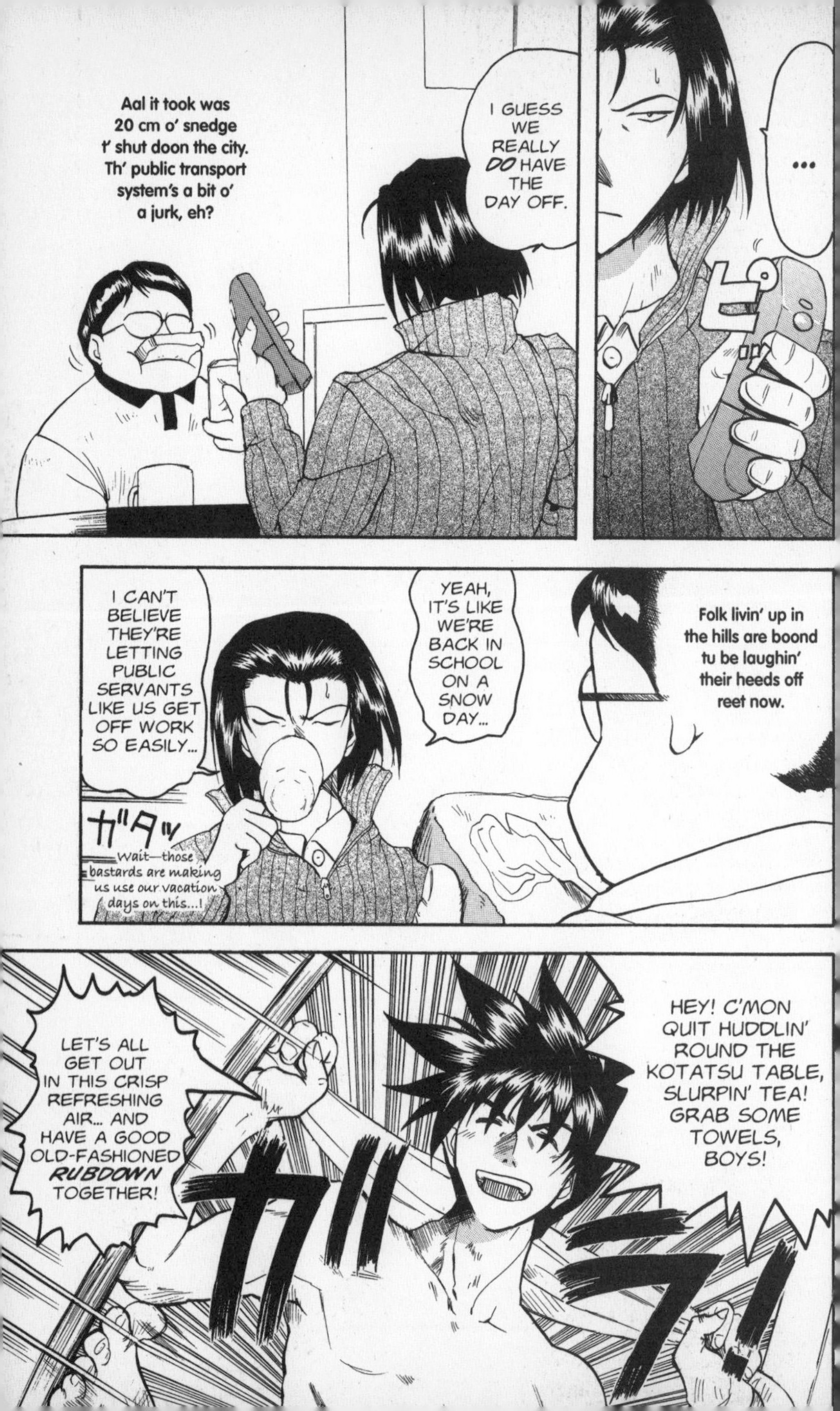
...
I GUESS WE REALLY DO HAVE THE DAY OFF.
Aal it took was 20 cm o' snedge t' shut doon the city. Th' public transport system's a bit o' a jurk, eh?
Folk livin' up in the hills are boond tu be laughin' their heeds off reet now.
YEAH, IT'S LIKE WE'RE BACK IN SCHOOL ON A SNOW DAY...
I CAN'T BELIEVE THEY'RE LETTING PUBLIC SERVANTS LIKE US GET OFF WORK SO EASILY...
ガタッ
Wait—those bastards are making us use our vacation days on this...!
HEY! C'MON QUIT HUDDLIN' ROUND THE KOTATSU TABLE, SLURPIN' TEA! GRAB SOME TOWELS, BOYS!
LET'S ALL GET OUT IN THIS CRISP REFRESHING AIR... AND HAVE A GOOD OLD-FASHIONED RUBDOWN TOGETHER!

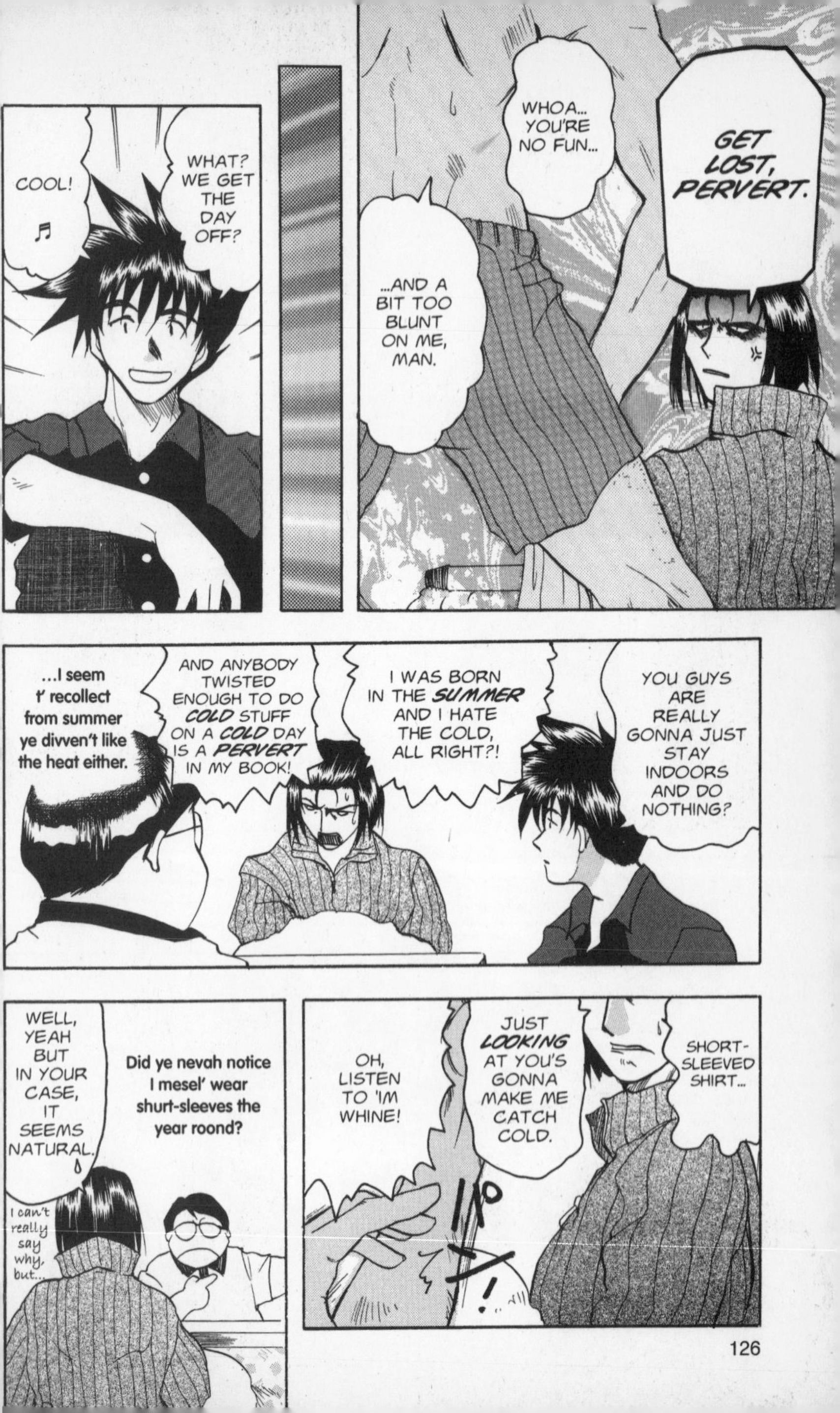

GET LOST, PERVERT.
WHOA... YOU'RE NO FUN...
...AND A BIT TOO BLUNT ON ME, MAN.
WHAT? WE GET THE DAY OFF?
COOL! ♬
YOU GUYS ARE REALLY GONNA JUST STAY INDOORS AND DO NOTHING?
I WAS BORN IN THE SUMMER AND I HATE THE COLD, ALL RIGHT?!
AND ANYBODY TWISTED ENOUGH TO DO COLD STUFF ON A COLD DAY IS A PERVERT IN MY BOOK!
...I seem t' recollect from summer ye divven't like the heat either.
SHORT-SLEEVED SHIRT...
JUST LOOKING AT YOU'S GONNA MAKE ME CATCH COLD.
OH, LISTEN TO 'IM WHINE!
Did ye nevah notice I mesel' wear shurt-sleeves the year roond?
WELL, YEAH BUT IN YOUR CASE, IT SEEMS NATURAL.
I can't really say why, but...

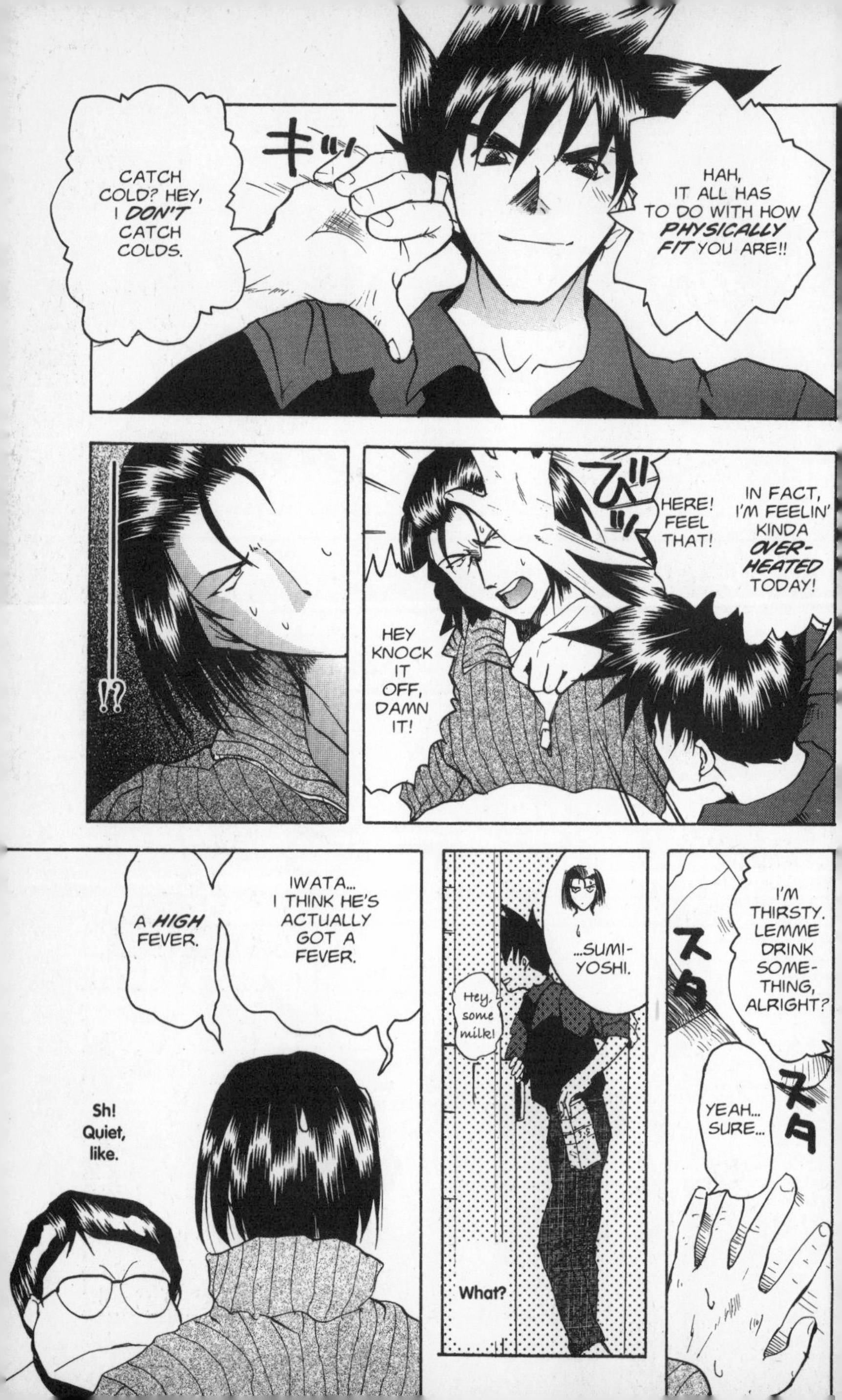
HAH, IT ALL HAS TO DO WITH HOW *PHYSICALLY FIT* YOU ARE!!
ギッ
CATCH COLD? HEY, I *DON'T* CATCH COLDS.
IN FACT, I'M FEELIN' KINDA *OVER-HEATED* TODAY!
HERE! FEEL THAT!
HEY KNOCK IT OFF, DAMN IT!
!?
I'M THIRSTY. LEMME DRINK SOME-THING, ALRIGHT?
スタ
YEAH... SURE...
スタ
...SUMI-YOSHI.
Hey, some milk!
What?
IWATA... I THINK HE'S ACTUALLY GOT A FEVER.
A *HIGH* FEVER.
Sh! Quiet, like.

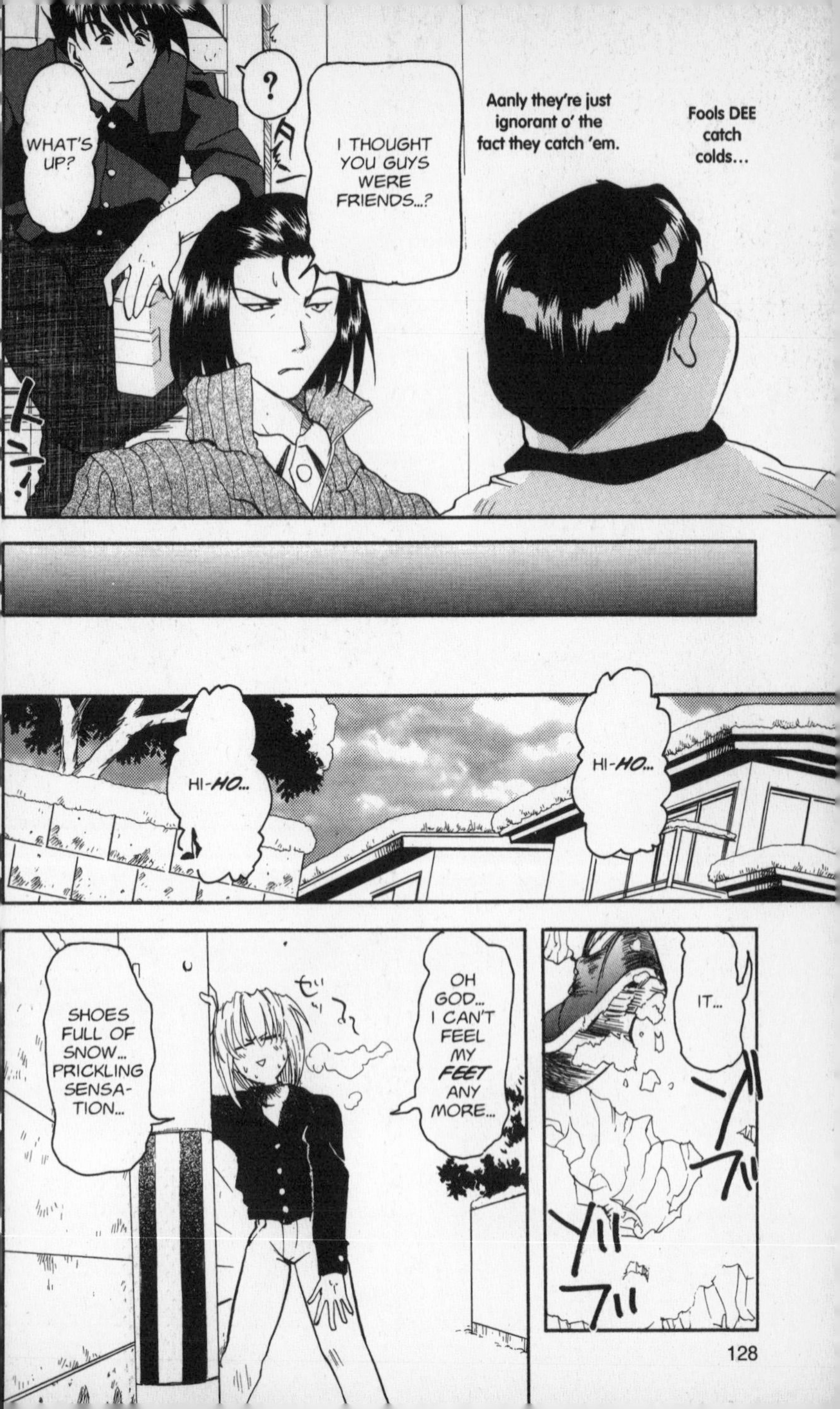
Fools DEE catch colds...
Aanly they're just ignorant o' the fact they catch 'em.
I THOUGHT YOU GUYS WERE FRIENDS...?
?
WHAT'S UP?
HI-HO...
HI-HO...
IT...
OH GOD... I CAN'T FEEL MY FEET ANY MORE...
SHOES FULL OF SNOW... PRICKLING SENSATION...

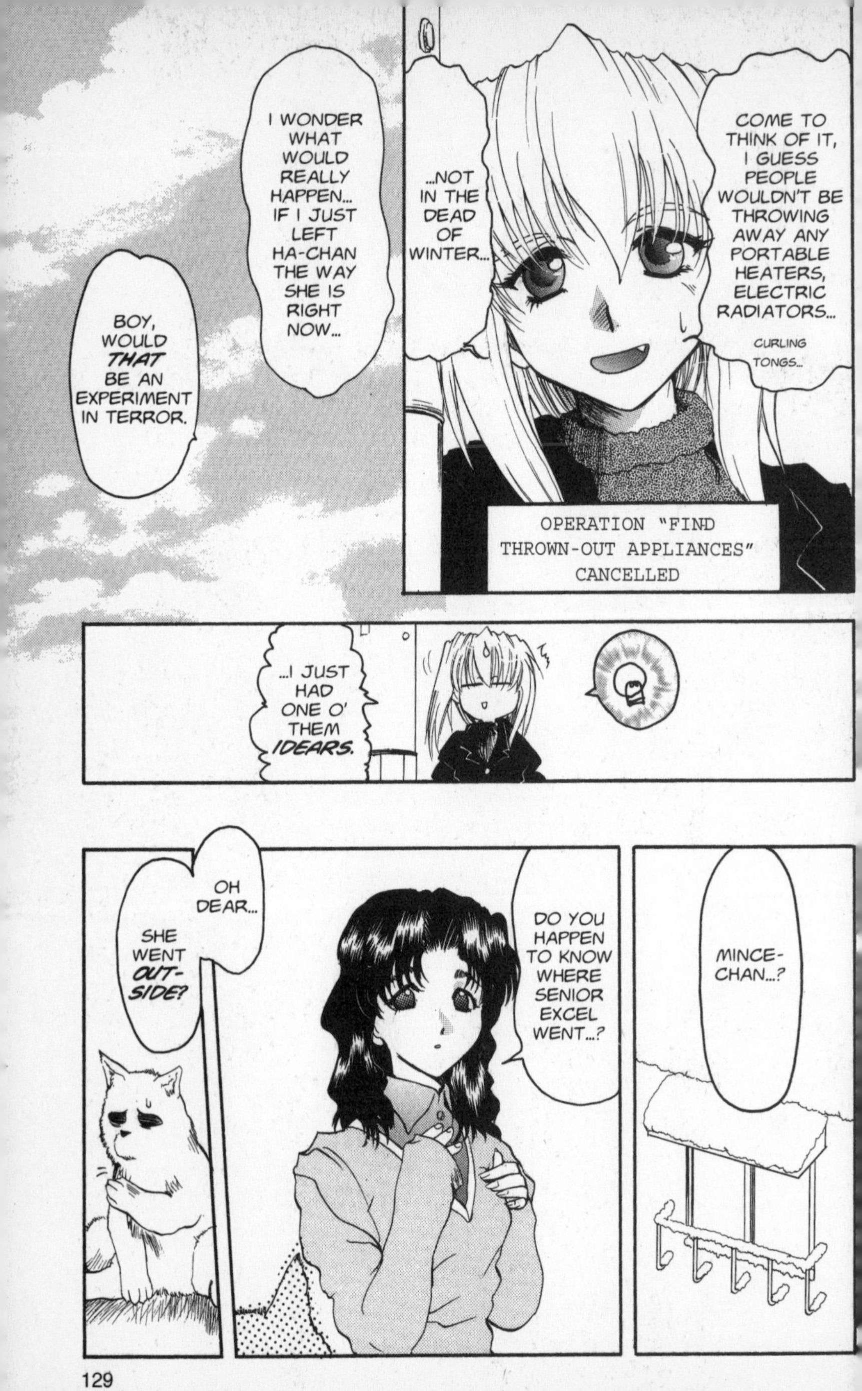

COME TO THINK OF IT, I GUESS PEOPLE WOULDN'T BE THROWING AWAY ANY PORTABLE HEATERS, ELECTRIC RADIATORS...
CURLING TONGS...
...NOT IN THE DEAD OF WINTER...
OPERATION "FIND THROWN-OUT APPLIANCES" CANCELLED
I WONDER WHAT WOULD REALLY HAPPEN... IF I JUST LEFT HA-CHAN THE WAY SHE IS RIGHT NOW...
BOY, WOULD *THAT* BE AN EXPERIMENT IN TERROR.
...I JUST HAD ONE O' THEM *IDEARS.*
MINCE-CHAN...?
DO YOU HAPPEN TO KNOW WHERE SENIOR EXCEL WENT...?
OH DEAR...
SHE WENT *OUT-SIDE?*

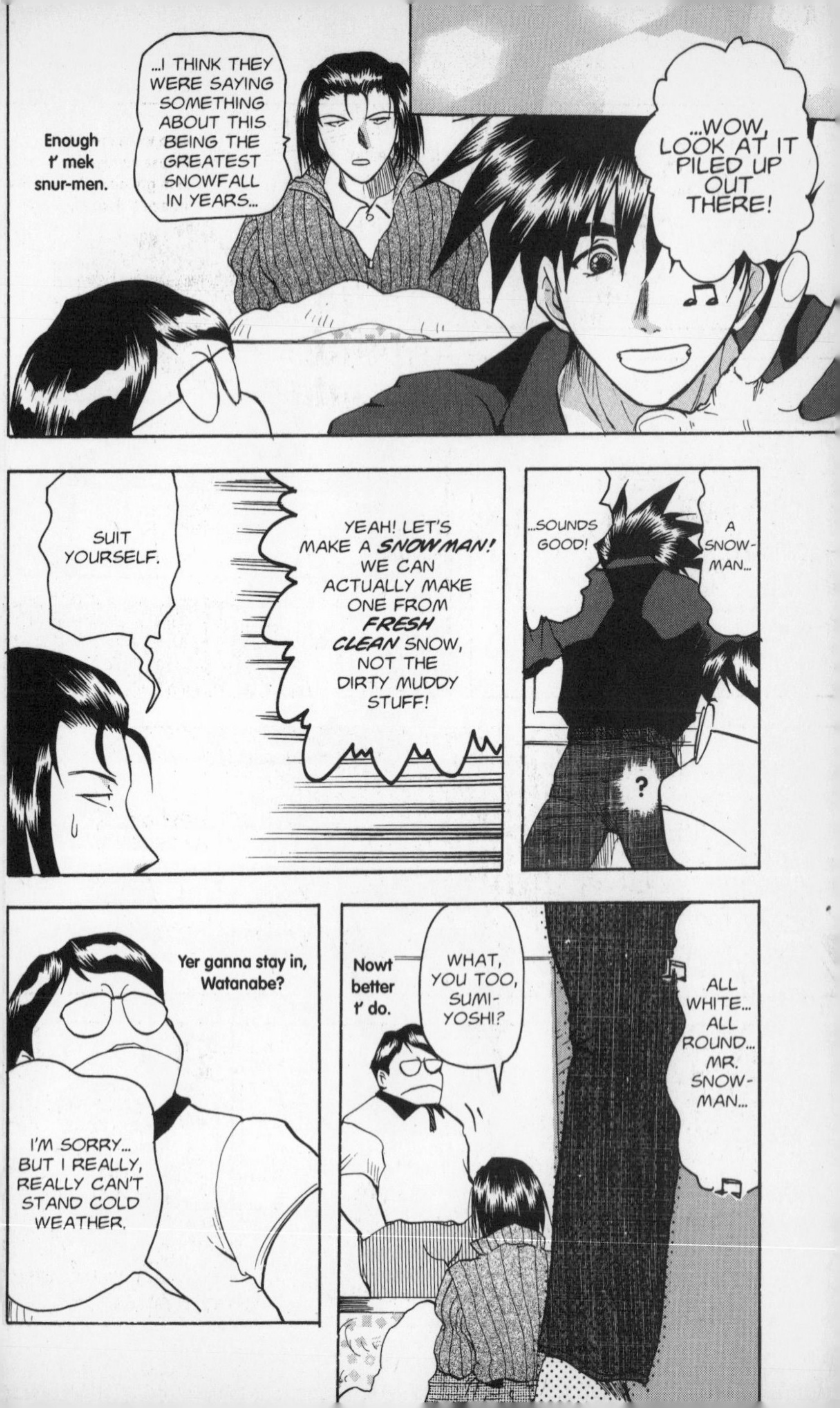
...WOW, LOOK AT IT PILED UP OUT THERE!
...I THINK THEY WERE SAYING SOMETHING ABOUT THIS BEING THE GREATEST SNOWFALL IN YEARS...
Enough t' mek snur-men.
A SNOW-MAN...
...SOUNDS GOOD!
?
YEAH! LET'S MAKE A SNOWMAN! WE CAN ACTUALLY MAKE ONE FROM FRESH CLEAN SNOW, NOT THE DIRTY MUDDY STUFF!
SUIT YOURSELF.
ALL WHITE... ALL ROUND... MR. SNOW-MAN...
WHAT, YOU TOO, SUMI-YOSHI?
Nowt better t' do.
Yer ganna stay in, Watanabe?
I'M SORRY... BUT I REALLY, REALLY CAN'T STAND COLD WEATHER.

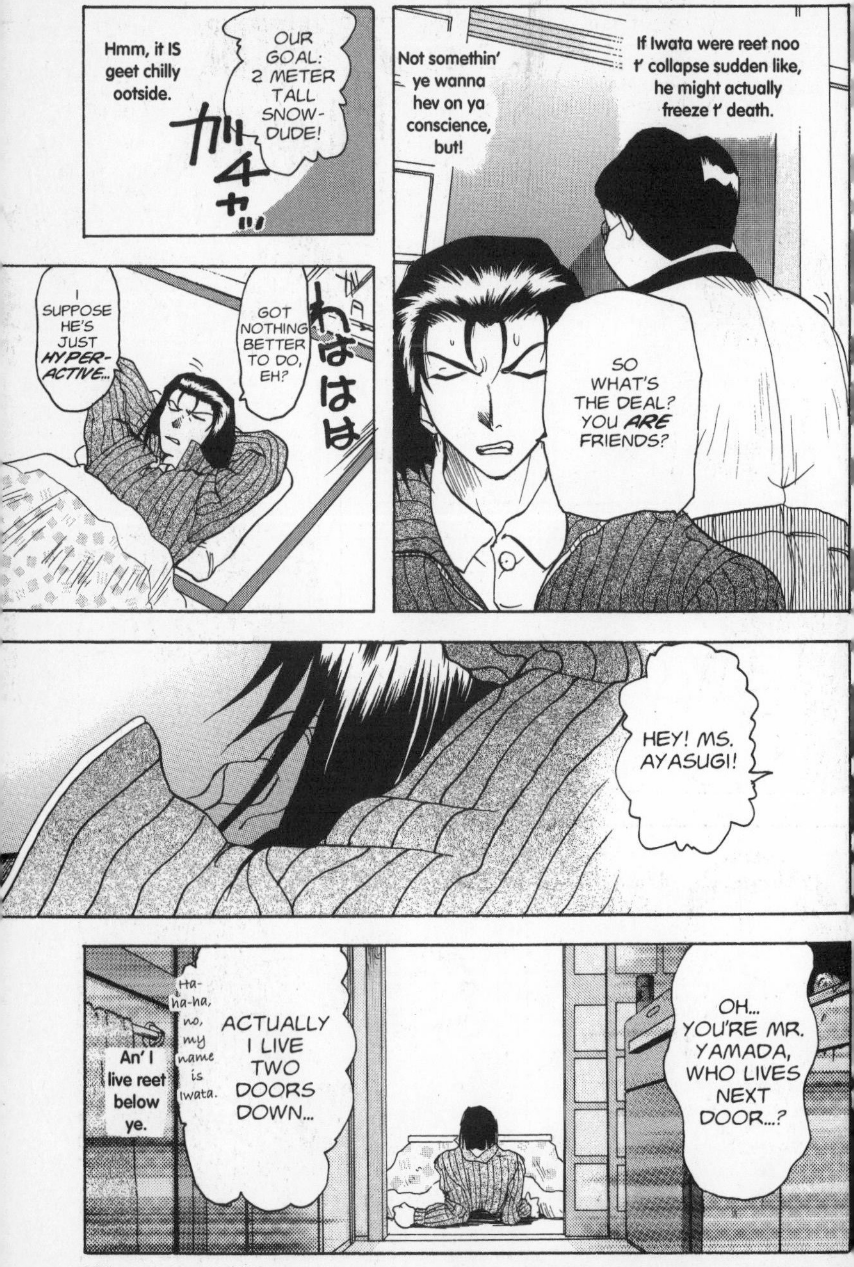
If Iwata were reet noo t' collapse sudden like, he might actually freeze t' death.
Not somethin' ye wanna hev on ya conscience, but!
OUR GOAL: 2 METER TALL SNOW-DUDE!
Hmm, it IS geet chilly ootside.
ガチャッ
SO WHAT'S THE DEAL? YOU *ARE* FRIENDS?
わははは
GOT NOTHING BETTER TO DO, EH?
I SUPPOSE HE'S JUST *HYPER-ACTIVE*...
HEY! MS. AYASUGI!
OH... YOU'RE MR. YAMADA, WHO LIVES NEXT DOOR...?
ACTUALLY I LIVE TWO DOORS DOWN...
Ha-ha-ha, no, my name is Iwata.
An' I live reet below ye.

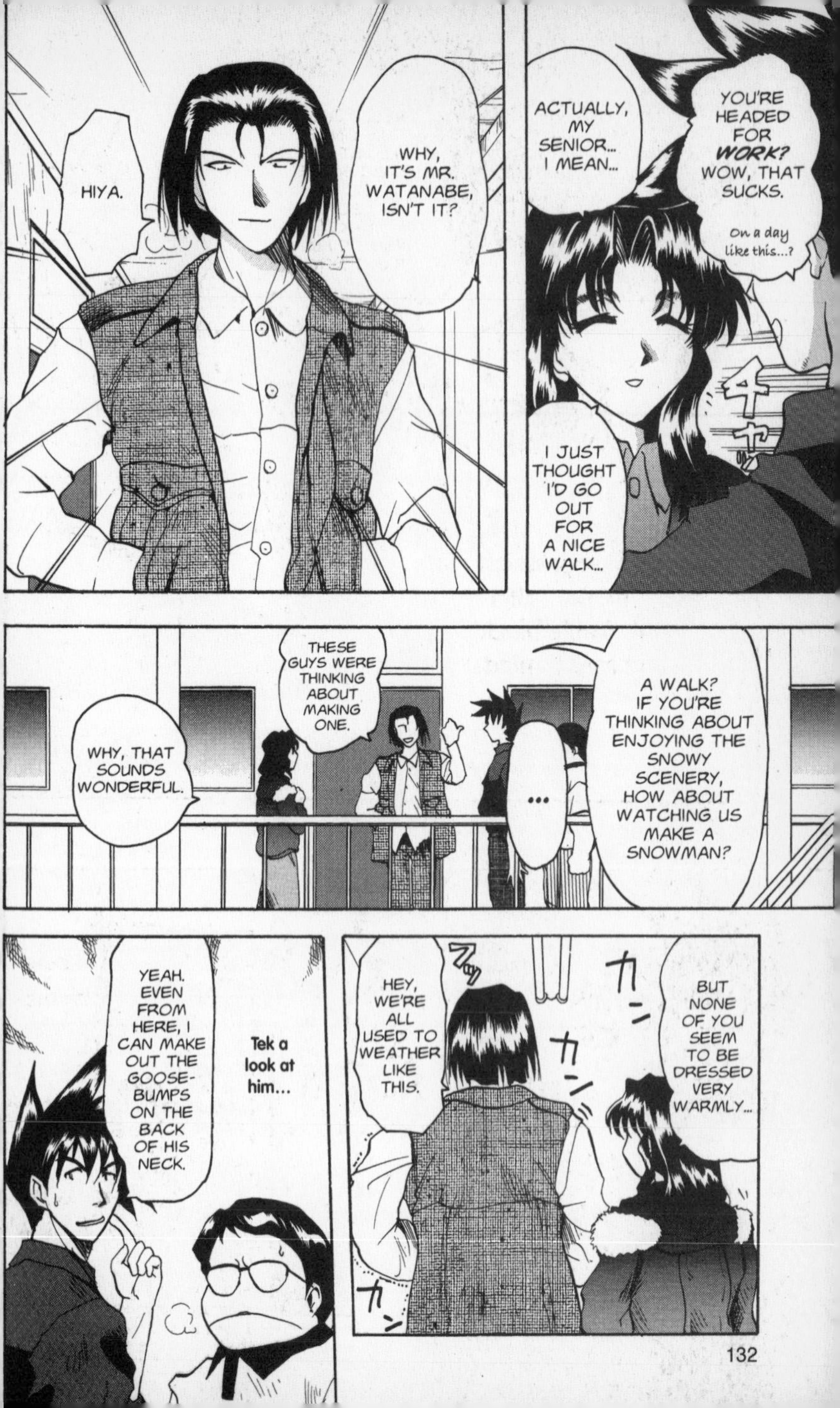

YOU'RE HEADED FOR **WORK?** WOW, THAT SUCKS.
On a day like this...?
ACTUALLY, MY SENIOR... I MEAN...
I JUST THOUGHT I'D GO OUT FOR A NICE WALK...
WHY, IT'S MR. WATANABE, ISN'T IT?
HIYA.
A WALK? IF YOU'RE THINKING ABOUT ENJOYING THE SNOWY SCENERY, HOW ABOUT WATCHING US MAKE A SNOWMAN?
...
THESE GUYS WERE THINKING ABOUT MAKING ONE.
WHY, THAT SOUNDS WONDERFUL.
BUT NONE OF YOU SEEM TO BE DRESSED VERY WARMLY...
HEY, WE'RE ALL USED TO WEATHER LIKE THIS.
YEAH. EVEN FROM HERE, I CAN MAKE OUT THE GOOSE-BUMPS ON THE BACK OF HIS NECK.
Tek a look at him...

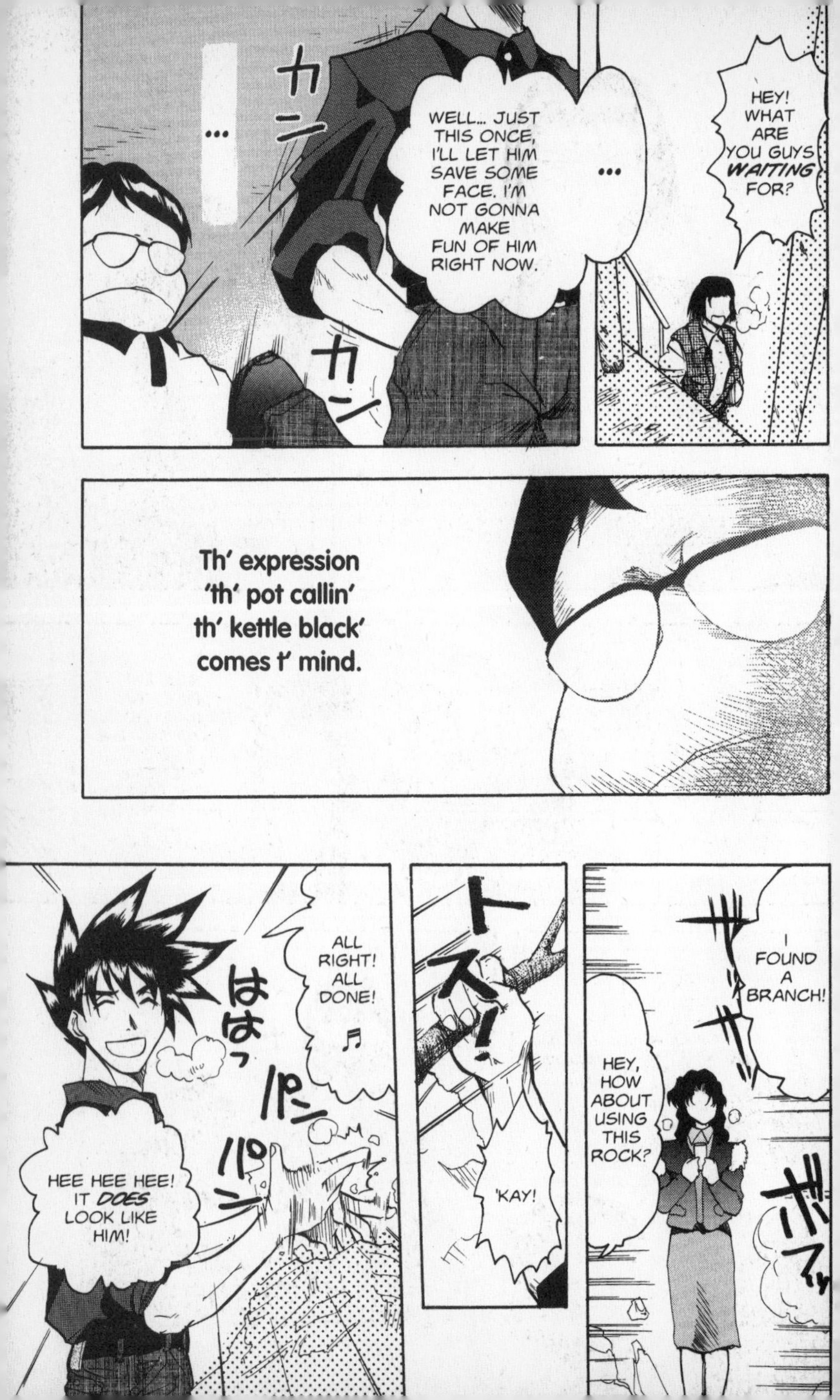
HEY! WHAT ARE YOU GUYS *WAITING* FOR?
...
WELL... JUST THIS ONCE, I'LL LET HIM SAVE SOME FACE. I'M NOT GONNA MAKE FUN OF HIM RIGHT NOW.
カン
...
カン
Th' expression 'th' pot callin' th' kettle black' comes t' mind.
I FOUND A BRANCH!
ザザッ
HEY, HOW ABOUT USING THIS ROCK?
ボフッ
トスッ
'KAY!
ALL RIGHT! ALL DONE! ♫
はは
パンパン
HEE HEE HEE! IT *DOES* LOOK LIKE HIM!

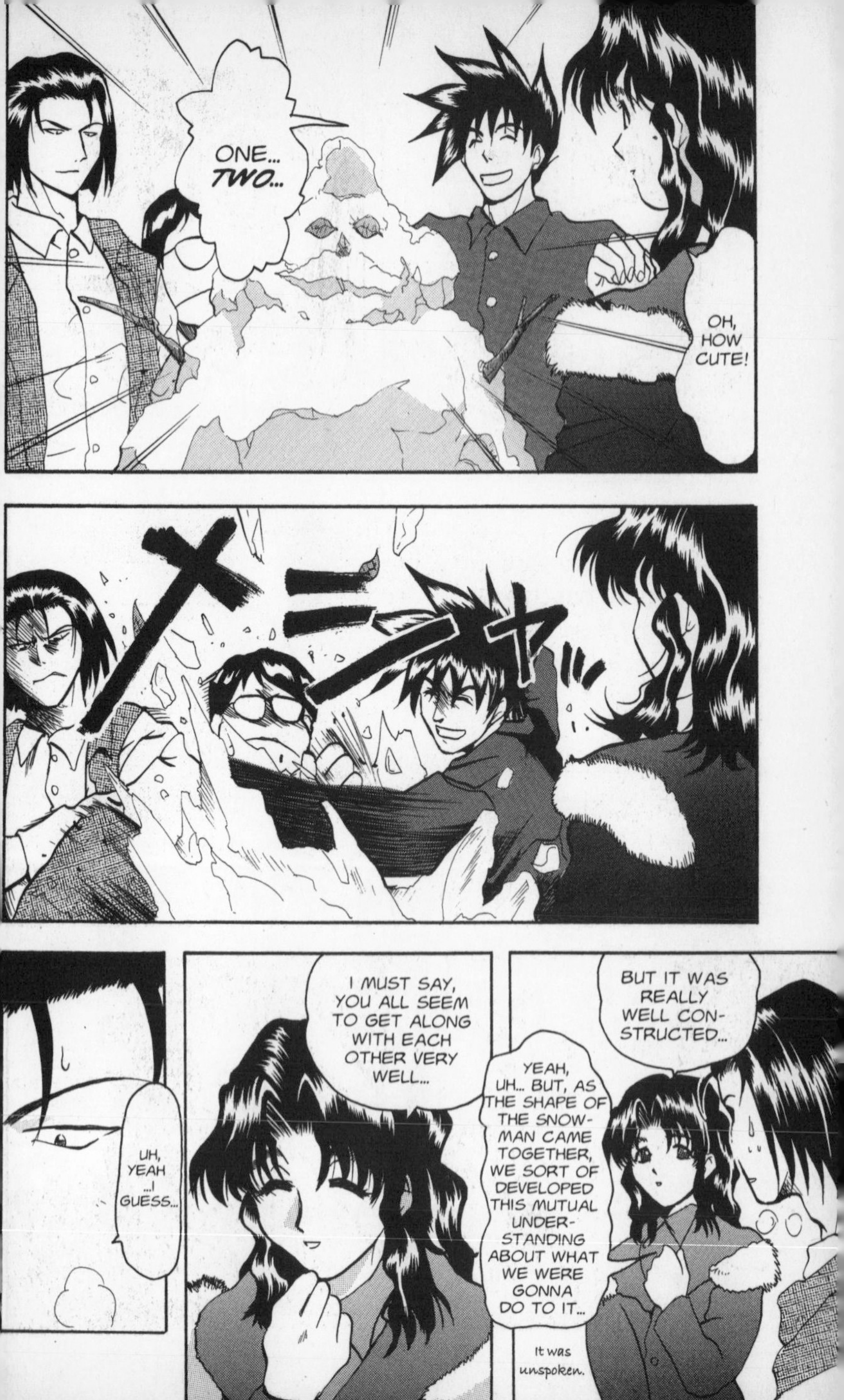

OH, HOW CUTE!
ONE... TWO...
BUT IT WAS REALLY WELL CON- STRUCTED...
YEAH, UH... BUT, AS THE SHAPE OF THE SNOW- MAN CAME TOGETHER, WE SORT OF DEVELOPED THIS MUTUAL UNDER- STANDING ABOUT WHAT WE WERE GONNA DO TO IT...
It was unspoken.
I MUST SAY, YOU ALL SEEM TO GET ALONG WITH EACH OTHER VERY WELL...
UH, YEAH ...I GUESS...

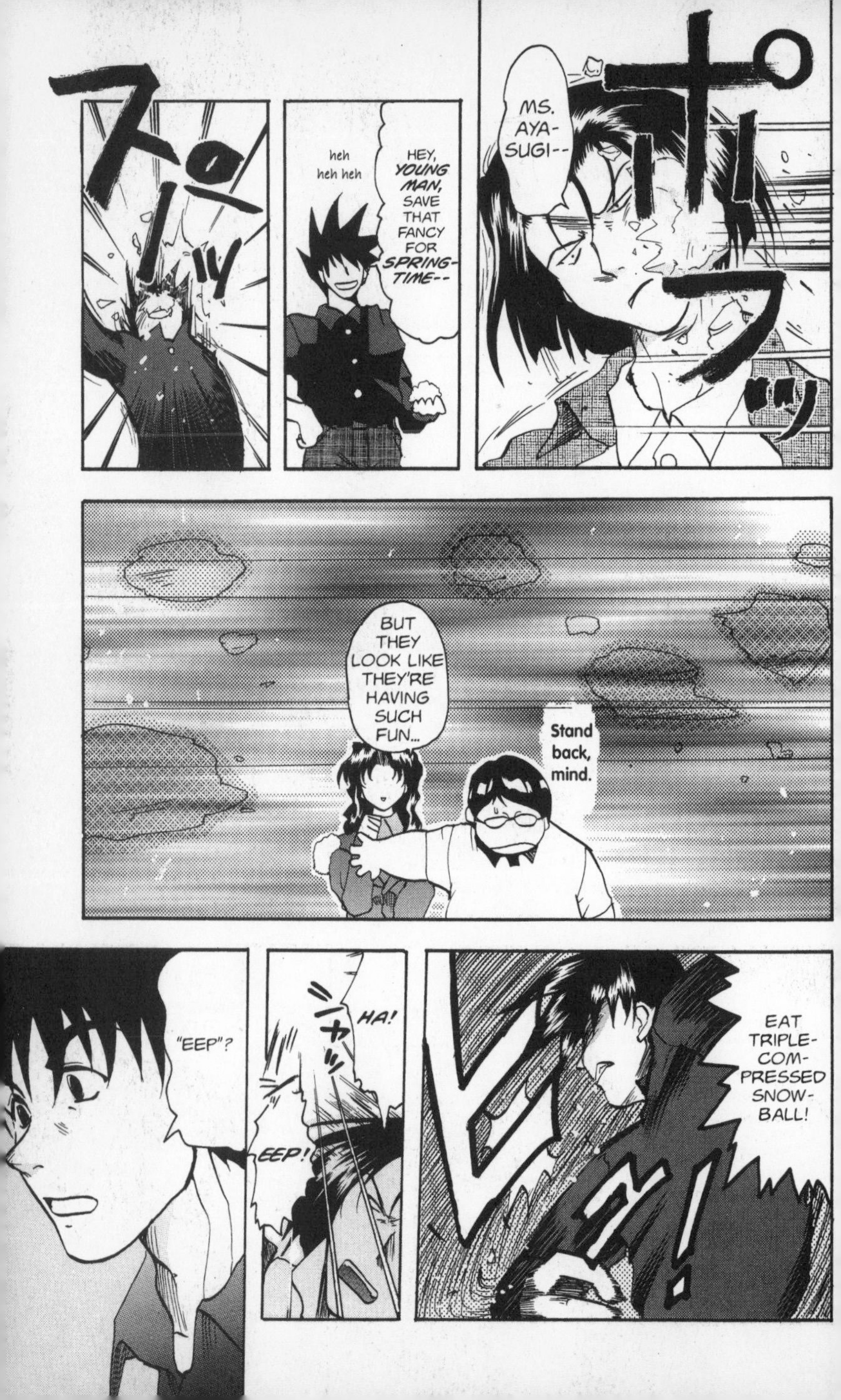
MS. AYA-SUGI--
HEY, YOUNG MAN, SAVE THAT FANCY FOR SPRING-TIME--
heh heh heh
BUT THEY LOOK LIKE THEY'RE HAVING SUCH FUN...
Stand back, mind.
EAT TRIPLE-COM-PRESSED SNOW-BALL!
HA!
EEP!
"EEP"?

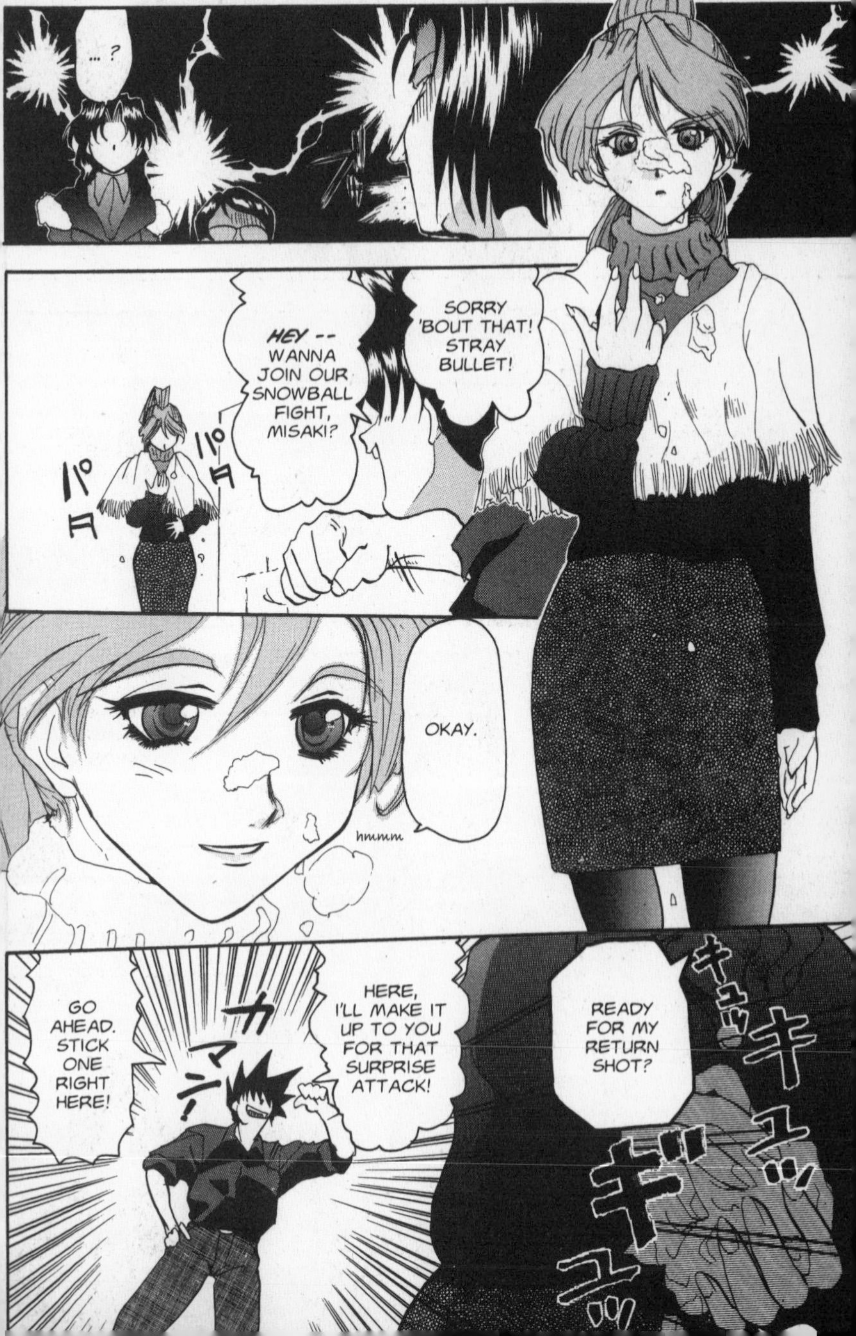
...?
SORRY 'BOUT THAT! STRAY BULLET!
HEY -- WANNA JOIN OUR SNOWBALL FIGHT, MISAKI?
パタ
パタ
OKAY.
hmmm
READY FOR MY RETURN SHOT?
キュッ
キュッ
ギュッ
HERE, I'LL MAKE IT UP TO YOU FOR THAT SURPRISE ATTACK!
カマン!
GO AHEAD. STICK ONE RIGHT HERE!

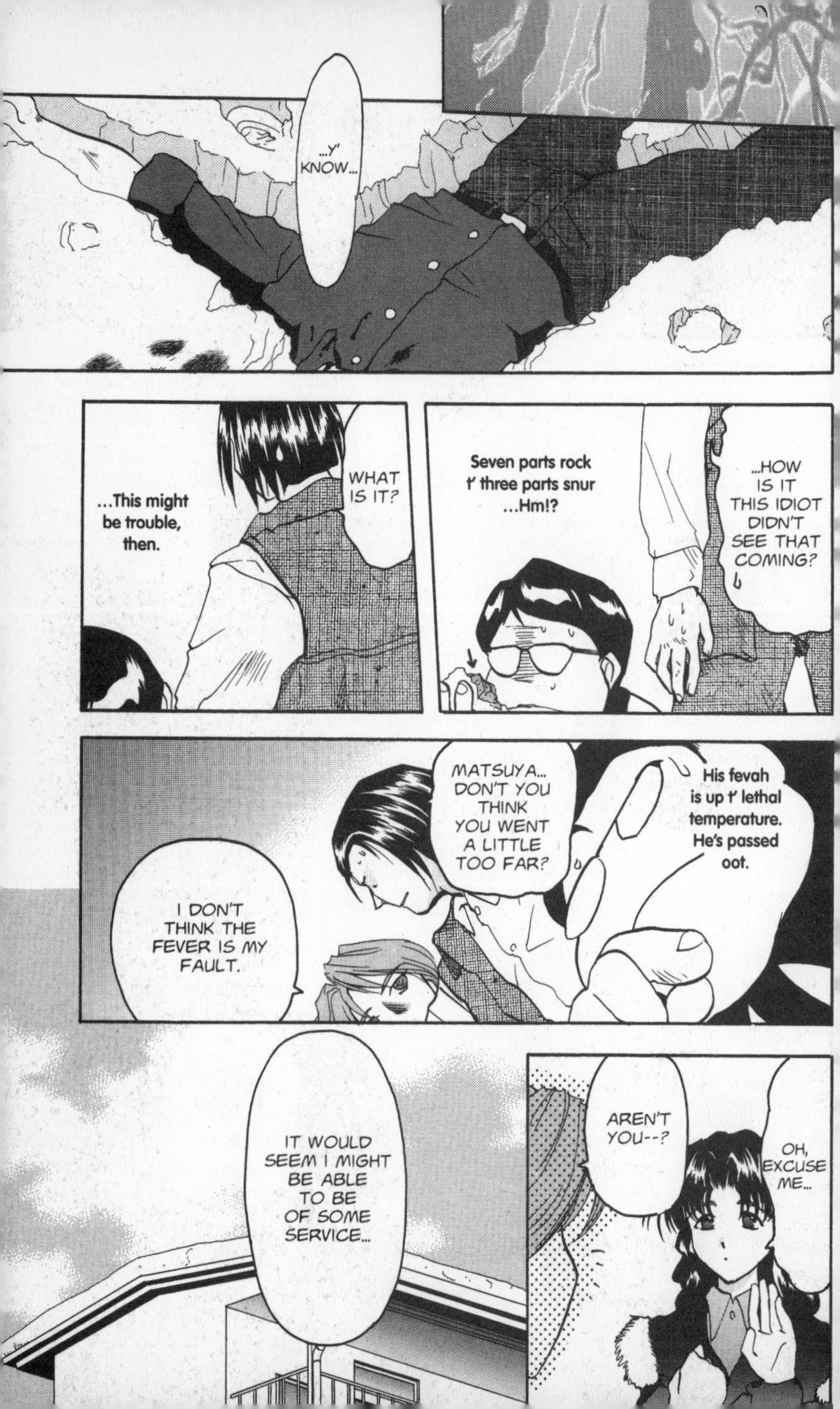
...Y' KNOW...
...HOW IS IT THIS IDIOT DIDN'T SEE THAT COMING?
Seven parts rock t' three parts snur ...Hm!?
WHAT IS IT?
...This might be trouble, then.
His fevah is up t' lethal temperature. He's passed oot.
MATSUYA... DON'T YOU THINK YOU WENT A LITTLE TOO FAR?
I DON'T THINK THE FEVER IS MY FAULT.
OH, EXCUSE ME...
AREN'T YOU--?
IT WOULD SEEM I MIGHT BE ABLE TO BE OF SOME SERVICE...

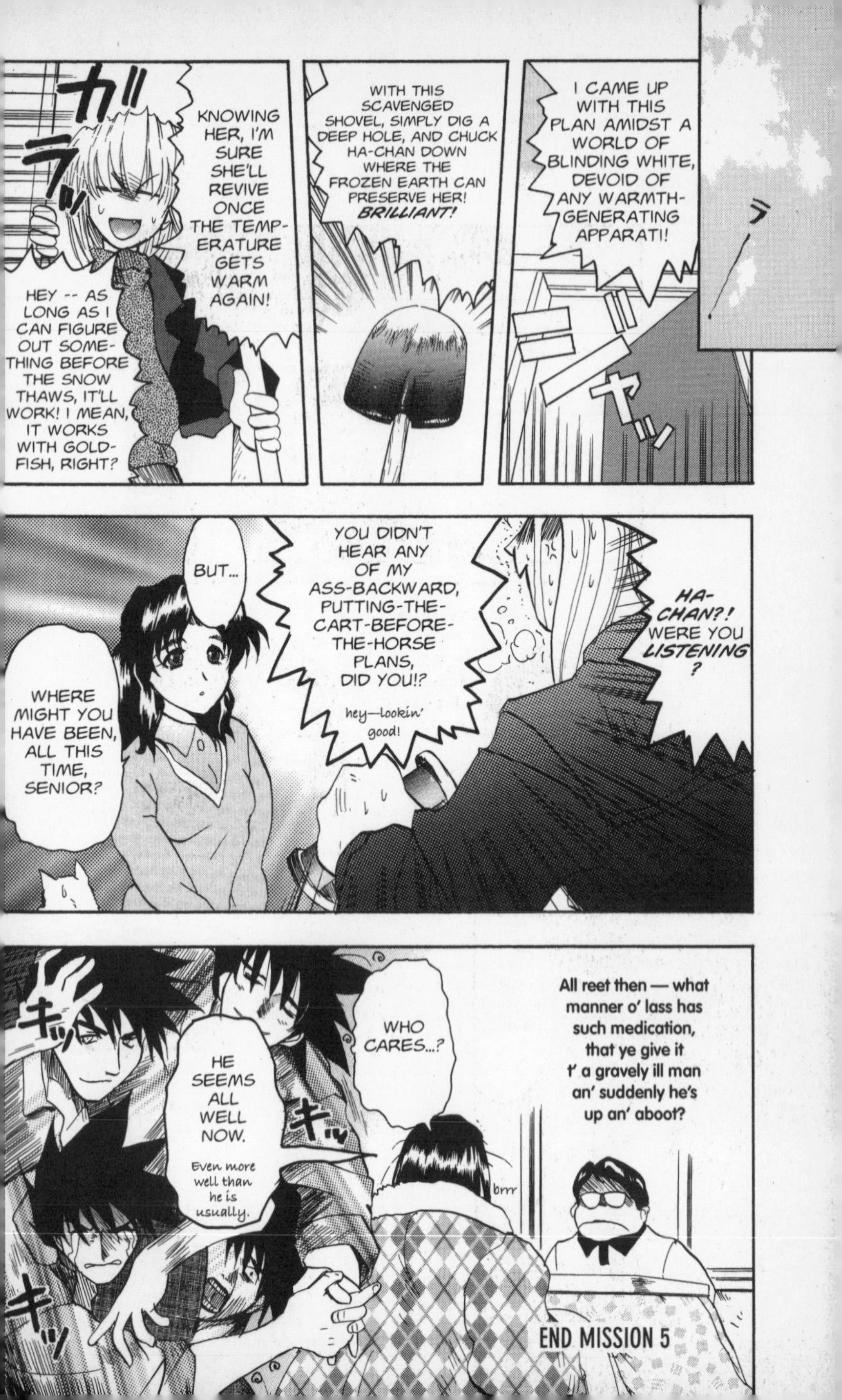

I CAME UP WITH THIS PLAN AMIDST A WORLD OF BLINDING WHITE, DEVOID OF ANY WARMTH-GENERATING APPARATI!
WITH THIS SCAVENGED SHOVEL, SIMPLY DIG A DEEP HOLE, AND CHUCK HA-CHAN DOWN WHERE THE FROZEN EARTH CAN PRESERVE HER! BRILLIANT!
KNOWING HER, I'M SURE SHE'LL REVIVE ONCE THE TEMPERATURE GETS WARM AGAIN!
HEY -- AS LONG AS I CAN FIGURE OUT SOMETHING BEFORE THE SNOW THAWS, IT'LL WORK! I MEAN, IT WORKS WITH GOLDFISH, RIGHT?
HA-CHAN?! WERE YOU LISTENING?
YOU DIDN'T HEAR ANY OF MY ASS-BACKWARD, PUTTING-THE-CART-BEFORE-THE-HORSE PLANS, DID YOU!?
hey—lookin' good!
BUT...
WHERE MIGHT YOU HAVE BEEN, ALL THIS TIME, SENIOR?
All reet then — what manner o' lass has such medication, that ye give it t' a gravely ill man an' suddenly he's up an' aboot?
WHO CARES...?
HE SEEMS ALL WELL NOW.
Even more well than he is usually.
brrr
END MISSION 5

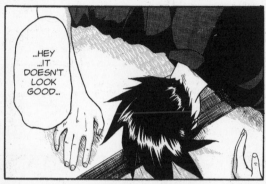

...HEY ...IT DOESN'T LOOK GOOD...

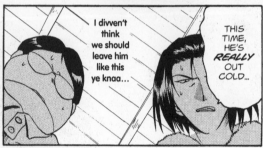

THIS TIME, HE'S *REALLY* OUT COLD...
I divven't think we should leave him like this ye knaa…

EXCEL SAGA

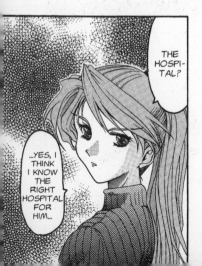

THE HOSPI-TAL?
...YES, I THINK I KNOW THE RIGHT HOSPITAL FOR HIM...

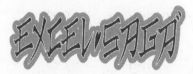

EXCEL SAGA

I HEARD YOU'RE IWATA'S BROTHER, SO I BROUGHT HIM -- BUT CAN YOU REALLY HELP HIM IN THIS STATE?
I'm not joking around here.
WELLLL, THIS IS THE SURGERY WING, AND HE'S NOT MY BROTHER, JUST A COUSIN... BUT HEY! THAT'S NOT IMPORTANT!
I'm glad you came.
ALL RIGHT THEN, GET HIM PREPPED FOR O.R.!
TO DO WHAT, DOCTOR...?

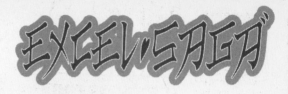

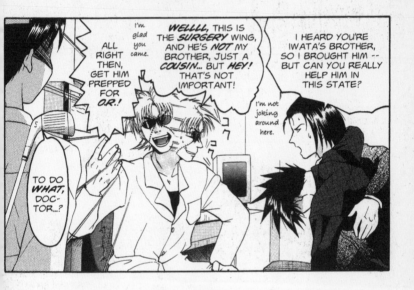

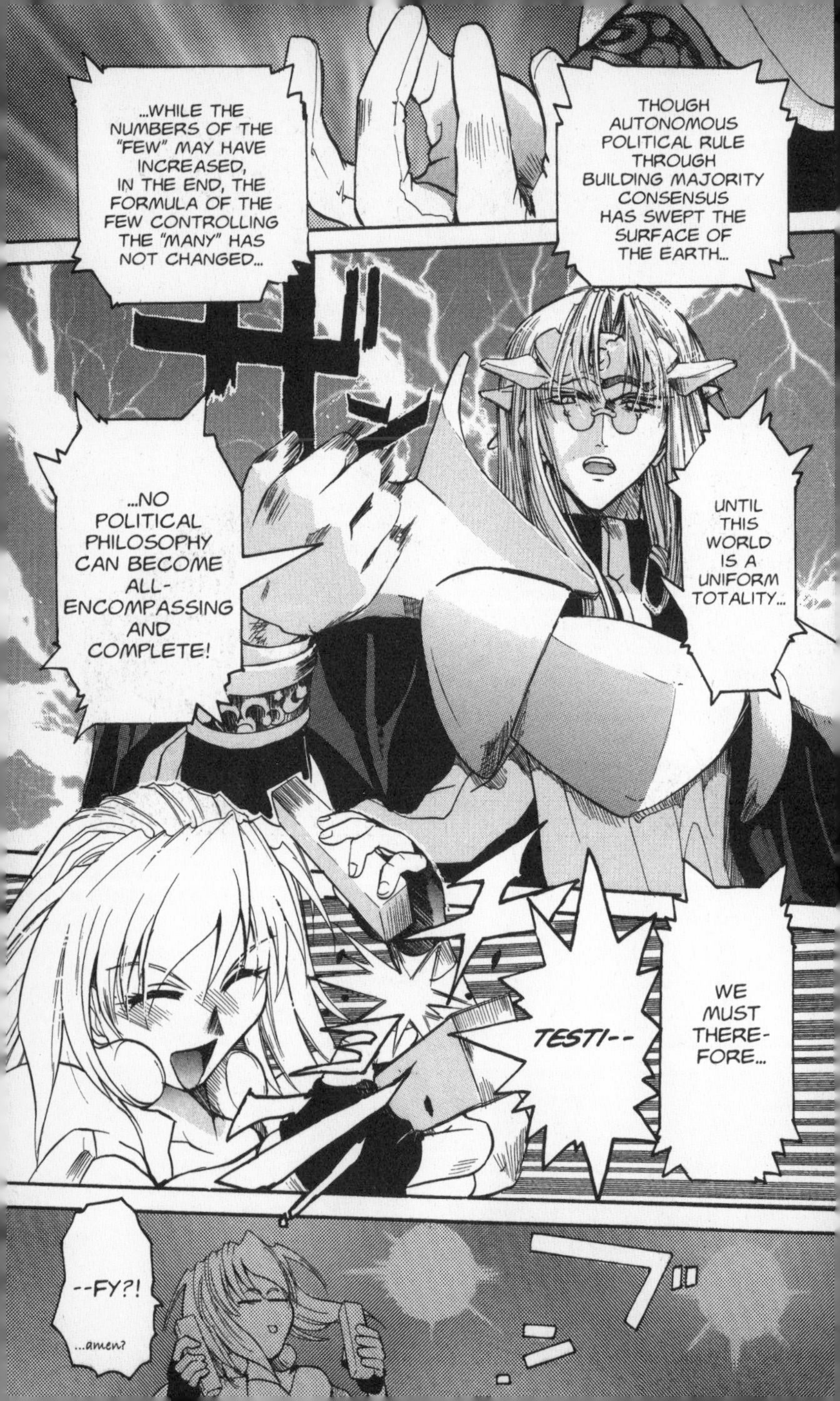
THOUGH AUTONOMOUS POLITICAL RULE THROUGH BUILDING MAJORITY CONSENSUS HAS SWEPT THE SURFACE OF THE EARTH...
...WHILE THE NUMBERS OF THE "FEW" MAY HAVE INCREASED, IN THE END, THE FORMULA OF THE FEW CONTROLLING THE "MANY" HAS NOT CHANGED...
UNTIL THIS WORLD IS A UNIFORM TOTALITY...
...NO POLITICAL PHILOSOPHY CAN BECOME ALL-ENCOMPASSING AND COMPLETE!
WE MUST THEREFORE...
TESTI--
--FY?!
...amen?

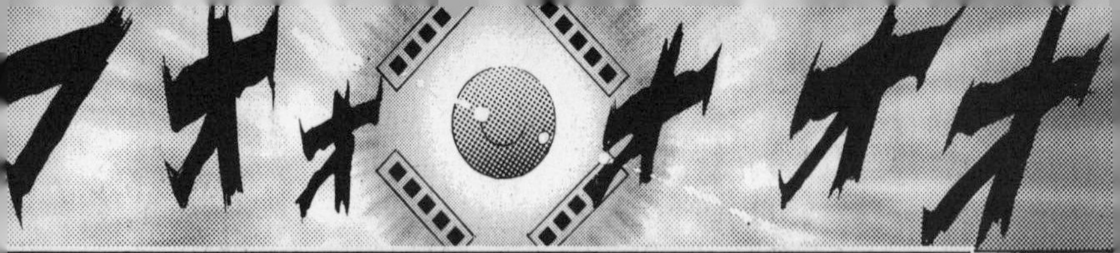
フオォオオオ

MISSION 6
HE WHO DOES NOT OPEN THE TREASURE BOX HIMSELF

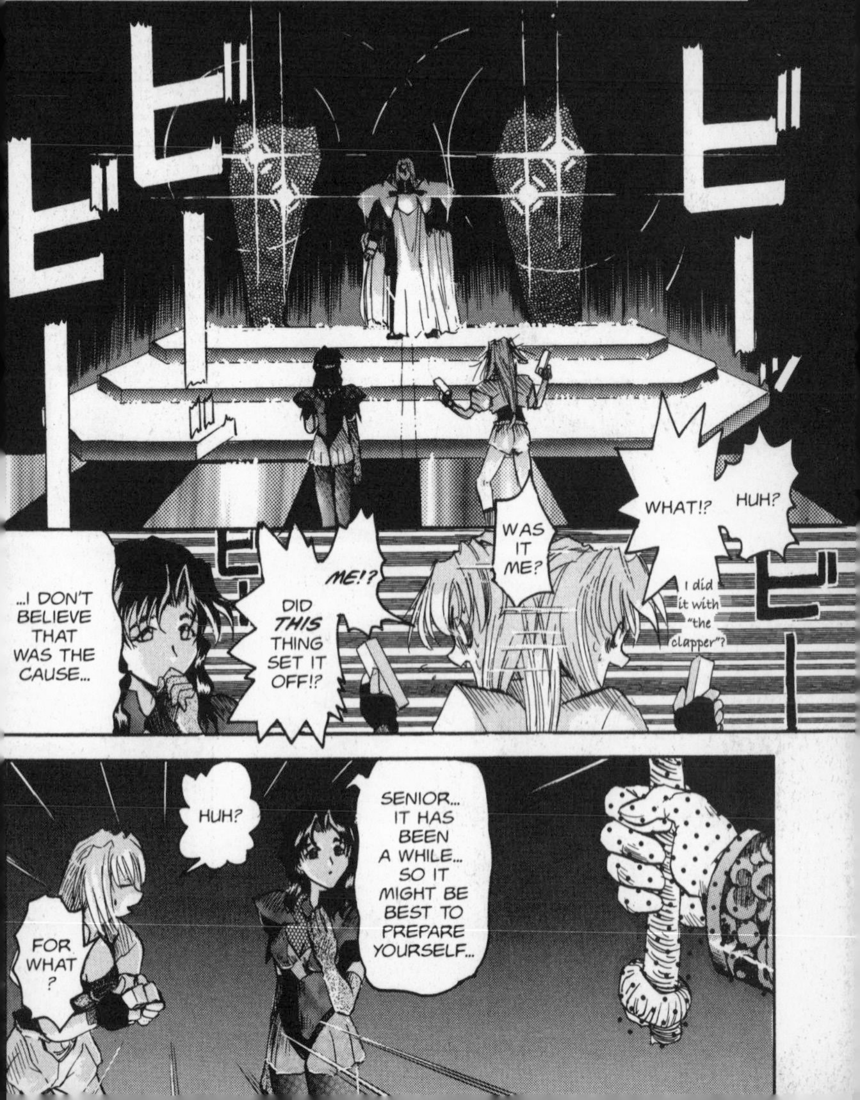
ビビー
ビビー
HUH?
WHAT!?
WAS IT ME?
I did it with "the clapper"?
ME!?
DID *THIS* THING SET IT OFF!?
...I DON'T BELIEVE THAT WAS THE CAUSE...
SENIOR... IT HAS BEEN A WHILE... SO IT MIGHT BE BEST TO PREPARE YOURSELF...
HUH?
FOR WHAT?

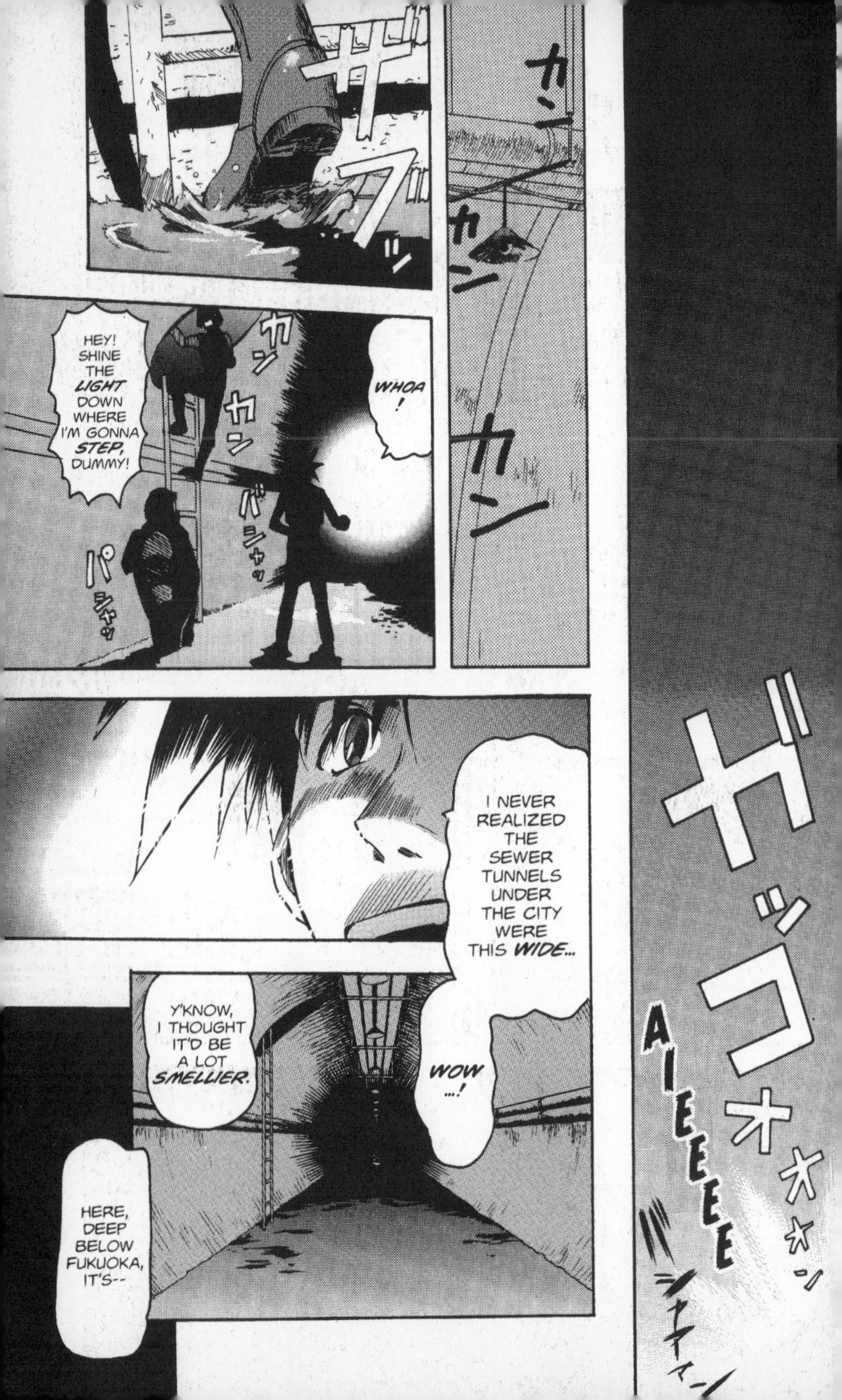
AIEEEE
WHOA!
HEY! SHINE THE LIGHT DOWN WHERE I'M GONNA STEP, DUMMY!
I NEVER REALIZED THE SEWER TUNNELS UNDER THE CITY WERE THIS WIDE...
WOW...!
Y'KNOW, I THOUGHT IT'D BE A LOT SMELLIER.
HERE, DEEP BELOW FUKUOKA, IT'S--

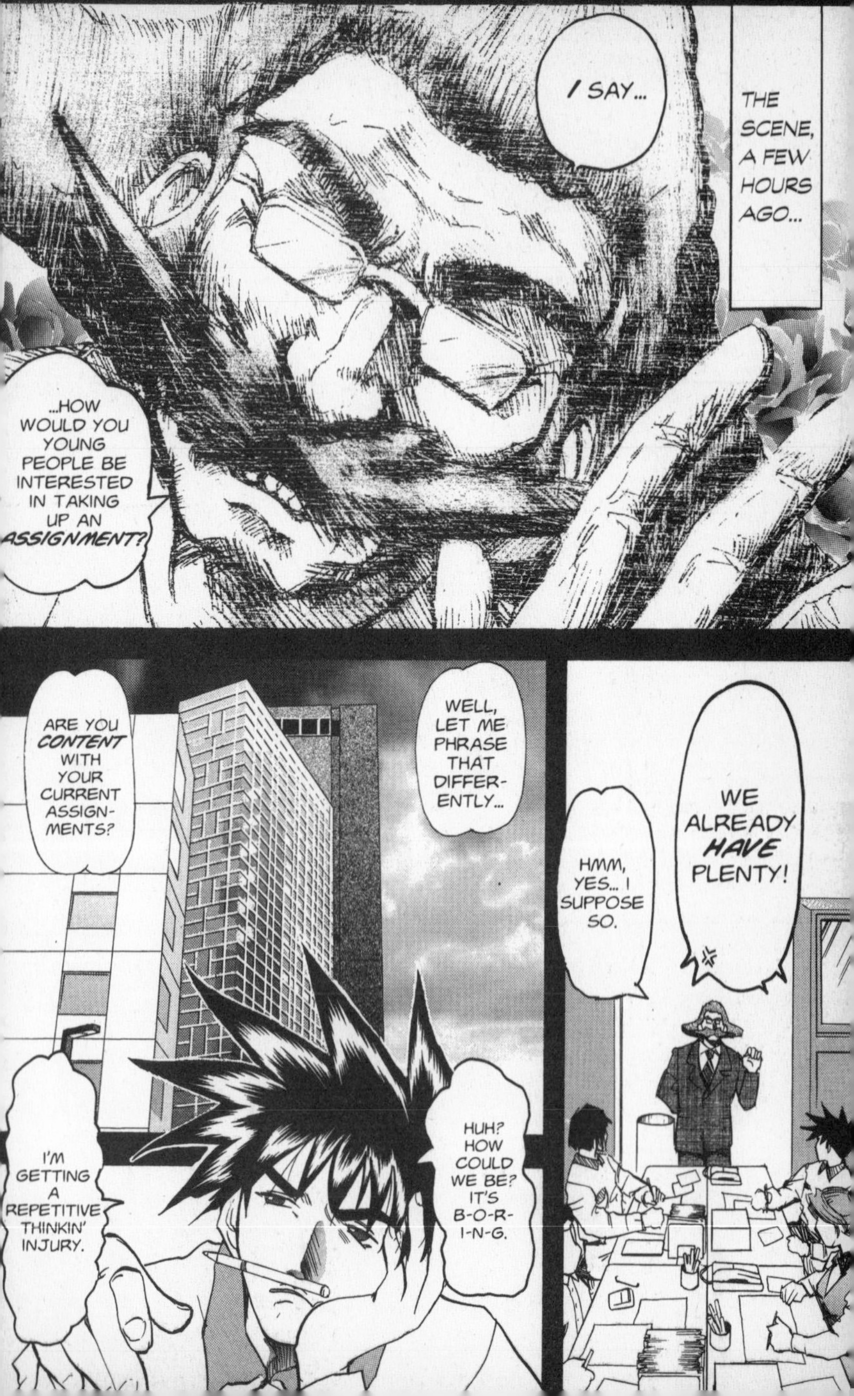
THE SCENE, A FEW HOURS AGO...
I SAY...
...HOW WOULD YOU YOUNG PEOPLE BE INTERESTED IN TAKING UP AN ASSIGNMENT?
WE ALREADY HAVE PLENTY!
HMM, YES... I SUPPOSE SO.
WELL, LET ME PHRASE THAT DIFFER-ENTLY...
ARE YOU CONTENT WITH YOUR CURRENT ASSIGN-MENTS?
HUH? HOW COULD WE BE? IT'S B-O-R-I-N-G.
I'M GETTING A REPETITIVE THINKIN' INJURY.

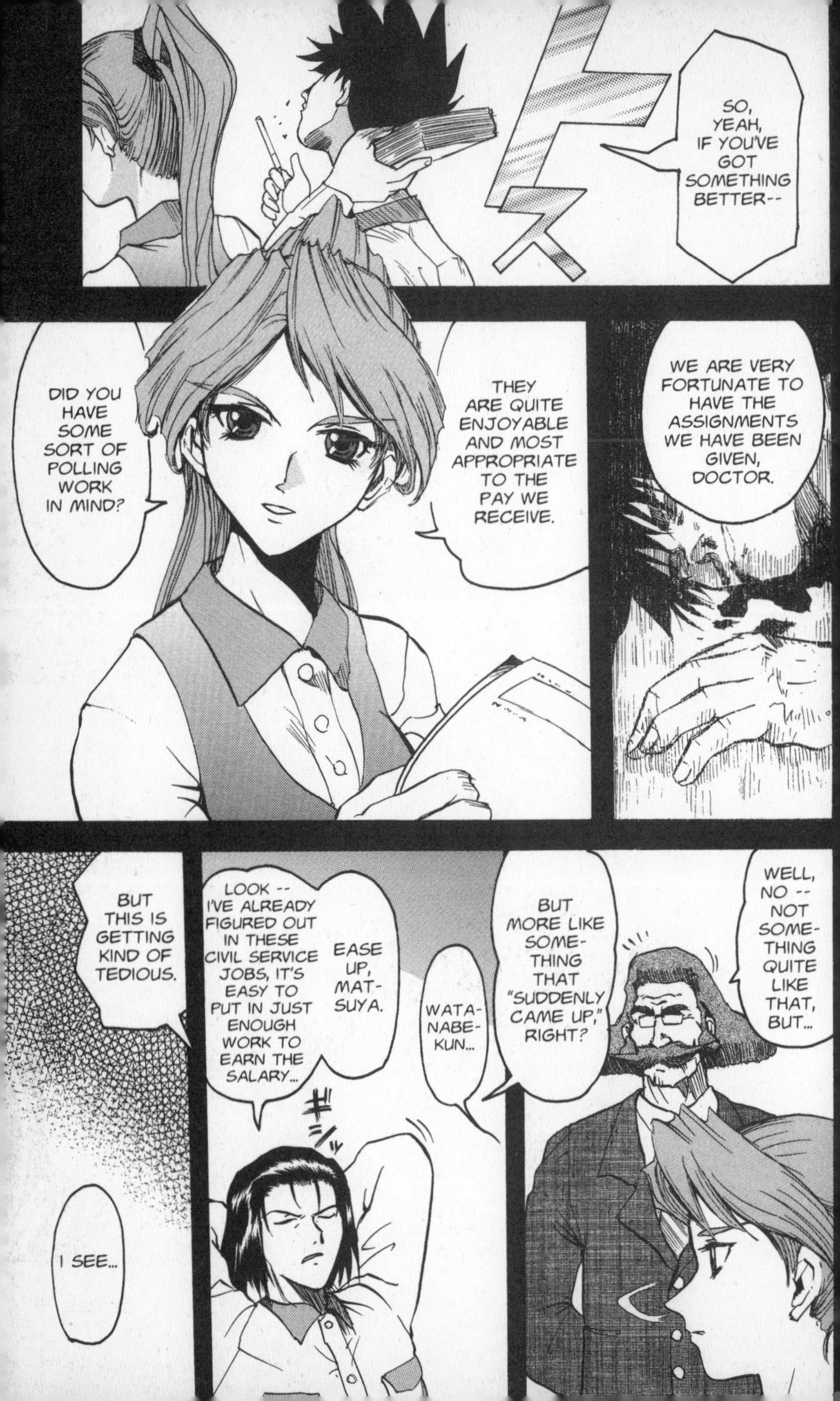
SO, YEAH, IF YOU'VE GOT SOMETHING BETTER--
WE ARE VERY FORTUNATE TO HAVE THE ASSIGNMENTS WE HAVE BEEN GIVEN, DOCTOR.
THEY ARE QUITE ENJOYABLE AND MOST APPROPRIATE TO THE PAY WE RECEIVE.
DID YOU HAVE SOME SORT OF POLLING WORK IN MIND?
WELL, NO -- NOT SOME-THING QUITE LIKE THAT, BUT...
BUT MORE LIKE SOME-THING THAT "SUDDENLY CAME UP," RIGHT?
WATA-NABE-KUN...
EASE UP, MAT-SUYA.
LOOK -- I'VE ALREADY FIGURED OUT IN THESE CIVIL SERVICE JOBS, IT'S EASY TO PUT IN JUST ENOUGH WORK TO EARN THE SALARY...
BUT THIS IS GETTING KIND OF TEDIOUS.
I SEE...

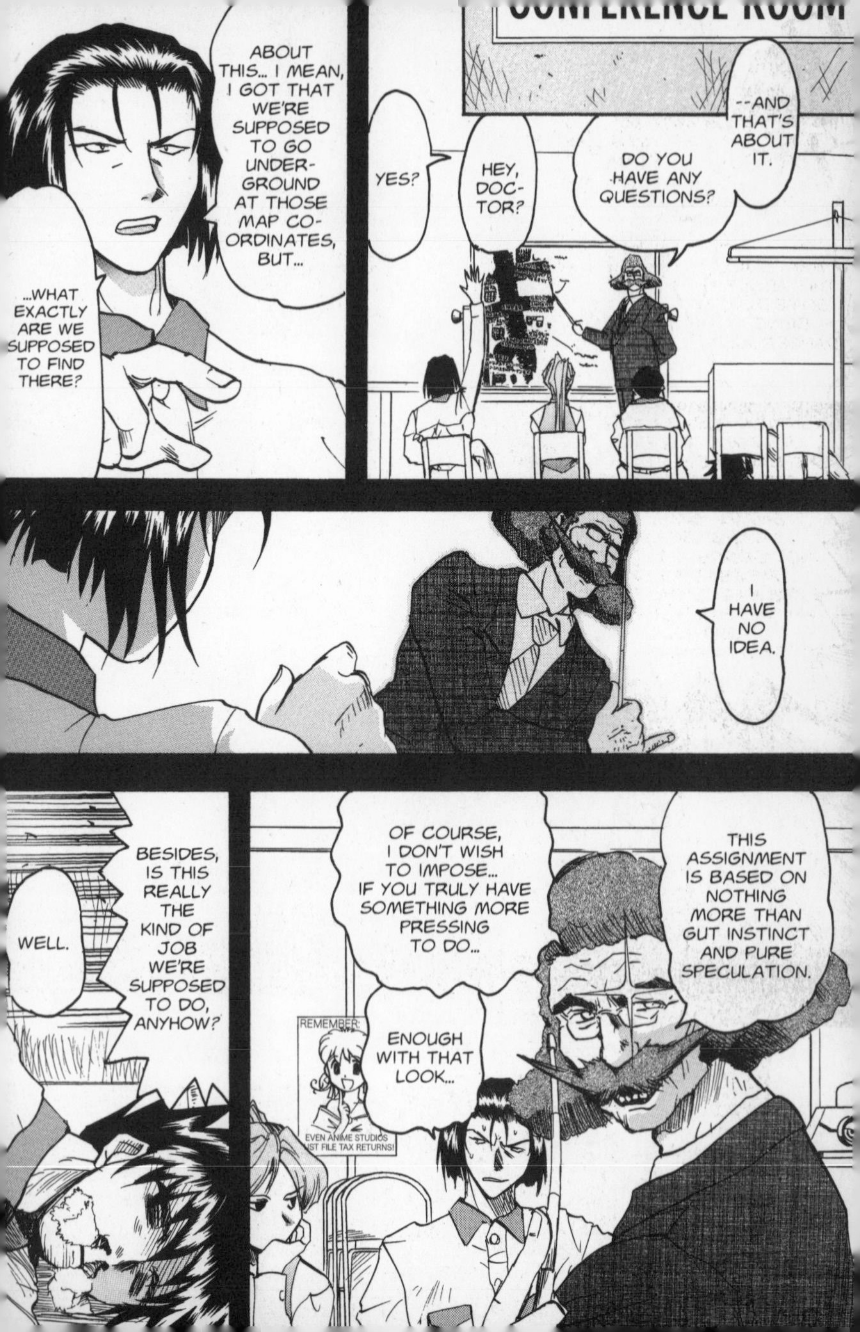
--AND THAT'S ABOUT IT.
DO YOU HAVE ANY QUESTIONS?
HEY, DOCTOR?
YES?
ABOUT THIS... I MEAN, I GOT THAT WE'RE SUPPOSED TO GO UNDER-GROUND AT THOSE MAP CO-ORDINATES, BUT...
...WHAT EXACTLY ARE WE SUPPOSED TO FIND THERE?
I HAVE NO IDEA.
THIS ASSIGNMENT IS BASED ON NOTHING MORE THAN GUT INSTINCT AND PURE SPECULATION.
OF COURSE, I DON'T WISH TO IMPOSE... IF YOU TRULY HAVE SOMETHING MORE PRESSING TO DO...
ENOUGH WITH THAT LOOK...
REMEMBER:
EVEN ANIME STUDIOS
BESIDES, IS THIS REALLY THE KIND OF JOB WE'RE SUPPOSED TO DO, ANYHOW?
WELL.

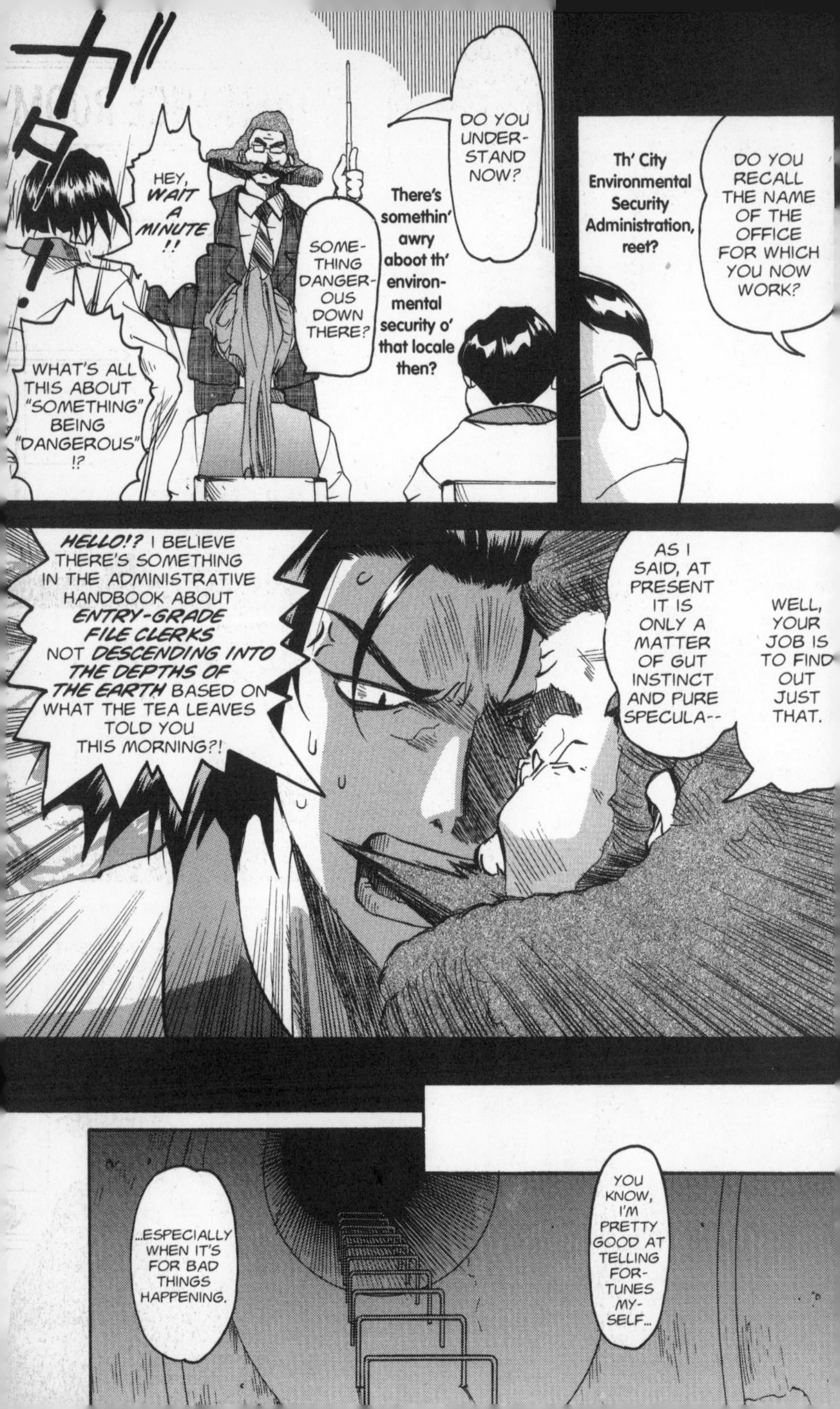
DO YOU RECALL THE NAME OF THE OFFICE FOR WHICH YOU NOW WORK?
Th' City Environmental Security Administration, reet?
DO YOU UNDERSTAND NOW?
There's somethin' awry aboot th' environmental security o' that locale then?
SOMETHING DANGEROUS DOWN THERE?
ガタッ!
HEY, WAIT A MINUTE!!
WHAT'S ALL THIS ABOUT "SOMETHING" BEING "DANGEROUS"!?
WELL, YOUR JOB IS TO FIND OUT JUST THAT.
AS I SAID, AT PRESENT IT IS ONLY A MATTER OF GUT INSTINCT AND PURE SPECULA--
HELLO!? I BELIEVE THERE'S SOMETHING IN THE ADMINISTRATIVE HANDBOOK ABOUT ENTRY-GRADE FILE CLERKS NOT DESCENDING INTO THE DEPTHS OF THE EARTH BASED ON WHAT THE TEA LEAVES TOLD YOU THIS MORNING?!
YOU KNOW, I'M PRETTY GOOD AT TELLING FORTUNES MYSELF...
...ESPECIALLY WHEN IT'S FOR BAD THINGS HAPPENING.

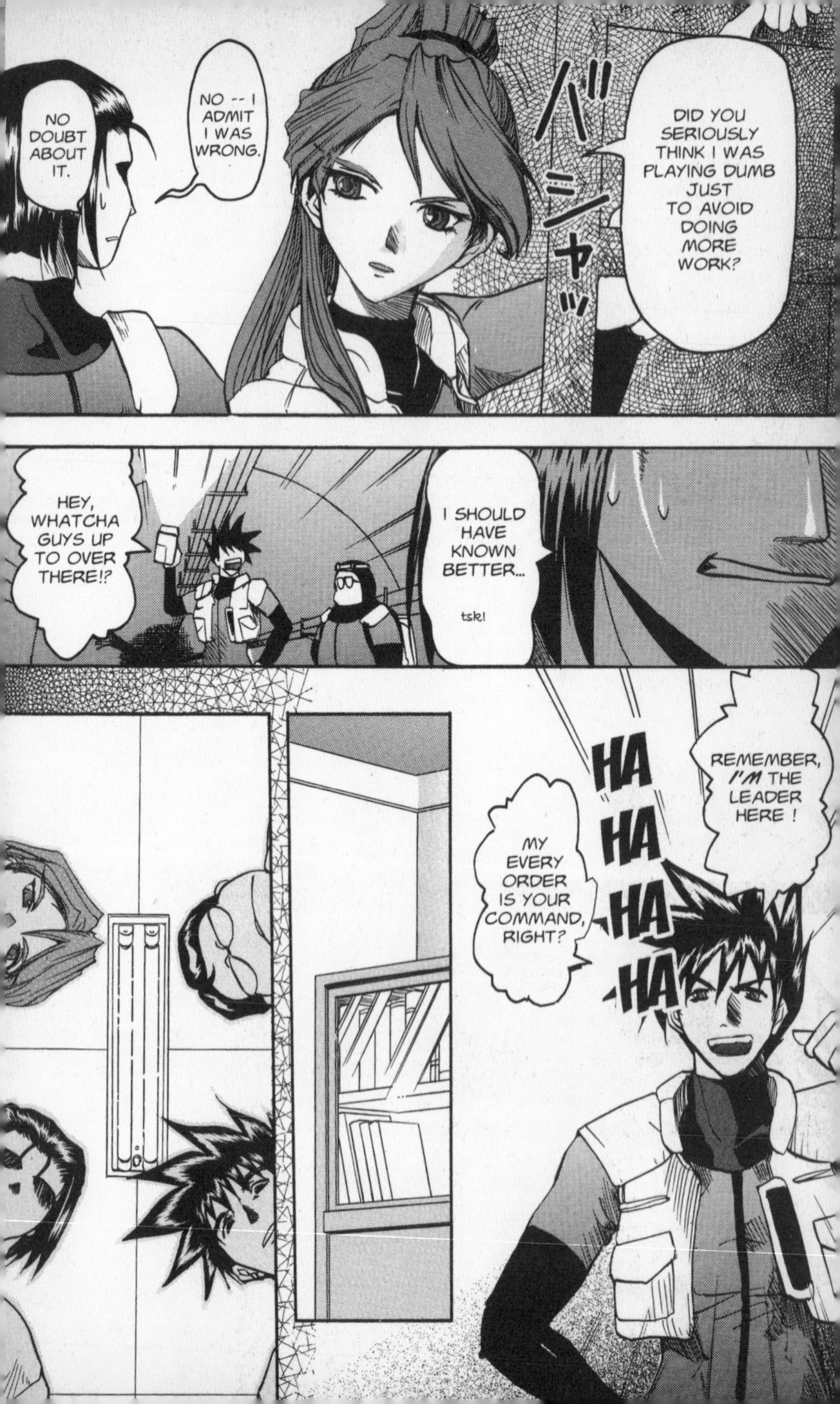
DID YOU SERIOUSLY THINK I WAS PLAYING DUMB JUST TO AVOID DOING MORE WORK?
NO -- I ADMIT I WAS WRONG.
NO DOUBT ABOUT IT.
I SHOULD HAVE KNOWN BETTER...
tsk!
HEY, WHATCHA GUYS UP TO OVER THERE!?
REMEMBER, *I'M* THE LEADER HERE !
HA HA HA HA
MY EVERY ORDER IS YOUR COMMAND, RIGHT?

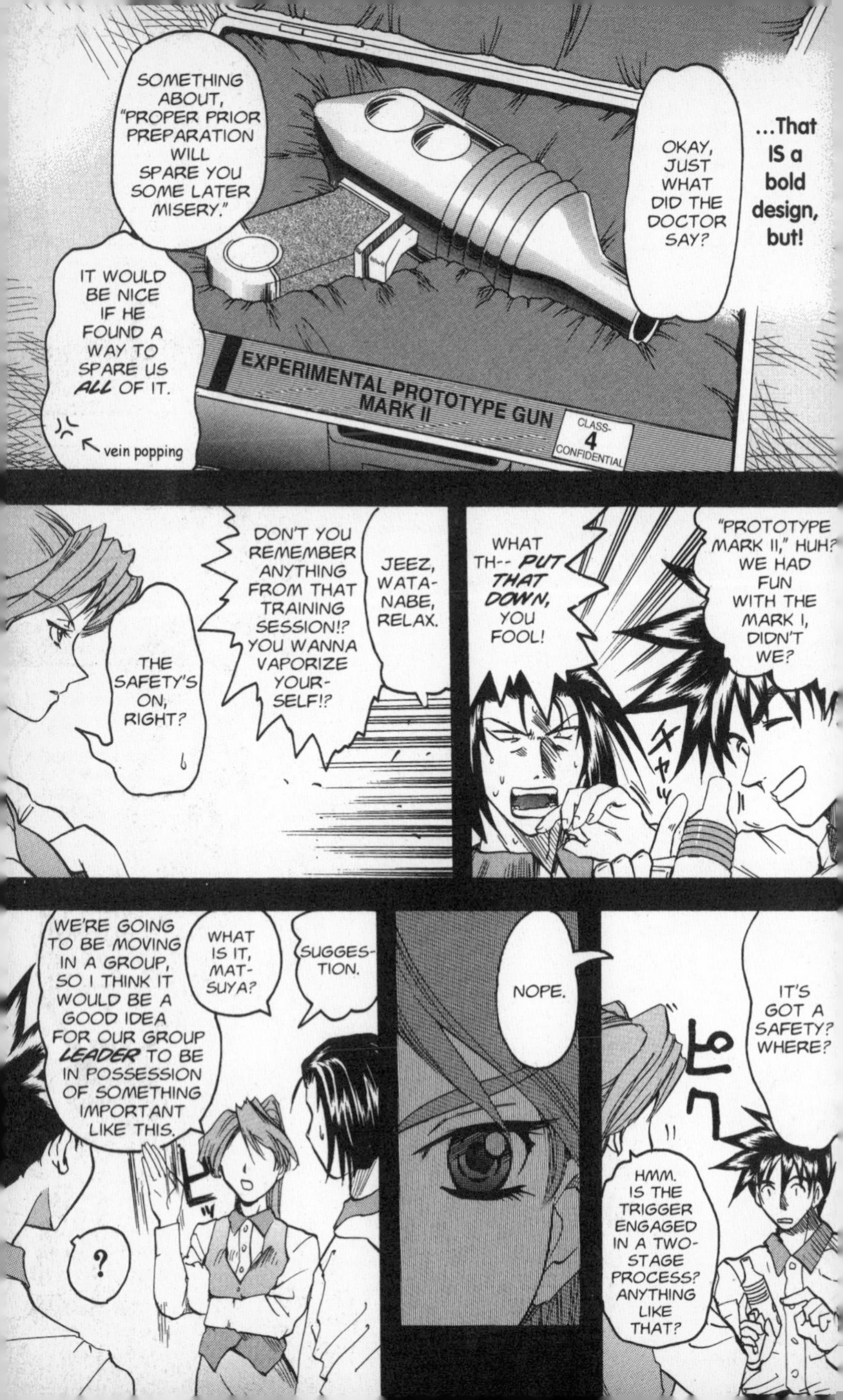
...That IS a bold design, but!
OKAY, JUST WHAT DID THE DOCTOR SAY?
SOMETHING ABOUT, "PROPER PRIOR PREPARATION WILL SPARE YOU SOME LATER MISERY."
IT WOULD BE NICE IF HE FOUND A WAY TO SPARE US ALL OF IT.
vein popping
EXPERIMENTAL PROTOTYPE GUN MARK II
CLASS-4 CONFIDENTIAL
"PROTOTYPE MARK II," HUH? WE HAD FUN WITH THE MARK I, DIDN'T WE?
WHAT TH-- PUT THAT DOWN, YOU FOOL!
JEEZ, WATA-NABE, RELAX.
DON'T YOU REMEMBER ANYTHING FROM THAT TRAINING SESSION!? YOU WANNA VAPORIZE YOUR-SELF!?
THE SAFETY'S ON, RIGHT?
IT'S GOT A SAFETY? WHERE?
HMM. IS THE TRIGGER ENGAGED IN A TWO-STAGE PROCESS? ANYTHING LIKE THAT?
NOPE.
SUGGES-TION.
WHAT IS IT, MAT-SUYA?
WE'RE GOING TO BE MOVING IN A GROUP, SO I THINK IT WOULD BE A GOOD IDEA FOR OUR GROUP LEADER TO BE IN POSSESSION OF SOMETHING IMPORTANT LIKE THIS.
?

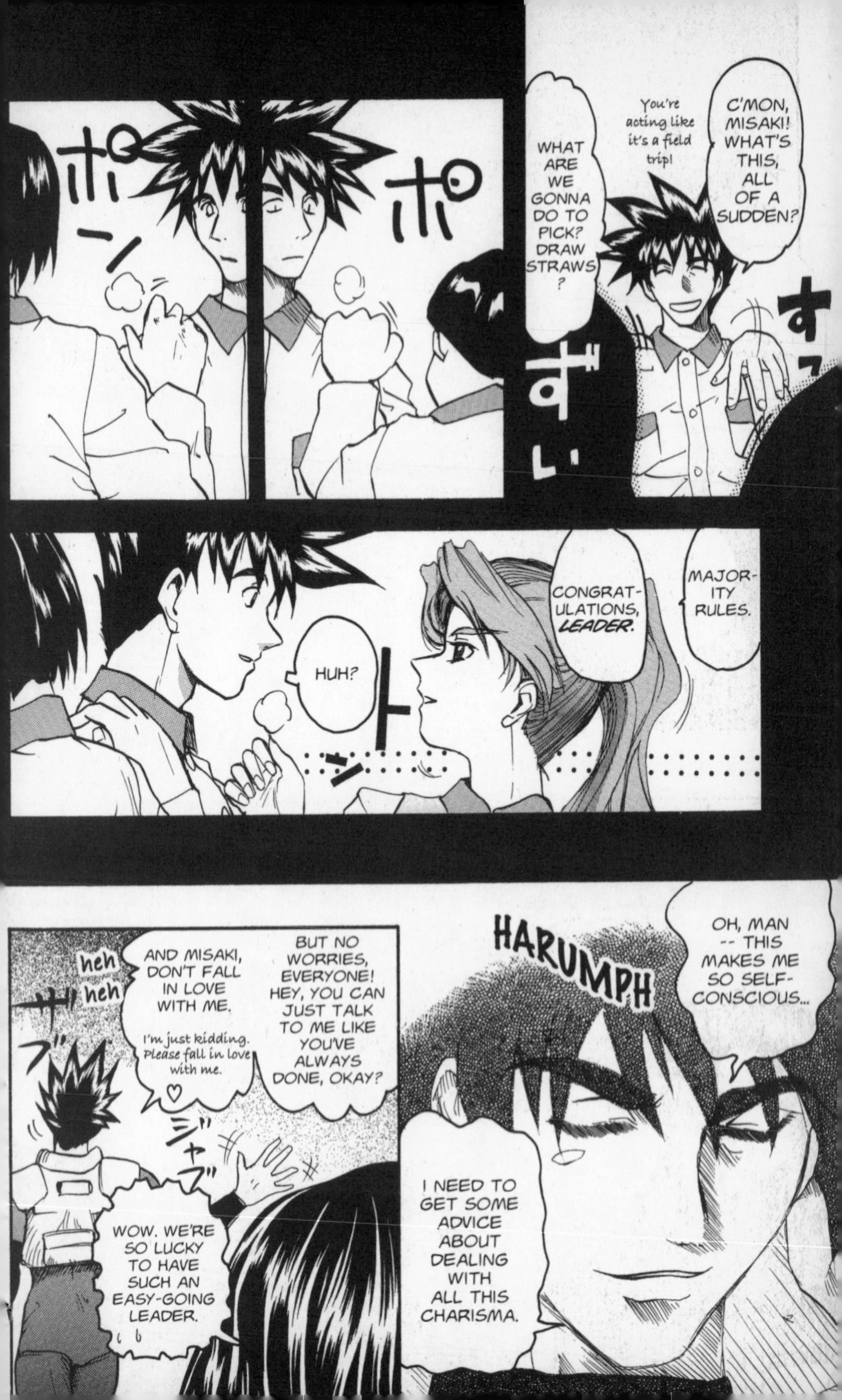
C'MON, MISAKI! WHAT'S THIS, ALL OF A SUDDEN?
You're acting like it's a field trip!
WHAT ARE WE GONNA DO TO PICK? DRAW STRAWS?
すっ
ずい
ポ
ポン
MAJORITY RULES.
CONGRATULATIONS, *LEADER*.
HUH?
ト
OH, MAN -- THIS MAKES ME SO SELF-CONSCIOUS...
HARUMPH
I NEED TO GET SOME ADVICE ABOUT DEALING WITH ALL THIS CHARISMA.
BUT NO WORRIES, EVERYONE! HEY, YOU CAN JUST TALK TO ME LIKE YOU'VE ALWAYS DONE, OKAY?
AND MISAKI, DON'T FALL IN LOVE WITH ME.
I'm just kidding. Please fall in love with me. ♡
heh heh
WOW. WE'RE SO LUCKY TO HAVE SUCH AN EASY-GOING LEADER.

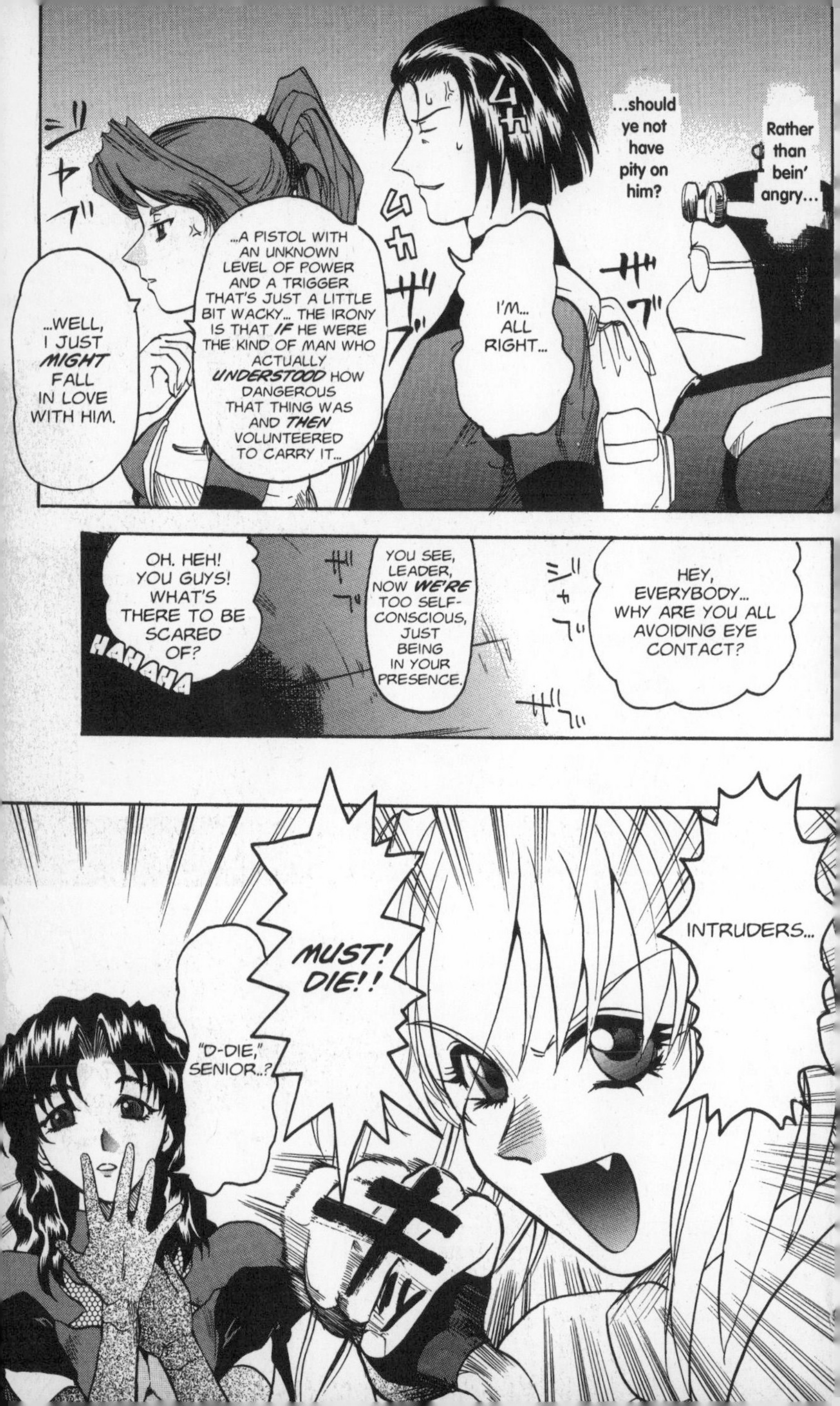
Rather than bein' angry…
…should ye not have pity on him?
I'M… ALL RIGHT…
…A PISTOL WITH AN UNKNOWN LEVEL OF POWER AND A TRIGGER THAT'S JUST A LITTLE BIT WACKY… THE IRONY IS THAT *IF* HE WERE THE KIND OF MAN WHO ACTUALLY *UNDERSTOOD* HOW DANGEROUS THAT THING WAS AND *THEN* VOLUNTEERED TO CARRY IT…
…WELL, I JUST *MIGHT* FALL IN LOVE WITH HIM.
HEY, EVERYBODY… WHY ARE YOU ALL AVOIDING EYE CONTACT?
YOU SEE, LEADER, NOW *WE'RE* TOO SELF-CONSCIOUS, JUST BEING IN YOUR PRESENCE.
OH. HEH! YOU GUYS! WHAT'S THERE TO BE SCARED OF?
HAHAHA
INTRUDERS…
MUST! DIE!!
"D-DIE," SENIOR..?

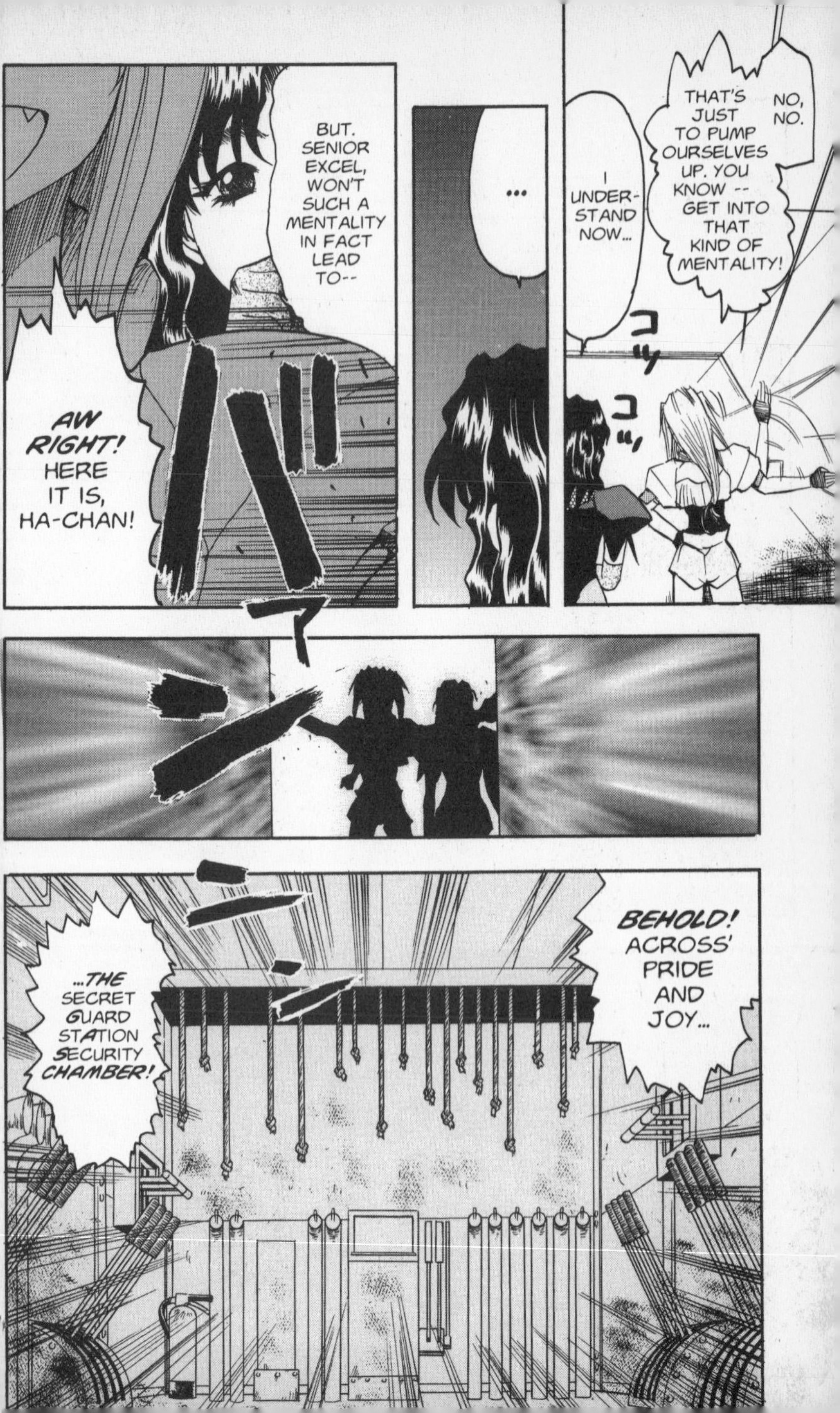
NO, NO.
THAT'S JUST TO PUMP OURSELVES UP. YOU KNOW -- GET INTO THAT KIND OF MENTALITY!
I UNDERSTAND NOW...
...
BUT. SENIOR EXCEL, WON'T SUCH A MENTALITY IN FACT LEAD TO--
AW RIGHT! HERE IT IS, HA-CHAN!
BEHOLD! ACROSS' PRIDE AND JOY...
...THE SECRET GUARD STATION SECURITY CHAMBER!

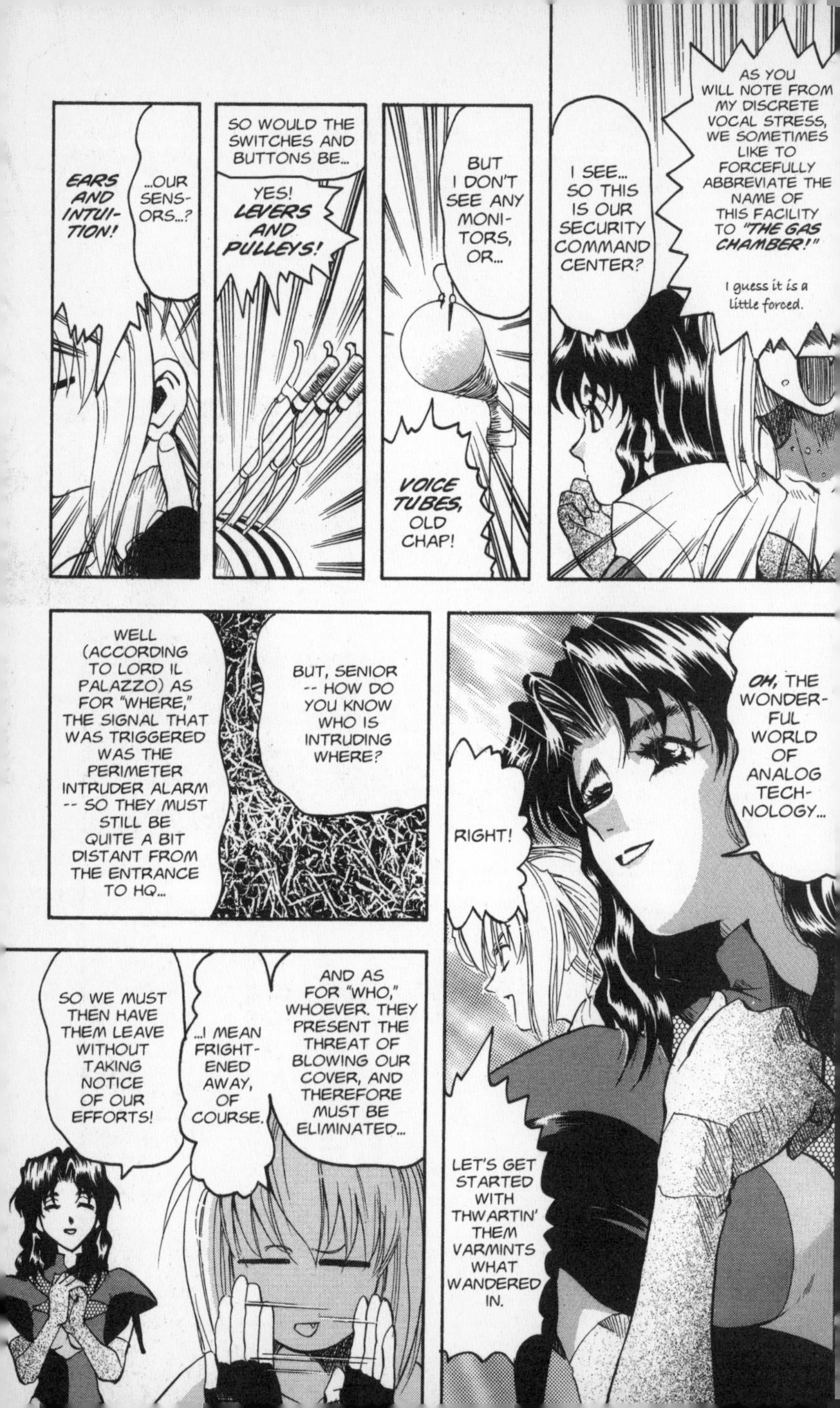

AS YOU WILL NOTE FROM MY DISCRETE VOCAL STRESS, WE SOMETIMES LIKE TO FORCEFULLY ABBREVIATE THE NAME OF THIS FACILITY TO ***"THE GAS CHAMBER!"***
I SEE... SO THIS IS OUR SECURITY COMMAND CENTER?
I guess it is a little forced.
BUT I DON'T SEE ANY MONITORS, OR...
VOICE TUBES, OLD CHAP!
SO WOULD THE SWITCHES AND BUTTONS BE...
YES! ***LEVERS AND PULLEYS!***
...OUR SENSORS...?
EARS AND INTUITION!
OH, THE WONDERFUL WORLD OF ANALOG TECHNOLOGY...
RIGHT!
LET'S GET STARTED WITH THWARTIN' THEM VARMINTS WHAT WANDERED IN.
BUT, SENIOR -- HOW DO YOU KNOW WHO IS INTRUDING WHERE?
WELL (ACCORDING TO LORD IL PALAZZO) AS FOR "WHERE," THE SIGNAL THAT WAS TRIGGERED WAS THE PERIMETER INTRUDER ALARM -- SO THEY MUST STILL BE QUITE A BIT DISTANT FROM THE ENTRANCE TO HQ...
AND AS FOR "WHO," WHOEVER. THEY PRESENT THE THREAT OF BLOWING OUR COVER, AND THEREFORE MUST BE ELIMINATED...
...I MEAN FRIGHTENED AWAY, OF COURSE.
SO WE MUST THEN HAVE THEM LEAVE WITHOUT TAKING NOTICE OF OUR EFFORTS!

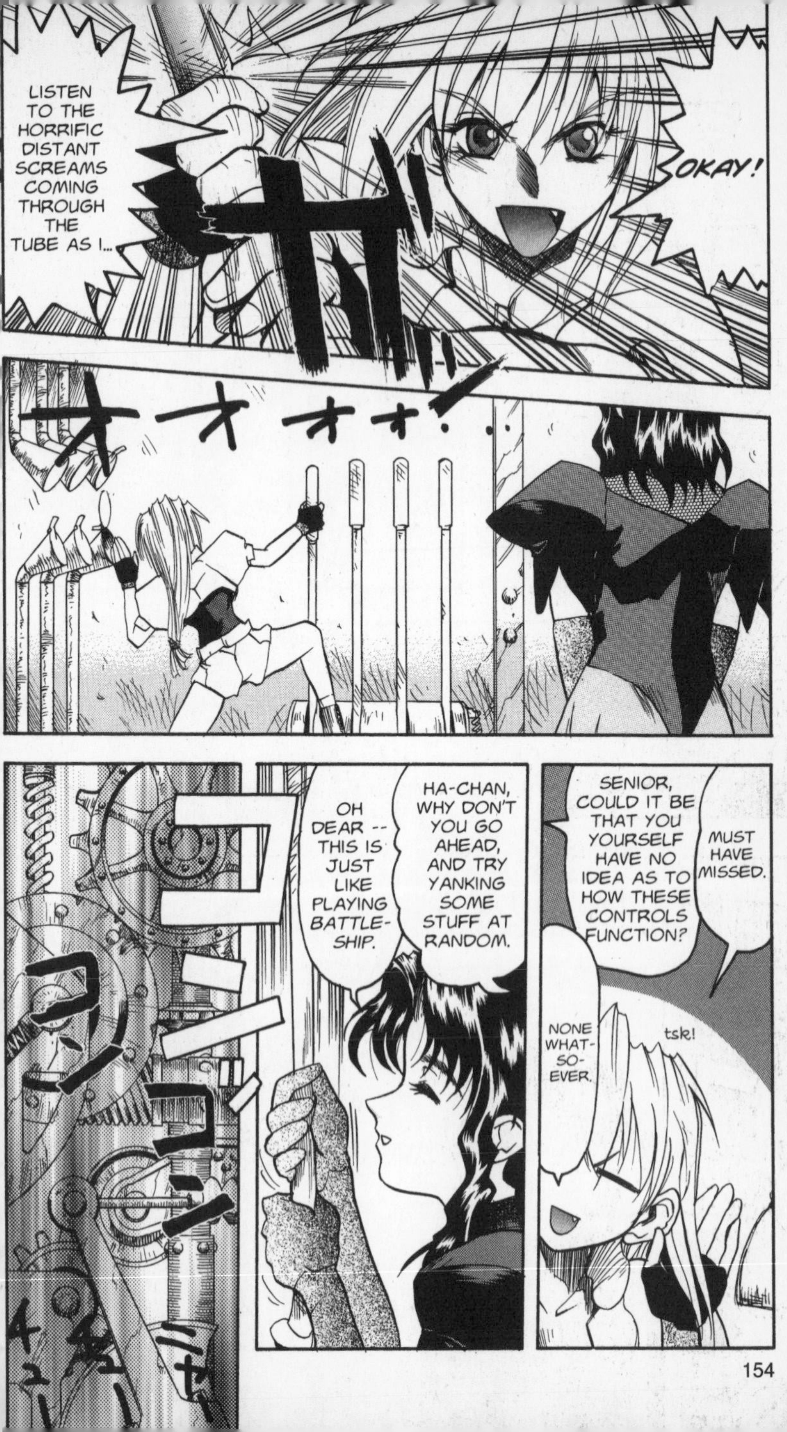
OKAY!
LISTEN TO THE HORRIFIC DISTANT SCREAMS COMING THROUGH THE TUBE AS I...
MUST HAVE MISSED.
SENIOR, COULD IT BE THAT YOU YOURSELF HAVE NO IDEA AS TO HOW THESE CONTROLS FUNCTION?
tsk!
NONE WHAT-SO-EVER.
HA-CHAN, WHY DON'T YOU GO AHEAD, AND TRY YANKING SOME STUFF AT RANDOM.
OH DEAR -- THIS IS JUST LIKE PLAYING BATTLE-SHIP.

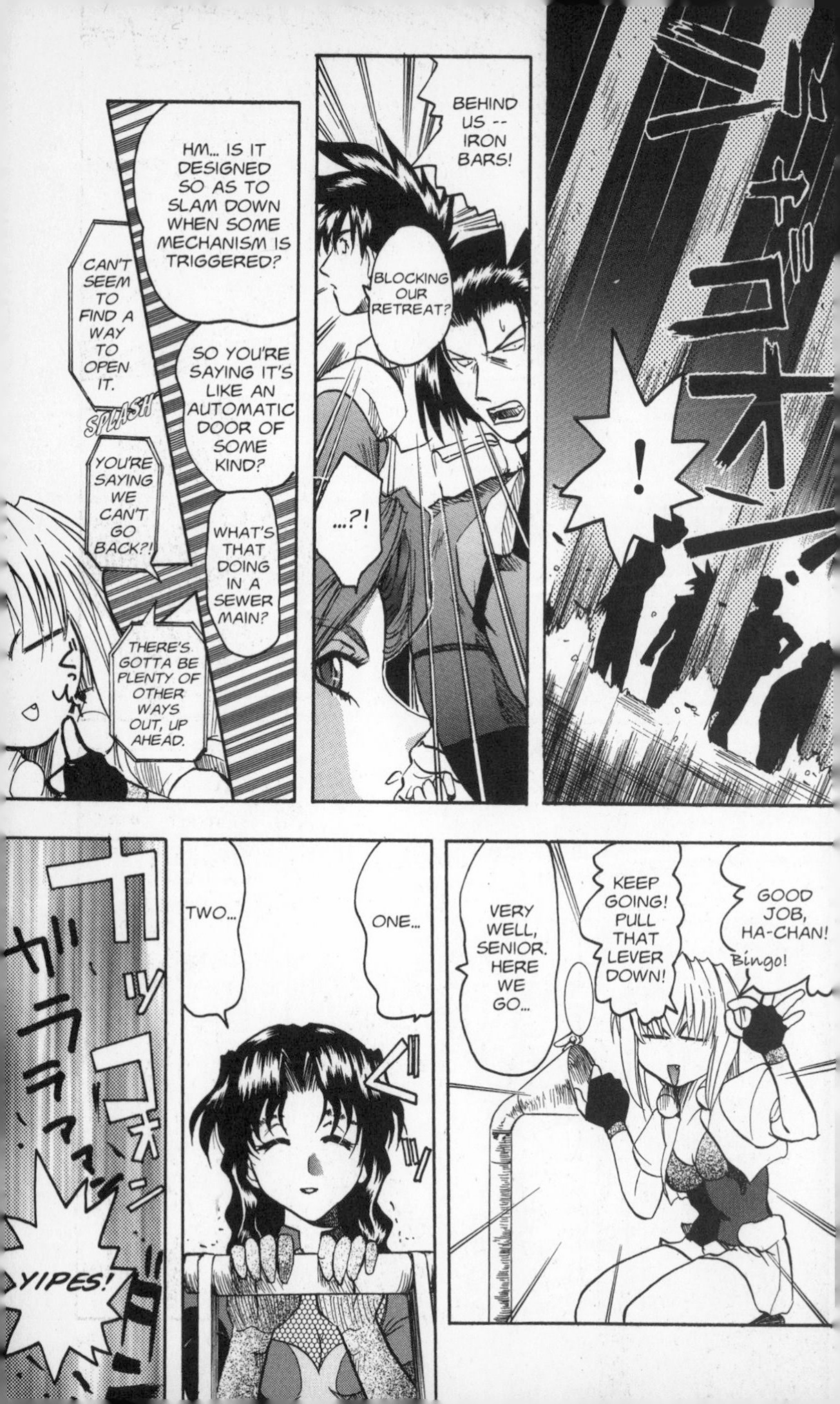
!
BEHIND US -- IRON BARS!
BLOCKING OUR RETREAT?
...?!
HM... IS IT DESIGNED SO AS TO SLAM DOWN WHEN SOME MECHANISM IS TRIGGERED?
CAN'T SEEM TO FIND A WAY TO OPEN IT.
SO YOU'RE SAYING IT'S LIKE AN AUTOMATIC DOOR OF SOME KIND?
SPLASH
YOU'RE SAYING WE CAN'T GO BACK?!
WHAT'S THAT DOING IN A SEWER MAIN?
THERE'S GOTTA BE PLENTY OF OTHER WAYS OUT, UP AHEAD.
GOOD JOB, HA-CHAN!
Bingo!
KEEP GOING! PULL THAT LEVER DOWN!
VERY WELL, SENIOR. HERE WE GO...
ONE...
TWO...
YIPES!

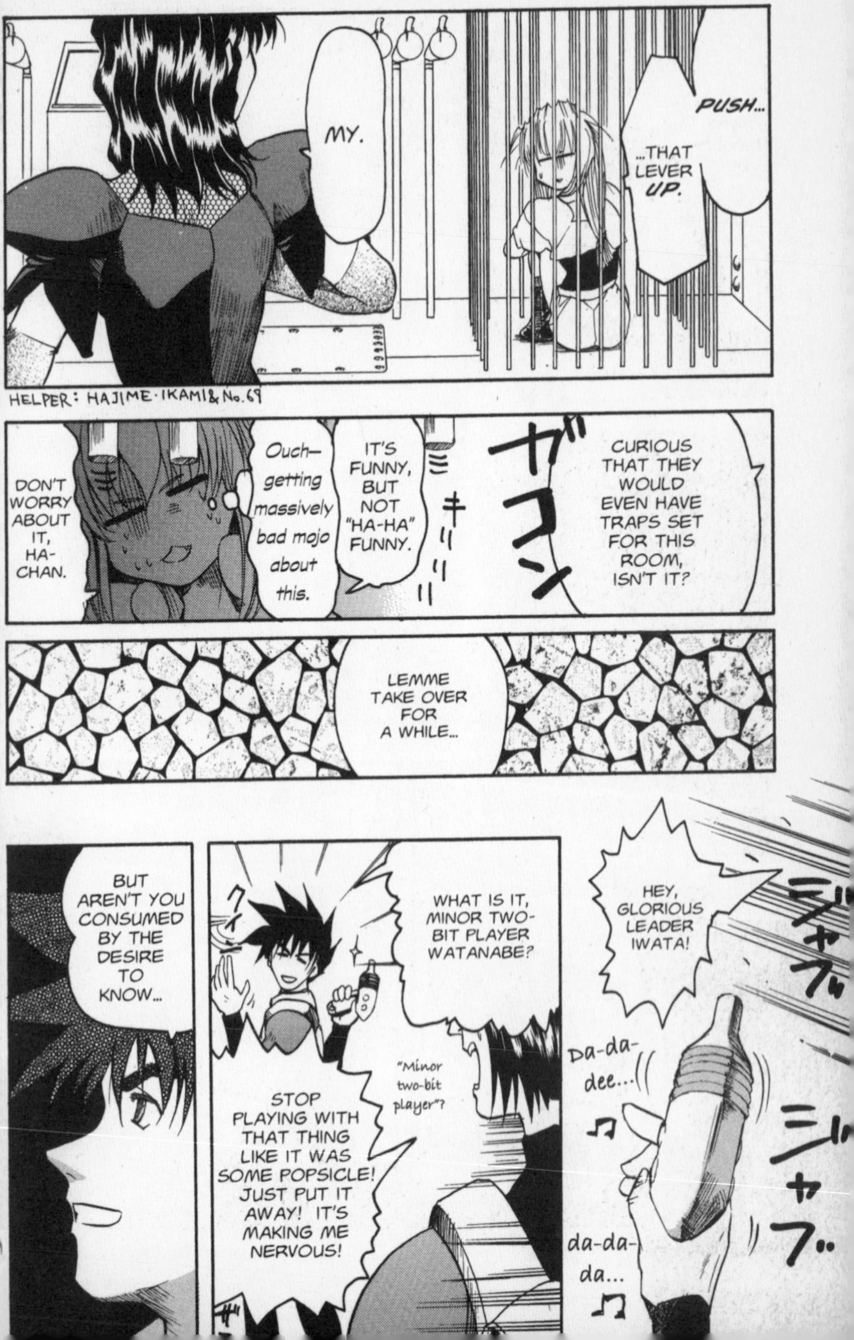
PUSH...
...THAT LEVER UP.
MY.
HELPER: HAJIME·IKAMI & No.69
CURIOUS THAT THEY WOULD EVEN HAVE TRAPS SET FOR THIS ROOM, ISN'T IT?
ガコン
キリリ
IT'S FUNNY, BUT NOT "HA-HA" FUNNY.
Ouch—getting massively bad mojo about this.
DON'T WORRY ABOUT IT, HA-CHAN.
LEMME TAKE OVER FOR A WHILE...
HEY, GLORIOUS LEADER IWATA!
ジャブ
ジャブ
Da-da-dee... ♫
da-da-da... ♫
WHAT IS IT, MINOR TWO-BIT PLAYER WATANABE?
クイ
"Minor two-bit player"?
STOP PLAYING WITH THAT THING LIKE IT WAS SOME POPSICLE! JUST PUT IT AWAY! IT'S MAKING ME NERVOUS!
BUT AREN'T YOU CONSUMED BY THE DESIRE TO KNOW...

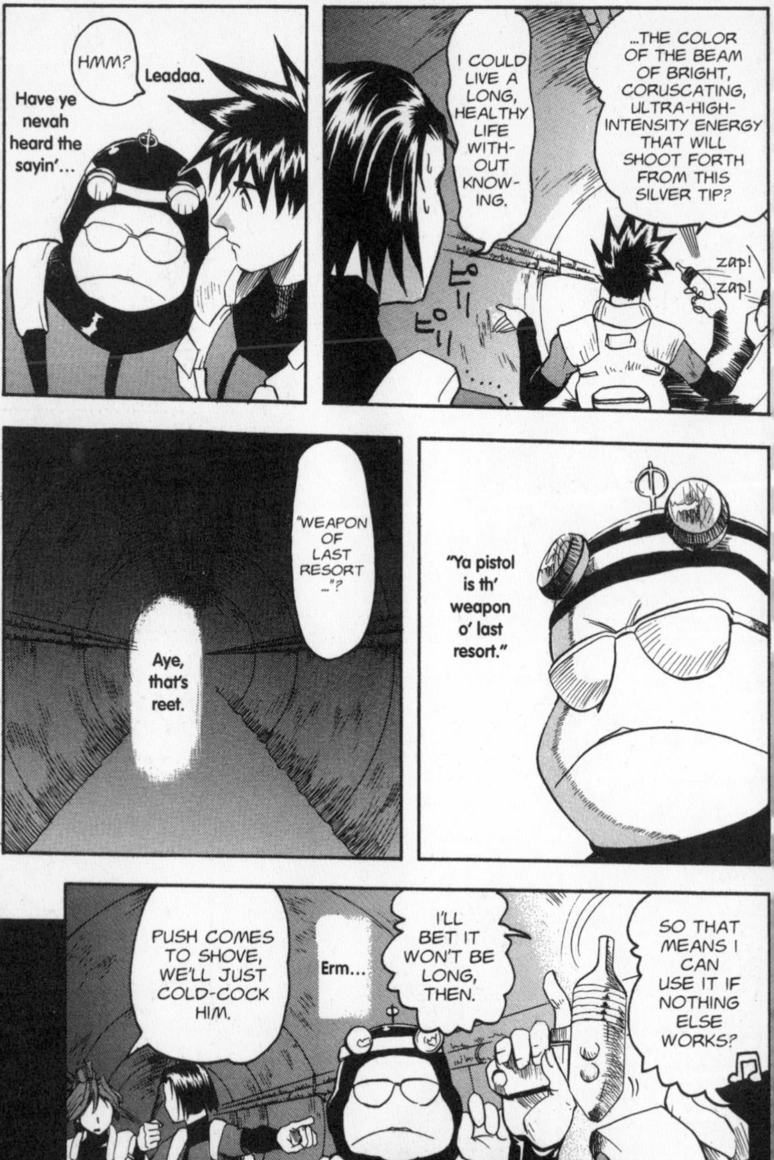
...THE COLOR OF THE BEAM OF BRIGHT, CORUSCATING, ULTRA-HIGH-INTENSITY ENERGY THAT WILL SHOOT FORTH FROM THIS SILVER TIP?
zap! zap!
I COULD LIVE A LONG, HEALTHY LIFE WITHOUT KNOWING.
Leadaa.
HMM?
Have ye nevah heard the sayin'...
"Ya pistol is th' weapon o' last resort."
"WEAPON OF LAST RESORT ..."?
Aye, that's reet.
SO THAT MEANS I CAN USE IT IF NOTHING ELSE WORKS?
I'LL BET IT WON'T BE LONG, THEN.
Erm...
PUSH COMES TO SHOVE, WE'LL JUST COLD-COCK HIM.

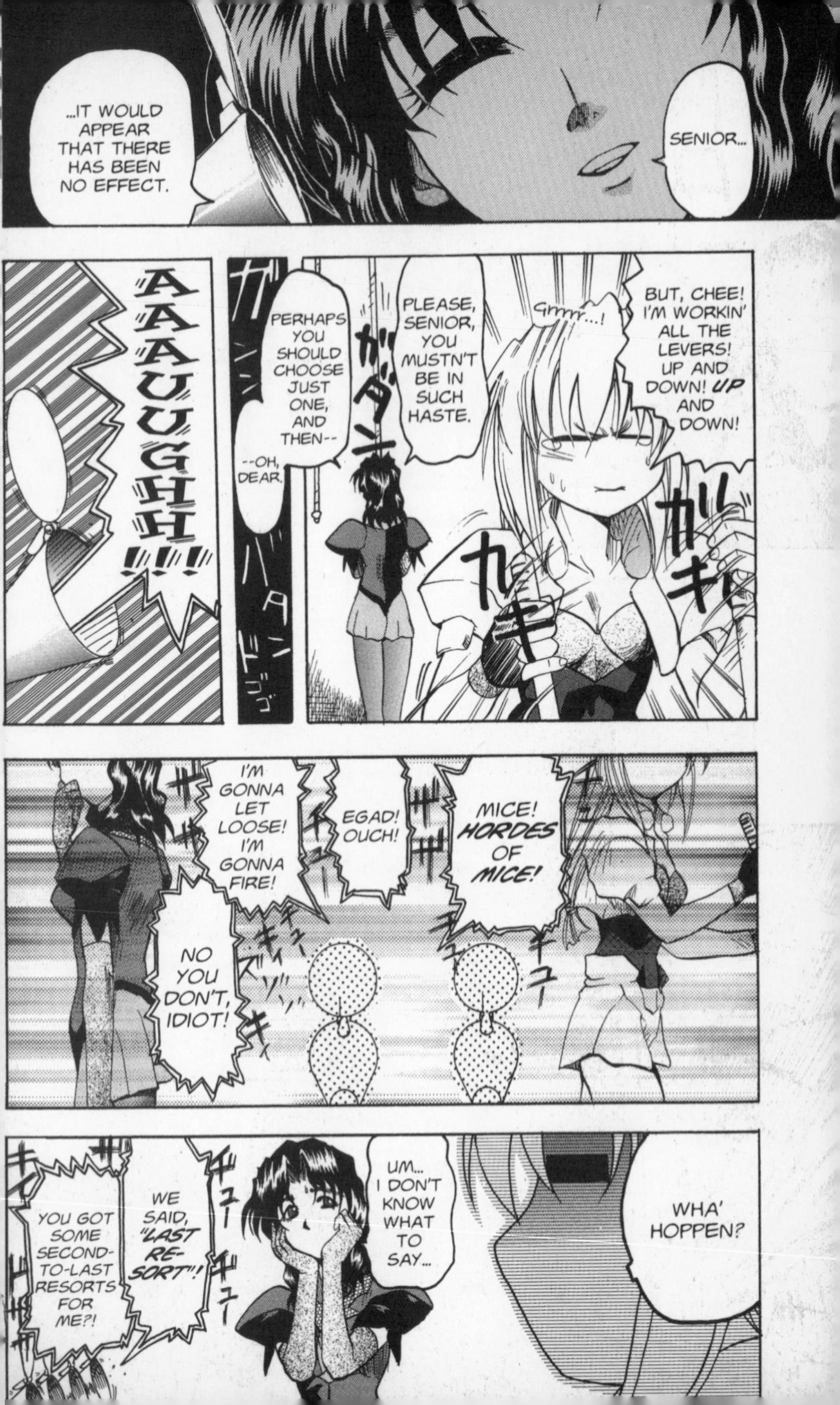
SENIOR...
...IT WOULD APPEAR THAT THERE HAS BEEN NO EFFECT.
Grrrr...!
BUT, CHEE! I'M WORKIN' ALL THE LEVERS! UP AND DOWN! UP AND DOWN!
PLEASE, SENIOR, YOU MUSTN'T BE IN SUCH HASTE.
PERHAPS YOU SHOULD CHOOSE JUST ONE, AND THEN--
--OH, DEAR.
AAAUUGHH!!!!
MICE! HORDES OF MICE!
EGAD! OUCH!
I'M GONNA LET LOOSE! I'M GONNA FIRE!
NO YOU DON'T, IDIOT!
WHA' HOPPEN?
UM... I DON'T KNOW WHAT TO SAY...
WE SAID, "LAST RESORT"!
YOU GOT SOME SECOND-TO-LAST RESORTS FOR ME?!

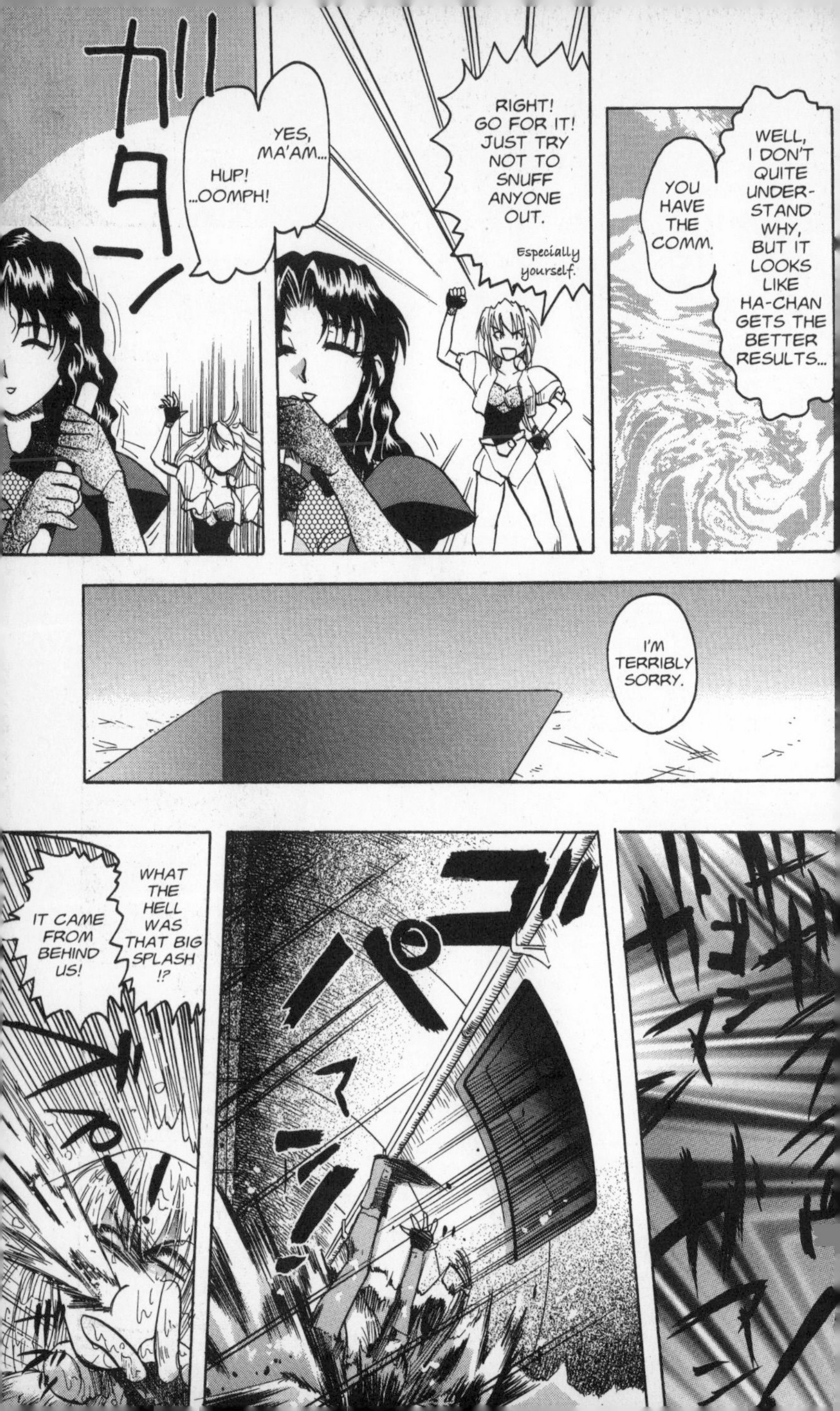
WELL, I DON'T QUITE UNDER-STAND WHY, BUT IT LOOKS LIKE HA-CHAN GETS THE BETTER RESULTS...
YOU HAVE THE COMM.
RIGHT! GO FOR IT! JUST TRY NOT TO SNUFF ANYONE OUT.
Especially yourself.
YES, MA'AM...
HUP! ...OOMPH!
I'M TERRIBLY SORRY.
WHAT THE HELL WAS THAT BIG SPLASH !?
IT CAME FROM BEHIND US!

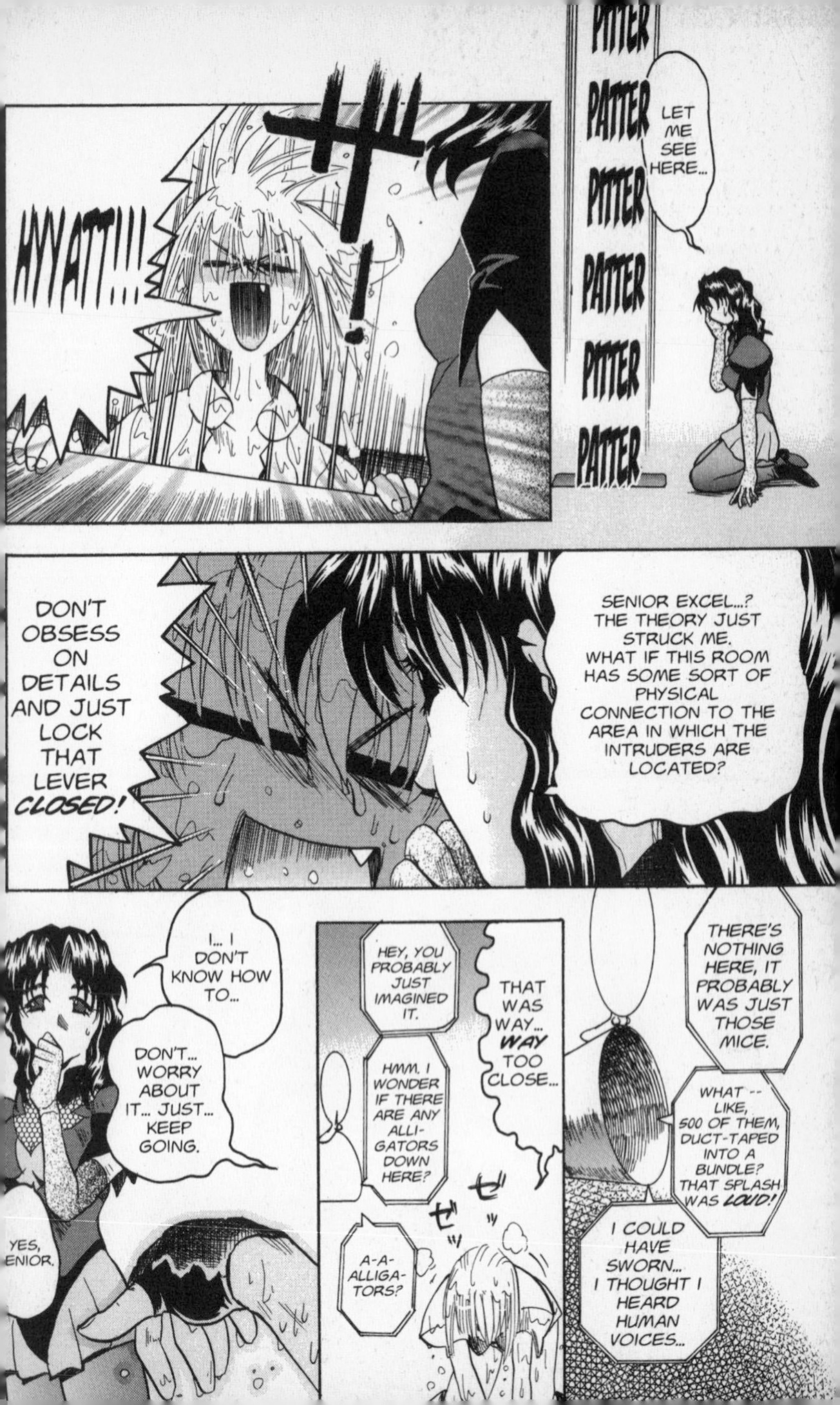

PITTER PATTER PITTER PATTER PITTER PATTER
LET ME SEE HERE...
HYYATT!!!
SENIOR EXCEL...? THE THEORY JUST STRUCK ME. WHAT IF THIS ROOM HAS SOME SORT OF PHYSICAL CONNECTION TO THE AREA IN WHICH THE INTRUDERS ARE LOCATED?
DON'T OBSESS ON DETAILS AND JUST LOCK THAT LEVER CLOSED!
THERE'S NOTHING HERE, IT PROBABLY WAS JUST THOSE MICE.
WHAT -- LIKE, 500 OF THEM, DUCT-TAPED INTO A BUNDLE? THAT SPLASH WAS LOUD!
I COULD HAVE SWORN... I THOUGHT I HEARD HUMAN VOICES...
HEY, YOU PROBABLY JUST IMAGINED IT.
THAT WAS WAY... WAY TOO CLOSE...
HMM, I WONDER IF THERE ARE ANY ALLI-GATORS DOWN HERE?
A-A-ALLIGA-TORS?
I... I DON'T KNOW HOW TO...
DON'T... WORRY ABOUT IT... JUST... KEEP GOING.
YES, ENIOR.

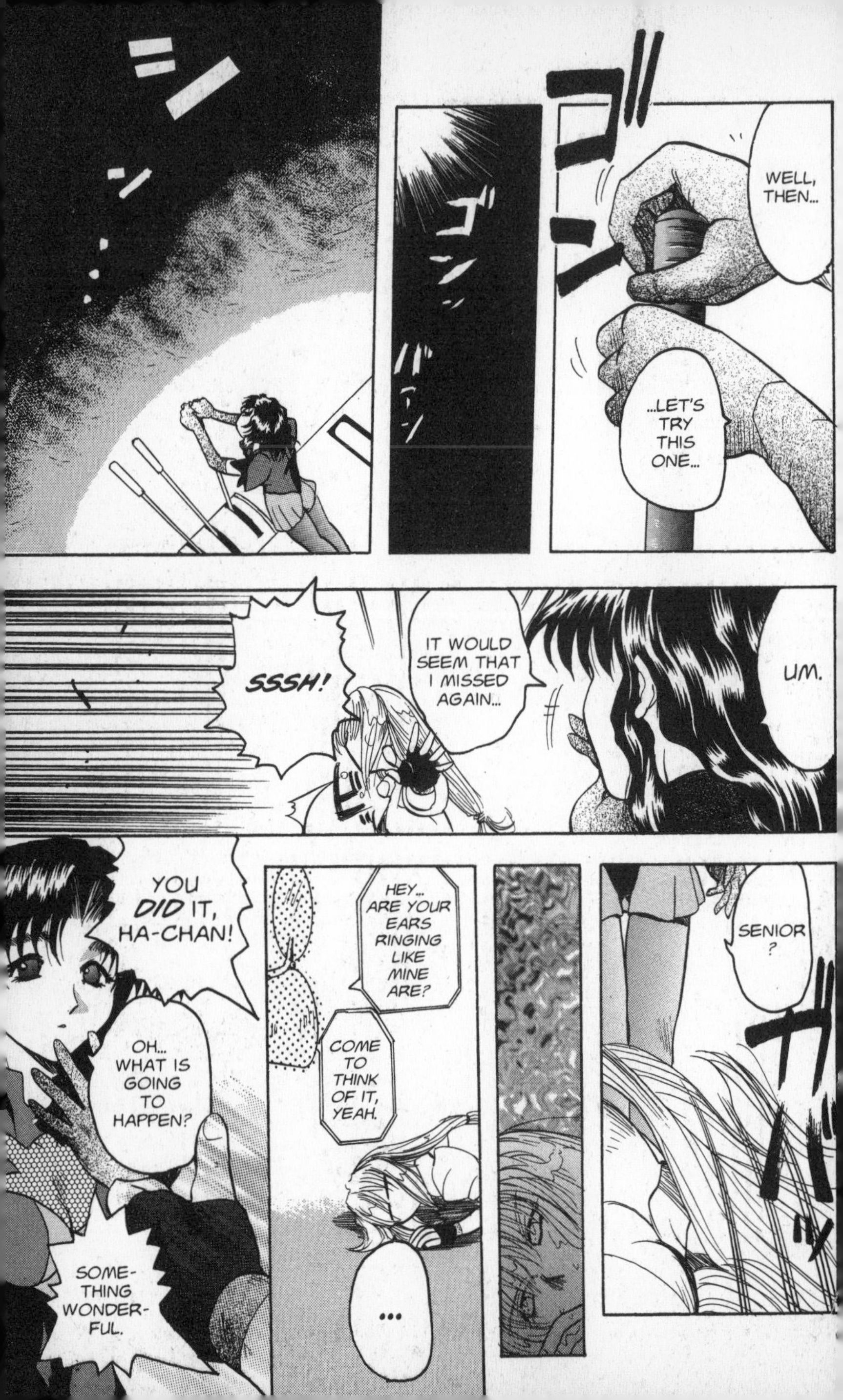
WELL, THEN...
...LET'S TRY THIS ONE...
UM.
IT WOULD SEEM THAT I MISSED AGAIN...
SSSH!
SENIOR?
HEY... ARE YOUR EARS RINGING LIKE MINE ARE?
COME TO THINK OF IT, YEAH.
...
YOU *DID* IT, HA-CHAN!
OH... WHAT IS GOING TO HAPPEN?
SOMETHING WONDERFUL.

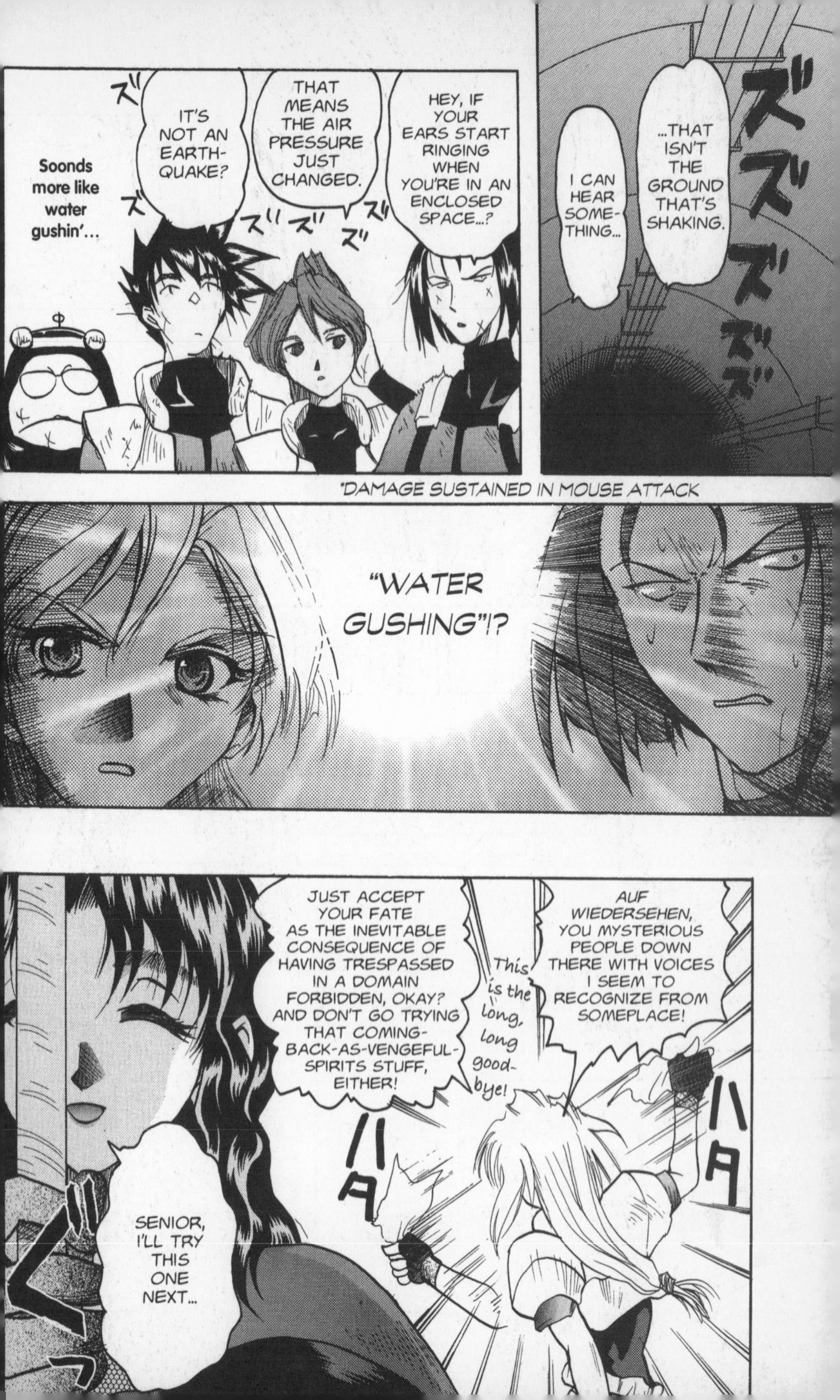

ズズズズズ
...THAT ISN'T THE GROUND THAT'S SHAKING.
I CAN HEAR SOMETHING...
HEY, IF YOUR EARS START RINGING WHEN YOU'RE IN AN ENCLOSED SPACE...?
THAT MEANS THE AIR PRESSURE JUST CHANGED.
IT'S NOT AN EARTHQUAKE?
Soonds more like water gushin'...
*DAMAGE SUSTAINED IN MOUSE ATTACK
"WATER GUSHING"!?
AUF WIEDERSEHEN, YOU MYSTERIOUS PEOPLE DOWN THERE WITH VOICES I SEEM TO RECOGNIZE FROM SOMEPLACE!
This is the long, long good-bye!
JUST ACCEPT YOUR FATE AS THE INEVITABLE CONSEQUENCE OF HAVING TRESPASSED IN A DOMAIN FORBIDDEN, OKAY? AND DON'T GO TRYING THAT COMING-BACK-AS-VENGEFUL-SPIRITS STUFF, EITHER!
SENIOR, I'LL TRY THIS ONE NEXT...

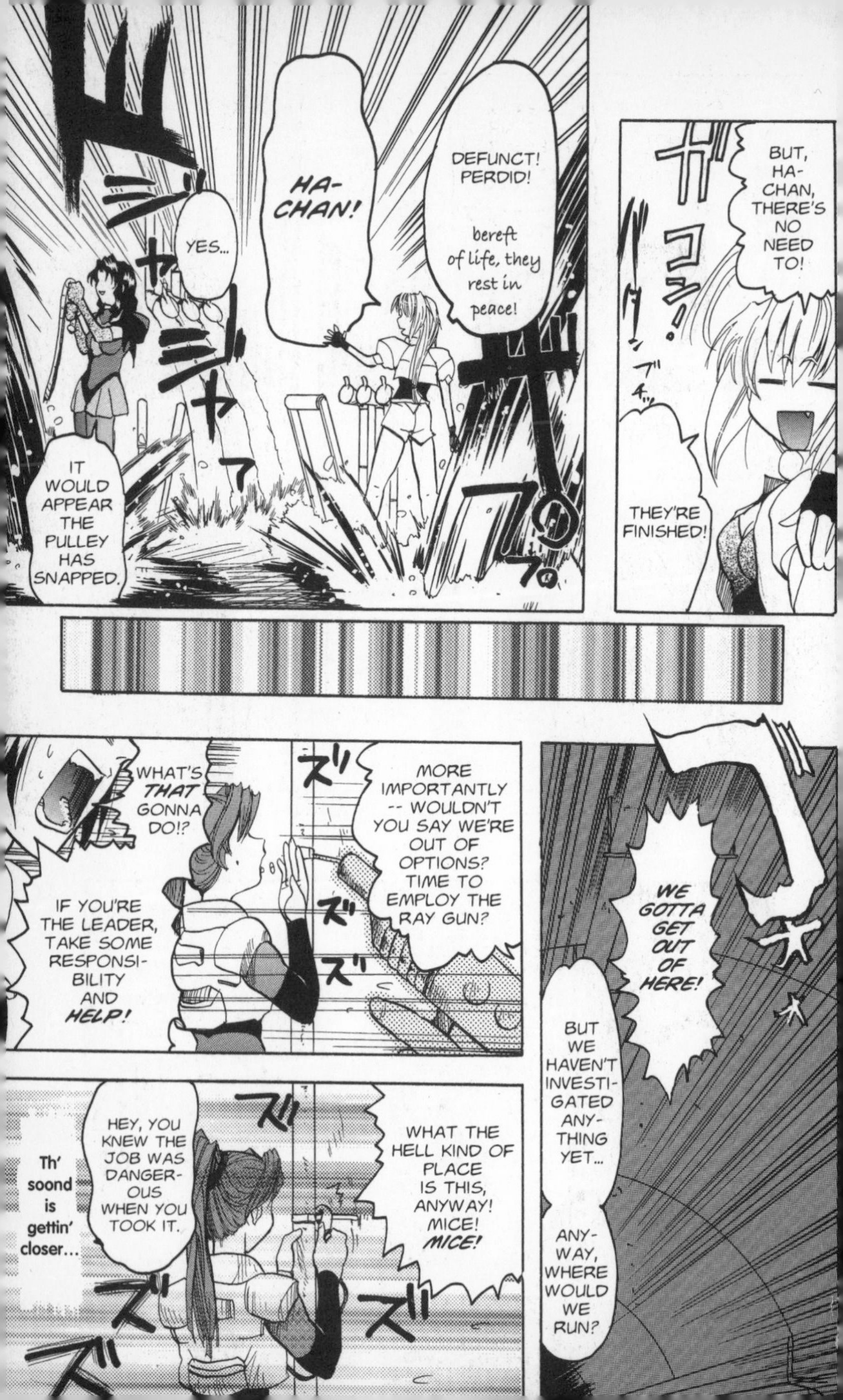
BUT, HA-CHAN, THERE'S NO NEED TO!
THEY'RE FINISHED!
DEFUNCT! PERDID!
bereft of life, they rest in peace!
HA-CHAN!
YES...
IT WOULD APPEAR THE PULLEY HAS SNAPPED.
WE GOTTA GET OUT OF HERE!
BUT WE HAVEN'T INVESTIGATED ANYTHING YET...
ANYWAY, WHERE WOULD WE RUN?
MORE IMPORTANTLY -- WOULDN'T YOU SAY WE'RE OUT OF OPTIONS? TIME TO EMPLOY THE RAY GUN?
WHAT'S THAT GONNA DO!?
IF YOU'RE THE LEADER, TAKE SOME RESPONSIBILITY AND HELP!
WHAT THE HELL KIND OF PLACE IS THIS, ANYWAY! MICE! MICE!
HEY, YOU KNEW THE JOB WAS DANGEROUS WHEN YOU TOOK IT.
Th' soond is gettin' closer...

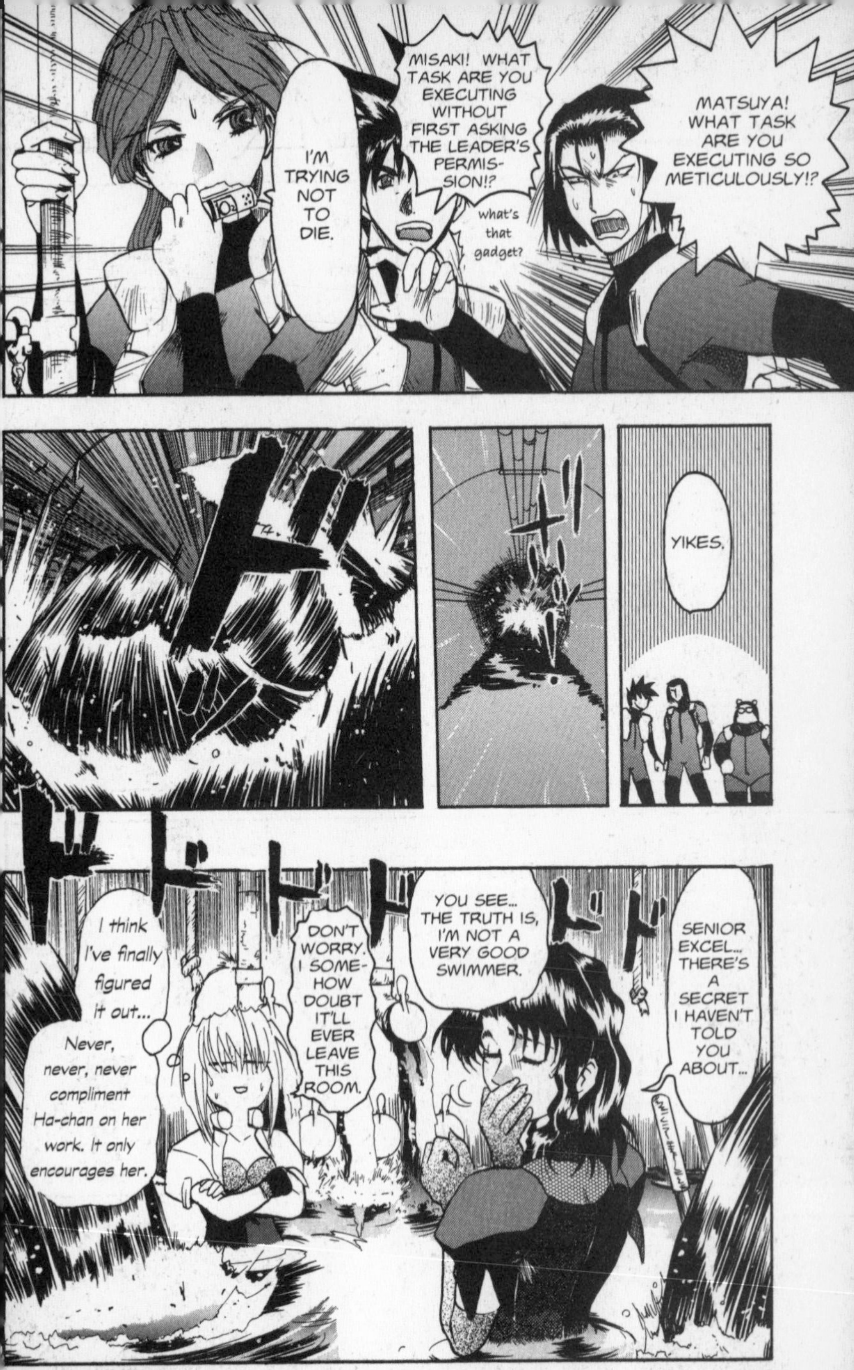
MATSUYA! WHAT TASK ARE YOU EXECUTING SO METICULOUSLY!?
MISAKI! WHAT TASK ARE YOU EXECUTING WITHOUT FIRST ASKING THE LEADER'S PERMISSION!?
what's that gadget?
I'M TRYING NOT TO DIE.
YIKES.
SENIOR EXCEL... THERE'S A SECRET I HAVEN'T TOLD YOU ABOUT...
YOU SEE... THE TRUTH IS, I'M NOT A VERY GOOD SWIMMER.
DON'T WORRY. I SOMEHOW DOUBT IT'LL EVER LEAVE THIS ROOM.
I think I've finally figured it out...
Never, never, never compliment Ha-chan on her work. It only encourages her.

END MISSION 6

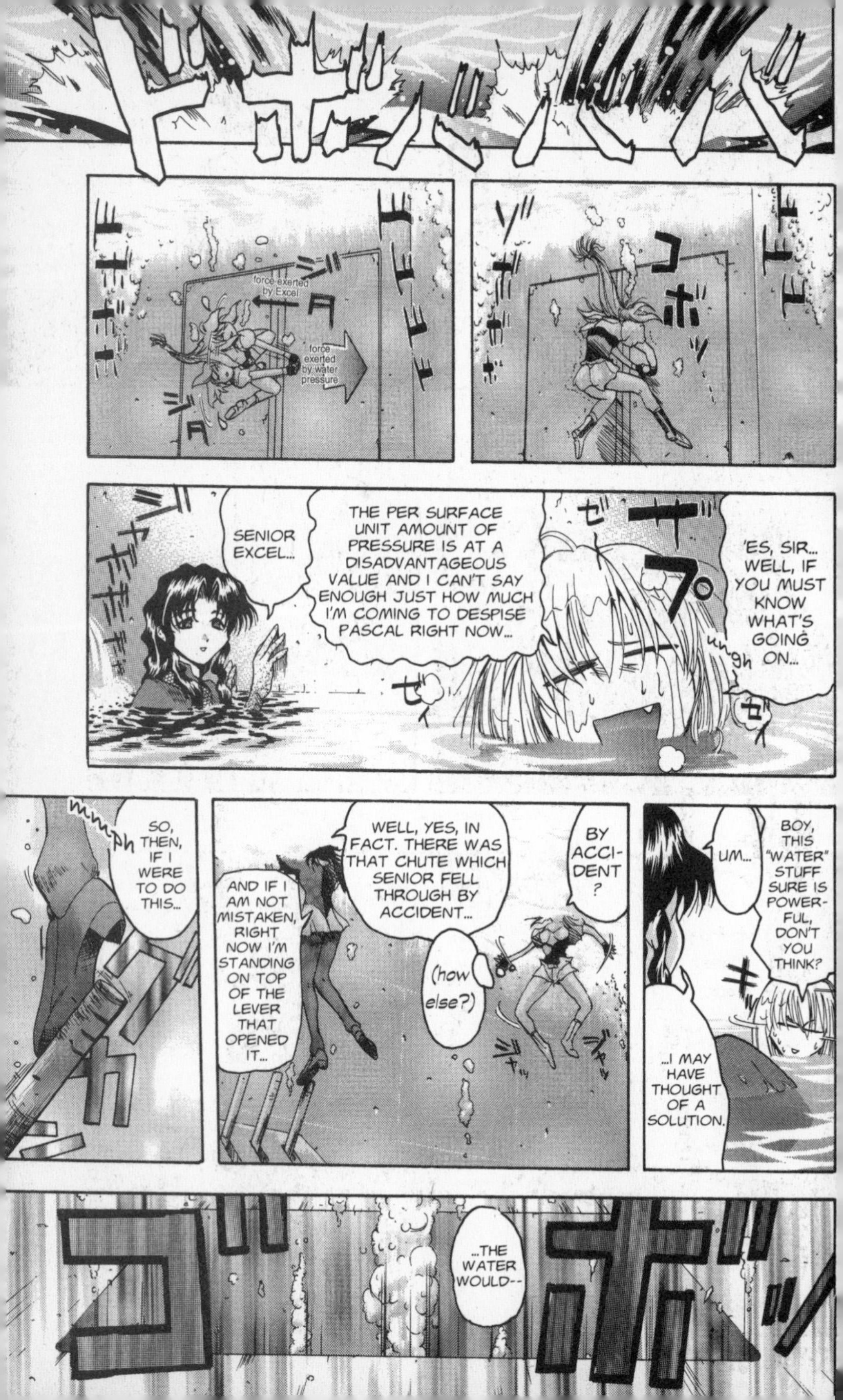
force exerted by Excel
force exerted by water pressure
'ES, SIR... WELL, IF YOU MUST KNOW WHAT'S GOING ON...
ungh
THE PER SURFACE UNIT AMOUNT OF PRESSURE IS AT A DISADVANTAGEOUS VALUE AND I CAN'T SAY ENOUGH JUST HOW MUCH I'M COMING TO DESPISE PASCAL RIGHT NOW...
SENIOR EXCEL...
BOY, THIS "WATER" STUFF SURE IS POWERFUL, DON'T YOU THINK?
UM...
...I MAY HAVE THOUGHT OF A SOLUTION.
BY ACCIDENT?
WELL, YES, IN FACT. THERE WAS THAT CHUTE WHICH SENIOR FELL THROUGH BY ACCIDENT...
(how else?)
AND IF I AM NOT MISTAKEN, RIGHT NOW I'M STANDING ON TOP OF THE LEVER THAT OPENED IT...
mmmph
SO, THEN, IF I WERE TO DO THIS...
...THE WATER WOULD--

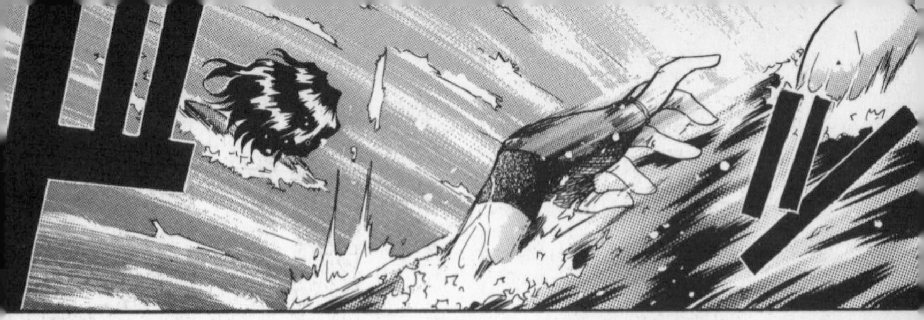

MISSION 7 "WE CAME...WE LEFT."

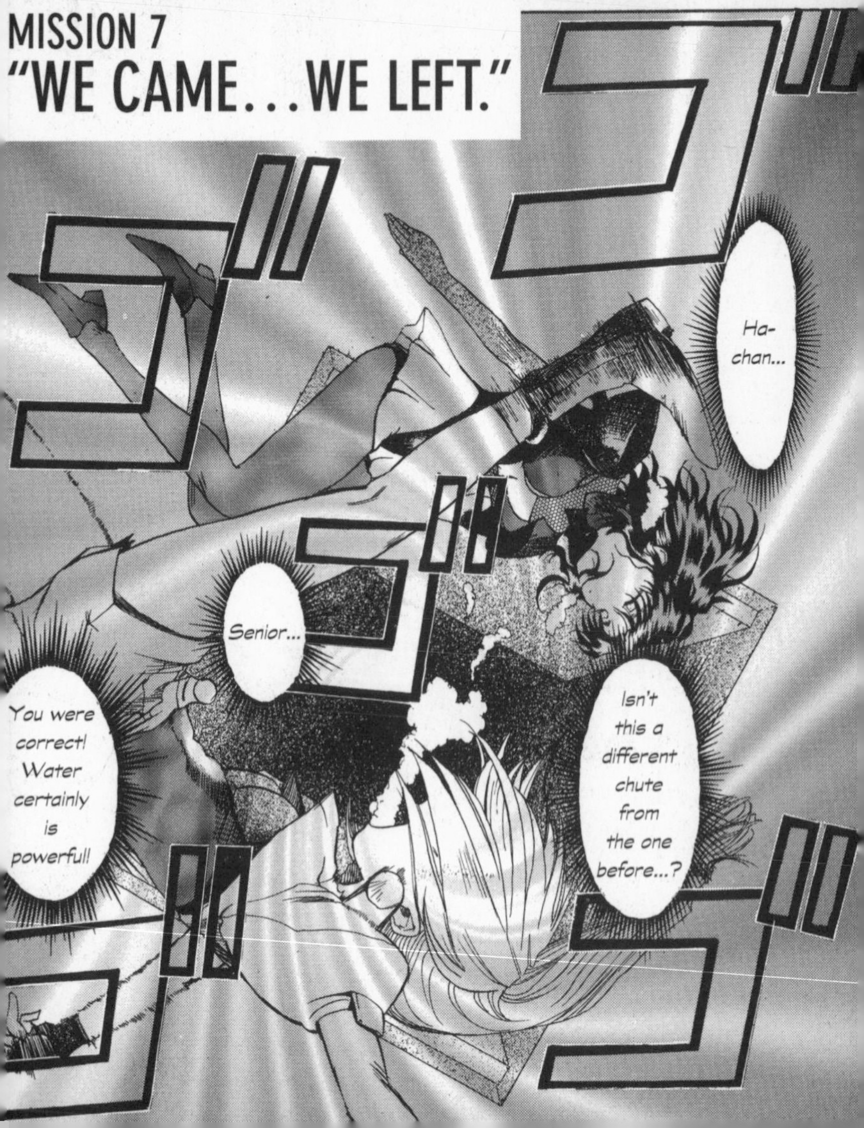
Ha-chan...
Senior...
Isn't this a different chute from the one before...?
You were correct! Water certainly is powerful!

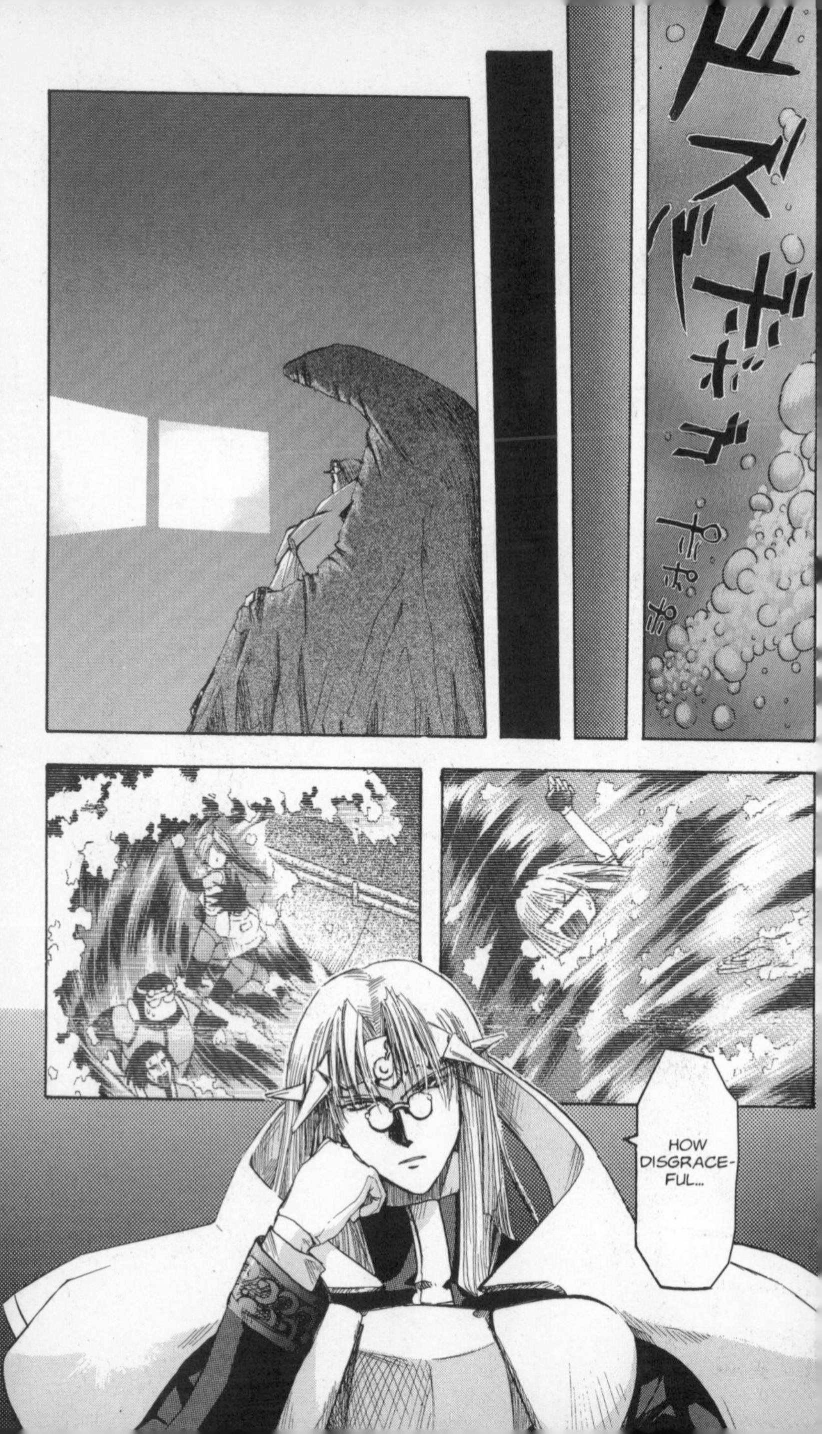
HOW DISGRACE-FUL...

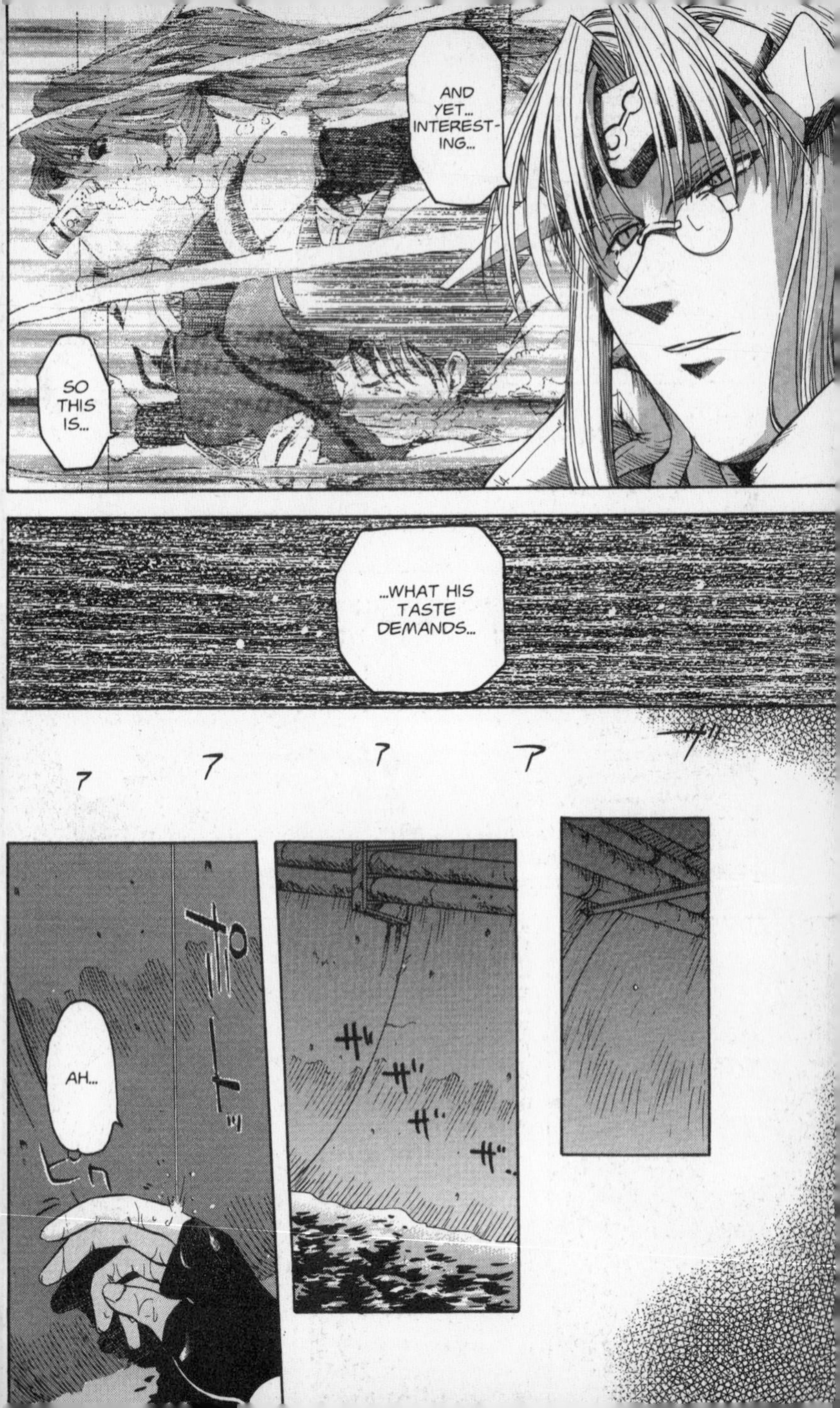
AND YET... INTERESTING...
SO THIS IS...
...WHAT HIS TASTE DEMANDS...
AH...

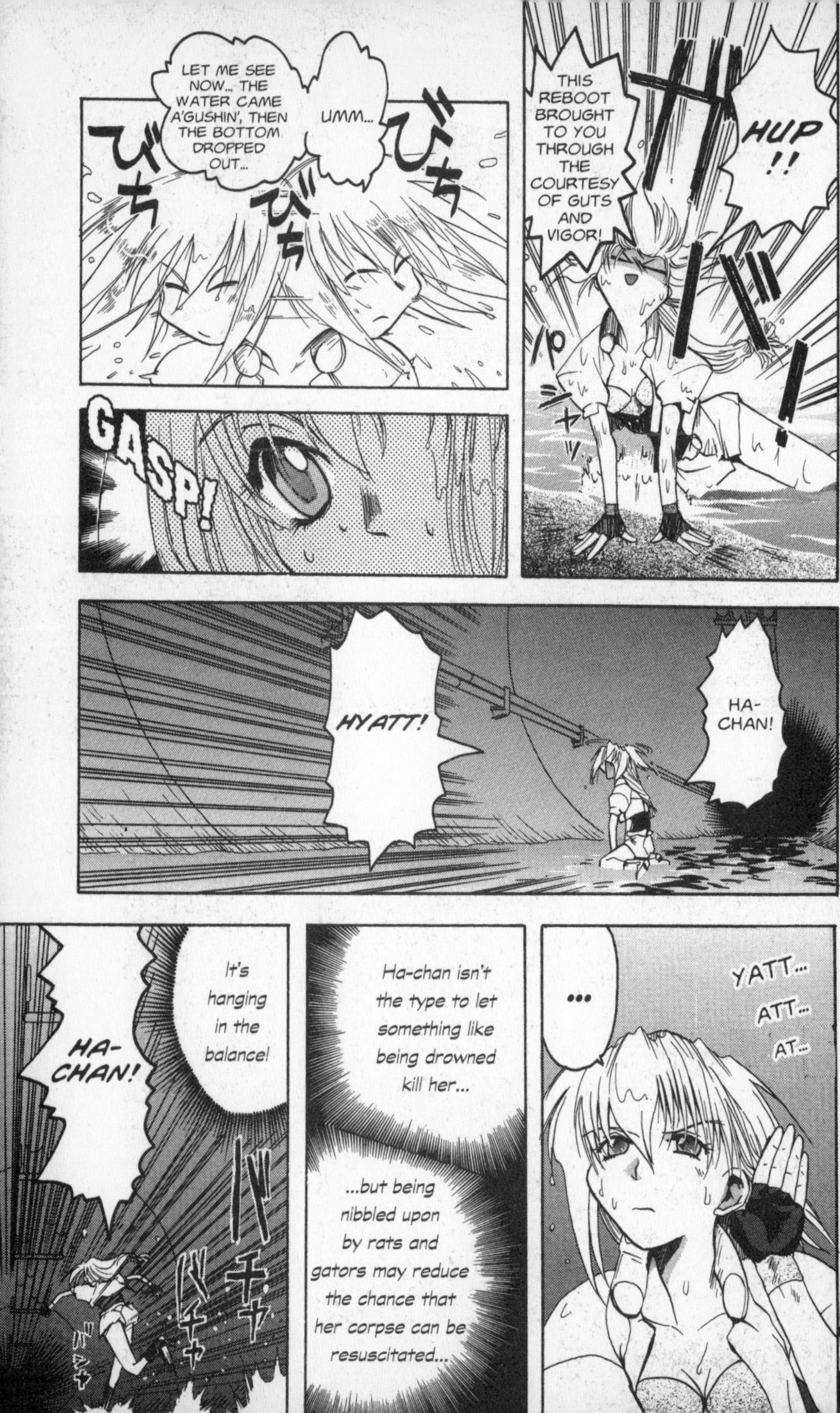
HUP!!
THIS REBOOT BROUGHT TO YOU THROUGH THE COURTESY OF GUTS AND VIGOR!
LET ME SEE NOW... THE WATER CAME A'GUSHIN', THEN THE BOTTOM DROPPED OUT...
UMM...
GASP!
HA-CHAN!
HYATT!
YATT... ATT... AT...
...
Ha-chan isn't the type to let something like being drowned kill her...
...but being nibbled upon by rats and gators may reduce the chance that her corpse can be resuscitated...
It's hanging in the balance!
HA-CHAN!

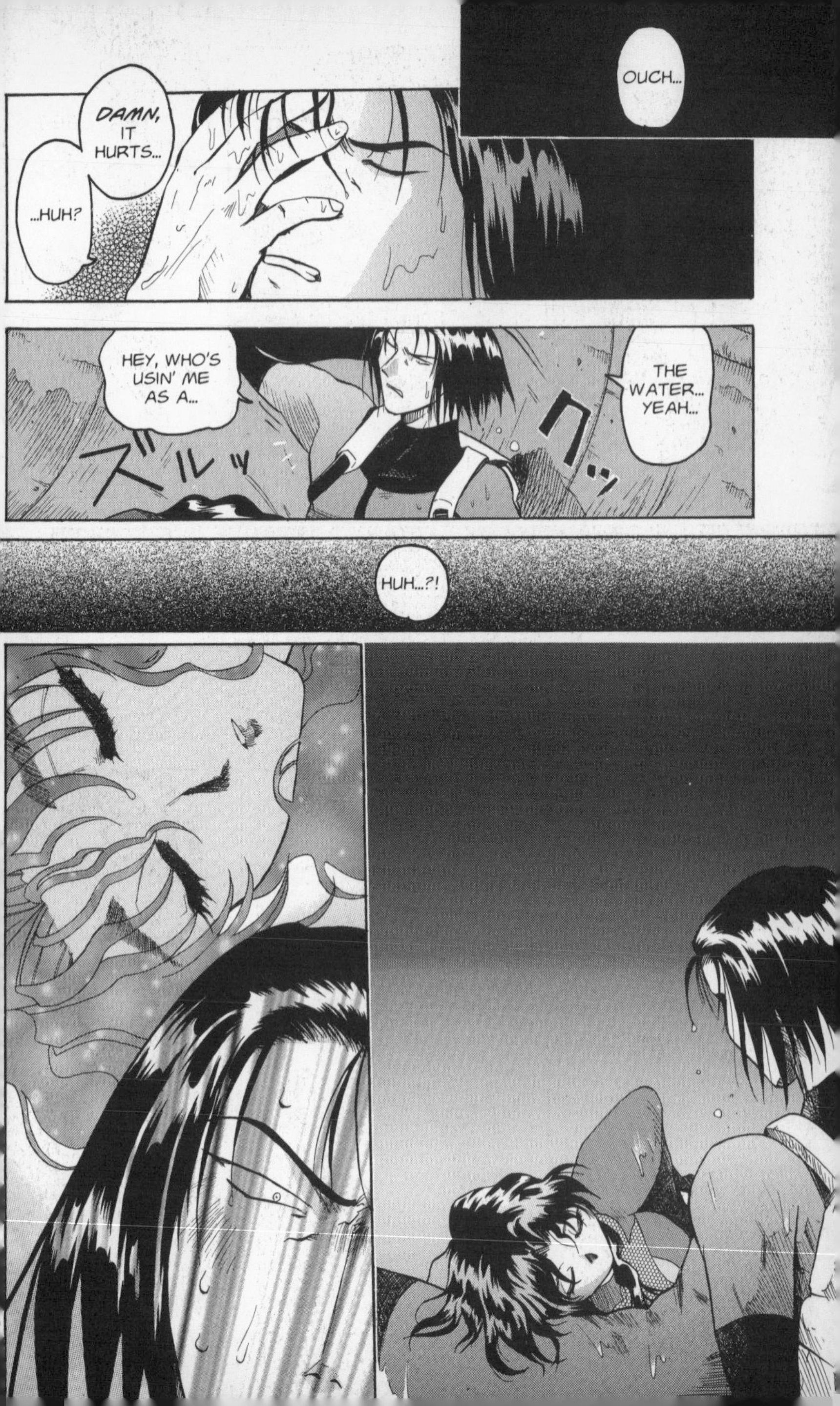
OUCH...
DAMN, IT HURTS...
...HUH?
THE WATER... YEAH...
クッ
HEY, WHO'S USIN' ME AS A...
ズルッ
HUH...?!

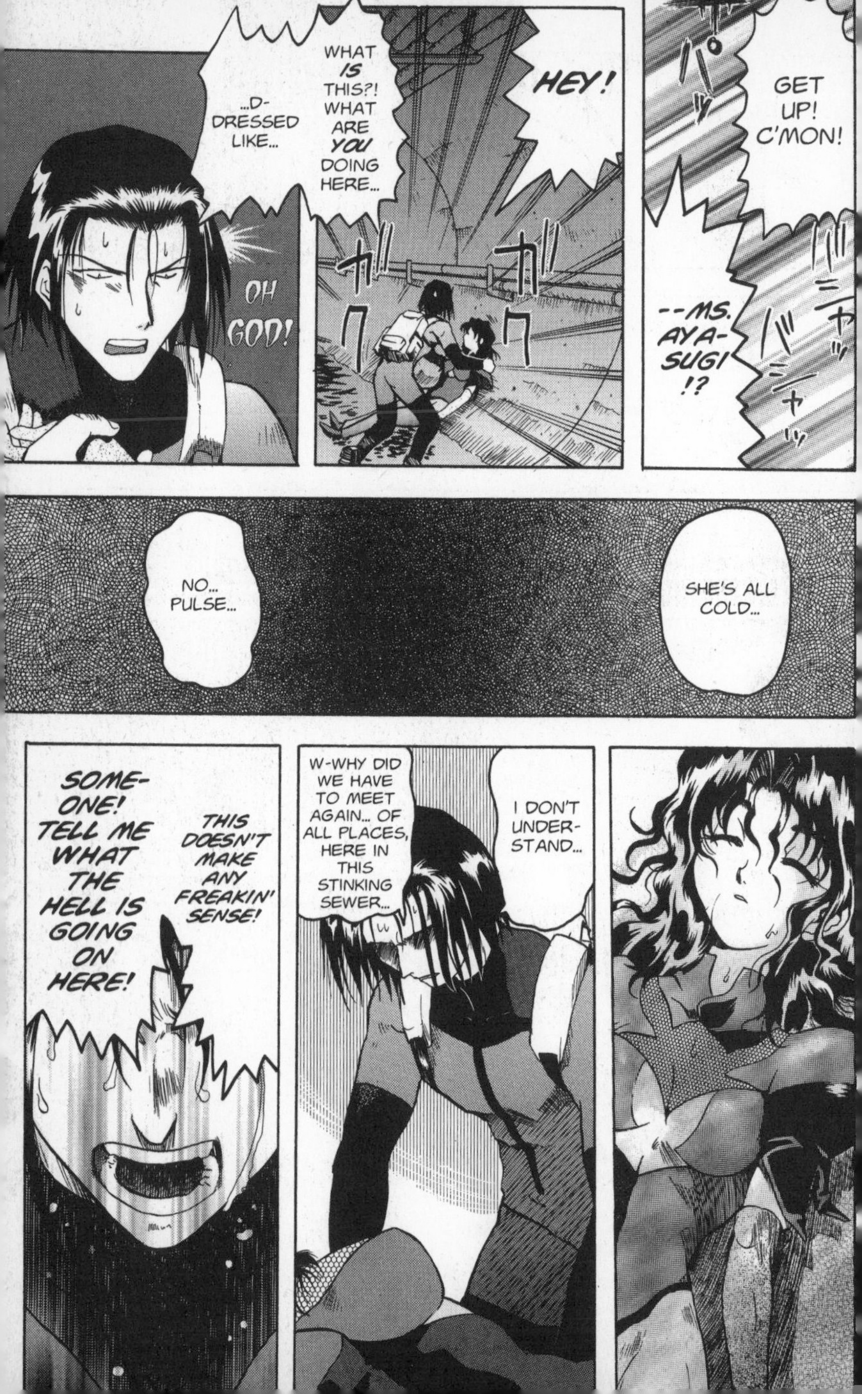
GET UP! C'MON!
--MS. AYA-SUGI !?
HEY!
WHAT IS THIS?! WHAT ARE YOU DOING HERE...
...D-DRESSED LIKE...
OH GOD!
SHE'S ALL COLD...
NO... PULSE...
I DON'T UNDER-STAND...
W-WHY DID WE HAVE TO MEET AGAIN... OF ALL PLACES, HERE IN THIS STINKING SEWER...
THIS DOESN'T MAKE ANY FREAKIN' SENSE!
SOME-ONE! TELL ME WHAT THE HELL IS GOING ON HERE!

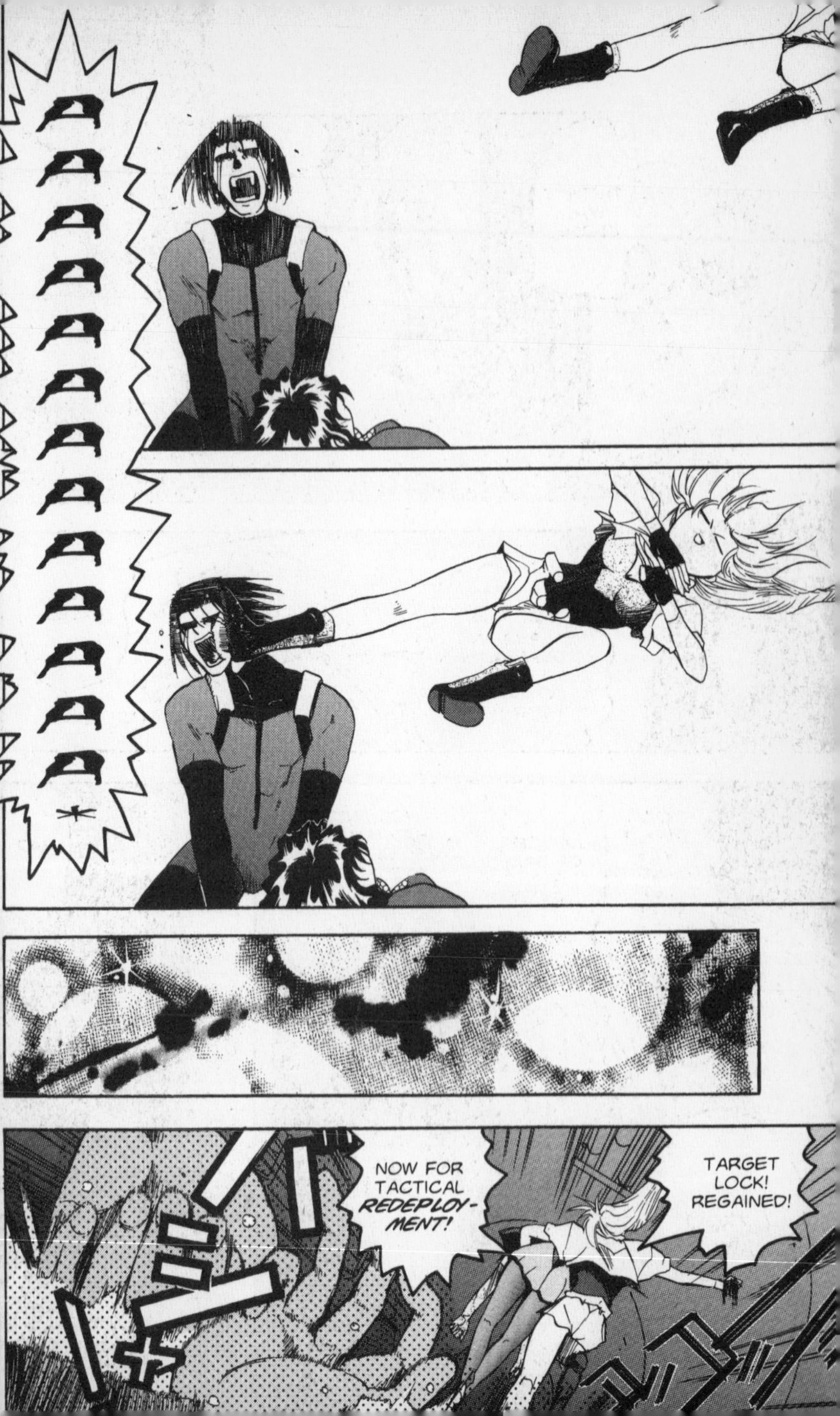
AAAAAAAAAAAAA*
TARGET LOCK! REGAINED!
NOW FOR TACTICAL REDEPLOYMENT!

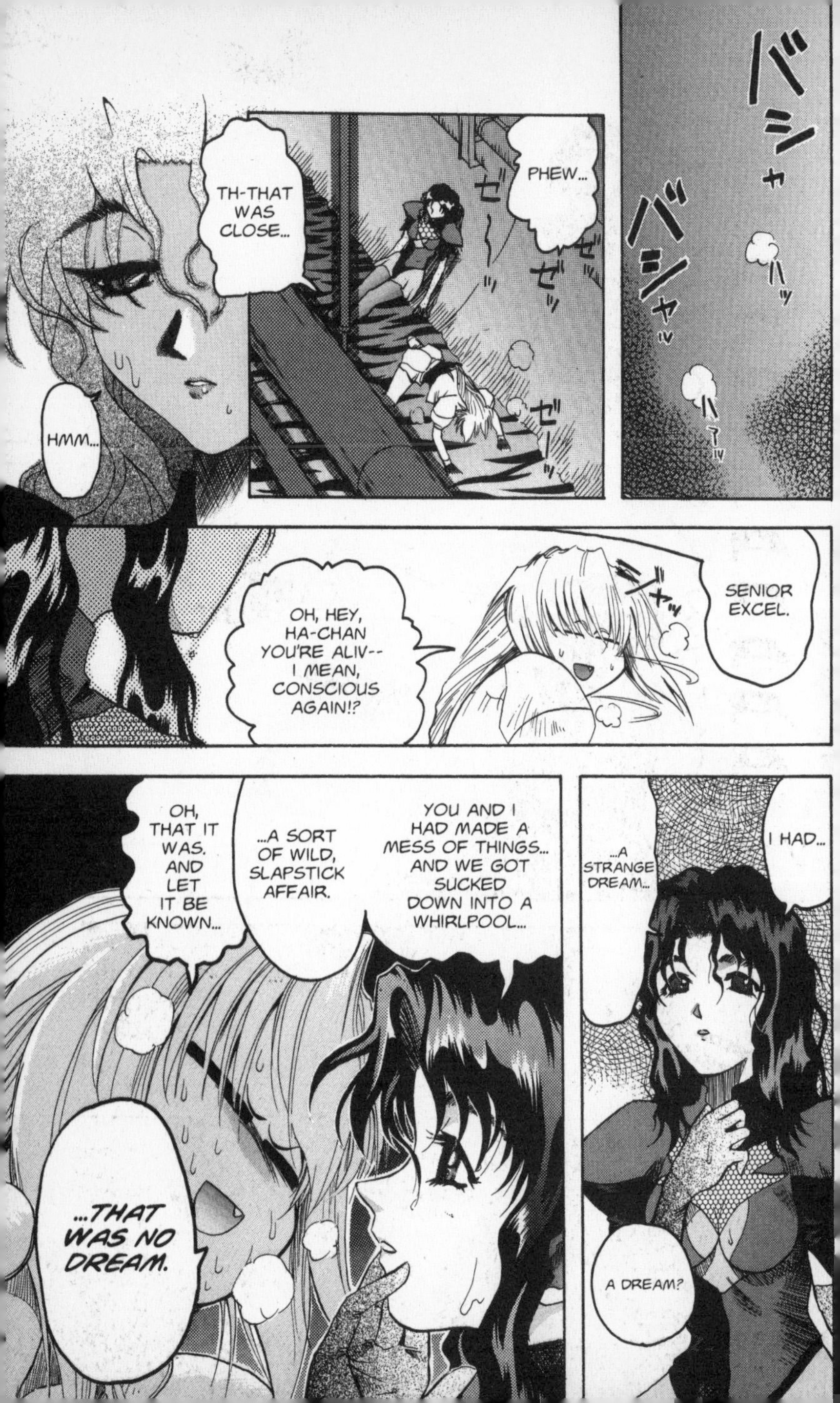

バシャ
バシャッ
ハッ
ハァッ
PHEW...
TH-THAT WAS CLOSE...
HMM...
SENIOR EXCEL.
OH, HEY, HA-CHAN YOU'RE ALIV-- I MEAN, CONSCIOUS AGAIN!?
I HAD...
...A STRANGE DREAM...
A DREAM?
YOU AND I HAD MADE A MESS OF THINGS... AND WE GOT SUCKED DOWN INTO A WHIRLPOOL...
...A SORT OF WILD, SLAPSTICK AFFAIR.
OH, THAT IT WAS. AND LET IT BE KNOWN...
...THAT WAS NO DREAM.

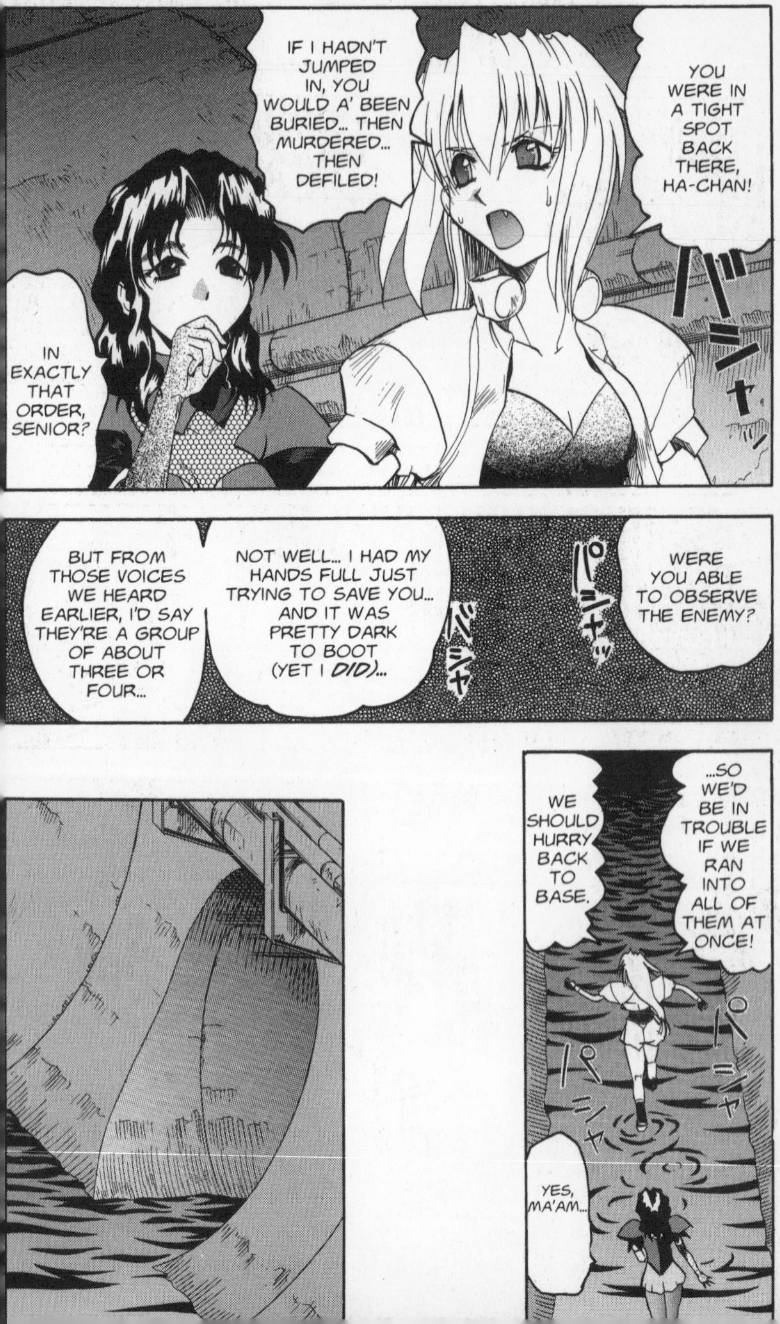
YOU WERE IN A TIGHT SPOT BACK THERE, HA-CHAN!
バシャッ
IF I HADN'T JUMPED IN, YOU WOULD A' BEEN BURIED... THEN MURDERED... THEN DEFILED!
IN EXACTLY THAT ORDER, SENIOR?
WERE YOU ABLE TO OBSERVE THE ENEMY?
パシャッ
バシャ
NOT WELL... I HAD MY HANDS FULL JUST TRYING TO SAVE YOU... AND IT WAS PRETTY DARK TO BOOT (YET I *DID*)...
BUT FROM THOSE VOICES WE HEARD EARLIER, I'D SAY THEY'RE A GROUP OF ABOUT THREE OR FOUR...
...SO WE'D BE IN TROUBLE IF WE RAN INTO ALL OF THEM AT ONCE!
WE SHOULD HURRY BACK TO BASE.
パシャ
パシャ
YES, MA'AM...

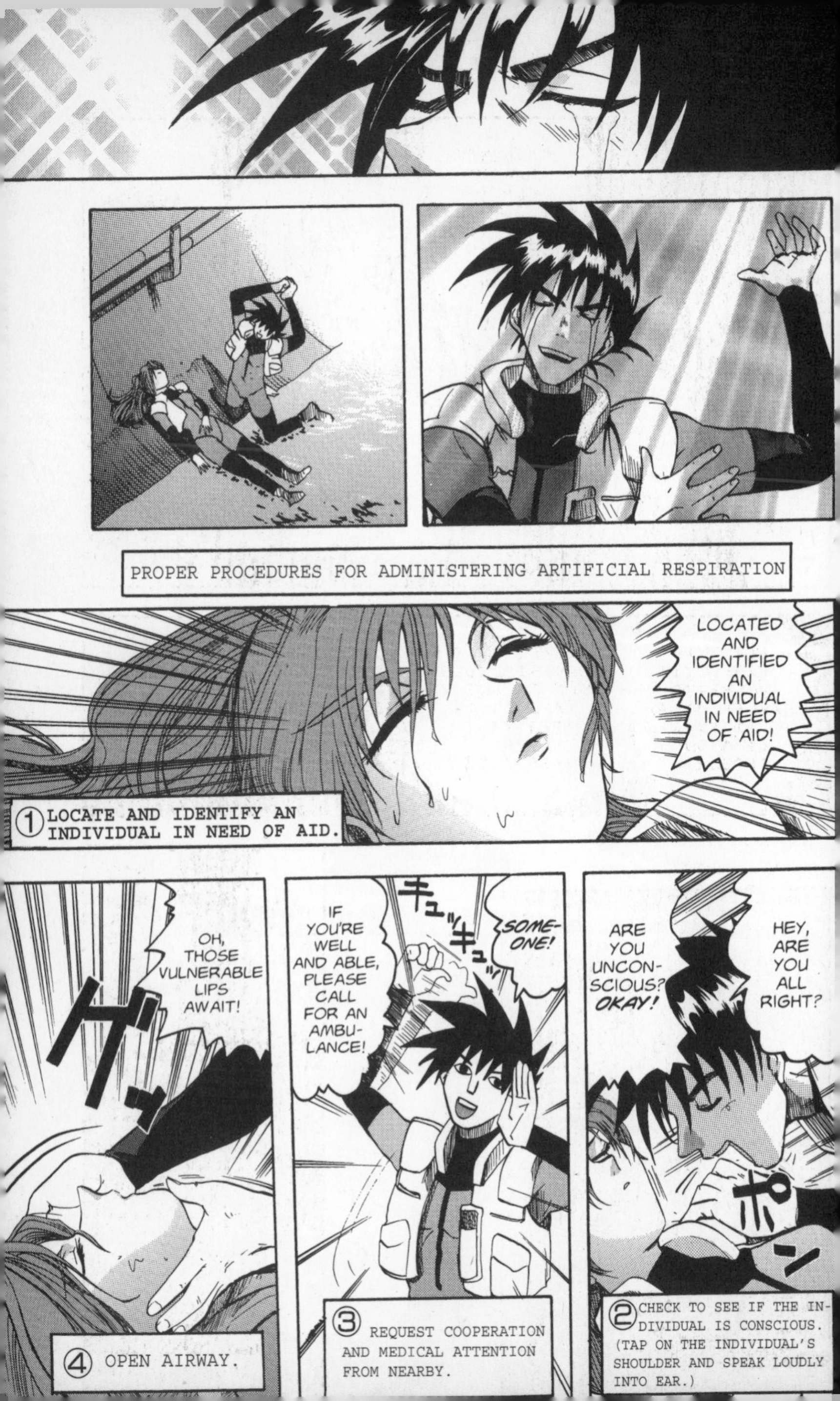
PROPER PROCEDURES FOR ADMINISTERING ARTIFICIAL RESPIRATION
LOCATED AND IDENTIFIED AN INDIVIDUAL IN NEED OF AID!
① LOCATE AND IDENTIFY AN INDIVIDUAL IN NEED OF AID.
HEY, ARE YOU ALL RIGHT?
ARE YOU UNCONSCIOUS? OKAY!
ポン
② CHECK TO SEE IF THE INDIVIDUAL IS CONSCIOUS. (TAP ON THE INDIVIDUAL'S SHOULDER AND SPEAK LOUDLY INTO EAR.)
SOME-ONE!
キュッキュッ
IF YOU'RE WELL AND ABLE, PLEASE CALL FOR AN AMBULANCE!
③ REQUEST COOPERATION AND MEDICAL ATTENTION FROM NEARBY.
OH, THOSE VULNERABLE LIPS AWAIT!
グッ
④ OPEN AIRWAY.

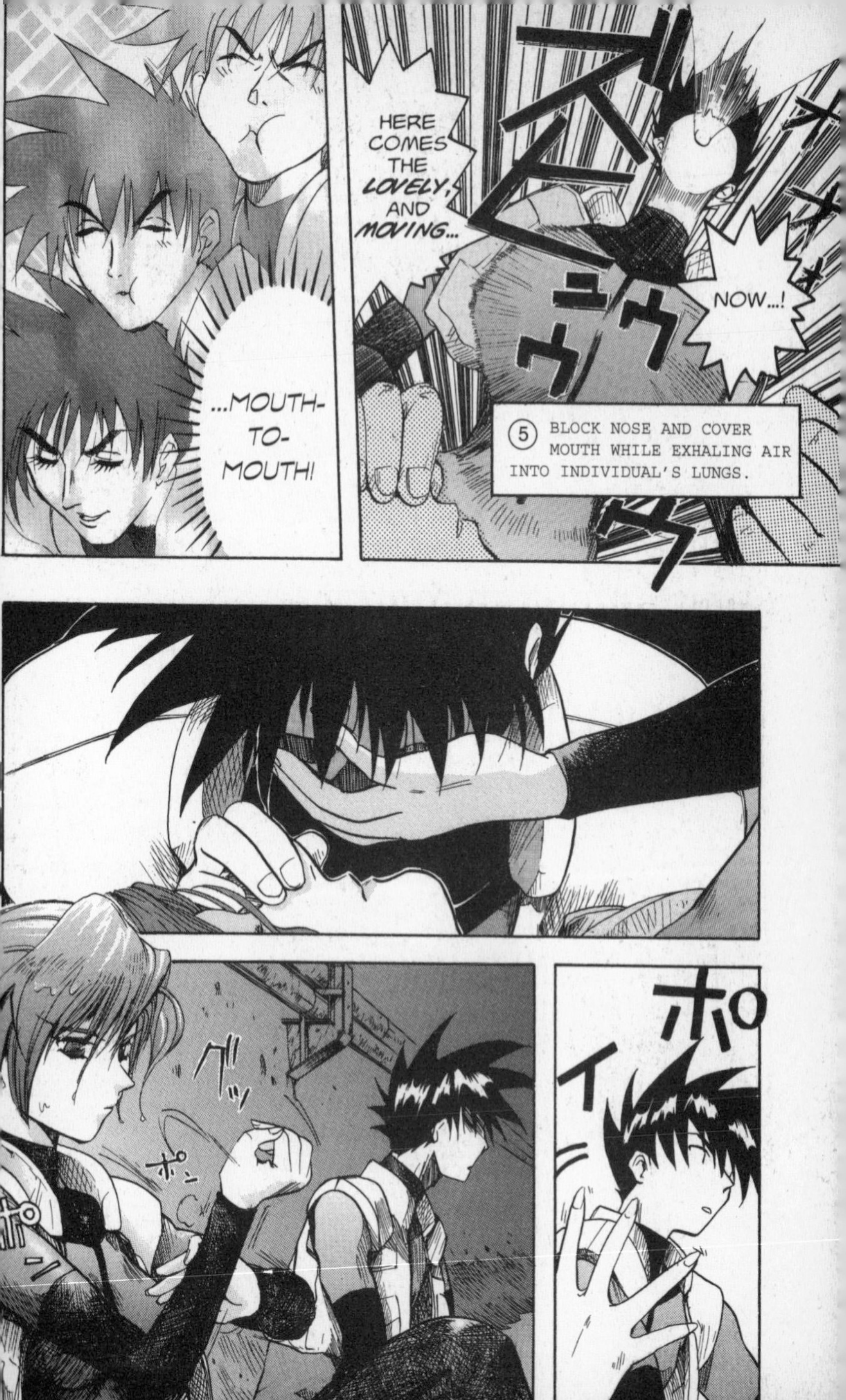
HERE COMES THE LOVELY, AND MOVING...
NOW...!
⑤ BLOCK NOSE AND COVER MOUTH WHILE EXHALING AIR INTO INDIVIDUAL'S LUNGS.
...MOUTH-TO-MOUTH!

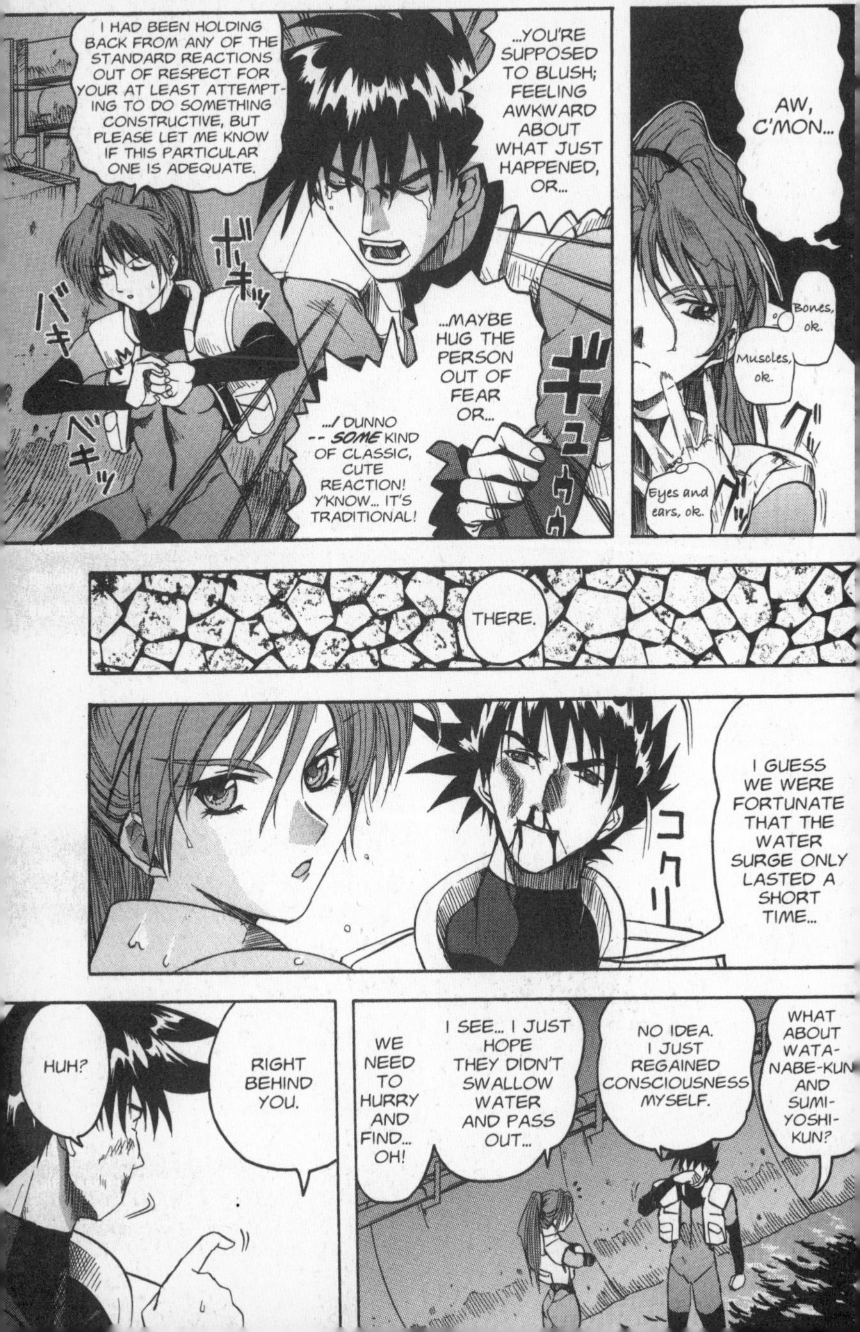
AW, C'MON...
Bones, ok.
Muscles, ok.
Eyes and ears, ok.
グッ
グッ
...YOU'RE SUPPOSED TO BLUSH; FEELING AWKWARD ABOUT WHAT JUST HAPPENED, OR...
...MAYBE HUG THE PERSON OUT OF FEAR OR...
ギュウウ
...I DUNNO -- *SOME* KIND OF CLASSIC, CUTE REACTION! Y'KNOW... IT'S TRADITIONAL!
I HAD BEEN HOLDING BACK FROM ANY OF THE STANDARD REACTIONS OUT OF RESPECT FOR YOUR AT LEAST ATTEMPTING TO DO SOMETHING CONSTRUCTIVE, BUT PLEASE LET ME KNOW IF THIS PARTICULAR ONE IS ADEQUATE.
ボキッ
バキ
ベキッ
THERE.
I GUESS WE WERE FORTUNATE THAT THE WATER SURGE ONLY LASTED A SHORT TIME...
コクリ
WHAT ABOUT WATA-NABE-KUN AND SUMI-YOSHI-KUN?
NO IDEA. I JUST REGAINED CONSCIOUSNESS MYSELF.
I SEE... I JUST HOPE THEY DIDN'T SWALLOW WATER AND PASS OUT...
WE NEED TO HURRY AND FIND... OH!
RIGHT BEHIND YOU.
HUH?

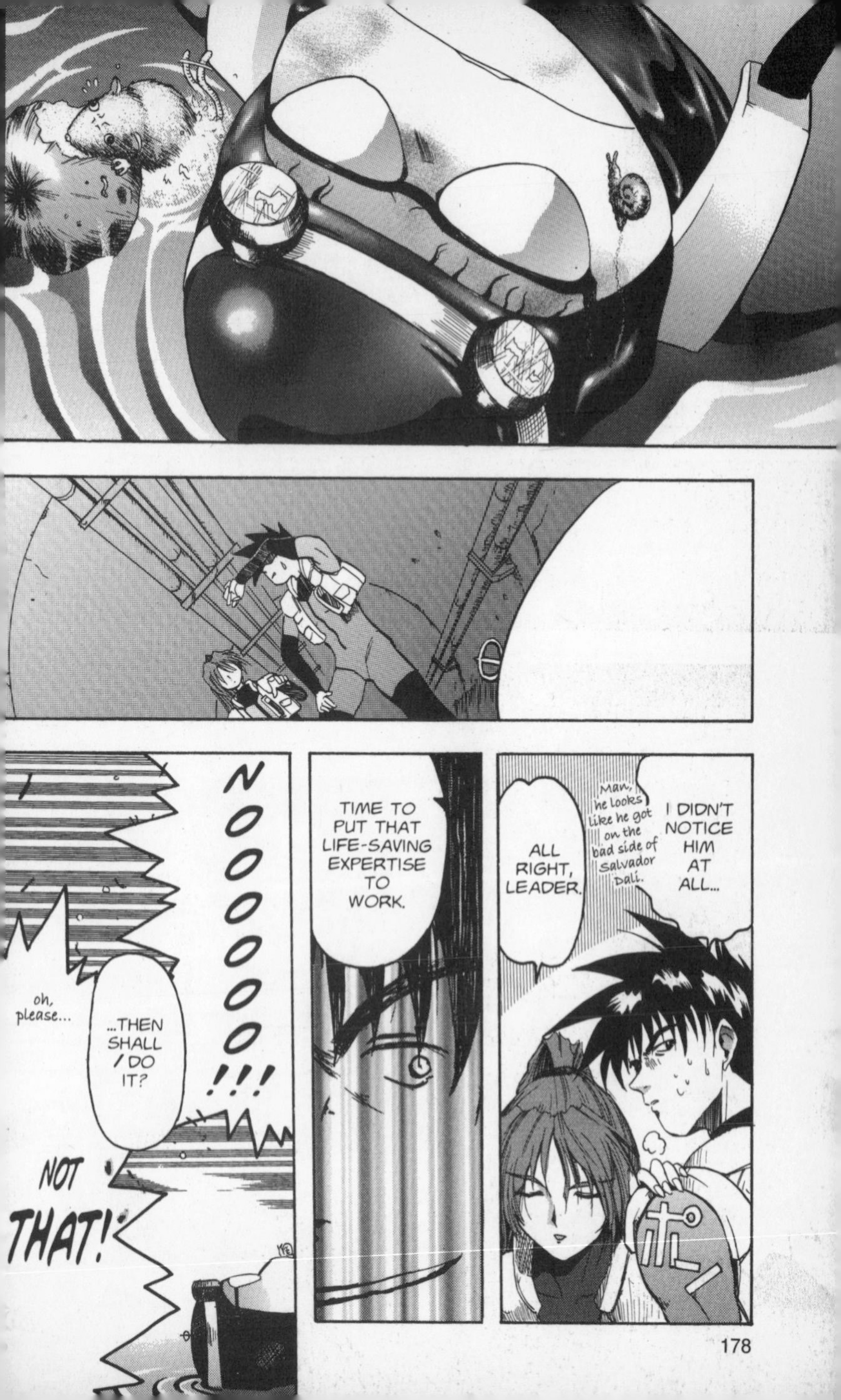
I DIDN'T NOTICE HIM AT ALL...
Man, he looks like he got on the bad side of Salvador Dalí.
ALL RIGHT, LEADER.
TIME TO PUT THAT LIFE-SAVING EXPERTISE TO WORK.
NOOOOOOO!!!
...THEN SHALL I DO IT?
oh, please...
NOT THAT!

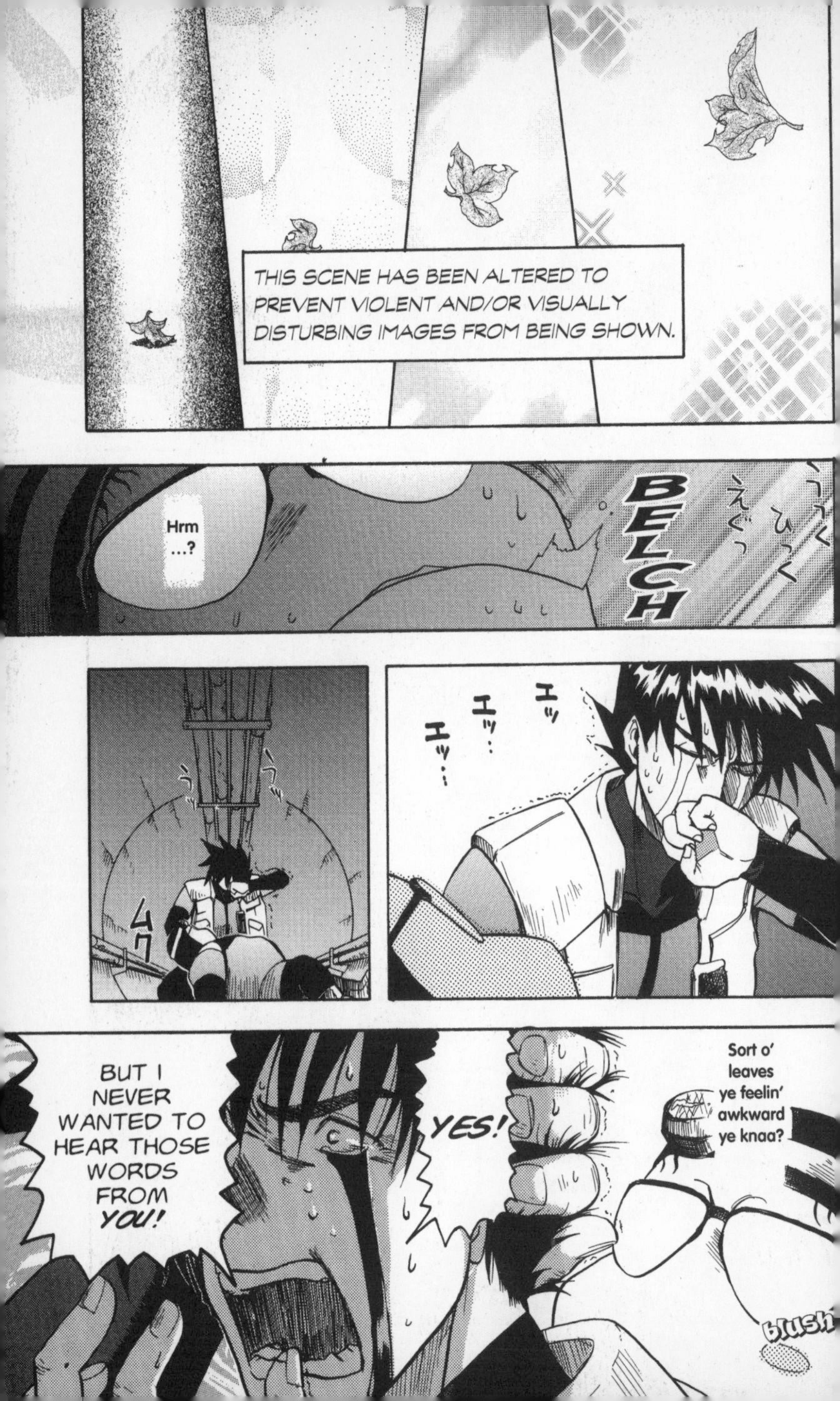
THIS SCENE HAS BEEN ALTERED TO PREVENT VIOLENT AND/OR VISUALLY DISTURBING IMAGES FROM BEING SHOWN.
ひっく
えぐっ
BELCH
Hrm ...?
エッ
エッ…
エッ…
うっ
うっ
ムク
Sort o' leaves ye feelin' awkward ye knaa?
blush
YES!
BUT I NEVER WANTED TO HEAR THOSE WORDS FROM *YOU!*

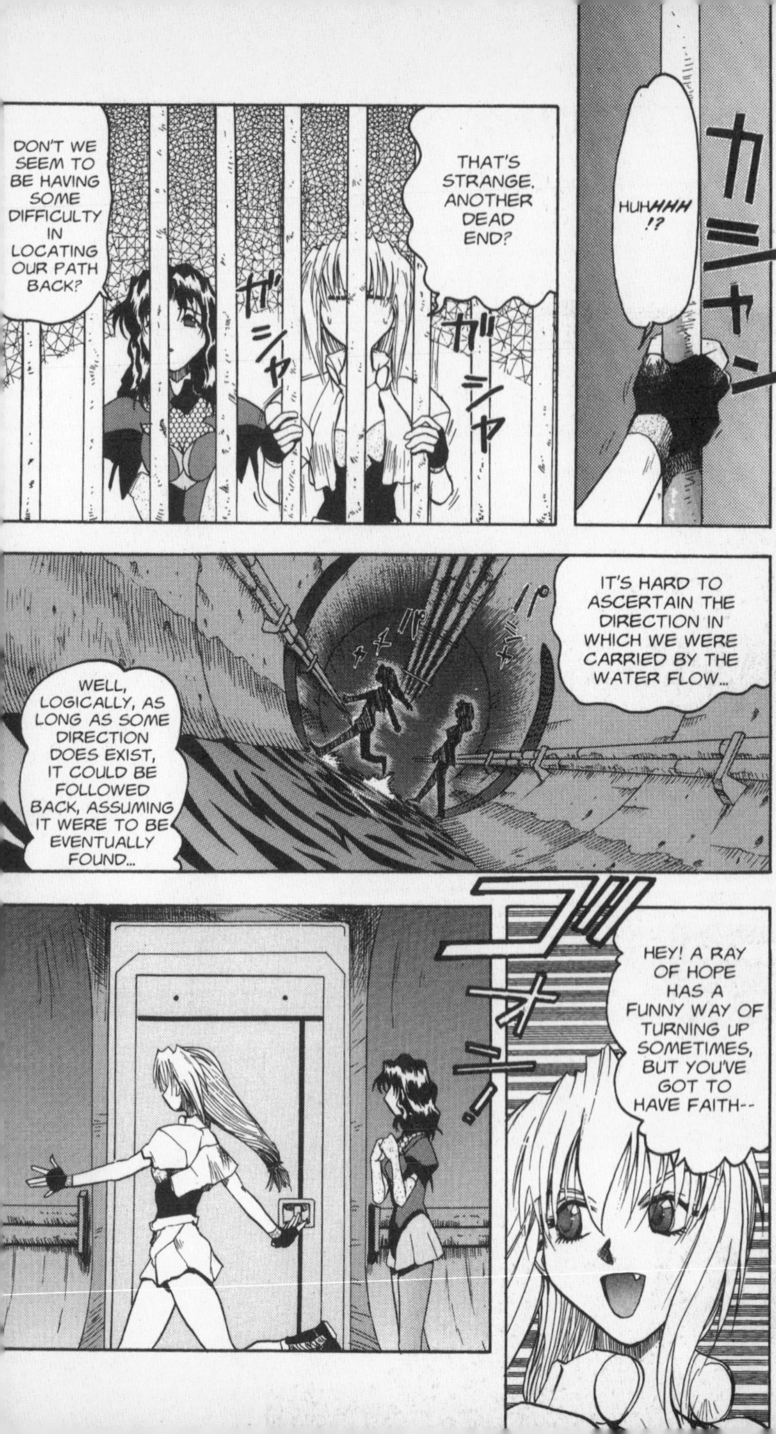
HUHHHH!?
カシャン
THAT'S STRANGE. ANOTHER DEAD END?
ガシャ
ガシャ
DON'T WE SEEM TO BE HAVING SOME DIFFICULTY IN LOCATING OUR PATH BACK?
IT'S HARD TO ASCERTAIN THE DIRECTION IN WHICH WE WERE CARRIED BY THE WATER FLOW...
WELL, LOGICALLY, AS LONG AS SOME DIRECTION DOES EXIST, IT COULD BE FOLLOWED BACK, ASSUMING IT WERE TO BE EVENTUALLY FOUND...
HEY! A RAY OF HOPE HAS A FUNNY WAY OF TURNING UP SOMETIMES, BUT YOU'VE GOT TO HAVE FAITH--

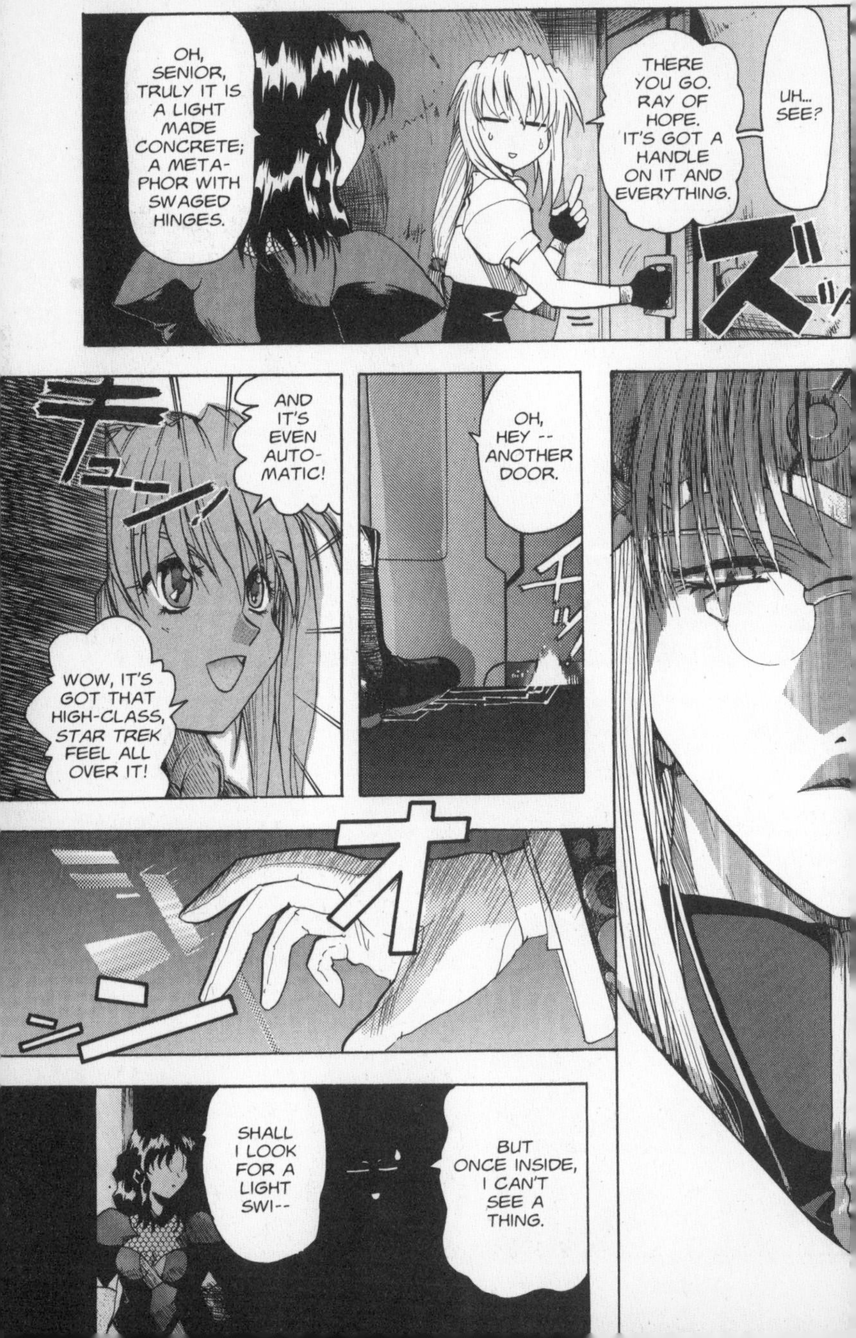
UH... SEE?
THERE YOU GO. RAY OF HOPE. IT'S GOT A HANDLE ON IT AND EVERYTHING.
OH, SENIOR, TRULY IT IS A LIGHT MADE CONCRETE; A METAPHOR WITH SWAGED HINGES.
OH, HEY -- ANOTHER DOOR.
AND IT'S EVEN AUTOMATIC!
WOW, IT'S GOT THAT HIGH-CLASS, STAR TREK FEEL ALL OVER IT!
BUT ONCE INSIDE, I CAN'T SEE A THING.
SHALL I LOOK FOR A LIGHT SWI--

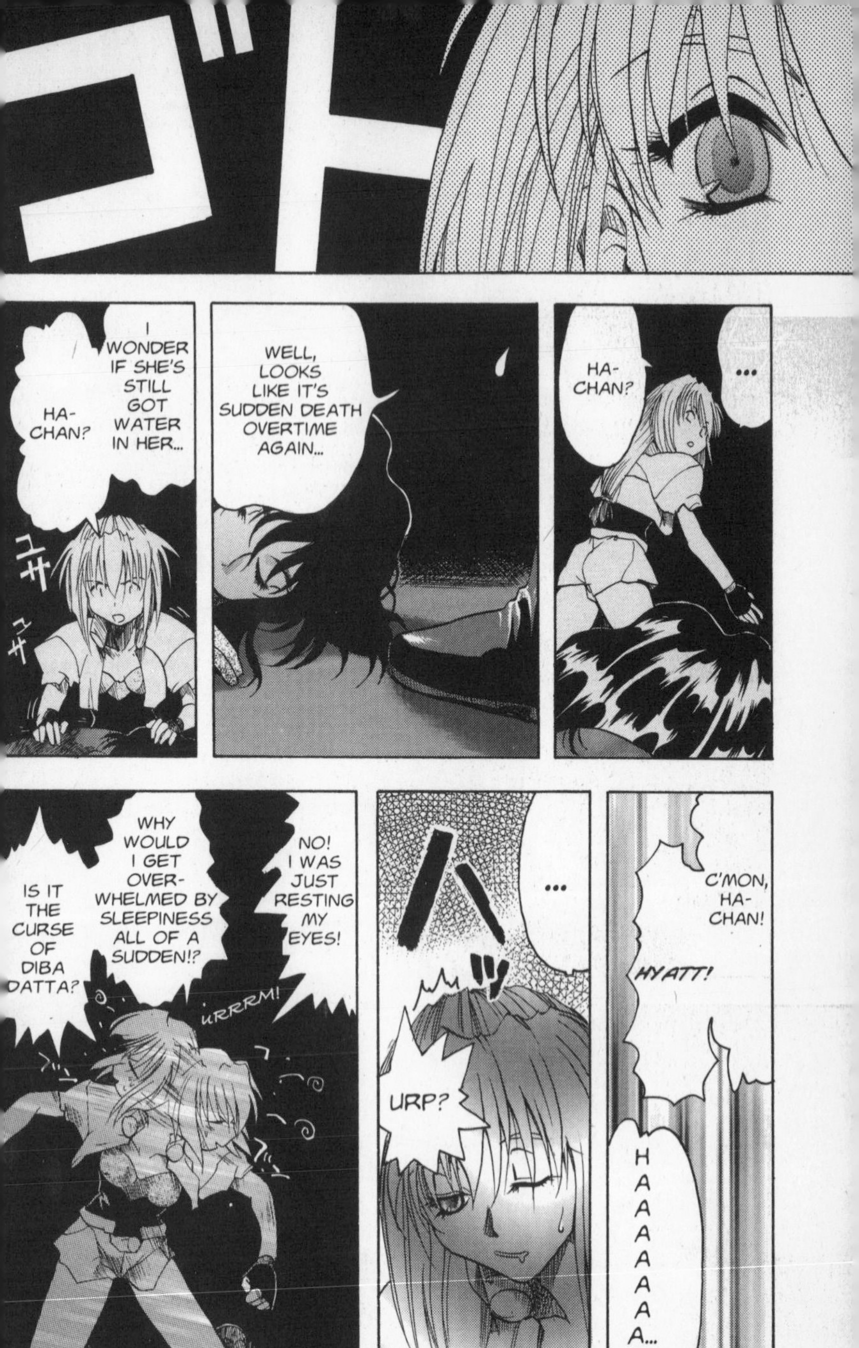

ゴト
...
HA-CHAN?
WELL, LOOKS LIKE IT'S SUDDEN DEATH OVERTIME AGAIN...
I WONDER IF SHE'S STILL GOT WATER IN HER...
HA-CHAN?
ユサユサ
C'MON, HA-CHAN!
HYATT!
HAAAAAAAA...
...
URP?
NO! I WAS JUST RESTING MY EYES!
WHY WOULD I GET OVERWHELMED BY SLEEPINESS ALL OF A SUDDEN!?
IS IT THE CURSE OF DIBA DATTA?
URRRM!

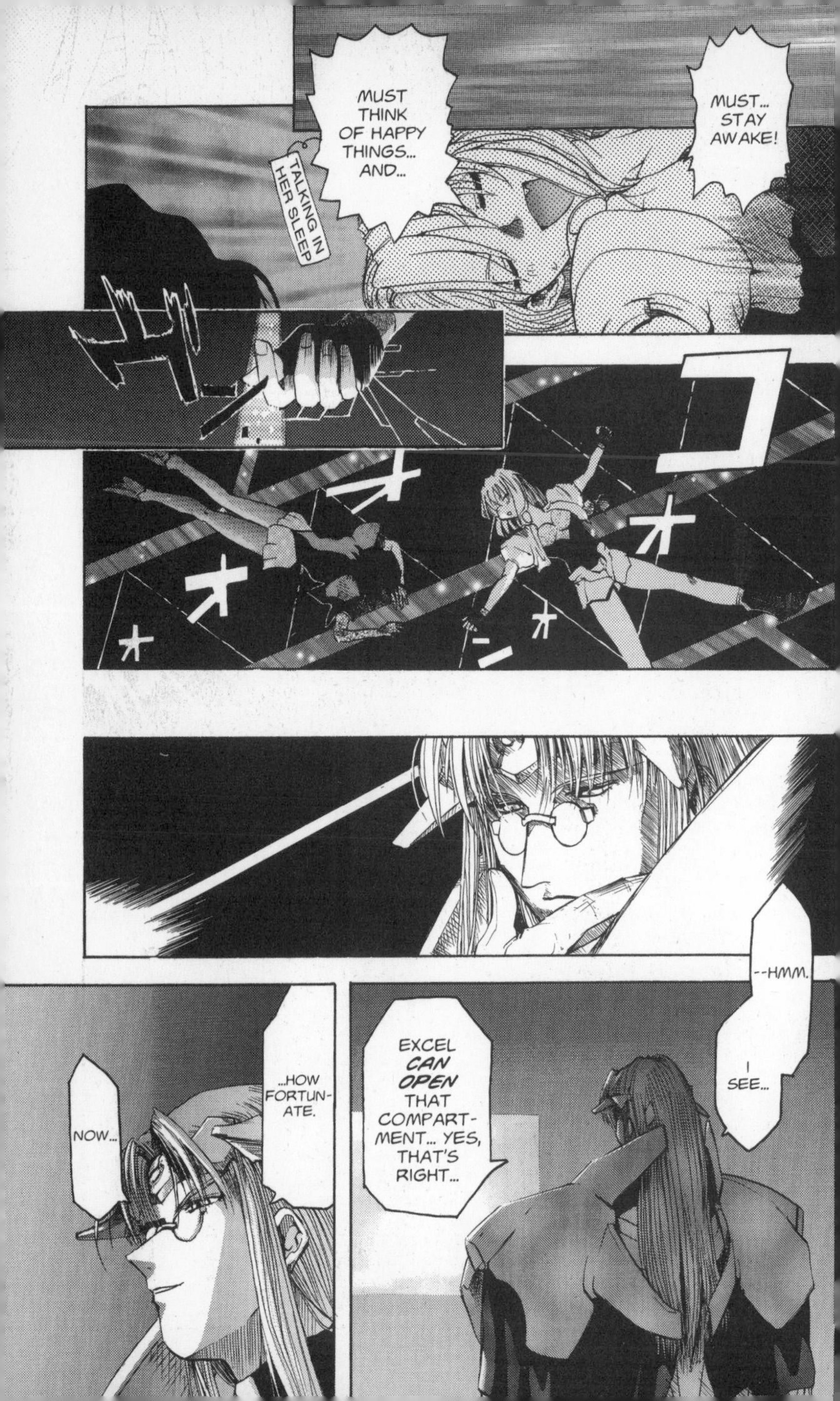
MUST... STAY AWAKE!
MUST THINK OF HAPPY THINGS... AND...
TALKING IN HER SLEEP
--HMM.
I SEE...
EXCEL *CAN OPEN* THAT COMPARTMENT... YES, THAT'S RIGHT...
...HOW FORTUNATE.
NOW...

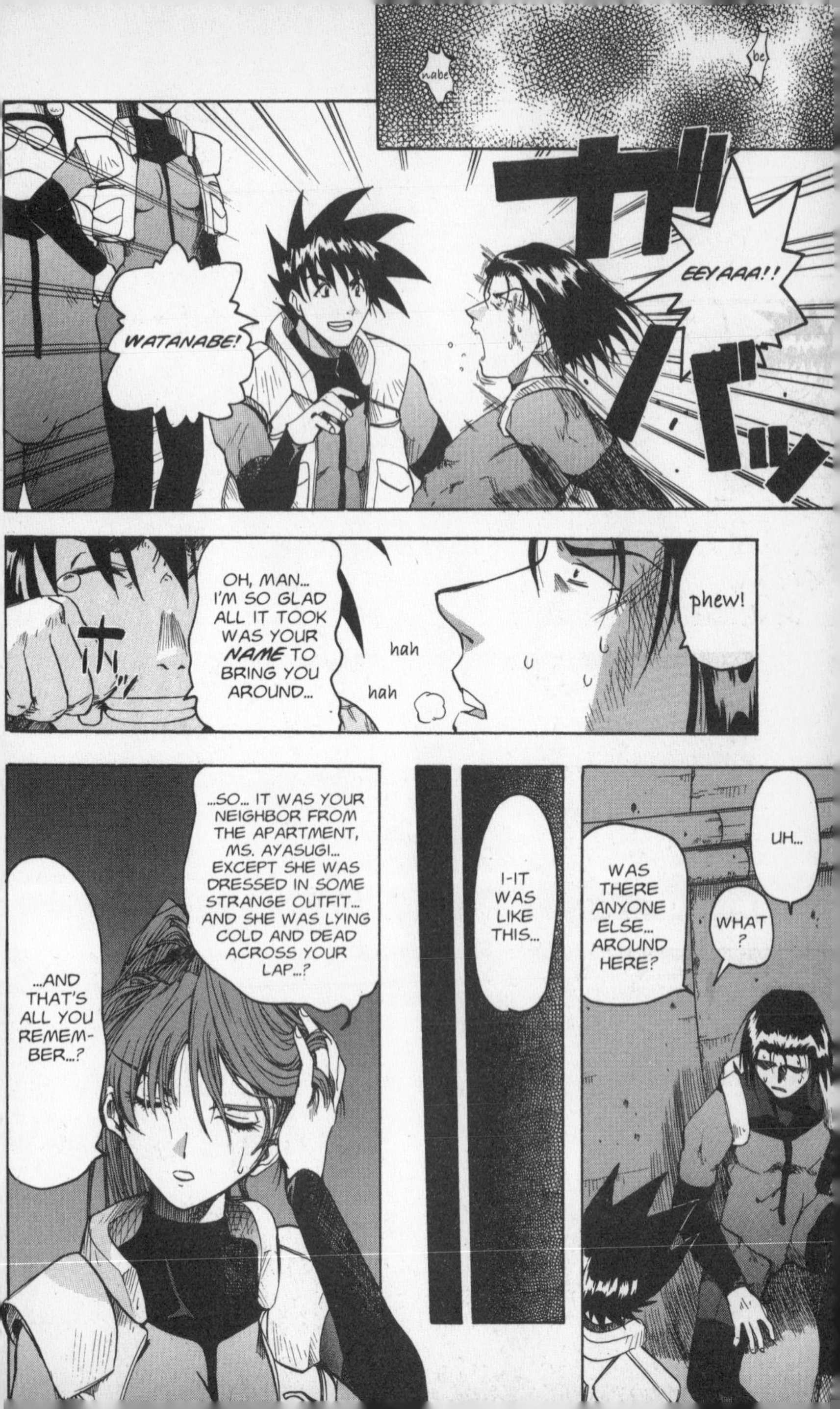
be
nabe
EEYAAA!!
WATANABE!
phew!
hah
hah
OH, MAN... I'M SO GLAD ALL IT TOOK WAS YOUR *NAME* TO BRING YOU AROUND...
UH...
WHAT?
WAS THERE ANYONE ELSE... AROUND HERE?
I-IT WAS LIKE THIS...
...SO... IT WAS YOUR NEIGHBOR FROM THE APARTMENT, MS. AYASUGI... EXCEPT SHE WAS DRESSED IN SOME STRANGE OUTFIT... AND SHE WAS LYING COLD AND DEAD ACROSS YOUR LAP...?
...AND THAT'S ALL YOU REMEMBER...?

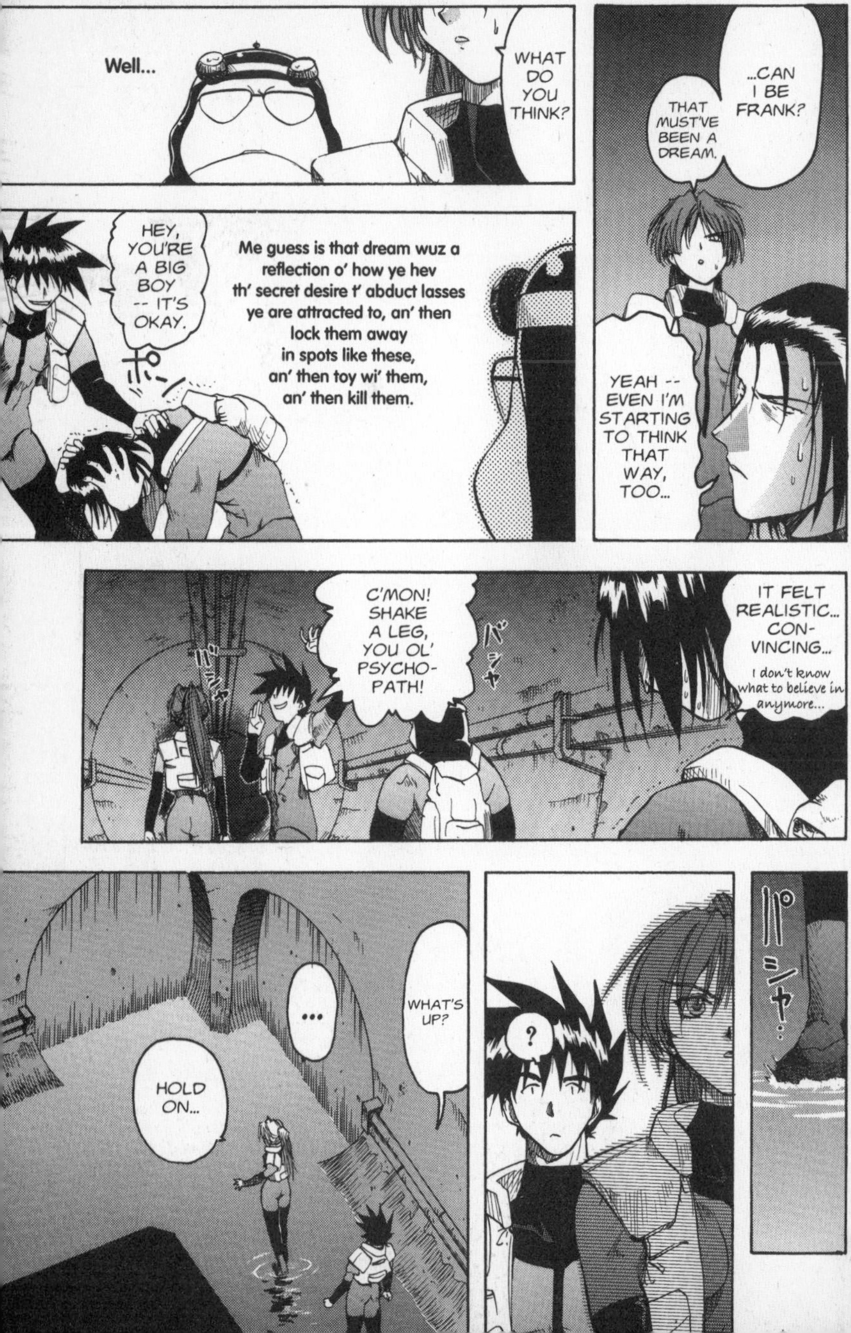
...CAN I BE FRANK?
THAT MUST'VE BEEN A DREAM.
YEAH -- EVEN I'M STARTING TO THINK THAT WAY, TOO...
WHAT DO YOU THINK?
Well...
Me guess is that dream wuz a reflection o' how ye hev th' secret desire t' abduct lasses ye are attracted to, an' then lock them away in spots like these, an' then toy wi' them, an' then kill them.
HEY, YOU'RE A BIG BOY -- IT'S OKAY.
IT FELT REALISTIC... CON-VINCING...
I don't know what to believe in anymore...
C'MON! SHAKE A LEG, YOU OL' PSYCHO-PATH!
バシャ
パシャ…
?
WHAT'S UP?
...
HOLD ON...

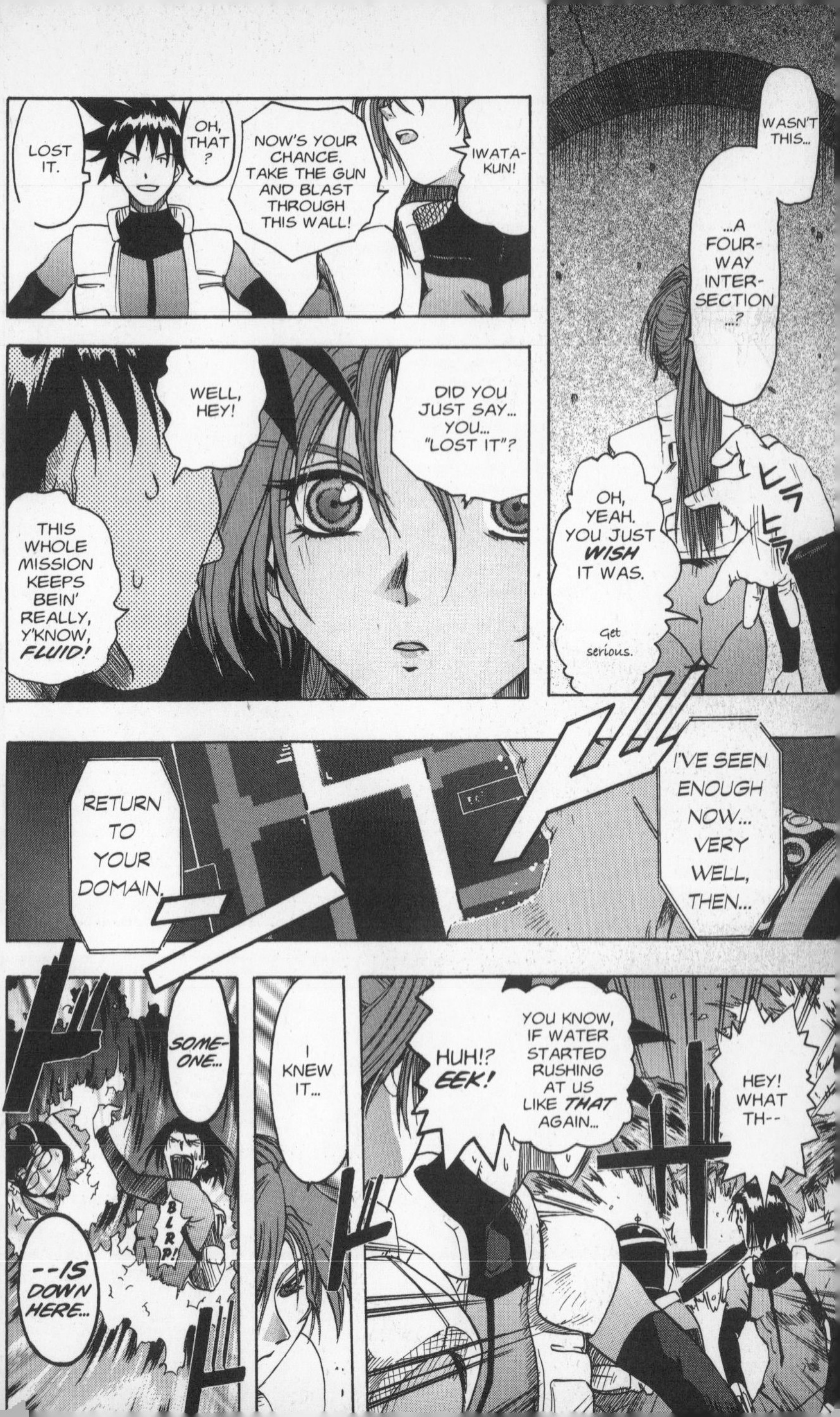
WASN'T THIS...
...A FOUR-WAY INTERSECTION ...?
OH, YEAH. YOU JUST *WISH* IT WAS.
Get serious.
IWATA-KUN!
NOW'S YOUR CHANCE. TAKE THE GUN AND BLAST THROUGH THIS WALL!
OH, THAT?
LOST IT.
DID YOU JUST SAY... YOU... "LOST IT"?
WELL, HEY!
THIS WHOLE MISSION KEEPS BEIN' REALLY, Y'KNOW, *FLUID!*
I'VE SEEN ENOUGH NOW... VERY WELL, THEN...
RETURN TO YOUR DOMAIN.
HEY! WHAT TH--
YOU KNOW, IF WATER STARTED RUSHING AT US LIKE *THAT* AGAIN...
HUH!? *EEK!*
I KNEW IT...
SOME-ONE...
BLRP!
--IS DOWN HERE...

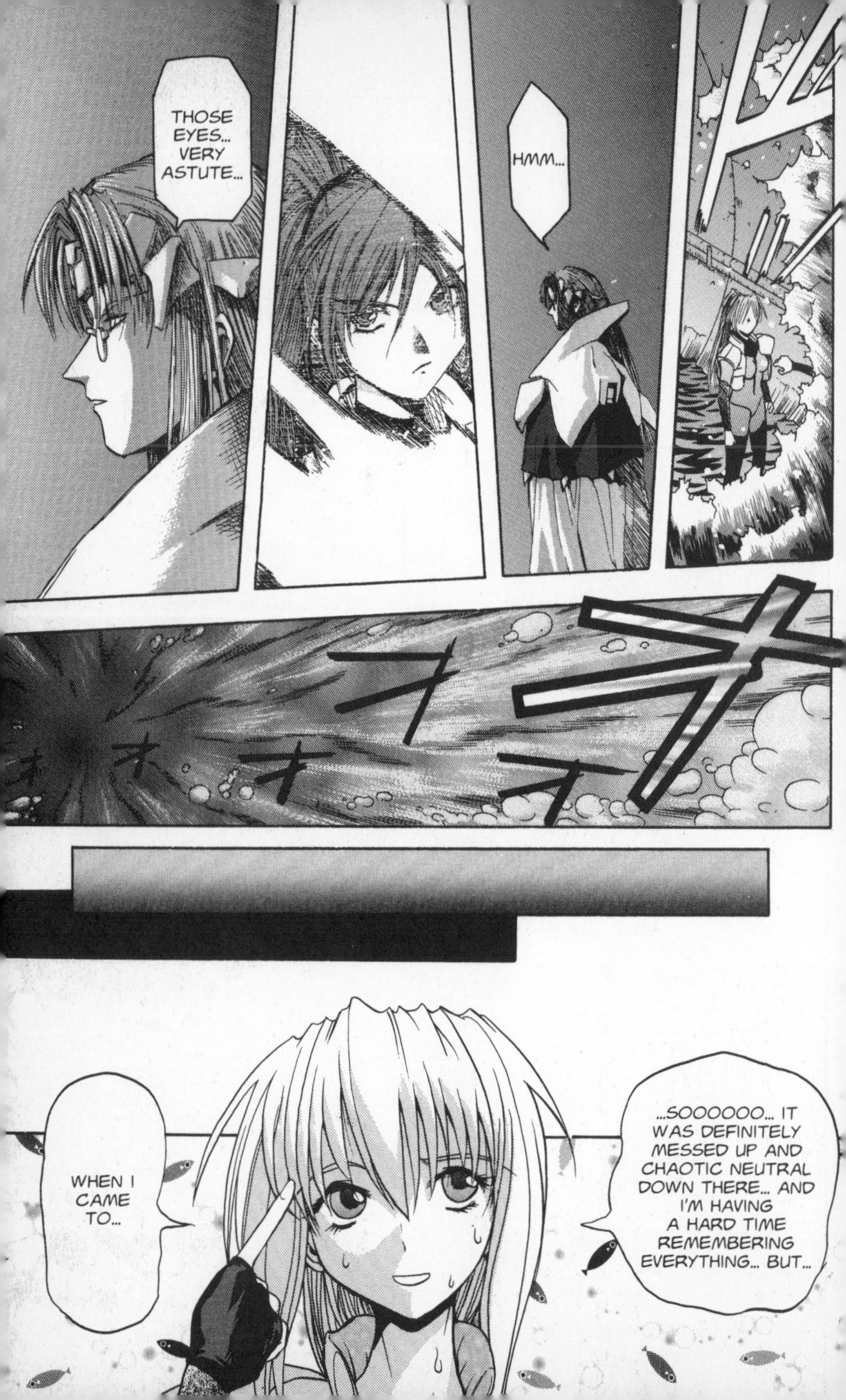
HMM...
THOSE EYES... VERY ASTUTE...
...SOOOOOO... IT WAS DEFINITELY MESSED UP AND CHAOTIC NEUTRAL DOWN THERE... AND I'M HAVING A HARD TIME REMEMBERING EVERYTHING... BUT...
WHEN I CAME TO...

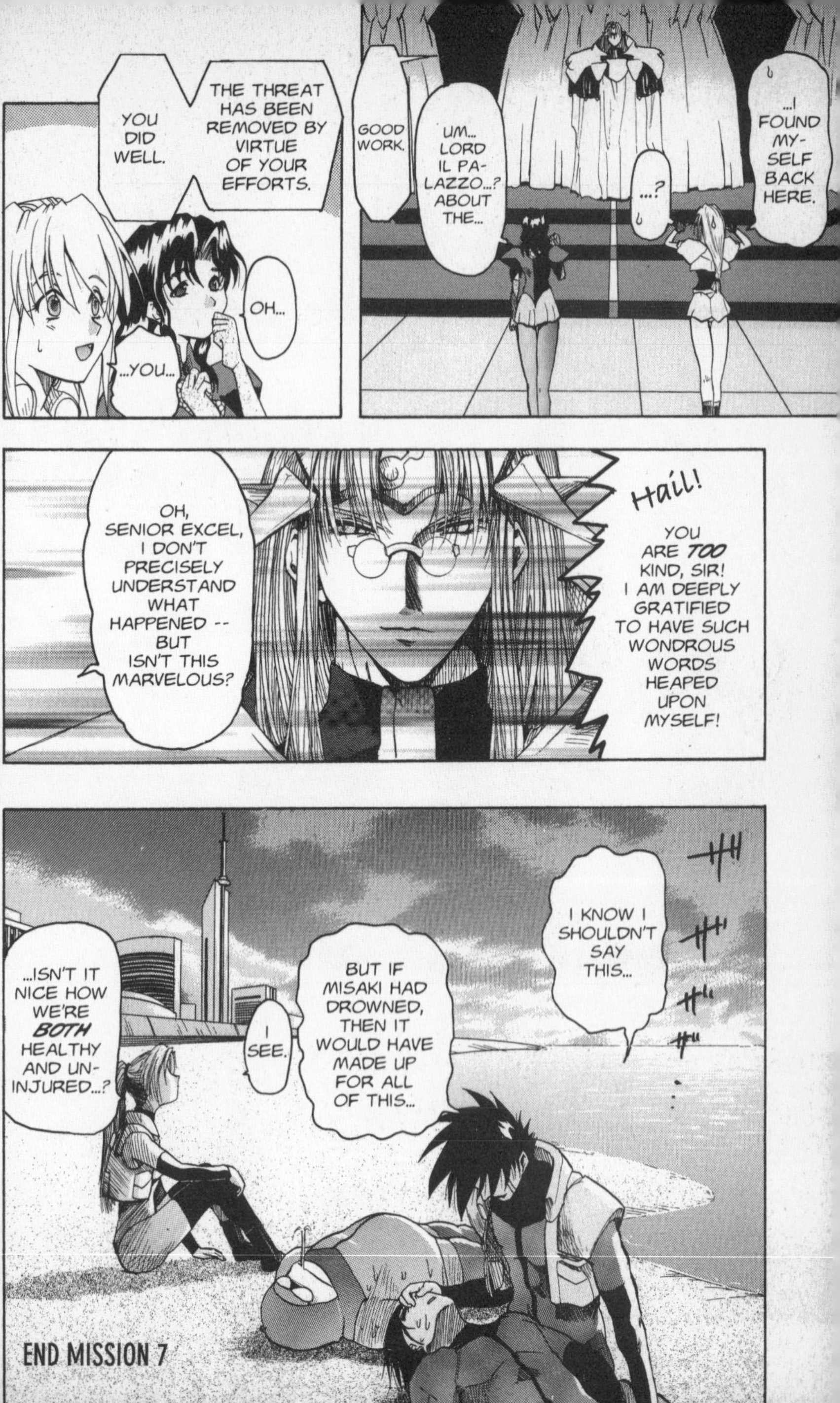
...I FOUND MY-SELF BACK HERE.
...?
UM... LORD IL PA-LAZZO...? ABOUT THE...
GOOD WORK.
THE THREAT HAS BEEN REMOVED BY VIRTUE OF YOUR EFFORTS.
YOU DID WELL.
OH...
...YOU...
Hail!
YOU ARE *TOO* KIND, SIR! I AM DEEPLY GRATIFIED TO HAVE SUCH WONDROUS WORDS HEAPED UPON MYSELF!
OH, SENIOR EXCEL, I DON'T PRECISELY UNDERSTAND WHAT HAPPENED -- BUT ISN'T THIS MARVELOUS?
I KNOW I SHOULDN'T SAY THIS...
BUT IF MISAKI HAD DROWNED, THEN IT WOULD HAVE MADE UP FOR ALL OF THIS...
I SEE.
...ISN'T IT NICE HOW WE'RE *BOTH* HEALTHY AND UN-INJURED...?
END MISSION 7

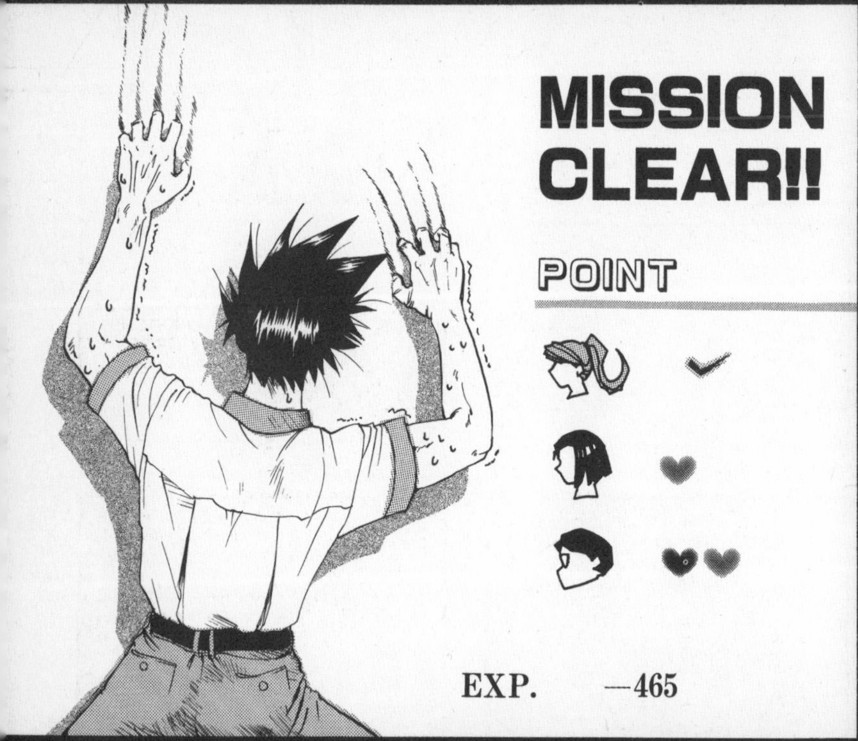
MISSION
CLEAR!!
POINT
EXP. —465

Scenes of the Personal Life of Rikdo Koshi Vol.③

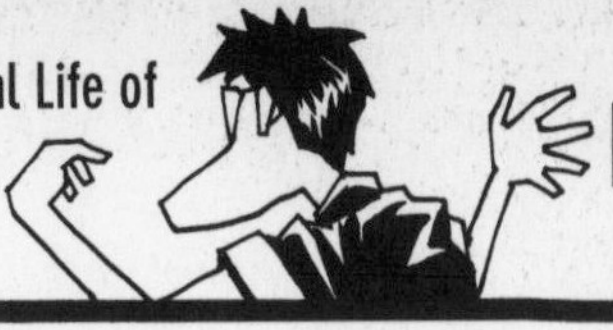

The People Without Manners

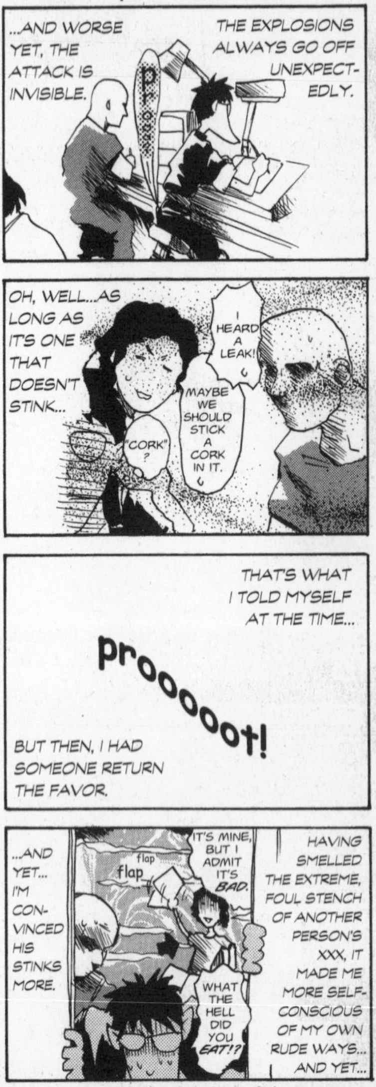
THE EXPLOSIONS ALWAYS GO OFF UNEXPECT-EDLY.
...AND WORSE YET, THE ATTACK IS INVISIBLE.
I HEARD A LEAK!
OH, WELL...AS LONG AS IT'S ONE THAT DOESN'T STINK...
MAYBE WE SHOULD STICK A CORK IN IT.
"CORK"?
THAT'S WHAT I TOLD MYSELF AT THE TIME...
proooooot!
BUT THEN, I HAD SOMEONE RETURN THE FAVOR.
HAVING SMELLED THE EXTREME, FOUL STENCH OF ANOTHER PERSON'S XXX, IT MADE ME MORE SELF-CONSCIOUS OF MY OWN RUDE WAYS... AND YET...
IT'S MINE, BUT I ADMIT IT'S *BAD*.
flap flap
...AND YET... I'M CON-VINCED HIS STINKS MORE.
WHAT THE HELL DID YOU *EAT!?*

These days, we hardly take notice of them anymore...

We Who Get Wrapped Up, Part II

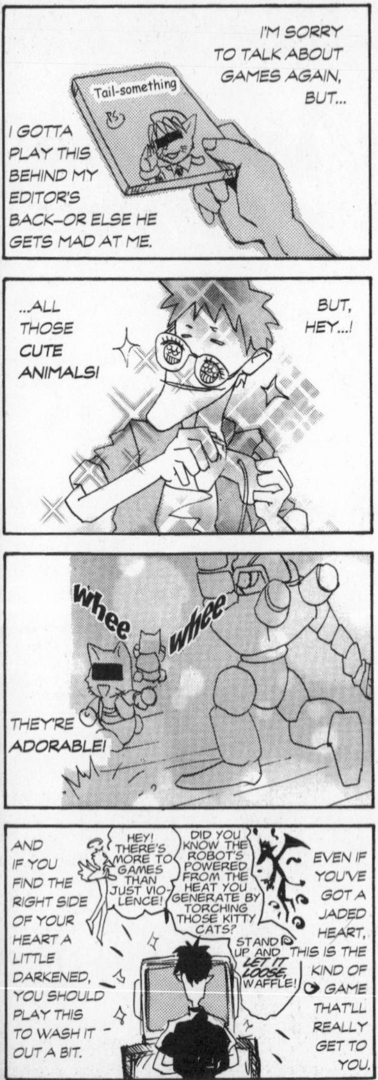
I'M SORRY TO TALK ABOUT GAMES AGAIN, BUT...
Tail-something
I GOTTA PLAY THIS BEHIND MY EDITOR'S BACK—OR ELSE HE GETS MAD AT ME.
BUT, HEY...!
...ALL THOSE CUTE ANIMALS!
whee
whee
THEY'RE ADORABLE!
EVEN IF YOU'VE GOT A JADED HEART, THIS IS THE KIND OF GAME THAT'LL REALLY GET TO YOU.
DID YOU KNOW THE ROBOT'S POWERED FROM THE HEAT YOU GENERATE BY TORCHING THOSE KITTY CATS?
HEY! THERE'S MORE TO GAMES THAN JUST VIO-LENCE!
STAND UP AND *LET IT LOOSE,* WAFFLE!
AND IF YOU FIND THE RIGHT SIDE OF YOUR HEART A LITTLE DARKENED, YOU SHOULD PLAY THIS TO WASH IT OUT A BIT.

Doesn't this have the exact opposite message of We Who Get Wrapped Up, Part I?

EXCEL SAGA RETURNS IN DECEMBER!

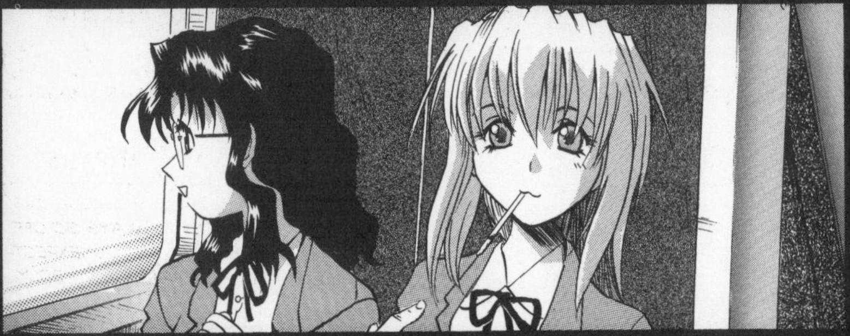

IT'S THE BIG SCHOOL FIELD TRIP EXTRAVAGANZA!

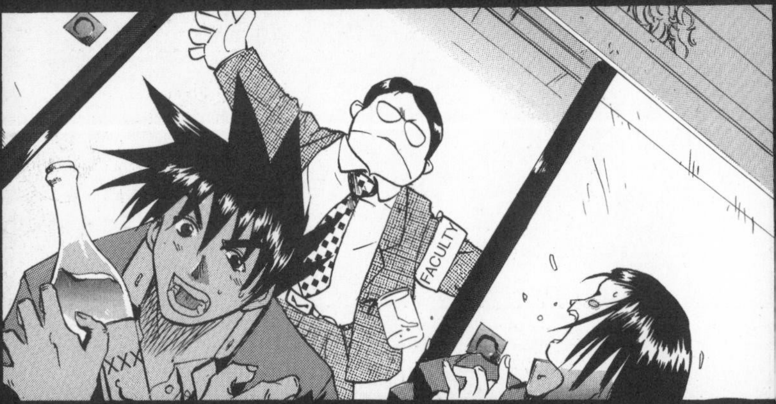
FACULTY

YES…IT'LL NO DOUBT BRING UP MEMORIES OF YOUR OWN STUDENT DAYS

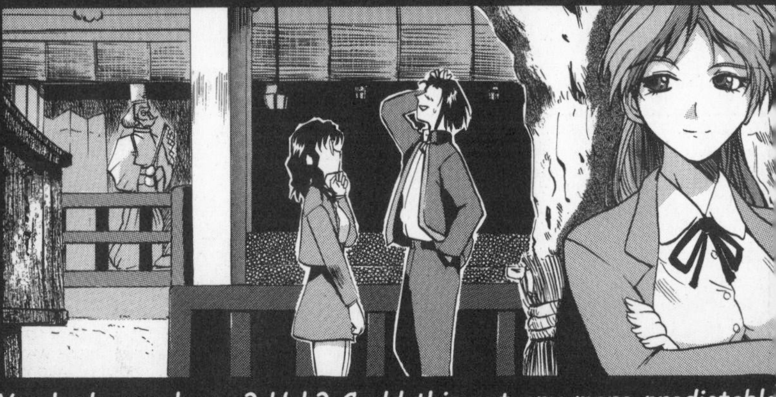

You had enough now? Huh? Could this get any more predictable

Guide to Excel Saga 03's Sound Effects!

8-2——FX: G'ThuK (gosu, sound, placing something heavy)

9-1——FX: peel peel (shyu shyu, movement, peeling)

9-3——FX: munch munch (kori kori, depiction)

9-4——FX: klak klak (ka', sound)

9-5——FX: g'ThuDd! (gatan, sound)

10-1-1——FX: kREEEK! (kiin, sound, loud feedback)

10-1-2——FX: v'BANGg (zudon, depiction)

10-3/4-FX: k'KREEK K'CRACK kREEKRIK! (bikiki, sound and depiction, something being strained excessively)

10-5——FX: GASP (hata, depiction)

11-1-1——FX: kreek kreek (kirikiri, sound)

11-1-2——FX: f'SHshSHshSH (fushuuu, sound and depiction, all spent)

12-3——FX: klak (kotsu, sound)

12-5——FX: kla'chak (kochi', sound)

13-2-1——FX: thok thok (ton ton, sound)

13-2-2——FX: k'chak k'chak (chiki chiki, sound, mechanical)

13-5——FX: thh'chakk (kasa..., sound and depiction, moving things about)

14-5——FX: kla'chak (kochi', sound)

15-1——FX: priririrr pririri (piriri', sound)

15-2——FX: clak'shnnk (suka, sound and depiction, no more staples)

15-4——FX: puu˜˜˜ (pu-, sound, the phone sound after being hung up)

15-6——FX: vV'RI˜˜˜P (biririr, sound and depiction, ripping)

15-7——FX: (background) thh'chakk thh'chakk thh'chakk thh'chakk thh'chakk (kuki, sound and depiction, moving things about)

Most of Rikdo Koshi's original sound FX are left in their original Japanese in the Viz edition of Excel Saga; exceptions being handwritten dialogue and "drawn" notes that have the character of captions. Although these sounds are all listed as "FX," they are of two types: onomatopoeia (in Japanese, giseigo) where the writing is used in an attempt to imitate the actual sound of something happening, and mimesis (in Japanese, gitaigo) where the writing is used to attempt to convey rhetorically a state, mood, or condition.

Whereas the first type of FX will invariably be portrayed with kana, the second may use kana and/or kanji. One should note that there is often overlap between these two types. Onomatopoeia notes: Sound refers to audible sounds being generated somehow. Movement refers to the physical movement, or lack of movement, of something; not audible or mostly not audible. Depiction refers to the psychological state of something or someone. In the unlikely event the matter slipped your mind during the two-month gap between vol. 02 and 03, all numbers are given in the original Japanese reading order: right-to-left.

Thanks to all of you out there reading Excel Saga who made Vol. 01 such a success! You might have seen (you could have hardly avoided) the life-size cardboard standees of Excel that landed in August in over 1,000 bookstores throughout North America. Makes it look as if ACROSS has speeded up its agenda for world conquest, doesn't it? As always, please feel free, dear member of the masses, to write Oubliette c/o Excel Saga, VIZ, LLC, P.O. Box 77064, San Francisco, CA, 94107.

25-5 ——FX v'WOOF! (gau!, sound)

26-1 ——FX CH'anK CH'anK CH'anK CH'anK CH'anK (gakin, sound)

26-2 ——FX v'WOOF! vV'RooF v'WOOF (gau' bau, sound)

26-3-1 –FX v'V... (ga', sound)

26-3-2 –FX th-THUMP (pita, depiction, sudden freeze -> changed to heart beat)

26-5 ——FX ph'TiNG! (biku', depiction, alarm)

27-1 ——FX Huff huff (dialog)

27-2-1 –FX fssk (nosori, depiction, appear slowly -> movement)

27-2-2 –FX wheeze wheeze (ze~, sound)

27-2-3 –FX k'thuk (koton..., sound)

27-3 ——FX ja'jangle! (zyaran!, sound chains)

27-7-1 –FX gGriKk..kK (kiri, depiction and sound, something strung up)

27-7-2 –FX gGriKk..kK (kiri, depiction and sound, something strung up)

27-3 ——FX wheeze wheeze wheeze (ze, sound)

28-2 ——FX wobble (tere~~~, depiction and movement)

28-4 ——FX jika (sound, step forward)

28-5 ——FX kla'chank (gacha, sound)

29-2 ——FX th-Thut (suta, movement)

29-5 ——FX fssk (kuru, movement, turn -> movement)

30-3 ——FX whisk! (sui', movement)

31-5 ——FX flap flap (pata, movement)

32-2 ——FX Hah haha haha! (dialog)

32-4-1 –FX p'THAp' (pata, movement)

32-4-2 –FX thh'chakk (kasa..., sound and depiction, moving things about)

33-1 ——FX ph'fft (pon, depiction)

16-3 ——FX: k'tak k'tak kreek kreek k'tak k'tak kreek (kata, sound, typing) (kari, sound, writing)

16-4 ——FX: klak klak klak (kaki, sound, typing into calculator)

16-5 ——FX: k'tak k'tak k'tak k'tak k'tak k'tak (kata, sound, typing)

17-3 ——FX: k'thud (gata', sound)

17-5 ——FX: kla'CHAKk (gachya, sound, door knob)

18-1 ——FX: b'THUmp (batan, sound)

18-4 ——FX: fssk fssk (suru suru, depiction, opening poster)

20-1 ——FX: v'VumphV b'BRRm v'RRRmmm (basun, sound, coughing engine) (bosu, sound) (burororo, sound, engine noise)

20-2-1 –FX: v'VumphV' (gofun, sound)

20-2-2 –FX: s'creek' (ki, sound)

20-3 ——FX: b'THmp! (batan!, sound)

20-4 ——FX: b'THmp (batan, sound)

21-1 ——FX: zsh'SHINGg! (babi', depiction)

21-3 ——FX: zZ'rak zZ'rak (zuru, depiction, dragging)

21-4 ——FX: v'THUd! (dosa!, sound)

21-5 ——FX: ggrip (kyu, depiction)

22-1 ——FX: A'RATHH! (gabaa', movement)

23-5 ——FX: t'thutt t'thutt t'thutt (ta', movement)

24-2 ——FX: zz'rak zz'rak (za' za', sound, gathering something)

24-4-1 –FX: (up and down) t'thutt (ta', movement)

24-4-2 –FX th'THUNK! (sukon!, sound)

25-3 ——FX What the!? (dialog)

25-4 ——FX gGRgRgRgRgRgRgR (urghghgh~~~,sound)

50-1——FX	eh'eeek eh'eeek eh'eeek (gea, sound, ominous sounding bird)	
50-4——FX	thBPLth (bu', sound, plosive bilabial)	
51-4——FX	ta-DAH (don, depiction)	
52-1-1–FX	thak thak thak thak (do ga gaga ka, sound and depiction, series of images being presented)	
52-1-2–FX	tltltlt'tut tut (dara' da' da', sound and depiction, improvised drumroll?)	
54-3——FX	ph'Wwoo… (hyu~, sound, wind blowing and rustling leaves)	
54-5——FX	yank! (gu', movement)	
56-3——FX	shake shake (bun bun, movement)	
57-5——FX	b'Thump (batan, sound)	
59-6——FX	th'chakk (goso, sound and depiction, moving things about)	
59-7——FX	peel (pi', movement)	
60-1——FX	phBLrp! (bu', sound, plosive bilabial)	
60-2——FX	GASP (ha', depiction)	
60-5——FX	(all the same one) a'Rath a'Rath a'Rath (bun, movement, violent shaking)	
61-6——FX	hHISSS~~~ (shagya~~~, sound)	
63-2——FX	zsh'SHINGg! (babi', depiction)	
64-3——FX	klak klak (ka', sound)	
64-4-1–FX	Hahaha (dialog)	
64-4-2–FX	b'Thump (batan, sound)	
66-1——FX	clap clap (pachi pachi, sound)	
67-1——FX	poink poink poink (pata pota, depiction, a droplet falling)	
67-4——FX	zZ'SHrk! (zuza', sound)	
67-5——FX	zZINGg' (bi', depiction and movement, fast movement followed by sudden stop)	
68-3——FX	klakla'chak klakla'chak (kasha, sound, flipping score board like sign)	

33-3——FX	kreek kreek k'kree~~~k (kukyu kaki kekya' kyu~, sound, writing)	
33-4——FX	wh'THUD (doka, sound)	
34-2-1–FX	wh'THUD (doka, sound)	
34-2-2–FX	k'KRAK! (meri, sound)	
34-4——FX	phPH~~~ (goha~, depiction, lot of smoke billowing out)	
35——FX	ph'fft (pon, depiction)	
38-2——FX	vNnNNNN (ooo, sound, dramatic space)	
38-4——FX	vNnnn (ooo, depiction and sound, dramatic space)	
39-2——FX	sh'ZINGg' (bi', depiction and movement, fast movement followed by sudden stop)	
44-4-1–FX	ggrab (hishi, movement)	
44-4-2–FX	fssk (suka, movement)	
45-1——FX	Shattered… (ga~n, depiction)	
46-4-1–FX	g'GRAB! (munzu!, movement)	
46-4-2–FX	YANK! (gu', movement)	
47-1——FX	Hya!! (dialog)	
47-3——FX	fssk (su, movement)	
47-5——FX	th'chakk (goso, sound and depiction, moving things about)	
47-6——FX	peel (pira, movement)	
48-1——FX	ffssk!! (ka', depiction, sudden movement and dramatic close up -> movement)	
48-2-1–FX	a'rath vW'rth (basaan, sound)	
48-2-2–FX	honk honk (pafu, sound)	
48-4-1–FX	wheeze wheeze (ze~, sound)	
48-4-2–FX	honk… (pafu, sound)	
49-1-1–FX	ggrip (kyu, movement)	
49-1-2–FX	ffsk'! (bi', movement)	
49-2——FX	ggri~~~p (gigigi, depiction)	

79-7 ——FX kKla´chaK (gacha, sound)

80-1 ——FX k´thudd k´thudd k´thudd (doya, depiction and sound, noisily moving about)

80-3-1 ---FX v´thump (don!, sound, sitting down)

80-3-2 –FX (small) thud! (go´, sound)

80-4-1 –FX kreek´o kreek´o (kuge, depiction and sound, comic)

80-4-2 –FX Tsk! (dialog)

81-1 ——FX g´ThuDd! (gatan, sound)

81-5 ——FX Humph (dialog)

82-6 ——FX th´oink (to´, movement and depiction, sudden)

83-2 ——FX kthnkt (gaku, depiction and movement, collapsing and/or prone movement)

84-3 ——FX ggrip (gu´, depiction)

85-7-1 –FX thlbpt (bu!, depiction)

85-7-2 –FX g´thunk! (gata, sound)

86-3-1 –FX (in wb) ph´ting! (piku, depiction)

86-3-2 –FX th-THUMP (giku, depiction)

86-3-3 –FX BamMP (don!, sound)

87-4 ——FX th´phat th´phat th´phat (pata, sound, panicky walk)

88-5 ——FX ZZZ (su, sound)

91-2 ——FX gacha (kachnk, sound of door)

92-1 ——FX BANG ! (ban!, sound and depiction)

93-3 ——FX ggrind (giri, depiction, grinding teeth)

93-4 ——FX z´zLuRRRP (zuzu, sound, fill in back as needed)

93-5 ——FX th-THUMp (biku´, depiction)

94-1 ——FX gak! (u´, dialog)

94-5 ——FX ph´Zz… (za´, sound, wind)

68-6 ——FX fssk´ fssk´ (kuri´, movement, turning -> movement)

72-4 ——FX phew (fu´, depiction, sighing)

72-5 ——FX klak (ka´, sound)

72-6 ——FX kk´lak kk´lak (zuka, sound, reinforced)

73-3 ——FX k´reek k´reek k´ree~~k (kyu, depiction)

74-4-1 —FX kKRACKk (baki´, sound, breakage)

74-4-2 –FX kLa´chankK-chank (garan, sound, rolling)

74-4-3 —FX th´RAAAAASHshshsh (ka´shan, sound)

74-6 ——FX rustle bustle (zawa, depiction)

75-2-1 —FX pu´PREEP (pu´po~n, sound, electronic)

75-2-2 —FX (small, white) pip (pu´, sound)

75-2-3 —FX (small text) click (kachi´, sound)

75-3-1 —FX zZak´ (bu´, sound)

75-3-2 —FX k´thath… (ka´, sound)

75-4-1 —FX kla´chak (gasha, sound)

75-4-2 –FX yank (zui´, movement and depiction, getting close -> movement)

75-5 ——FX t´thut t´thut t´thut (suta, movement, quick)

76-3 ——FX shashashashake (kakaka, depiction, shaking)

76-4 ——FX THBPLTH (bu´, sound, plosive bilabial expletive)

76-6 ——FX huff puff (hufu, sound)

77-1 ——FX fsk fsk (te´, depiction, fast and accurate movement)

77-2 ——FX fssk fsk fssk fsk (as above)

77-3 ——FX kla´chak (kacha´, sound)

77-5 ——FX B´thump (batann…, sound)

78-4 ——FX fssk´ (ku´, movement, quick turn -> movement)

101-3 —FX	worry worry worry worry (oro oro, depiction)	
101-4 —FX	th'sss… (su~, depiction and sound, inhaling)	
101-5 —FX	gCH'cOaUGHh (gopu', sound, coughing up something)	
102-1-1 -FX	th'phat (pata, sound, flapping like)	
102-1-2 -FX	th'sss… (su~, depiction and sound, inhaling)	
102-5 —FX	kyu'whine~~~ (kyu~~, sound, whining)	
102-6 —FX	a'roo~~~f (hyu-n, sound, whine)	
102-8 —FX	fF'lash' (ka', depiction)	
102-9 —FX	ph'VLupVLupVLupVLup (dodo~, sound, gushing water)	
103-1 —FX	thok (ton', sound)	
103-4 —FX	thok thok thok (ton' tom' ton', sound)	
104-1 —FX	TH'THUMP!! (do biku', depiction)	
104-4 —FX	Heh heh heh heheee (dialog)	
104-5 —FX	ph'WwooWoo (hyu~, sound, wind blowing, dramatic)	
105-1 —FX	z'ZNORree (fuga~, sound)	
105-4-1 -FX	kK'BLAAAMmm (zubaaan, sound, explosion)	
105-4-2-FX	vGRGGGRRRGR (gogogoooo, sound, smoldering)	
107-3 —FX	rroarrrr (ooo, sound, residual)	
108-2 —FX	b'BlamM (daaan, sound)	
109-6 —FX	z'ZNORree (fuga~, sound)	
110-1-1 -FX	SNORRRE (gu~, sound)	
110-1-2-FX	Grngnrnnn (goo', depiction, gaunt and vast atmosphere)	
110-2 —FX	kla'CHAnG kla'CHAnG (gashakon gashakon, sound, metal armor)	
110-3 —FX	zz'RAK (zya', sound)	

94-6 —FX	ph'arUTH AruTH z'RTHth (bababa, sound, wind fluttering clothing)	
94-7 —FX	v'phWOo'zZrth'woo… (baa' sound and depiction, wind plus dramatic)	
95-3 —FX	rROAR' (oo', sound and depiction, roaring crowds)	
95-4 —FX	(in background) Hail! RA ~~~ ! U'RAAA~~~ (etc., dialog)	
96-5 —FX	zZINGg' (bi', depiction and movement, fast movement followed by sudden stop)	
97-1 —FX	a'RhuTH' (ba', sound and depiction, clothing)	
97-3 —FX	GASP (ha', depiction)	
98-3 —FX	wheeze wHEEz wheeze (ze-, sound)	
98-6 —FX	th'chrunch th'crunch (kusha', sound and depiction)	
98-7-1 -FX	th'chrunch (kusha', sound and depiction)	
98-7-2 -FX	munch munch (mofu, sound and depiction)	
99-1-1 —FX	hg'gnk! (gokun!, sound, swallowing)	
99-1-2 -FX	z'Rathh (basa', sound)	
99-3 —FX	zZ'Chak! (zaa', sound)	
99-4 —FX	zZ'claksh zZ'claksh zZ'claksh (za, sound, lot of loose items)	
99-6 —FX	ka'CHINk ka'CHINk ka'CHINk ka'CHINk (ka', sound)	
99-7 —FX	ka'CHINk ka'CHINk ka'CHINk ka'CHINk (ka', sound)	
99-8 —FX	KA'CHIN'K (ka', sound)	
100-2 —FX	ph'Wwoo'ArathrTH… (zaa', sound, wind blowing and rustling leaves)	
101-1 —FX	GASP (ha', depiction)	
101-2-1 -FX	th'chakk (goso, sound and depiction, moving things about)	
101-2-2 -FX	th-THMP th-THMP (doki doki, depiction, pounding heart)	

119-3 —FX WHEEZE z'WEEz WHEEZE (ze-ha-, sound, heavy breathing)

121-2 —FX KTHNKT KTHNKT (gaku gaku, depiction and movement, collapsing and/or prone movement)

122-1 —FX t'DuTHh (da', movement, dashing movement)

122-2 —FX b'Thump (batan, sound)

122-4 —FX waddle waddle (noso noso, movement)

122-5 —FX pfft (pofu, sound)

123-4 —FX s'SHINnnn (saaa', depiction, sun starting to shine through)

125-1 —FX pip (pí', sound, electronic)

125-3 —FX k'thud (gata', sound)

125-4 —FX kR'clacla! (gara!, sound, opening sliding door resting on bearings)

126-5 —FX ph'ap! (pan', sound)

127-1 —FX fssh'k! (ki', movement, rapid movement followed by stop)

127-2 —FX ph'tap (bi', movement)

127-4 —FX t'thut t'thut (sutasuta, movement and depiction, walking away)

128-1-1 -FX ph'thap (tan', sound, closing door)

128-1-2 -FX th'that! (ton', sound, sitting down)

128-4 —FX zz'thunk zz'thunk (zobu zobu, sound, snow crunching)

128-5 —FX huph wheeze (ze' fu', sound)

131-2 —FX Kla'chak! (gacha', sound)

131-3 —FX Hahaha (dialog)

132-1 —FX K'chnk (cha, sound, sudden behind)

132-4-1 -FX klang klang (kan', sound)

132-4-2 -FX (white) Humph (dialog)

132-4-3 -FX klang (kan, sound)

133-2 —FX klang klang (kan kan, sound)

110-4 —FX zz'THRAzthAzthAz (zu'shaaa, depiction, something ominous and large appearing)

110-5 —FX sh'SHINGg! (zya'kiin', depiction)

111-1 —FX fidget fidget (niki niki, movement)

111-2 —FX arath' (muku, movement, getting up)

111-3—FX th'chak (gara, sound and depiction, moving things about)

111-4 —FX kla'chank (kapa, sound)

111-5 —FX kla'chankmpp' (gapan, sound)

111-8 —FX b'thmpt (batan, sound)

112-1-1 -FX b'Thump (batamu, sound)

112-1-2 -FX v'rrommm (burorororo, sound)

112-2 —FX klang klang (kan, sound)

112-3/4-FX STARE (zi͂, depiction)

115-1 —FX k'blup k'bluv k'blup k'bluv (kato koto, sound, boiling quietly)

115-4 —FX k'blup k'bluv k'blup k'bluv (kato koto, sound, boiling quietly)

115-5 —FX ppPSSSHTt' (pushuu, sound, gas release ending)

117-3 —FX flap flap (pata pata, movement)

118-1 —FX shiver shiver (kata kata, depiction)

118-2 —FX pfft pfft (posu posu, depiction, soft tapping)

118-3 —FX b'fft B'ffTt bB'fft (bon dosu, depiction and sound, a little stronger)

118-4-1 -FX Hup! Hup! Hup! (dialog)

118-4-2 -FX gG'fssk fG'fssk gG'fssk (ki', movement, massaging)

118-5 —FX Shla'CHAK! (zya', depiction, getting something ready)

119-1-1 -FX HurPH!! (dialog)

119-1-2 -FX zzZRACKK! (bikon, sound and depiction, electric shock)

143-1-1 -FX k'CHAK'tnn (ga'kooon, sound, trap door opening)

143-1-2 -FX kK'SPALASHsh (bashaan', sound)

143-2 —FX klang klang klang (kan kan kan, sound)

143-3 —FX sp'lurshss (zabu', sound)

143-4-1 -FX klang klang (kan kan, sound)

143-4-2 -FX sp'lash sp'latch (basha pasha, sound)

145-1 —FX thoink (tosu', sound, deceptively not loud but crucial blow)

145-5 —FX creeeak (kishi,' sound, chair leaning back)

147-2 —FX k'thud (gata', sound)

148-1 —FX sp'lash (basha, sound)

149-2 —FX kla'chack (cha', sound)

149-4 —FX ph'ting! (piku, depiction)

149-6 —FX whisk (pi', sound)

150-1-1 -FX fssk (su', movement)

150-1-2 -FX zz'rk (zui', movement and sound, abrasive)

150-2 —FX p'fft (po', depiction)

150-3 —FX ph'fft (pon, depiction)

150-4 —FX thunk (ton, depiction)

150-6 —FX zup'lash sp'lash (zabu zyabu, sound)

151-1-1 -FX sp'lash (zabu, sound)

151-1-2 -FX sp'lash (zabu, sound)

151-1-3 -FX zup'lash (zyabu, sound)

151-2-1 -FX zup'lash (zyabu, sound)

151-2-2 -FX grumble grumble (muka muka, depiction, anger building up)

151-2-3 -FX sp'lash (zabu, sound)

151-2-4 -FX sp'lash (zabu, sound)

133-4-1 -FX zz'rak zz'rak (za' za', sound, gathering something)

133-4-2 -FX vV'fufft (bofu', sound, something light being piled on)

133-5 —FX k'thunk! (tosu!, movement)

133-6-1 -FX haha (dialog)

133-6-2 -FX ph'ap ph'ap (pan', sound)

134-2 —FX th'CRSHsh (mesha', depiction and sound)

135-1 —FX ff'fuMP! (pofu', sound)

135-3 —FX ph'THOK! (supa, sound)

135-5 —FX f'ffsshk'! (hyu', movement, throwing)

135-6-1 -FX ffsk (shya', movement)

135-6-2 -FX phap (bashi', sound)

136-2 —FX phBLrp! (bu', sound, plosive bilabial)

136-3 —FX ph'ap ph'ap (pata, sound)

136-5 —FX zz'KriK zz'Krik ZZ'KRNCH! (kyu' gyu', sound)

138-1 —FX Ta da ~~~… (ra~~, depicion)

138-2 —FX zz'shing! (zya', depiction)

138-4 —FX kR'clacla! (gara!, sound, opening sliding door resting on bearings)

138-6 —FX fssk! fssk! fssk! (ki', ki', ki', movement)

140-1 —FX nod nod (koku, movement)

141-2 —FX zz'sSHING (zan, depiction, posing)

141-3 —FX ch'CHING (chon', sound, clapper)

141-4 —FX vVRM… (bun', depiction, lighting change)

142-1 —FX vVREEEE~~~ (fuooo, sound, siren)

142-2 —FX VREEEP VREEEP VREEEP (bi~', sound, siren)

142-3-1 -FX VREEP (bi~', sound, siren)

142-3-2 -FX VREEP (bi~', sound, siren)

158-5-1 -FX squeak squeak (chu~, sound)

158-5-2 -FX squeak (chu~, sound)

158-5-3 -FX zz'plashzz (zaza, sound)

158-5-4 -FX squeak (chu~, sound)

158-5-5 -FX squeak (chu~, sound)

158-5-6 -FX squeak (chu~, sound)

158-5-7 -FX zz'plashzz (zaza, sound)

158-5-8 -FX zz'plashzz (zaza, sound)

158-6-1 -FX zqueak zqueak (zu~, sound)

158-6-2 -FX zz'plash (za, sound)

158-6-3 -FX squeak (kii, sound)

158-6-4 -FX k'thudthud (dosasa, sound)

159-3 —FX k'klunkk (gatan, sound)

159-4-1 -FX wha-thud thracsh (dogaragashan, sound)

159-4-2 -FX k'thud (gon, sound)

159-4-3 -FX thrash (gaan, sound)

159-5 —FX wV'splaSHsh! (gopaan!, sound)

159-6-1 -FX phbBLuRRP (bupu~, sound, plosive bilabial)

159-6-2 -FX zz'plash (zabu', sound)

160-2—FX zz'rKk! (za!, movement)

160-5 —FX whezz whezz (ze' ze', sound)

161-1 —FX kk'KTHNK (gon', sound)

161-2 —FX k'thuk kla'chunk (gon' baan, sound)

161-3 —FX nnNNNN ~~~ (shinnn, depiction, silence)

161-4 —FX ffsk'! (bi', movement)

161-5 —FX Aaruth (gaba', movement)

162-1 —FX zVRzRzRzR (zuzuzu, sound, rumbling)

162-2 —FX zVRzRzRzR (zuzuzu, sound, rumbling)

151-3 —FX fssk' (ki', movement)

152-1 —FX klak klak (ko', sound)

152-3/5 FX va'VaUMPp! (baannn, sound and depiction, dramatic opening of door)

154-1 —FX ggrip! (ga', depiction)

154-2 —FX vgrrnnnn (ooon, sound, residual)

154-5-1 -FX thoink (kon', movement, light heart ed yank)

154-5-2 -FX (black) ka'chank ka'chank (kon kon, sound, mechanical)

154-5-3 -FX (black, lower) squeak squeak (chuu~, sound)

154-5-4 -FX meow (nya~, sound)

155-1 —FX f'shSHUnk!!

155-4 —FX Ggrip (gu', movement)

155-6 —FX ggrip (gu', depiction)

155-7-1 -FX kla'CHUNK! (jagoon!, sound)

155-7-2 -FX kR'clacla (gara!, sound, something sliding)

155-7-3 -FX wud'THUD (dan)

156-1 —FX kla'chunk (gakon, sound)

156-2 —FX kreek kreek kreek (kririri, sound)

156-4 —FX zup'lash zup'lash (zyabu zyabu, sound)

156-5-1 -FX twirl (kuin', movement)

156-5-2 -FX (lower) zup'lash (zyabu zyabu, sound)

157-1 —FX quiver quiver (piri piri, depiction, fidgeting from extreme tension)

158-2-1 -FX kla'klunk kla'klunk (gaki kaki, sound)

158-2-2 -FX k'thunk (gadan, sound)

158-3-1 -FX kla'thud (gann, sound)

158-3-2 -FX b'thump (batan, sound)

158-3-3 -FX vGRRRR (dogogo, sound)

162-4-1 -FX ph'thap (hata, movement)

162-4-2 -FX ph'thap (hata, movement)

162-4-3 -FX yank (gu', depiction)

163-1-1 -FX kla'chunk (gakon, sound)

163-1-2 -FX b'thump (batan, sound)

163-1-3 -FX ph'snap (buchi, sound and depic tion, something snapping)

163-2-1 -FX zz'PLASSH (zapupu, sound)

163-2-2 -FX v'pLURSSSSH (dozayazyaaa, sound)

163-4 —FX vV'Whoosh (goo, sound and depic tion, incoming large mass)

163-5 —FX zVRzRzRzR (zuzuzu, sound, rum bling)

163-6 —FX zVRzRzRzR (zuzuzu, sound, rum bling)

164-3 —FX vV'umpP! (bo'!, sound and move ment)

164-4 —FX vV'Whoosh' (do', sound and depic tion, incoming large mass)

164-5 —FX v'VLupVLupVLupVLup (dodo~, sound, gushing water)

165-1 —FX th'VLupVLupVLupVLup (dobobaba ba, sound, gushing water)

165-2-1 -FX VlupVLupVLupVLup (dododo, sound)

165-2-2 -FX blub (kobo, sound)

165-2-3 -FX zZ'VlupVLupVLupVLup (zobobobo, sound)

165-3-1 -FX VlupVLupVLupVLup (dododo, sound)

165-3-2–FX struggle struggle (zita zita, depic tion)

165-3-3–FX VlupVLupVLupVLup (dododo, sound)

165-4-1 -FX wheeze (ze' ze', sound)

165-4-2 -FX Zz'plash (zapu, sound)

165-4-3 -FX wheeze wheeze (ze' ze', sound)

165-4-4 -FX zZ'plashplashplashplash (zyabobobo, sound)

165-5 —FX glare (ki', depiction)

165-6 —FX thrash thrash (zya', movement)

165-7 —FX kla'channnk (gukan', sound, heavy)

165-8 —FX v'VLUBb' (gobo', sound)

166-1 —FX vV'WHOOSSH (do', sound)

166-2 —FX zVLzBRzRzR (zuzuzu, sound, rum bling)

167-1 —FX vV'LuBbVLupVLupblopblopblop... (dozubabobogopopopo', sound)

168-3 —FX z'thrshshshshs (zaa, sound, run ning water)

168-5 —FX z'thrshshshshs (zaa, sound, run ning water)

168-6-1–FX poink (poto, depiction, a droplet falling)

168-6-2 -FX p'TinK (piku, depiction)

169-1-1 -FX a'RrUTHh! (gaba, movement, get ting up)

169-1-2 -FX ph'lashsh (pasha', sound)

169-2 —FX sSH'plash sSH'plash sSH'plash (bichi, movement, shaking head, shaking free of liquid)

169-7 —FX th'PLASH th'PLASH th'PLASH (bachya, sound)

170-3-1 -FX A'RuTH (ku', movement, getting up)

170-3-2 -FX zz'Rth... (zuru, depiction, abrasive slipping movement)

171-1-1 -FX sup'lash sp'lash sup'lashsh (zapa' basha basha, sound)

171-2 —FX KTHNKT KTHNKT (gaku gaku, depiction and movement, collaps ing and/or prone movement)

172-4-1 -FX th'plash th'plash th'plash (badada da, movement, running)

180-3 —FX	sp'lash sp'latch (basha pasha, sound)	
180-4/5 -FX	gG'Thuk! (goon!, sound, heavy mechanical)	
181-1 —FX	gG'Zkreek (zu', sound, heavy)	
181-3 —FX	pHUp (chi´, depiction, light turned on, minute)	
181-4 —FX	ffSHink! (kyun!, sound and movement, Star Trek doors)	
181-5 —FX	vVRM... (bun', depiction, lighting change)	
182-1 —FX	wh'THUD (goto, sound)	
182-4 —FX	rock rock (yusa yusa, depiction and movement)	
182-6 —FX	gasp (ha´, depiction)	
182-7 —FX	shake shake (bun bun, movement)	
183-3 —FX	vVRM... (bun´, depiction, lighting change)	
183-4 —FX	vVRMMMmmm (kooon ooo, sound, some computer like)	
184-2 —FX	A'RUTH! (gaba', movement, sound)	
185-3 —FX	ph'fft (pon, depiction)	
185-4-1 -FX	sp'lash (basha, sound)	
185-4-2 -FX	sp'lash (basha, sound)	
185-5 —FX	sp'lash (pasha, sound)	
186-1 —FX	flap flap (hira, movement)	
186-4 —FX	VRMMM! (don´, sound, command being issued like effect)	
186-5 —FX	zZ'Whoosh! (zan, sound)	
186-6/7 FX	v'VLupVLupVLupVLup (dodo¯, sound, gushing water)	
187-1 —FX	vV'oosh! (do, sound)	
187-5 —FX	rR'whoosshshsh (ooo, sound, residual)	
188-4 —FX	thrPLAsh SuPLAsh thrPLAsh SuPLAsh (zazazaza..., sound, waves)	

172-4-2 -FX	zZp'lash! (basha!, sound)	
173-1-1 -FX	zZp'lash zZp'lash (basha, basha sound)	
173-1-2 -FX	wheez wheez (ha haa, sound)	
173-2 —FX	wheeze whezz' whezz' wheeze (ze' ze¯', sound)	
173-4 —FX	fssk (zya', movement)	
174-1 —FX	zZp'lashhh (bashaa, sound)	
174-2 —FX	zup'lash sp'lash (pasha' basha, sound)	
174-3 —FX	zup'lash sp'lash (pasha, sound)	
175-6 —FX	p'fft (pon, movement)	
175-7 —FX	fssk' fssk' (kyu' kyu', movement)	
175-8 —FX	zz'gripp (gu', movement)	
176-1 —FX	zV'phREEEeee (zuhyuuu ooo, depiction and sound, dramatic enhancement of inhaling sound)	
176-4 —FX	p'phft' (poi, movement and depiction, tossing something away)	
176-5-1 —FX	ggrip (gu', movement)	
176-5-2 —FX	p'fft (pon, movement)	
176-5-3 —FX	p'fft (pon, movement)	
177-1 —FX	ggrip ggrip (gu', gu' movement)	
177-2-1 -FX	ggrip~~~ (gyuuu, depiction)	
177-2-2 -FX	pop snap crackle (boki, baki, beki', sound)	
177-4 —FX	nod (koku, movement)	
178-4 —FX	p'fft (pon, movement)	
179-2 —FX	hg'sob hk'sob hrk'sob (ukku hikku egu, sound, sobbing)	
179-3 —FX	hg'sob hk'sob hrk'sob (e', sound, sobbing)	
179-4 —FX	a'rath (muku, movement)	
180-1 —FX	kla'chak (kashan, sound)	
180-2 —FX	klang'chank klang'chank (gacha, gacha sound)	

public appearances in military uniform, being active at top-level military planning sessions, and of course, all military orders being issued in the Emperor's name.

But part of the reason the US occupation of Japan seemed better-organized than that of, say, Iraq, is that America decided keeping the top leader in place (i.e., the Emperor) would help to better keep order. Since, unlike Saddam Hussein, Hirohito was not personally cruel or vicious, many people were willing to buy the idea that he had been a man of peace, when in fact he hadn't—forgetting that's not the same thing as being a peaceful man, which in fact he always was.

19-2 This SDF recruitment poster is the second, but by no means the last goof by Rikdo-san on Saint Tail. The use of anime characters on government posters is no joke, though. It isn't just classics like Astro Boy (a.k.a. Tetsuwan Atom) being on the customs and immigrations posters at Narita Airport (the fact that he can fire machine guns from his ass, while they retain the option to search yours with a gloved hand, is presumably intended to remind you of the power of the state). Near Shinjuku Station, in a police box—the one between that open plaza below the stairs were people pass out flyers and samples, and the place where they put up all the huge movie ads—the editor has witnessed with his own eyes Ruri-Ruri from Nadesico on a poster urging the use of safety belts low and tight. There were also back in 1997 public-service ads using Shinji and Asuka from Evangelion to promote saving water (wouldn't Misato have been more appropriate?).

Evangelion's co-producer, Hiroyuki Yamaga, once told the editor that he never knew a Japanese cop who wasn't an otaku (this may be the real reason Mamoru Oshii told Animerica magazine he hates cops), because where else are you going to get a chance to carry a gun and dress in a uniform on a daily basis? In the SDF, also, of course—but bear in mind that any prospective recruit grew up watching giant monster (kaiju) films which give the impression you if you join up you'll get to fight Gamera.

24-3-3 No. At the time this story was published (and perhaps today as well) door-to-door canvassing by political candidates was forbidden by law; furthermore Japan has severe restrictions on campaign advertising, usually allowing it no earlier than a month before the election. Robert Whiting's "A Note About Continued Corruption" (p. 345–346) in the back of his biography (another "Oubliette Pick") Tokyo Underworld: The Fast Times and Hard Life of an American Gangster in Japan (a sort of true-crime version of Megatokyo) suggests Rikdo's portrayal of "direct retail" money politics is hardly an exaggeration. A Harris poll conducted in Japan and the U.S. only a few weeks after this volume's original Japanese publication found that 75% of Japanese agreed with the statement "there are many dishonest people who manage our national politics," while only 30% of Americans felt that way about their own country's government. Only 40% of Japanese agreed with the statement "their vote counts for much," compared to 60% of Americans. Of course, the 2000 Presidential election was just around the corner, after which we might begin perhaps to see things more from the Japanese point of view.

25-3 Excel originally used the English letter "W," which is so employed in Japanese real estate listings to indicate a "double." This is exactly the original meaning it had in Rumiko Takahashi (creator, Inu-Yasha)'s manga story "1 or W," collected in the graphic novel Rumic Theater: 1 or Double which, by amazing coincidence, is also available from Viz.

48-2-1 PHS (Personal Handy-phone System) is a service provided by NTT in Japan, where the signal is carried by numerous (relatively) low powered antennas, such as those attached to public telephone boxes. One of the largest sticking points is that the roaming range is limited, and if you are moving quickly (i.e. in a train or car) the "passing off" of the connection of the phone from one access point to another access point may not work all the time. It is still in service in Japan as it is considered to be the cheaper (but limited) alternative to the more versatile regular cell phone services, such as CDMA One and FOMA.

61-1 Yeah, the Pokémon slogan, although the original Japanese version of it is half-English already: "Getto [i.e., "get"] da ze!" meaning "Gotta get 'em!"

83-4-1 The "killer move" that Kikaida uses to defeat his opponent. Jinzo

14-1 Excel Saga Vol. 3 had its original Japanese date of publication on September 1, 1998. Rikdo-san, despite his remarks at the beginning of Vol. 2, appears to get each "Mission" into Excel's monthly home magazine, Young King Ours, like clockwork. Since this reference is in the first part of Vol. 3, it would imply it was originally written in early 1998. But Ryutaro Hashimoto was PM then (see, American youth aren't interested either) and he don't look like this ghoul. Hashimoto was born in Okayama Prefecture, like Sumiyoshi, although it is interesting that his official Ministry of Foreign Affairs bio claims he was born in Tokyo and makes no mention of the fact he represented Okayama in the Diet (inheriting his father's seat, something that would never happen in our country) for thirty-five years.

He looks a bit more like the man who followed Hashimoto in July 1998, Keizo Obuchi, who in fact did die in office less than two years later. Obuchi (who was Foreign Minister at the time this story must have run in Young King Ours—as in Hashimoto's case, the post of Foreign Minister, Japan's equivalent of Secretary of State, is usually considered a stepping-stone to becoming PM) was actually a pretty good guy (his program of tax cuts and deficit spending actually boosted the Japanese economy for a while, something that would also never happen in our country) and proved that even an English Lit. major like himself (Waseda '62) can make good. I wonder if Rikdo Koshi, in checking over the collected stories for Vol. 3, decided to re-write the joke at the last minute?

Of course, there's also the possibility that this guy is just supposed to look like some generically godawful Japanese politician. It might have been funny to rewrite the joke to make it contemporary, and have this Eugene Levy-lookin' campaign worker say, "Well, eventually he got a hair transplant, and now he's the Prime Minister." But I would never insert a historically inaccurate political allusion such as that.

14-5-2 ishh is how it sounds when they scratch "shit" from hip-hop on the radio. I've noticed that in tracks by less dusky musicians (see your exam on p. 207, question 1), the radio tends to either blank out the word entirely (as in NIN's "I wear this crown of _____/Upon my liar's chair") or demand a substitute version (as in AiC's "I'm the man in the box/Shove my nose in _____"). Of course, hip-hop does the drop-out and the clean versions, too, but I kind of like literally doing it with the turntable. Not that Excel said "shit" in the original or anything; there's actually very little swearing in Excel Saga. Not that she was doing a Geto Boys track in the original, either. But because there's actually very little swearing in Excel Saga, that's why she's doing the radio version.

14-5-two-and-a-half: What she said was "I'm sorry, but they don't really interest us," accompanied by a musical note.

17-5 Watanabe originally said to Iwata, "What are you, a lower form of life than a persimmon?" The translator notes that "one way to make persimmons last is to have them air dried, like tomatoes in Italy," but the editor went for making beef jerky.

18-2 Sumiyoshi is referring to the JGSDF, or the Japanese Ground Self-Defense Forces, or what countries without a clause in their constitution forbidding them to have an army would call the "army." In fact, the air, sea, and ground units of the SDF are a well-funded (Japan has a larger military budget than either Britain or France) well-equipped, and reasonably well-trained organization. But for perfectly sensible historical reasons, the military is held in less respect in Japan than it is in the US.

The editor agrees with the school of analysis argued in Yoshikuni Igarashi's book Bodies of Memory (highly recommended last issue, and still highly recommended) that when the US occupied Japan after the Second World War, both countries' dominant policy-makers decided to base Japan's reconstruction efforts on the theory that the disastrous war in Asia had come about because of decisions made by Japan's military leaders.

Many historians today feel that one problem with this theory is not so much that it isn't true, but in the way the theory ignored the fact that the Japanese Emperor at the time, Hirohito (both he, and the era of Japanese history when he reigned—1926-1989—is posthumously known under the name Shōwa [meaning "Enlightened Peace"]; we are now in year 15 of the Heisei [meaning "Achieved Peace"] Emperor, Hirohito's son Akihito) himself acted as one of the top military leaders, having received an education in military issues, making

157-3 "Your pistol is the weapon of last resort" is a line from a wild live-action ninja show (as opposed to those respectable, sedate live-action ninja shows) from the mid-60s, Ninja Butai Gekkou ("Ninja Force Moonlight"). Check out an image from it and the original manga it was based on at http://user.shikoku.ne.jp/yanotesk/SF/Na/gekkou.htm. This is an old reference even for Japanese readers; kind of like saying you're "the new Number Two."

165-4-2 Blaise Pascal, brilliant 17th century French physicist and mathematician. Not only did he invent this awesome geared mechanical calculator, the Pascaline, that was literally centuries ahead of its time, he also founded probability theory with Pierre de Fermat, in order to help out a friend of his who was a professional gambler! His name is used for the scientific unit, the pascal—the pressure or stress on a surface caused by a force of one newton spread over a surface of one square meter. A newton (check out Neal Stephenson's new novel Quicksilver for more info on this dude) is the force required to cause an acceleration of one meter per second squared of a mass of one kilogram in the direction of that force. Remarks like this support my theory that Excel was a high-school girl who snapped while cramming for her college entrance exams.

168-2 Il Palazzo is inferring that the selection of the members in the City Environmental Security Administration is a reflection of the tastes of Kabapu.

187-7-2 A reference to Warrior of Love—Rainbowman, an even more incredibly f-d up sentai show than usual that was on the air 1972-73 (also on KIKU-TV back in the day; for a contemporary article from the Honolulu Star-Bulletin & Advertiser explaining how to tell Rainbowman and Kikaida apart, dial up http://incolor.inebraska.com/stuart/kikaida/hawaii.htm.) For a contemporary retrospective, read all about it in Patrick Macias's article on p. 52 of the September 2003 issue of Animerica (Vol. 11, No. 9). In the show, "scrawny Takeshi Yamato, a name . . . so patriotic you'd figure he snores the Japanese national anthem in his sleep" gets his semi-impressive abilities from the training of Daibadatta, an "old coot in the mountains of India." According to tradition, Daibadatta (a.k.a. Devadatta) was the Buddha's cousin. Sort of like the Iwata family.

Daibadatta is remembered in Buddhist tradition as one of the movement's early villains, who tried to gank the sangha (the community of monks and later, nuns, who lead and guide the Buddhist church) from the Buddha. Interestingly, Daibadatta was said to have super-powers such as flight and the ability to change shape, although Buddhist priests have traditionally explained these powers as a curse upon his bad karma that only led him to disaster. Daibadatta tried to assassinate the Buddha by first sending a giant elephant against him and then by dropping a large boulder; tactics with overtones of both sentai shows and Wile E. Coyote. Daibadatta, by the way, eventually reincarnated into a good guy in Buddhism, as sometimes happens even in the second series of actual sentai shows.

I'm not entirely sure what Excel means by "the curse of Daibadatta," but one theory is that she is referring to an incident where Daibadatta recruited 500 naïve disciples who believed he was a genuine follower of the Buddha. While Daibadatta was preaching to them, Maudgalyayana and Shariputra—two great apostles loyal to the Buddha's teachings—showed up to audit the course; but Daibadatta was so arrogant he told himself they must have come around to his own point of view. After many hours, Daibadatta became tired, and asked Shariputra to take over the sermon. Once Daibadatta was asleep, Shariputra and then Maudgalyayana began to subtly move the teaching over to the Buddha's true doctrine, and then led the whole congregation away while Daibadatta was still snoring.

190-4 Rikdo censored it in the original. I'm guessing the word was ass, as in, the extreme, foul stench of another person's ass. The editor's favorite term for this event is bowel-howl, courtesy of the British magazine Viz (to which Sumiyoshi also owes his accent). The sound FX, however, is Texan, courtesy of Gilbert Shelton.

190-8 To end on a somewhat more wholesome note: the game is Tail Concerto from Altus, which some consider to be one of the best "E"-rated games ever released for the U.S. version of the PS2. In this very cute disc, you play Officer Waffle, a doggie who protects the land of Prairie from the equally cute kittens of the Black Cats Gang in a powered, robotic suit.

Ningen Kikaida, a Watergate-era sentai (Japanese superhero) show. Peep game from a player and chikki-chikki-check out the ad for the re-run on its Honolulu TV site, http://www.kikutv.com/shows/kikaida/. Like the Irish in the Dark Ages translating ancient Greek and Roman knowledge and then bringing it back to the European mainland, the Hawaiians were responsible for producing just about the only subtitled versions of sentai and anime TV shows you could lay hands on before the mid-80s; and hence Beta tapes of them made their way through missionaries to the benighted 48. Original text of Kikaida's slogan is deenji-eendo! (a stretched-out denji-endo), and I've seen it translated as "Electro-End." You might have caught the new anime version, going under the spelling Kikaider, on Adult Swim.

Recently we had a minor blackout at the V-I-Z to the L-L-C. Some people keep candles or a flashlight on hand for such an occasion, but my man Patrick Macias keeps a battery-powered Panasonic LV-75 portable DVD player fully strapped with Kikaida on disc. Together with fellow editors Urian Brown and Kit Fox and designer Benjamin Wright (the fabled "community of man" that comes together during natural disasters), we played vingt-en-un with a remarkably filthy deck of cards and watched it until the power came back on, intercutting Kikaida with a little Star Blazers: The Bolar Wars, which is oh-so-isshy.

88-4 This is not quite correct. In Japan, hospitals are many times equipped with both a morgue (shitai-o(ki)ba) and a "temporary visitation and grieving room" (reianshitsu.) The recently deceased would have been pronounced dead in either their hospital room or the emergency room, then carried to the temporary visitation and grieving room for a certain duration while various final arrangements are made. If, for some reason, the body was to be kept on the premises for an extended duration, then they would go into the morgue.

89-1-3 We have a pun here in the original Japanese; hameru means both "to con someone" and "to fit something back."

94-1 Technically, polygamy means something similar (in that both terms signify multiple spouses), but whereas polygamy refers to one husband having multiple wives (as practiced today by some fundamentalist Mormon sects) the rarer practice of polyandry refers to a social situation where one wife has multiple husbands (as practiced today by the Nyinba people of northwestern Nepal and, more informally, in many American suburbs).

98-4 It's considered in Japan to be especially auspicious if your first dream of the New Year consists of these three items. The tradition goes back to stories pertaining to Tokugawa Ieyasu, founder of the noble house of samurai that ruled Japan for over 250 years (the Viz manga Vagabond is set right at the beginning of this era) but beyond that, there are numerous theories regarding as to how the belief got started.

107-1 The original text made a reference to the Apacchi Yakyuugun ("The Apache Baseball Army") a wacky Toei anime series that ran during 1971-72 (as a matter of fact, it ran at the same hour and during almost exactly the same period—but not the same evening—as the original Lupin III anime series; the one showing on Adult Swim recently is the second Lupin series, from 1977-80). Apacchi Yakyuugun featured eccentric characters doing the sort of stuff you could get away with in those Red Army days of the early 70s. Since this reference is almost guaranteed to be super-obscure to a US audience, I substituted like my name was Pete Townshend (or, in Excel Saga terms, Dr. Shinoji, who makes his first appearance in Vol. 05).

125-6 The kanpu masatsu ("rubbing-dry-cloth-on-body") health technique in Japan is pretty old-fashioned, and not too many people do it these days. It involves rubbing a dry cloth against your naked skin in an abrasive manner while being outside in the cold outdoor air.

128-1 There is a popular myth (and saying) in Japan that says baka (fools) don't catch colds.

141-4 Excel's use of the clapper is in the tradition of old Japanese oratory, a use not entirely dissimilar to the tradition in certain African-American religious denominations where interjections by the audience to the preacher's sermon are an expected part of the service (sometimes called that part of the congregation who are in the "amen corner").

If you enjoy
EXCEL SAGA,
the editor
recommends,
also from VIZ:

SANCTUARY

"You can't be a politician if you're embarrassed to show your ass…a politician has no need for common sense" And I *quote* from the first of nine volumes of *Sanctuary*, which illustrates (art by Ryoichi Ikegami) and describes (story by Sho Fumimura) that *Excel Saga*'s portrayal of corruption and absurdity in Japanese politics is more realistic than cynical. And unlike Excel's relatively nonviolent ways (no doubt from being unable to afford even Wal-Mart prices on ammunition), in *Sanctuary*'s world all your problems are solved with a pop pop, another politician drop, and you feel relief like plop, plop, fizz.

© 1995 Sho Fumimura/
Ryoichi Ikegami/
Shogakukan, Inc.

BLACK JACK

You're old enough, and it's time you knew who Dr. Iwata is in fact based on: Black Jack, the medical mercenary created by Osamu Tezuka (*Phoenix*) in his manga of the same name. Tezuka—in his spare time from being the modern manga industry's greatest pioneer—earned a medical degree, and in *Black Jack* created the story of a mysterious, scarred drifter/surgeon rejected by the health-care establishment, yet able to work miracles on baffling wounds and conditions when all hope is lost. Really sort of the complete opposite of Dr. Iwata; now that I think about it, I guess Rikdo-san was right.

© 2003 Tezuka
Productions

FLOWERS AND BEES

Unlike *Sanctuary* or *Black Jack*, this manga is brand new—so it *must* be good! You may have noticed that in *Excel Saga* there's no time for love, Dr. Jones. But just for the sake of variety I kind of admire Excel and Hyatt's more spiritual infatuation with Il Palazzo; you don't see them having a high-school crush over him (although that happens in *Excel Saga* Vol. 10) or cooking and cleaning for him like a punk (although that happens in *No Need For Tenchi!*). Every once in a while, though, you want to read a manga about teenage affairs of the heart and other, more "M"-rated organs. You'll find it in *Flowers and Bees* Vol. 1, out this month—maybe even on the same collapsible cardboard rack where you found this very book! It may even be shrink-wrapped, which makes it all the more enticing, doesn't it?

© 2000 Moyoco
Anno/Kodansha